CAMBRIDGE NAVAL AND MILITAR

General Editors—SIR JULIAN S. CORBETT, LL.M., F.S.A.
H. J. EDWARDS, C.B., M.A.

THE NAVY IN THE WAR OF 1739–48

IN 3 VOLUMES

VOLUME I

CAMBRIDGE UNIVERSITY PRESS
C. F. CLAY, MANAGER
LONDON : FETTER LANE, E.C. 4

BOMBAY }
CALCUTTA } MACMILLAN AND CO., LTD.
MADRAS }
TORONTO : J. M. DENT AND SONS, LTD.
TOKYO : MARUZEN-KABUSHIKI-KAISHA

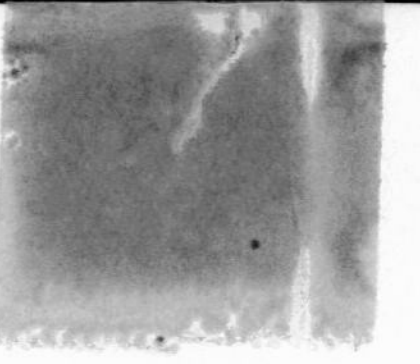

T. Burford ad vivum delin. et fecit 1741.

The Right Honble Sr John Norris – Vice Admiral of England, Admiral and Commander in Chief of His Majesties Fleets &c. and one of His Majesties most Honourable Privy Council.

Sold by T. Burford at the Golden Eagle in Villers Street York Buildings.

ADMIRAL SIR JOHN NORRIS

THE NAVY IN THE WAR OF 1739–48

BY

H. W. RICHMOND
REAR-ADMIRAL

VOLUME I

CAMBRIDGE
AT THE UNIVERSITY PRESS
1920

PREFACE

THIS book was begun in 1907 as during the preceding two or three years I had tried in vain to understand the part played by the Navy in the wars between 1739 and 1748. I therefore began to study the original papers and the result of my researches gradually developed into this book. As opportunity was scanty and odd hours only could be given to the work I took some years to complete it. The book was finished in August 1914 and would have been published that autumn if it had not been for the outbreak of war. Although the story affords many analogies with, and abundant matter for comment on, the course of the War with Germany, it has been thought best to issue it as originally written, without any knowledge of the events which lay so close ahead.

I was the fortunate recipient of help from the late Sir John Laughton who was always ready to give to others the benefit of his own great store of knowledge; from Mr W. G. Perrin and Mr Carr Laughton who have procured papers and undertaken research for me when I was unable to do it for myself; from Lord Hawke and the late Lord Sandwich who allowed me to examine their family papers at Womersley and Hinchinbrooke; and finally from Sir Julian Corbett who has given me invaluable advice on many matters and to whom I owe more than I can express for his never-failing assistance and encouragement.

I am indebted to Mr Emery Walker for the use of his copyright photographs of the portraits, and to the authorities of the National Portrait Gallery for permission to reproduce that of Admiral Vernon.

To all of these my grateful thanks are due.

H. W. R.

H.M.S. 'CONQUEROR,'
March 1918.

Gl

CONTENTS

CHAP.		PAGE
	INTRODUCTION	ix
I.	PRELIMINARIES OF THE SPANISH WAR	1
II.	THE CONSIDERATION OF THE WAR PLANS	14
III.	THE OPENING OPERATIONS IN THE WEST INDIES	39
IV.	BEGINNING OF THE WAR IN THE MEDITERRANEAN . .	59
V.	EVENTS IN HOME WATERS, 1740	73
VI.	THE EXPEDITION TO CARTAGENA, SANTIAGO AND PANAMA .	101
VII.	THE BEGINNING OF THE WAR OF THE AUSTRIAN SUCCESSION	138
VIII.	OPERATIONS IN THE MEDITERRANEAN, 1741	151
IX.	EVENTS IN EUROPE AND HOME WATERS, 1742—1743 . .	179
X.	REINFORCEMENT OF THE MEDITERRANEAN COMMAND WITH THE DEVELOPMENT OF THE WAR IN ITALY, 1742 . .	197
XI.	THE MEDITERRANEAN COMMAND (*continued*)	221
XII.	THE WEST INDIES. END OF COLONIAL OFFENSIVE. OCTOBER 1742 TO FEBRUARY 1744	241
	APPENDIX I. A LIST OF SHIPS IN SEA PAY IN SEPTEMBER 1739 WITH THEIR STATIONS	261
	„ II. CONTEMPORARY CRITICISM (1740) OF THE CONDUCT OF THE WAR	264
	„ III. THE MARINES AND THE MANNING QUESTION	267
	„ IV. CONSIDERATIONS ON WAR WITH FRANCE AND SPAIN	276
	INDEX	279

ILLUSTRATIONS

ADMIRAL OF THE FLEET SIR JOHN NORRIS	*Frontispiece*
THE TRADE ROUTES TO THE WEST INDIES AND CENTRAL AMERICA (*Carte Marine*)	*between* 16 *and* 17
THE ATTACK ON PORTO BELLO	„ 48 *and* 49
THE ATTACK ON CHAGRES	„ 52 *and* 53
FERROL HARBOUR AND APPROACHES	*to face* 84
CARTAGENA	*between* 112 *and* 113
THE FORT OF SAN LAZAR	*to face* 120
GUANTANAMO BAY	„ 126
THE ISTHMUS OF PANAMA	*between* 132 *and* 133
THE WESTERN MEDITERRANEAN	*to face* 151
THE ITALIAN COAST	*between* 196 *and* 197
THE CARACCAS COAST	*to face* 245
PUERTO CABELLO	„ 254

"The next great war has now passed almost entirely out of memory, not having brought to light any very great commander, nor achieved any definite result. But we have all heard speak of the fable of Jenkins' ears, and we have heard of the battles of Dettingen and Fontenoy, though perhaps few of us could give a rational account either of the reason for fighting them or of the result that came of them."

SEELEY, Expansion of England.

INTRODUCTION

THE war which lasted from 1739 to 1748 marks a definite phase in English naval history. The seventeenth century, which in an historical sense may be said to have lasted until the peace of Utrecht, had been a period in which the sea had played a supremely important part. It had been a century in which colonial expansion had held the foremost place in the external policy of England. As the sixteenth century had witnessed the discoveries of the Portuguese and Spaniards, and the acquisition by those powers of vast dominions and trading interests oversea, so the following hundred years had seen Holland, England and France stretching out their arms both in the East and in the West. England had become a truly maritime power on a new scale. She had taken her place as a factor to be reckoned with in the Mediterranean, as a colonial power in the West Indies and America and as a trading power in the Far East, where the first year of the century was marked by the establishment of the East India Company. The eighteenth century inherited the effects of this development, which shewed themselves in a struggle, lasting through a series of wars, to decide whether France or the United Kingdom should finally become the great colonial power. "The explanation of that second Hundred years' war between England and France which fills the eighteenth century is this, that they were rival candidates for the possession of the New World, and the triple war which fills the middle of the century is, as it were, the decisive campaign in that great world struggle[1]."

In considering therefore the strategy of this war the great struggles on the continent must not be allowed to obscure the fundamental contention between France and England; and the importance attached to colonies and trade was the direct outcome of the prevailing national sentiment. The significance of naval power was fully appreciated by the statesmen of the day, and naval strategy took the colour of the objects of national policy. With this object—the development of colonial power and trade—crystallised in their minds they saw clearly the means of reaching their ends. That a supreme navy was the

[1] *Expansion of England*, p. 34, Sir John Seeley. The "triple war" referred to is the series 1739–1748, 1755–1762, 1778–1783. Cf. also A. Sorel *Essais d'histoire et de critique*, for a parallel French view.

essential instrument formed an article of faith; but they had an equally unshakeable conviction as to the general principles governing the employment of that weapon. Whether it were the trade of the enemy to be attacked or our own to be protected, whether the kingdom were to be defended or military operations to be supported, it was an accepted formula that these ends could only be fully attained by the destruction of the sea forces of the enemy. If these were swept away or rendered impotent the enemy's trade, without protection, must collapse; the enemy's troops, undefended, could not risk themselves upon the water; and the troops and stores of ourselves or our allies could pass unmolested across the sea, or our small vessels could combine tactically with the troops on shore to the extent of the range of their guns because the sea forces of the enemy would be unable to interfere with them. Whatever the ends might be the means were governed by the one main principle—the necessity for destroying the enemy's sea forces.

There was however a link wanting in the chain of the factors necessary for success. However sound may be national policy, and however correct the tactical doctrines, the desired results cannot be reached unless the principles of the strategy are equally appreciated and acted upon. The overwhelming navy manned by expert tacticians and seamen must still fail fully to exercise its strength if the fleets and squadrons are not correctly disposed. This was the case in the early years of this war, and the country was, and had reason to be, dissatisfied with the results obtained by the navy. Commerce suffered heavy losses at the hands of the privateers of Spain alone and Spanish fleets sailed, effected junctions and escorted armies apparently as they pleased. A great oversea expedition, prepared in high hopes of conquests which should outshine those of any previous time came to a standstill before the walls of an inconsiderable city, whence it eventually retired reduced by sickness and battle to a fourth of its original strength. French squadrons sailed from their harbours and convoyed, unattacked, transports of troops and rich fleets of merchants across the Atlantic. There were, besides, inconclusive engagements between squadrons in more than one of which there were suggestions of misconduct; and to crown all, in the eyes of the British public, a British fleet engaged an approximately equal fleet of the enemy and parted without a victory.

The common habit of accounting for things by establishing generalisations or employing catchwords has led to the failures of this war being ascribed entirely to a want of professional ability on the part of the naval officer of the day. The degree of responsibility borne by the direction of operations and the state of naval thought, as influenced by precedent, have not been sought for; yet in any study of war this should be one of the first points to be investigated. A navy, however well conducted, officered and manned, can do nothing in the shadow of inefficient strategical direction; the best manned fleet will be impotent if its tactical government embodies a wrong doctrine. Although these statements are platitudes and should seem to need no repetition, yet they continue to lie, in spite of experience, at the root of the cause of failure in war.

Infinite pains at different times have gone to the making of officers, as experts in seamanship and gunnery, but little towards instructing them in the design and conduct of operations. War, in its higher aspects, in what Kempenfelt called its "more sublime parts," has too often in the course of our history received only a Cinderella's share of attention.

This defect existed in that part of the eighteenth century to which this book refers both in the British and French navies. Indeed, in the French service the conditions were worse than in our own. At the Académie de Marine[1] sea military knowledge was in the background, while mathematics, hydrography, astronomy, navigation, construction of instruments, naval architecture, medicine, botany, agriculture, philosophy and even gynaecology found their places. Mineralogy and gun manufacture, "les productions d'ingénieur d'artillerie et non d'officier de marine cannonier," as M. Castex pertinently remarks—were included, but military studies only appear in an anecdotal historical form[2].

While the British navy did not err in the direction of a worship of mathematics, science and other matters unconnected with seamanship and sea fighting, there was a tendency to put purely nautical acquirements so high that sea military knowledge suffered in consequence. This was not peculiar to the fifth decade of the eighteenth century. It had existed earlier and continued to exist later. Yet, like Kempenfelt in 1779, there were men of the earlier period who had recognised the same defect in their time. Curtis Barnett and Vernon were both well aware that an officer must be something more than a seaman alone, and apparently Anson had had an idea of doing something to remedy

[1] Although the Académie de Marine at which the extraordinary education described was not instituted until 1752 the ideas which permeated the curriculum must have been long in existence or they could not have obtained a hold sufficient so completely to dominate the training. Castex, *Les idées militaires de la Marine du XVIIIième siècle*, chap. 5.

[2] Out of 274 units of instruction, two only were accorded to strategy and tactics, "a particularly edifying percentage. It is equal to that of agriculture." Castex, *Les idées etc.*, chap. 5. The causes of the successes of the British navy in the eighteenth century are largely to be found in this book, and in particular, in this chapter.

matters before 1739. In a letter from Barnett to Anson, written in 1745 on hearing of the latter's appointment to the Admiralty, the following sentence occurs:

I expect a great deal from you. I am stupid enough to think that we are worse officers though better seamen than our neighbours; our young men get wrong notions early, and are led to imagine that he is the greatest officer who has the least blocks in his rigging. I hope you will give a new turn to our affairs and form a society for the propagation of sea-military knowledge. I think you had formerly such a scheme[1].

Barnett and Anson moreover were not solitary in their views even at this time. A senior officer, writing in 1747, says

It is certainly necessary that a sea officer should have some natural courage: but it is equally just that he should have a good share of sense, be perfect master of his business, and have some taste for honour; which last is usually the result of *a happy education, moderate reading, and good company, rarely found in men raised on the mere credit of being seamen.*

And, continuing, he complains that "the art of offensive and defensive sea fighting" and fitness to govern others are not so much as thought about in the examination for lieutenant.

The general notion about sea officers is that they should have the courage of brutes, without any regard to the fine qualities of men, which is an error themselves too often fall into. This levels the officer with the common seaman, gives us a stark wrong idea of the nature design and end of the employment, and makes no distinction between the judgement skill and address of a Blake, and a mere fighting blockhead without ten grains of common sense[2].

While the business of sea-fighting belongs to the seaman, the direction of a war concerns also and in a greater measure, the statesman, who in time of war becomes a member of Committees or Council, Inner Cabinets, War Councils or whatever name or form suits best the taste of the day. If therefore some study of strategy is incumbent on the seaman it is none the less incumbent on the statesman, lest when war breaks out there should be no definite doctrine as to how the national resources—navy, army and finance—can most effectively be employed in bringing about a victory which shall give a satisfactory and lasting peace. If this has not been determined, and the resultant course of action decided upon, there can be no national strategy, no clear plan of operations. Internal dissensions which hamper the full development of our strength, such as those caused by the Jacobites or the Chartists or their modern counterparts will not have been provided for and guarded against. In such cases the consequence must be indecision, vacillation and controversy in the execution of such immature plans as are eventually made. The war of 1739 to 1748 was no exception to this, and furnishes indeed an excellent example of the working of a system in

[1] Anson correspondence Add. MS. 15955.
[2] An article, probably by Vernon in *The Fool*, Feb. 25, 1747. B.M., 12530, c. 30.

which preparation for war finds too small a place in the activities of government.

Until the general European war began in the end of 1740 Great Britain's main strategy presented no very controversial points. Since Spain for want of an adequate naval force could not invade England nor England for want of a military force invade Spain on any large scale, the problem of the utilisation of the army of each kingdom was fairly restricted. Each country had in its power to attack the outlying possessions of the other, or to make feints against the home country. But in case of an invasion of foreign territory it is not sufficient merely to carry the troops thither in safety; the command of the sea must be sufficient to maintain the army and to prevent the enemy from sending out a counter expedition to recapture it. The only places in which England was seriously vulnerable abroad were Jamaica, Barbados, Antigua and some lesser West Indian islands of no great importance, Minorca and Gibraltar. Jamaica, great in area and equipped with a numerous local militia of white and black servants, would have required an expedition greater both to convoy and maintain than Spain could hope successfully to send across the Atlantic. The Leeward Islands and the Bahamas might have been taken with smaller forces, but would have been difficult to hold. Gibraltar and Malta remain. The former had proved its power of resistance in 1727: its capture would not involve the sending of a force by water, but it could not be invested unless reliefs could be intercepted by sea. Minorca might however be attacked swiftly by a considerable force despatched from the neighbouring ports of Carthagena and Barcelona, and its subsequent supply would not have been impossible owing to the large number of local Catalan small craft whose interception would be difficult. But provided that England retained the command of those seas its eventual recapture would depend only upon whether England could send a sufficient military force to reduce it by siege and blockade.

In consequence of these difficulties, inherent to her weakness at sea, Spain chose commerce attack as her principal strategical measure and used her army to assist this by threatening to attack the most important British points—the United Kingdom, Gibraltar and Minorca—in the hope that by preoccupying the British fleet with their defence, the high seas would be left open for the operations of her cruisers and privateers against trade.

England, with her larger fleet was able to undertake larger military operations against the distant and valuable possessions of the enemy. Attacks upon the principal naval ports of Spain lay also within her compass, for with the slowness of communication on land reinforcements took so long to reach a threatened point that a well prepared and informed expedition, carried out by surprise, had great promise of success even against places on the mainland. Rebuffs at Cadiz on earlier occasions had however been experienced and there was no great desire to incur them again, though an expedition was suggested. There was also a school of military thought—and the experienced Duke of Argyll was amongst its exponents—which advocated the employment of combined raiding expeditions on the lines of that carried out by Lord Cobham in 1719 against Vigo and Pasages, the object of such expeditions being the destruction of enemy privateers, their bases and the shipping. For warfare of this kind a comparatively small military force which could be carried in the fleet together with a few transports was sufficient. One definite proposal was made to use the army to assist the navy in obtaining command of the sea by the capture of Ferrol, but this was rejected in favour of the colonial attack. The ruling opinion however was that it was preferable to use the army in a more comprehensive way in capturing places on which Spanish prosperity depended. Such part of the army therefore as was available when the defence of the kingdom against internal rebellion on the part of the Jacobites had been allowed for, as well as external attack from a dubiously neutral France, was to be used in large bodies against the oversea possessions whence Spain drew the wealth on which her capacity for continuing the war depended. The innumerable discussions however which were heard before any decision was arrived at as to how and where war should be made against Spain, and the lamentable result of the constant procrastinations, provide examples for all time of the need of thinking out the employment of the national forces before war begins.

When the continental war broke out English main strategy received a new orientation. The great problem of whether British policy were to be mainly naval or mainly military divided the opinions of the day into two separate camps. There was on the one hand a body of opinion which would have conducted the war entirely at sea and in the colonies, sending no troops to the continent; and on the other a school which urged our taking a considerable share in the continental war and making that our principal effort. Both recognised the necessity of furnishing subsidies to our allies. The numerous debates in Parliament both on the question of sending troops to take part in the war on the continent, and on the subject of a standing army furnish interesting and important evidence of the way in which this question was regarded by the statesmen of the day. In the aims of the two schools there was no real difference. Both had the same objects in view—the security of the kingdom and the trade, the development of the colonies and the maintenance of the liberties of Europe, though the last of these was less considered by some supporters of the maritime and mercantile doctrine than by their opponents.

Those who advocated the strategy of a purely maritime and colonial war, leaving the continental battle fields severely alone, relied largely on arguments of a financial kind. As Britain was primarily a trading nation it was against her most important interests to hamper herself by the heavy expenses of an army. Continental struggles, they argued, did not concern this island nation; and if war were necessary it should only be such a war, waged in such a manner, as would advance our true interests, which were commercial. We should sweep the enemy's commerce from the sea, destroy his naval power and capture his colonies, the sources of his wealth; for by the monopolistic colonial system then in vogue we should thus become sole masters of the commerce, both export and import, of those colonies.

If we should take part in a land war the extra expense would involve extra taxation, which would cramp imports, hinder the re-exportation business, thus enhancing the prices of commodities sold to foreign countries, reducing trade and leading to borrowing and unsound finance[1].

A further argument, though of a different nature, was that if this country refused to afford military assistance on the continent it would not affect the war since the continental powers would then exert themselves more on their own account, as they could very well do, and would not look to the United Kingdom to repair their own sins of omission. It was argued that we should always be expected to bear the whole of the expense of the sea war to which there would be added the chief expense of the land war[2]. Moreover, if our army were used on the continent to defend Europe against France, the interested powers would leave to England the defence of those of their possessions as affected her—such as the Netherlands—and would themselves embark upon offensive operations for the increase of their own dominions. So, it was pointed out, had the Emperor behaved in King William's wars. When he saw that the Dutch and ourselves were ready to defend Flanders for him because of the great importance we attached to its not falling into the hands of France, he left us to fight these battles for him, and himself carried on a war of conquest against the Turks[3]. Indeed, an example

[1] *Parliamentary History*, vol. XIII, p. 176.

[2] Alderman Beckford's speech, *Parl. Hist.* vol. XIII. At a later date, see also Lord Strange and Beckford, *Parl. Hist.* vol. XIV, "Debate on the subsidy to the Elector of Hanover."

[3] Velters Cornewall's speech, *Parl. Hist.* vol. XIII, p. 159.

corroborating in no small measure this view arose later in this very war of the Austrian Succession. In 1745 Austria under the guidance of Kaunitz endeavoured to leave the defence of her territory in Lombardy to the King of Sardinia and the British fleet, while her own forces were used to conduct a campaign of conquest on Naples.

Finally, the supporters of the maritime policy urged that no success of France on land could affect us so long as we preserved our superiority at sea. No ignominious peace could be imposed upon us. By devoting our whole resources to the navy and to expeditions against the sources of wealth of the enemy we could ensure both the free flow and increase of our commerce, the destruction of that of the enemy, and the capture of the colonies of France and Spain; so that in the end the exhaustion of those powers would be brought about and a satisfactory peace obtained. As to the military operations on the continent our fleet alone, without the help of a single soldier landed in Europe, would render the most important service in the Mediterranean by commanding the sea communications, transporting where necessary the armies of our allies, and preventing the enemy from moving troops by sea from France or Spain into Italy, or from carrying supplies for his army by water. If on the other hand we should take upon us the burden of a continental war, we must abandon operations in America and the West Indies, and thus deny ourselves the only really profitable offensive in our own interests, for we could not conduct a strong war in two important theatres at the same time. Alderman Beckford summed up the views of this school.

> "The most effectual way," he said, "to assist our allies will always be to prosecute the war by sea and in America...We may conquer from our enemies, they can conquer nothing from us, and our trade will improve by a total extinction of theirs[1]."

Admiral Sir Peter Warren was a no less pronounced advocate of the purely maritime policy. While not believing that we could bring France to a peace solely by the operation of our squadrons at sea, he was strongly averse from our taking any part in a continental war.

> "We are not the weaker party," he said, "we have nothing to do with the continent; we do not stand in need of assistance from any state on the continent; let us confine ourselves to our own element, the ocean. There we may still ride triumphant, in defiance of the whole house of Bourbon[2]."

Warren considered it possible to keep a navy that could defy whatever force Europe brought against it, though he deplored the tendency he observed to neglect the navy, a tendency which would lead to our being "beat out of the ocean, and then we must contend not for any part of the continent of Europe, but for our own island."

[1] *Parliamentary History*, vol. XIII, p. 119.
[2] *Parliamentary History*, vol. XIV, p. 470.

The two postulates on which the maritime policy rested were that the continental powers alone should be able to withstand France without our help; and that we should be able, whatever the result of the continental campaign, to maintain our supremacy at sea in the face of such maritime confederations as might be arranged against us in succeeding years under the guidance of a Franco-Spanish alliance.

These views were disputed and their conclusions denied by the protagonists of the continental school. It was pointed out that in any case we were already engaged by treaty to furnish troops for the defence of Holland, and to uphold the rights of the Habsburg dynasty in the Netherlands. These countries could only be defended against French attack by an army on land, and our allies, in the dispositions of their forces, had counted upon our promised help. Whether this agreement were a right or a wrong one was now beside the case. We had entered into it and must act upon it.

Apart however from the question that honour dictated an abiding by our agreements, there was the fact that if Holland and the Austrian Netherlands were conquered owing to lack of cooperation on our part the ports of both and the maritime force of the latter would be at the disposal of France. The material assets of sea power of that country would thus be increased. But another, and possibly more important consideration would be that our allies, incensed at our desertion of their cause, would willingly turn to our enemies and execute vengeance upon the nation that had deserted them[1].

It was denied that our allies could stand against France unaided by us: in that case, they would be beaten; Europe would be at the feet of France. The conquests of the Netherlands by her, and of Lombardy by Spain would place the Bourbon Powers in so strong a military position that they would no longer have anything to fear on land. It would not be necessary for them to devote so large a proportion of their revenues to their armies and their attention would be devoted to developing their navies and that of Holland, who would fall under the Bourbon yoke. Then, with Portugal and the Italian states under the military thumb of the alliance and ordered to close their ports to us, with the Flemish and Dutch ports as bases of operation and trade, our navy though we should strengthen it to the utmost could not protect efficiently our kingdom, our colonies and our commerce. Tariffs and treaties would be arranged against us at the bidding of France for the destruction of our trade in peace, and, when the allied powers should feel themselves strong enough to engage us in war, first the trade and finally the kingdom would succumb to the superior forces they would bring out

[1] H. Fox, *Parliamentary History*, vol. XIII, p. 169.

upon the seas. Anticipating the policy of the Napoleonic decrees by sixty years, Mr James West, a member of Parliament, said:

> They might perhaps by threats or money get all the ports of the Baltic, except the Russian, shut against us; and in this case I should be glad to know how we could carry on even a naval war against the House of Bourbon, assisted by the Dutch. We might it is true fit out a most powerful navy, because all our merchant ships except those engaged in the East and West India trade would of course be laid up in our harbours. But as neither the French nor Spaniards would then have occasion to be at the expense of keeping up numerous land armies they might in a year or two be able with the assistance of the Dutch to provide a navy at least equal if not superior to ours.

As to possible conquests in America and at sea whose effect was so strongly represented by the maritime school, they would avail us nothing if the continental campaign were favourable to the Bourbons. The colonies would be reconquered in Europe, and their temporary loss by the enemy would not affect the final result. "I fear," said Hardwicke in a letter of August 17th, 1741 to the Duke of Newcastle, "that now America must be fought for in Europe, whatever success we may have in the former, I doubt it will always *finally* follow the fate of the latter[1]."

It was further argued that if we should abstain from sending troops, the Dutch would not move in defence of the Austrian Netherlands. Our abstention would thus have a double effect, and only a weak Austrian contingent would be left to defend that vital area. Austria without the aid of ourselves and the Dutch could not protect her Flemish and Italian provinces. First the former and then the latter would be over-run and reduced. Lord Perceval in a debate which took place three years after the continental war had been in progress gave a practical example of the value of the British contingent in the Dettingen campaign, the troops which took part in it being those British, Hessian and Hanoverian troops voted in 1743. It was owing to the presence of this pragmatic army that 60,000 French troops had been detained on the Maine and defeated at Dettingen. If these had been able to join the French armies in Bohemia and Bavaria, was it probable, asked the speaker, that the Queen of Hungary could have stood her own in Germany? or could the King of Sardinia have resisted France, Spain and Naples unless this diversion had been made?

The opinion of the Duke of Newcastle was that a military force upon the continent was necessary.

> "Naval force," said he, "tho' carried never so high unsupported with even the *appearance* of a force upon the continent, will be of little value.... France will outdo us at sea when they have nothing to fear by land.... I have always maintained that our marine should protect our alliances upon the continent; and they, by diverting the expense of France, enable us to maintain our superiority at sea[2]."

[1] *Life of Lord Hardwicke*, Yorke, vol. I, p. 263.

[2] Duke of Newcastle to Lord Hardwicke, Sept. 2, 1749. *Life of Lord Hardwicke*, Yorke, vol. II, p. 23.

Students of the later wars between this period and 1815 can consider whether the views of Newcastle or of Warren were borne out by the experience of those struggles.

The advocates of the continental policy were in the majority. Hence, from 1742 to 1748 we maintained an army in Europe which took part in the victory at Dettingen and shared the defeats at Fontenoy, Roucoux and Laffeldt; it was unable to prevent the Austrian Netherlands from falling into the hands of France, or the surrender of the great Dutch fortress of Bergen-op-zoom. The wished for attack upon Canada could not be carried out and was postponed until the second war of the trilogy. Whether the policy adopted were the one most in accordance with the national interests of the time will possibly be as much a matter of difference of opinion to-day as it was in 1740.

When the sea strategy of the war is examined an impressive evidence of continuity of tradition comes into view, a continuity broken only during the unhappy early years in which the advice given by the experienced seaman Norris, a veteran of Queen Anne's wars steeped in the doctrine of that time, was disregarded by those in whose hands the direction of the war rested. The Committee of Council frequently made their decisions in direct contradiction to the opinion of the Commander-in-Chief, and on many occasions made them without consultation with any of the sea-officers of the Admiralty. At one time, when Lord Winchelsea was first commissioner, the orders issued were such that the two Admirals then on the Board refused to put their names to them, that being the only way that lay in their power of expressing their disapproval. We have it on Vernon's authority that the basic principle of defence of the kingdom and of trade was a strong squadron operating in the Channel approaches from which detachments could be made as necessary. Norris continually urged this course in the early years of the war with Spain but without result; and Vernon revived it on his taking up a command in home waters after his return from the West Indies. Finally it fell to Anson to re-establish the squadron in the closing years of the war. The letters of the Duke of Bedford and Lord Sandwich in 1746[1] are important landmarks in this connexion, while Anson's later views on the western squadron as the corner-stone of our naval strategy in a war against France are well known.

The instructions to the Commanders in the Mediterranean at various periods of the war, which in many cases are reprinted at length in order fully to illustrate their form and the ideas which they express, shew how well accepted was the idea that in the event of a French squadron breaking out of the Mediterranean it should be followed to the West

[1] *Vide* vol. III.

Indies, as Nelson followed Villeneuve. The value of the West Indies was so great that they were considered to form the natural objective of a French naval force. Nelson, so far from creating a precedent, was in fact carrying out, perhaps instinctively, a practice the tradition of which extended over at least three generations.

While British strategy was comparatively consistent in its main lines, if not in its execution, French strategy was undecided. The operations of the French navy were not coordinated with those of its ally. The fleets of the two powers, except upon two occasions[1], worked separately, each pursuing its own policy. To criticise however is easy: but when the intense provincialism of the Spaniards themselves is remembered, and the difficulty of obtaining cohesion between the thirteen kingdoms, it is not hard to appreciate that full cooperation with a foreign power should be unattainable. This lack of cooperation gave England the greatest possible advantage throughout the war, combined as it was with a want of practical experience on the part of the enemy. Vernon's operations in the West Indies in 1741 were watched by France with grave and unconcealed anxiety in consequence of the loss to French trade, and the gain to English strength which would follow from an English capture of the more valuable Spanish possessions. To oppose such conquests France sent a fleet to Hispaniola, but, though it was expected by the Spaniards, cooperation was not provided; and lack of sea experience caused such illness in the fleet that it returned to Europe without having effected anything. When war broke out France began hostilities with two surprise attacks, one upon the British fleet in the Mediterranean, the other upon the United Kingdom itself, failing in both: in the former because it was not made clear that the destruction of the British fleet was the overwhelmingly important object, in the latter through a variety of causes which are not reducible to a generalisation. Immediately abandoning direct attack upon the British fleets, although the combined Franco-Spanish naval forces in European waters were superior to those of England, the French attempted a form of guerilla warfare upon the lines of communication of the Mediterranean fleet. It failed. A further attempt to invade England, and an endeavour to recover Louisbourg were made. The former again relied upon evasion, and upon the assistance of the Jacobites. The latter was conducted as though there was no enemy fleet to be considered nor communications to be maintained. Beyond these the strategy was concerned almost entirely with the protection of trade by convoy, that is by direct

[1] Viz., the scheme for the invasion of Italy in the last months of 1741, and the battle of Toulon in Feb. 1744. In the second case cooperation ceased after the battle.

tactical defence and not by attack upon the enemy's force which threatened it. Attack upon British trade was relegated to privateers, which, though they caused heavy losses were unable to bring about any serious dislocation of British commerce, and therefore no decisive effect upon the war. The French naval strategy of protection of trade by convoy alone, and of offence by sporadic attack failed.

When the strength of the British navy and the individual efficiency of its seamen are considered in relation to the divided forces, wrong ideas and inefficiency with which it was opposed, it is impossible not to regret that such great advantages should so largely have been thrown away by those who had to make use of our formidable weapon. What actually brought us through the war with some measure of success, was that the enemy made more mistakes than we did.

CHAPTER I

PRELIMINARIES OF THE SPANISH WAR

THE events which led up to the war with Spain in 1739 were the direct outcome of the exclusive colonial system which prevailed in the eighteenth century. Colonies were not established with any idea of civilisation, creating empires, extending the influence of the country or giving a home under the country's flag to a surplus population. They were regarded purely as a means of carrying on trade to a greater advantage. The colonies were an exclusive market for the products of the mother countries, and were themselves obliged to send their products to those mother countries exclusively. Monopoly of supply to the colonies, monopoly of manufacture and monopoly of colonial produce were the leading if not the sole principles of colonial intercourse[1]. Colonists could not supply their own wants from any market other than the home market, and were obliged to send their produce to the home countries. The restrictions did not end there. The produce must be sent in a raw or unmanufactured state, so that the profits of the processes of making the goods ready for consumption might accrue to the home manufacturer. A British example will illustrate the working of this system. Raw sugar—muscovado—paid an import duty of fifteen shillings per cwt.; refined sugar paid a duty of £4. 18*s*. 8*d*. By means of this duty the industry of refining sugar was made prohibitive in the West Indies in order that the British refiners might reap the profit, and although great waste of sugar through leakage took place on the voyage, with proportionate loss to all concerned, this duty was steadily retained. What applies to this one industry applies to others. The merchants, who were a class with the power of making their voices heard, insisted on retaining a system which provided them with a certain market, untainted by competition, and which forbade the raw materials from falling into any hands other than their own; the Molasses Act of 1733 and the Colonial Manufacturers Prohibition Act of 1750 are further examples of the idea in its practical application.

This vast system of monopoly extended also to shipping, and its influence is to be seen in the Navigation Act of Charles II. Colonial goods could not be sent to the British market except in British or Colonial bottoms, and, as freight at that time may be taken as 20 per cent.[2], no small portion of the benefits of the system fell to British

[1] Bryan Edwards, *History of the West Indies*.

[2] Bryan Edwards.

shippers. Finally, the Government came in for a share, since colonial produce had to pay an import duty which went direct into the coffers of the Treasury[1].

The same doctrine of monopoly which was held by Great Britain was held in essence, if not in detail, by the other European powers possessing colonies[2]. The right to prevent foreigners from trading with colonial possessions was recognised by all powers. A treaty of 1667 between England and Spain stipulated that if any ships belonging to the subjects or merchants of either nation entering into bays or in the open sea, were met by the ships-of-war of the other nation, such merchant ship might be examined and any prohibited goods taken out of her; and a further treaty of 1670 provided that British ships should not approach Spanish Colonial ports unless driven by stress of weather or provided with a licence to trade. By the Treaty of Utrecht of 1713 other trading facilities were wrung from Spain. A thirty years' monopoly of the slave trade, and permission to send one ship annually of not more than 500 tons burden was granted to the South Sea Company. The door to the Spanish colonies was thus opened, very slightly, to Great Britain.

Abuses on both sides were not long in coming. The South Sea Company exceeded their treaty rights by various devices and also conducted an extended smuggling trade in which they were imitated by a host of private adventurers—regarded by the company as interlopers—who came very largely from the North American Colonies. On the other hand, the Spaniards did not confine their attentions to vessels in the neighbourhood of their colonial ports, but extended the operations of their coastguard ships outside territorial waters, and a number of privateers, acting on commissions granted locally, pretended to be honest guarda-costas and acted in the same manner; so that a system not far removed from piracy prevailed in West Indian waters. The seamen taken on board the ships arrested were maltreated in a brutal manner, and on occasions lost not only their property and their liberty but their lives as well. On one occasion[3] at a later date a small British vessel was wrecked on the coast near a Spanish port; her crew were taken prisoners and as one man among them had been previously convicted of illicit trading, the whole crew of 26 men and the captain

[1] The average annual value of imports from the West Indies from 1739 to 1749 was £1,300,000: before the end of the century these had risen to over seven millions. Bryan Edwards.

[2] France, more liberal to her colonies, allowed them to manufacture. For a fuller account of the colonial system see *Cambridge Modern History*, vol. VI. pp. 50 *et seq.*, pp. 183–186; and G. L. Beer, *The Old Colonial System*.

[3] Commodore Brown, in letters, June 1739. Brown sent the 'Dragon' to Tolu and obtained the release of the crew.

were condemned to imprisonment, although there was no evidence whatever that they had been guilty of any malpractices.

Cool-headed men who looked at both sides of the question could see where the faults lay. Walpole summed the matter up very clearly in the House of Commons. "Spain," he said, "has never pretended to dispute our right of sailing from one of our own settlements to another: but she pretends, that in the course of that navigation, we ought not to touch upon her coasts, nor to trade with any of her subjects. We, on the other hand, admit that the Spaniards have a right to prevent any trade from being carried on by the subjects of other nations with hers, except that trade which is expressly stipulated by the Asiento treaty. But we deny that under that pretence her subjects ought to stop or search our ships[1]." Montijo, the President of the Council of the Indies expressed the matter with greater brevity but equal justice when he said to Mr Keene, our Ambassador at Madrid, that there were faults on both sides, that the British contrabandists ought to be punished and some of the Spanish Governors hanged[2]. Admiral Charles Steuart, who commanded in the West Indies in 1731, while complaining of the conduct of the guarda-costas and the privateers, was not blind to the fact that the British merchants were also to blame. "The question will be," he wrote, "whether we by carrying on the clandestine trade are not ourselves the authors of our complaints." He had no sympathy with those merchants who broke a nation's laws and then cried out at the results[3].

The Spanish claim to search vessels near their own coasts was indeed no more than our own to search vessels near the English coast. Thus, at this time, the exportation of wool and woollen goods from the United Kingdom was prohibited, and a squadron—known as 'Owlers'—of two frigates and eight or more armed sloops was maintained constantly to prevent such exportation. These ships, cruising in the Channel, had orders to search for vessels with contraband export goods of this nature, and were a parallel to the guarda-costas, searching British or foreign craft impartially. The difference lay in the manner in which they performed their duties and in their treatment of ships and men found infringing the law.

Complaints as to the conduct of the Spanish cruisers had been made as early as 1728; they continued throughout the next two years. In 1731 a commission was appointed to examine the claims made by certain merchants, but no conclusion was arrived at. It was during

[1] *Parliamentary History*, vol. x. p. 1311.
[2] "The Causes of the War of Jenkins' Ear." H. W. V. Temperley in the *Transactions of the Royal Historical Society*, vol. III. p. 204.
[3] Sir John Laughton in *The English Historical Review*.

this year that the incident which gave a name to the subsequent war took place. On April $\frac{9}{20}$, a Spanish privateer captain named Fandino captured the 'Rebecca,' Captain Jenkins, a ship belonging to Jamaica, which was on her way to England. The Spanish captain used Jenkins "in a most barbarous inhuman manner, taking all his money, cutting off one of his ears, plundering him of those necessaries which were to carry the ship safe home[1]." This incident, though sufficiently dramatic to have furnished the popular name for the war, was not brought to public notice until several years later.

For some years these high handed actions of the Spaniards continued, on one occasion—in 1734—even reaching so high a point as an attack on some ships engaged in the lawful occupation of gathering salt at the Tortugas under the convoy of a man-of-war—the 'Scarborough.' No redress was sought. The smuggling on the one hand and the piracy on the other continued, and a list exists which shews no fewer than 52 ships taken and plundered by the Spaniards up to the 18th December, 1737. A petition from the West Indian Merchants was submitted to the King in October of that year, and it became evident that popular feeling was becoming stirred. Counter complaints were made both by Spain and France in which the captains of two ships of the West Indian squadron, the 'Kinsale' and 'Antelope,' were accused by these Powers of using their ships to conduct an illicit trade in negroes to the Spanish and French colonies[2]—a complaint which was ordered immediately to be investigated, and which the Commodore on the station indignantly denied.

Under the influence of all these causes relations between England and Spain became seriously strained in the early part of 1738, and each began to make preparations for war. Both navies were on a peace footing, the bulk of the ships being kept in home waters. Only such small squadrons were maintained abroad as were necessary for the purposes of preventing piracy and smuggling, or for protecting traders in the less civilised regions, such as the coast of Africa.

Our foreign stations were classified under two main headings, the Plantations and the Mediterranean. The various Plantation stations comprised Jamaica, the Leeward Islands, Barbados, the coasts of the American colonies, Newfoundland and the West Coast of Africa. On all of them ships, principally small ones, were stationed, but the only area in which a squadron was permanently maintained was the Jamaica station. It was also the custom for vessels to go to the West Coast of

[1] Rear-Admiral Steuart to the Governor of Havana, September 12th, 1731, quoted in *Engl. Hist. Review*.

[2] Out letters. March, 1737–8.

Africa for some months and then pass on to the westward to the West Indies. At Jamaica a flag officer flew his flag or broad pendant on board a sixty gun ship. The Mediterranean was treated as one station and was policed by a squadron composed mainly of small frigates with a stiffening of heavy ships. The actual distribution in March 1738 was as follows:

Plantations			Mediterranean	
Ship	Guns	Station	Ship	Guns
'Dunkirk'	60	Jamaica	'Gloucester'	50
'Kinsale'	40		'Eltham'	40
'Drake' (sloop)	4.10*		'Dursley' galley	20
'Diamond'	40	Coast of Africa	'Greyhound'	20
'Greenwich'	50		'Gibraltar'	20
'Spence' (sloop)	6.10		'Dolphin'	20
'Roebuck'	40	Barbados	'Grampus'	20
'Tartar'	20	New York	'Deptford'	6
'Squirrel'	20	New England	(lighter)	
'Lowestoft'	20	Leeward Islands		
'Rose'	20	South Carolina		
'Seaford'	20			
'Seahorse'	20	Virginia		
'Shark' (sloop)	8.12*	Bahama Islands		
'Hawk' (sloop)	6.10*	Georgia		
'Falkland'	50	Newfoundland		
'Phoenix'	20	On her way to S. Carolina		

* The first figure denotes carriage guns; the second, 'swivels.'

It was with relations between the two powers in the highly strained condition described above that Captain Jenkins is said to have made his celebrated speech in March 1738. Whether he actually used the words attributed to him or not, the decision to strengthen the force in the West Indies had already been made two months earlier: in January a force of five ships[1] had been ordered to be prepared for service on the Jamaica station under Commodore Charles Brown.

Commodore Brown's instructions, which were dated February 10, 1738, directed him to take his squadron to Jamaica where he would be joined by two ships from the West Coast of Africa—the 'Falmouth,' 50, and 'Diamond,' 40. One of his frigates, the 'Anglesea,' was to reinforce the Leeward Islands, and the 'Dunkirk' and 'Kinsale,' which had been on the Jamaica station for some time, were to be sent home with the trade, so that a relief of fresh ships from England was provided in case of war. The duty of the squadron was to be the protection of

[1] 'Hampton Court,' 70; 'Windsor,' 60; 'Anglesea,' 40; 'Torrington,' 40; 'Sheerness,' 20.

Jamaica and the trade of those parts; in addition to which Brown was directed to observe closely all movements made by the French and Spaniards, information as to whose preparations he was constantly to send home. He was informed that as frequent complaints had been made that British ships had been seized by guarda-costas both on their outward and return journeys and condemned as prizes under pretence that they were intended to carry on illicit trade at the Spanish ports and settlements, he was to protect the trade from such attempts in all parts, particularly in the Windward Passage and the Gulf of Florida, the two main channels respectively for the outward and homeward bound trade. If any of his squadron should meet any Spanish armed vessels pretending to be guarda-costas which were known to have committed such depredations, they were to seize and bring them into port. If Georgia were said to be in danger of attack he was to protect it in conjunction with the stationed ships on the American coasts.

Subsequent movements of ships still further strengthened the Jamaica squadron. The 'Centurion,' 60, which had been sent to Barbados from the West Coast of Africa with instructions to convoy the trade to Barbados and back, was ordered to remain with Brown at Jamaica: the 'Saltash' and the 'Spence' from the African coast were also to join him, and he was directed to keep the 'Dunkirk' and 'Kinsale' with his squadron if he found they were still fit to remain abroad.

Thus the result of these dispositions was to concentrate a formidable squadron at Jamaica, and to strengthen the Leeward Islands command by one heavy ship[1]: the whole of the ships on the West Coast of Africa were transferred to the West Indies, except the 'Greenwich' which was ordered home. At the same time a squadron of four ships—two of 50 guns and two of 20—was fitted out for Newfoundland.

The care of the colony of Georgia also came under consideration. This colony was a most probable objective of any Spanish attack, as Spain disputed our right to the territory. It was the latest colony settled by Great Britain, and was an exception to the general rule which governed the establishment of colonies. Instead of being purely mercantile, its foundation was due partly to a desire to protect South Carolina from the Spaniards in Florida and the French in Louisiana, and partly to the efforts of Colonel James Oglethorpe, a soldier and

[1] The constitution of the intended squadron on April 1st was as follows, if 'Dunkirk' and 'Kinsale' were fit to remain:

With Brown at Jamaica: 'Hampton Court,' 70; 'Windsor Castle,' 60; 'Centurion,' 60; 'Dunkirk,' 60; 'Falmouth,' 50; 'Diamond,' 40; 'Torrington,' 40; 'Sheerness,' 20; 'Saltash,' 20; 'Drake' sloop; 'Spence' sloop.

At the Leeward Islands: 'Anglesea,' 40; 'Lowestoft,' 20.

philanthropist, who wished to provide a settlement for poor debtors in London prisons and for oppressed Protestants from the continent. Oglethorpe had visited England in the preceding winter and had obtained permission to raise a regiment for the defence of the Colony, the first detachment of which, 680 strong, had sailed in December in three transports convoyed by the 'Phoenix,' Captain Fanshaw[1]. A further reinforcement was sent in June, 1738, in five more transports, under convoy of the 'Hector,' Captain Sir Yelverton Peyton[2], and the 'Blandford.' These three ships were also to remain and reinforce the squadron on the colonial coasts, the 'Hector' at Virginia, the 'Phoenix' at South Carolina, and the 'Blandford' at Georgia.

Commodore Brown sailed from Spithead on the 19th February, but owing to bad weather was forced into Torbay and did not clear the coast till the 2nd March. The 'Anglesea' was dropped at the Leeward Islands in accordance with instructions, and the remainder of the squadron proceeded to Barbados where it arrived on April 17th. The Commodore then detached the 'Sheerness,' Captain Stapylton, to cruise off San Domingo and Cape Alta Vela, and sent orders to the 'Diamond,' Captain Knowles, to cruise off the north side of Porto Rico and Hispaniola and in the Windward Passage. He directed both of these commanders to use their utmost efforts to come up with any guarda-costas they might meet with in their cruising stations, "and if on a strict examination of them or by any other intelligence he might gain on his cruise it should appear that the Spaniards did continue to commit their usual depredations (which probably might be without any orders from his Catholic Majesty, in regard it was contrary to the Treaties subsisting between the two Crowns) I ordered him not only to seize such armed vessels as might have committed them but also all other ships and vessels of Spain that cruised and lurked about under the notion of Guarda costas, in order to take the ships and vessels of his Majesty's subjects. And whatever armed vessels he might so seize on, I directed him to take care that not anything belonging to them was embezzled on his way to Jamaica, to which port he was to carry them, where it would be determined in a judicial manner whether they ought or ought not to be condemned as prizes[3]." In similar terms he instructed the captains of his other ships as to their behaviour in regard to guarda-costas; and having made these arrangements he sailed for

[1] Fanshaw's instructions are dated December 3rd, 1737. Out letters.

[2] Peyton's instructions are dated May 19th, 1738. Out letters.

[3] Commodore Brown's *Journal*. The Commodore gives a very full and valuable account of his proceedings.

Jamaica where he arrived on April 29th. His line of battle, which he issued on May 3rd after his arrival, was as follows:

	'Sheerness,' 20;
	'Kinsale,' 40;
	'Dunkirk,' 60[1];
Repeating Ships { 'Spence' sloop	'Windsor,' 60;
'Drake' sloop	'Hampton Court,' 70;
	'Falmouth,' 50;
	'Diamond,' 40;
	'Torrington,' 40.

The squadron in the Mediterranean was under the command of Captain George Clinton, with his broad pendant on board the 'Gloucester,' 50. Clinton had been appointed in April, 1737, and his instructions, dated May 26 of that year, related principally to the protection of Mediterranean trade against the Barbary pirates—those useful people whose conduct had so often furnished a plausible reason for sending ships to the Mediterranean when diplomatic exigencies called for an increase of strength in that quarter. On this occasion the commodore was further instructed to keep himself constantly informed as to any naval preparations that might be made in the ports of France or Spain; and, when the strain between England and the latter power became acute in the early part of 1738, additional orders were sent him to be particularly watchful to prevent the Spaniards from making any attempt by surprise or otherwise on Minorca. If he should hear of any such intention he was to carry his squadron to that island, and, in cooperation with the Governor, to take all measures to protect it.

The Government did not confine themselves to these orders. Things were critical in March, and as Clinton's instructions shew, it was not considered impossible that Spain might act in the same manner as she had in 1726 and begin a war by an attack on one of the Mediterranean fortresses of which she had been deprived by the Treaty of Utrecht. She had broken her teeth on Gibraltar at that time. She now might make her attempt on Minorca. A reinforcement for the Mediterranean was therefore ordered to be prepared in April, consisting of nine ships[2] and two fireships, and this squadron was placed under the command of Rear-Admiral Nicholas Haddock.

Haddock's instructions, which were dated May 13th, directed him to sail for Gibraltar as soon as not less than five or six of his ships could be manned, and on arrival to inform himself of the strength of the Spanish naval forces. "Having done so," the instructions continued,

[1] The 'Dunkirk' sailed for England on May 28th.

[2] 'Somerset,' 80; 'Edinburgh,' 70; 'Dragon,' 60; 'Lancaster,' 80; 'Ipswich,' 70; 'Berwick,' 70; 'Plymouth,' 60; 'Canterbury,' 60; 'Jersey,' 60; 'Solebay,' 20 (fireship); and 'Alborough,' 20 (fireship).

"you are without loss of time to proceed to the island of Minorca and use your utmost endeavours to protect the same from any attacks the Spaniards may make thereon. And in case you shall find that the Spaniards actually attempt to attack the aforesaid island of Minorca, or come on the coast thereof with any number of ships of war and land soldiers in order to do the same, you are to do your utmost to frustrate them therein, and to seize and destroy such ships as may be employed on such an enterprize." Further clauses directed him to look out for the defence of Gibraltar; to send home constant accounts of the Spanish preparations; to defend trade; to demand immediate restitution of any British ships taken; and, if this were refused, to attack the Spanish captors whether they were privateers or King's ships. To sum up the sense of the orders: they were defensive but put power of retaliation into the Admiral's hands in the event of any attack by Spain.

Spain, very unready and already impressed by the attitude taken up by the British Government in its diplomatic correspondence, had been inclined to give way to the storm which she saw brewing[1]. The preparation of Haddock's squadron created no small stir at Madrid. Consul Strangford, writing from Alicante, said: "The notice of Admiral Haddock's coming out here with a squadron for these seas seems to have alarmed the court, so that everywhere they seem to be putting themselves in a posture of defence," and other writers from Spain reflect a similar apprehension[2]. The moving of squadrons or troops when diplomatic relations are strained invariably produces uneasiness, and Spain was no exception to the rule. She expected that a blow might be delivered at any moment, and she began taking measures of defence and at the same time preparing for counter-attack. The fortresses of Barcelona and Cartagena were hastily put in order, instructions were given to get the Cadiz squadron ready, 40,000 troops were ordered to move in the direction of Gibraltar, and another body towards the frontiers of Portugal[3]. Hostilities now appeared to be imminent and masters of British ships in Spanish ports were warned to be on the look out for an embargo. Haddock, who had arrived at Gibraltar in June, kept his squadron cruising between Cartagena and Gibraltar in order to be between the two main bodies of Spanish naval force at Cartagena and Cadiz. His information was that the Ferrol and Cadiz squadrons were coming to join the ships at Cartagena, and this intention

[1] Cf. "The Causes of the War of Jenkins' Ear," pp. 211–212.

[2] Enclosed in Haddock's letter of June. See also letters from Consuls, Ad. Sec. In letters.

[3] Haddock to Secretary. May and June, 1739. In letters.

he interpreted as indicating an attack on Minorca or Gibraltar. He therefore cruised in this station in order to be able to move quickly to either place if his surmise should be correct. Like his instructions, his movements were defensive, but not unnaturally Spain interpreted them in a different sense, believing that they portended an attack on some part of her dominions or her trade. It is however clear that if his intentions had been offensive he would more probably have cruised on the other side of the Straits, where an objective was to be found open to such attack as a squadron could make—viz., the Western Trade returning to or sailing from its headquarters at Cadiz.

While Haddock was thus covering Minorca and Gibraltar, Commodore Brown was similarly cruising to cover the trade and colonies in the West Indies and America. So early as March, 1738, a Spanish expedition had been in preparation at Havana directed against Georgia, and Brown detached the 'Torrington,' Captain Knight, to Havana to get intelligence as to its readiness, and also to find out the condition and strength of the Spanish squadron. In the then state of affairs Knight was not welcomed by the Spaniards. "We received some stiff civilities," he said, "but if we were not affronted it was easy to see we were not liked[1]." He found that an expedition of 3000 men had been made ready, but had been countermanded by orders from Madrid in March just at the time when Brown had sailed from England. The troops were to have been carried in flat-bottomed boats, "ridiculous things which could all be destroyed at sea by one ship of 40 guns and one of 20," and these were being kept ready against another occasion.

The main business of Brown's squadron was connected with the protection of the legal and the suppression of the illicit trade—British, colonial, and foreign—and though his instructions contain no reference to the suppression of the British illicit trader, the commodore issued orders to his captains to give no countenance to British or North American offenders whose actions, he pointed out, were doing so much to disturb the harmony between England and Spain[2]. Cases of all kinds concerning British, French, and Spanish ships occurred. Thus in June the 'Elizabeth,' a British ship homeward bound from Jamaica to London, was driven for water into Donna Maria Bay (at the west end of Hispaniola), where she was seized by a French 20 gun ship. Brown sent the 'Falmouth' to demand her release and redress, both of which were granted. On the other hand a French ship, the 'Volante,' was taken trading on the coast of Jamaica and condemned. In July the 'Kinsale' was sent to cruise in the Windward Passage to secure

[1] Captain Knight to Commodore Brown. June 21st, 1738. In letters.
[2] Brown's orders to Captain of 'Kinsale.' In letters.

our trade, as a Spanish guarda-costa, the 'Trionfo'[1], was reported to have plundered a British trader in that channel; while the 'Falmouth' arrested and brought into Jamaica a Rhode Island trader whom she found unloading a cargo on the coast of Hispaniola. It is worth noting that although this vessel was taken red handed and proved to have no licence for trading with the French, the local court at Jamaica acquitted the smuggler. Thus, while the admiral was endeavouring to suppress the traffic that was leading up to war, the legal gentlemen were upholding illegal acts. Nor was this the only occasion during these years in which the West Indian courts shewed a partiality to offenders which hampered the actions of the naval forces[2]. The presence of the squadron nevertheless reduced the practice of smuggling, and relations were not seriously strained during that year, at any rate not in the West Indies, where lay the original seat of the trouble. Brown was able to report in April, 1739, that the British trade had not lately suffered any interruption either from France or Spain.

In European waters the summer passed without matters proceeding to extremities. Although the first appearance of Haddock's squadron had given rise to great anxiety in Spain it had not only not precipitated war but had acted as one of the causes predisposing towards peace. It shewed Spain that England was in earnest. Behind these few ships loomed the remainder of the British fleet. "You ought not to be surprised," wrote Mr Trevor from the Hague, "at these pacifick appearances when I tell you that England has at present 107 ships of war of different force and denominations actually in commission[3]." The influence of Walpole, which was exerted towards finding a peaceful solution of the quarrel, and a strong measure of common sense on the part of the Spanish Ministers, were tending to produce the same result along other lines, and some months were spent in endeavouring to arrive at an agreement by which the claims of the British merchants and the rights of the Spanish Government should be satisfied. The result of these efforts was the Convention of the Pardo, in which it was stipulated that all losses which had been sustained at the hands of the guarda-costas up to December 10th, 1737, should be met by a payment of £95,000 by Spain, this sum to be paid within four months of the ratification of the convention. The treaty was signed on January $\frac{3}{14}$, 1739.

[1] She was subsequently taken at Porto Bello.

[2] Many similar cases occurred in the Seven Years' War: so great were the abuses that it was seriously discussed, Mr Temperley tells me, whether means should be used for over-awing the local courts.

[3] R. Trevor to Sir E. Fawkener, September 6th, 1738, quoted by Mr Temperley in his "Causes of the War, etc."

Everything now appeared to be making for peace and on January 29th Haddock was ordered to return with his squadron to England, leaving Clinton in command at Gibraltar with two ships only, the 'Gloucester,' 50, and the 'Dursley galley,' 20.

Haddock had gone to Minorca for the winter in order to refit his squadron. He could not return at once as several of his ships were on the careen, and it was only on March 13th that he sailed for Gibraltar on his way home. But in the interval since January the situation had taken a different turn. Parliament met on February 1st, and the convention was debated hotly in both houses. Petitions from merchants opposing the ratification rained in, their main objection being that the question of search was not settled. "No search" was the watchword. "No search, my Lords," said Lord Carteret, "is a cry that runs from the sailor to the merchant, from the merchant to Parliament, and from Parliament, my Lords, it ought to reach the Throne[1]." Party feeling was imported wholesale into the discussion and a matter which required cool handling between statesmen, became the subject of windy declamations from politicians. The peace, which the possession and use of a strong and ready fleet had so nearly secured, was to be wrecked at Westminster.

The debates came to an end on March 10th; the Ministry had a narrow majority in favour of the convention, but the country was stirred up by speeches and pamphlets against it. There can be little doubt that the nation was inclined to war. Men still looked back to the days of Cromwell and even those whose political views made them eye the Protector with no favour, sighed for a return to his conduct of foreign affairs. Throughout the debates in Parliament the days of Elizabeth and the Commonwealth were referred to constantly, and it would appear that the country was under one of those influences, perhaps the outcome of a long peace, which need war to exorcise them.

The Duke of Newcastle, the principal Secretary of State, kept his eye on the temper of the mob. He watched the trend of public feeling, and prepared to follow it. Suddenly another factor entered into the situation. The Ministry received intelligence that a Franco-Spanish treaty concluding an offensive and defensive alliance between the crowns was about to be arranged[2]. This news, in fact, was doubtful and premature, but nevertheless carried weight, and the net result of the combined causes was that the recall of Haddock's squadron was cancelled. On March 10th, the day the debates in Parliament on

[1] *Parliamentary History*, vol. x. p. 754.

[2] "Causes of the War of Jenkins' Ear," pp. 229–230.

the convention came to an end, Haddock was ordered to remain at Gibraltar[1].

Spain, who in consequence of the favourable turn of affairs had disarmed her fleet, now became anxious. To her it appeared that a double game was being played; and though Newcastle instructed Mr Keene at once categorically to deny that the counter orders had been sent to Haddock, the Spanish ministers, who could see the British squadron still at anchor in Gibraltar Bay, not unnaturally declined to accept the statement. When May 25th—the date on which the payment should have been made—arrived, no money was forthcoming from Spain. On May 29th the Spanish Minister informed Keene that nothing would be paid until Haddock's squadron was recalled. On May 31st the question was asked in Parliament whether the money had been paid and the reply, to make use of a formula familiar to us to-day, was in the negative.

Spain had broken the convention and thereby put herself in the wrong. War was now inevitable.

[1] Out letters. March 10th, 1739.

CHAPTER II

THE CONSIDERATION OF THE WAR PLANS

THE naval and military forces of the powers immediately concerned, and the probable attitude of the other powers, must now be taken in review.

The English fleet consisted, in May, 1739, of 124 ships of the line and fifty-gun ships; besides these there were many frigates of 40 and 20 guns, sloops, bomb-vessels, and smaller craft. Although the fifty-gun ship was not a ship of the line it was not unusual to include her among the heavy ships and to speak generally of "50 gun ships and above," but it is important to bear the difference in mind—a difference which was not only one of the number of guns, but of scantling and weight of guns as well. Of the 124 heavy ships, no fewer than 44 were, by the Admiralty accounts, unfit for service. Of the 80 remaining, only 35 were in sea-pay, that is to say actually ready for service, and of these 5 were in the West Indies with Commodore Brown and 10 in the Mediterranean with Haddock, so that the immediately ready force of ships of the line in home waters consisted of 20 ships, of which 10 were guard-ships.

The English army numbered about 29,000 to 30,000 men disposed in garrisons about the United Kingdom, at Gibraltar and in Minorca.

The Spanish navy consisted of 58 ships altogether, of which 41 were of 50 guns and upwards. It was however by no means ready; nor was it concentrated, since the necessity under which Spain lay to convoy her treasure fleet involved her always having a number of her heavy ships in the West Indies. The fleet in home waters was organised in three divisions at the ports of Cadiz, Ferrol and Carthagena, the whole being under the Infante don Philip as General-Admiral of the naval forces. Twenty-one of the great ships belonged to the first-named port, and out of the remaining twenty, eight belonged to the Flota (the armed ships which traded with South America), five to the Buenos Ayres service and two to the Barlovento, or Windward squadron. Her army, including about 23,000 militia, numbered some 110,000 foot and 20,000 horse[1].

France, whose exact diplomatic relationship with Spain was uncertain but suspected, had a fleet of about 50 ships of line, divided

[1] *Les préliminaires de la Guerre de la Succession d'Autriche*, M. Sautai, p. 388.

between the ports of Toulon, Rochefort and Brest: but according to the information in the possession of the Administration, very few of her ships were ready for service at this date. As a military power she was the strongest in Europe and could place over 300,000 men in the field[1].

The immediate struggle that was to take place was thus between a nation with a force of about 80 ships of the line and a small army, and another with about 40 ships of the line and a very large army, with the possibility that the latter might be assisted within a certain time by a third nation with a force of about 50 ships of the line and a larger army still. There could thus be no question of England's undertaking military operations on any large scale against Spain in Europe: the disproportion between the military forces of the two powers precluded any such possibility. Spain was only vulnerable in her colonial possessions overseas, and in the trade that passed between those possessions and the old country. Such pressure might be brought upon her by interference with that overseas trade and deprivation of the sources of wealth themselves, that the losses she would suffer by a continuation of hostilities, would exceed those incurred by a recognition of and subscription to the demands put forward by England. It was therefore obvious that the efforts of England would be directed towards sapping the wealth of Spain.

The wealth of Spain lay in her trade and in her colonies. But her colonies without trade were valueless to her; it was only because they were the sources of her trade that they contributed to her wealth. If the communication between those colonies and the home country were cut, or were interfered with to so great a degree that trade could not be carried on, the colonies lost their value. Thus as Spain could not be brought to an agreement by measures of military force, occupying the country and throttling the economic life, the pressure could only be brought to bear externally by throttling the channels on which that economic life depended. True, a certain degree of pressure might be brought to bear by the capture of oversea possessions, and their conversion into possessions of our own; but only so far as those possessions were of direct economic importance to Spain would this method affect her. The energies of Great Britain required therefore to be directed towards the destruction of Spanish trade. So much was clear; but when it came to consideration of the methods to be employed there was room for wide differences of opinion.

Trade could be attacked either by spreading ships fanlike over the

[1] Pajol, *Guerres sous Louis XV*, gives the state of the French army in 1745 as 322,000 men.

seas and capturing every vessel that sailed under the Spanish flag which came in sight: or by concentrating squadrons at the points of arrival and departure of that trade: or by seizing, by means of military force, the ports whence the trade sailed. Such ports as were seized might be held temporarily for the immediate purposes of the war, or, if favourably situated for strategic reasons, might be retained permanently afterwards. A still further development of such a trading war would be not only the seizure of a port, but the actual conquest of the territory in which the port was situated with the view of appropriating it to the Crown and settling colonists there, in order that that territory might be used to supply the wants or increase the riches of the kingdom, or because its occupation was essential to the secure tenure of an important strategic position in the territory.

The principal theatres of activity of the Spanish commerce were in the West Indies, Central and South America and the Philippine Islands; but the trade from all these parts came to Europe by the route across the Atlantic. On the continent the trade came down to the coast at Vera Cruz, Cartagena[1], Porto Bello (which received the trade from Peru) and Buenos Ayres. The trade from the Philippines which was embarked at Manila was carried across the Pacific to Acapulco and thence transported through Mexico City and re-embarked at Vera Cruz.

All of this trade was conducted by the Royal and privileged fleets. The South American trade was carried in the galleons, which, sailing from Spain went first to Cartagena where they awaited the news of the arrival of the Peru fleet at Panama. When this intelligence was received they proceeded to Porto Bello, whither the trade was brought from Panama either on mules over the stone-paved track which led across the Isthmus, or by water down the Chagres River, according to the season of the year. The arrival of the galleons was the occasion for the holding of a great market at Porto Bello. The merchandise brought out from Spain was then sold, the products of South America were embarked on board the ships, which then returned to Cartagena, received that part of the trade which came from the mainland and then stood over to Havana where all the Western trade collected on its return journey to Europe.

The trade between Spain and Mexico was carried out by the Flota. This fleet was fitted out at intervals—sometimes as much as three or four years apart—or as occasion required, and sailed from Cadiz taking

[1] In order to avoid confusion I have adopted the following arbitrary spelling to distinguish the two Cartagenas; the Spanish port, Carthagena; the Colombian one, Cartagena.

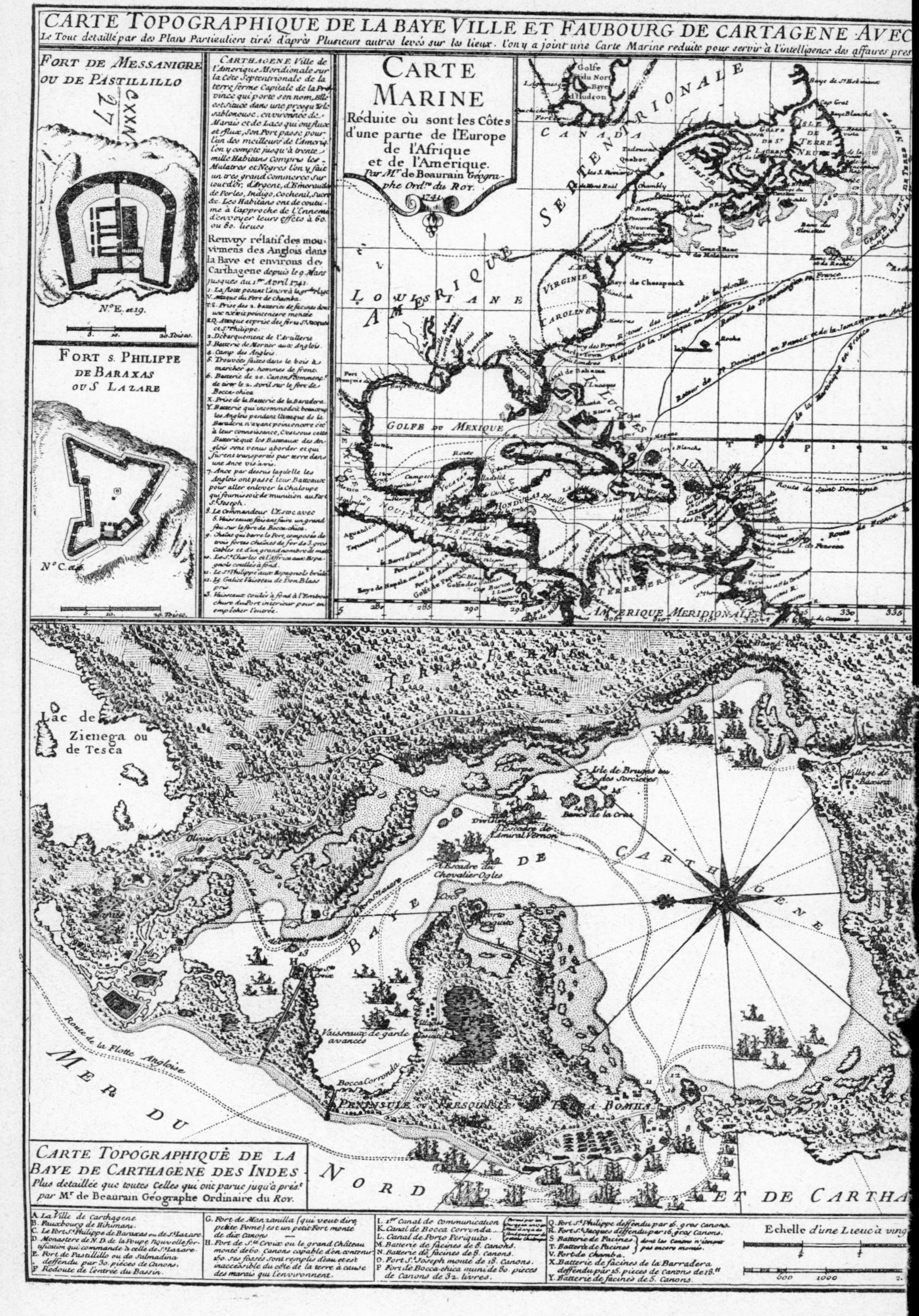

THE TRADE ROUTES TO THE WEST INDI

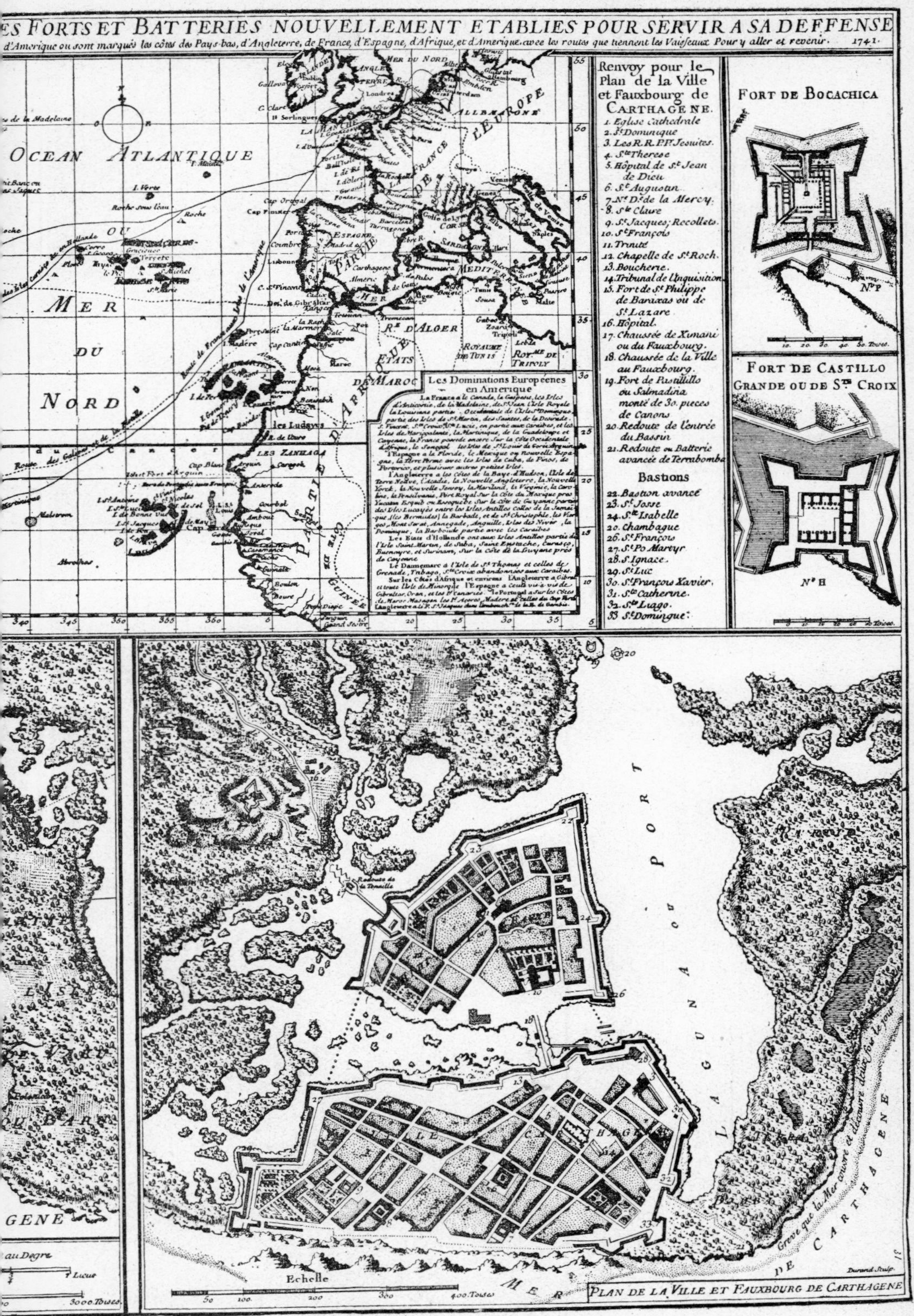

S AND CENTRAL AMERICA (*Carte Marine*)

out wine, oil, brandy, cloth and wearing apparel of all kinds. It called at Porto Rico to refresh and thence sailed to Vera Cruz. The harbour of Vera Cruz was very small and not more than 30 to 35 ships could lie in it; it was also weakly defended, so that any ships lying there were in danger of attack from the sea. The market was therefore not held at the port but at Jalapa, a town about a third of the way between the port and Mexico city. The treasure and trade were not brought down to the coast until the ships arrived and were ready to embark it, in order to shorten as much as possible the time during which they would be exposed to danger.

In the interval between the sailings of the Flota, vessels known as Azogues sailed between Spain, Havana and Vera Cruz, carrying quicksilver out from Spain for use in reducing the silver ore, and returning with the produce of Mexico and Havana. These ships, which figured among the men-of-war, were armed with about 60 guns.

The trade to Buenos Ayres, which was not as yet very extensive was conducted by ships which sailed separately from the great trading fleets. Their home port was Cadiz, and the imports they carried to Spain consisted largely of gold, silver and hides.

One other class of ship remains to be mentioned, the Register ships. These vessels belonged to merchants who by payment of a certain sum were privileged to carry goods to any part of the Spanish settlements. They were free to move independently, sailing when they wished and steering their own courses.

The Havana itself, besides being the principal port of Cuba where the products of that island—hides, sugar and tobacco—were embarked, was also an important shipbuilding centre not only for merchantmen but also for men-of-war of the largest classes. But its main importance lay in the fact that it was the rendezvous where the whole Western trade, except that of Buenos Ayres, collected before proceeding home under convoy. Porto Bello, Cartagena, La Vera Cruz and Chagres were minor trading bases at which the exports of the country immediately behind them, or of more distant parts such as China and Peru, were embarked, subsequently to be concentrated at Havana. Thus the capture of Havana, the focus of the trade, would be the most serious blow that could be inflicted on Spain, while the capture of any of the other ports would exercise a severely restraining effect upon the trade that they fed. In home waters Cadiz was the principal port: there a Casa de Contrataçion of the South Sea Company was established, and there the Flota collected for its outward sailing. The minor ports were Coruña, Santander, San Sebastian and Bilboa.

Sir Charles Knowles, an officer of whom we shall hear much during this war and a careful observer, writing in 1748, gave a fairly full account of the course of Spanish trade and its seasons. He said: "The Spanish ships generally arrive in May. The places to watch for them are off Cartagena, fifteen miles S.E. of Cape Tiberoon, and on the north side of Hispaniola to prevent their going through the old straits of Bahama, and between Cape Antonio and Cape Cartouche: which being so many different routes require the more ships.... In the middle of August or beginning of September the Spaniards generally bring up their treasure from Vera Cruz in two men-of-war, and three or four ships sail from the Havana much about that time over to the Dry Tortuga where they anchor and wait for those from Vera Cruz, when all proceed to the Havana. This has been the practice these eight years past, so that as the Hurricane months are not proper to arrive off Cape François[1], the time falls out well for the large ships upon this station going to waylay the Spaniards. The ships destined to carry the treasure generally sail from the Havana about the middle of October when they wait to see the first North (*i.e.* northerly gale) over before they sail: then they push through the gulf, so that if they were missed on the way from Vera Cruz with the treasure, our cruisers might run through the gulf and have a second chance of meeting them on their passage home; but then we must be very strong as the treasure ships are generally convoyed by most of the men-of-war from the Havana as far as the Bermudas." The treasure here referred to by Knowles was obtained from mines upon the American continent, the importance of which to Spain may be realized by the fact that the average annual receipt from them was at this time calculated at more than 4¼ million pounds sterling. The protection of this trade by convoy formed a perpetual duty of the navy even during peace. Privileged persons only were permitted to take part in the commerce, and the King himself was in effect the principal merchant of the kingdom. Instead of encouraging the trade to increase, those persons who could obtain permission to take a part in it held it jealously in their hands. "Kept under by absurd regulations, hindered by all kinds of obstacles, cramped by a thousand chains, yet this commerce is the richest in the universe." It was this rich commerce on which Spain so greatly depended that must be the first object of an attack, the successful issue of which would deprive her of the money she would require immediately for conducting a war.

The Ministry had a fairly clear field to work in so far as their offensive operations were concerned. If they decided to attack the

[1] The principal French station. The trade from the French settlements usually sailed for home in June, before the hurricane season set in.

headquarters of Spanish trade in the West Indies they required a combined force to capture the ports and a naval force to cover the operations, ensuring the immunity of the troops on their passage and holding the lines of communication at the required points to prevent either interference with our own supplies, or reinforcements from reaching the enemy. The main ports requiring observation would be Cadiz in the south, in connexion with which Carthagena would be included, and Ferrol in the north, which would include the ports on the Biscay coast. The security of our dominions—the British islands, Gibraltar and Minorca in the Mediterranean, and our scattered possessions in the West Indies and America had also to be provided for against counter attack; and so far as they were concerned the squadrons employed to cover our oversea offensive operations would, if properly disposed, secure those territories from invasion. There remained the defence of the trade. The large squadrons watching the enemy ports could not ensure its safety. While the squadrons off Carthagena, Ferrol or Cadiz could guard against the sailing of any similar body of ships, it was impossible for them to guarantee that single ships or small squadrons should not slip out from those ports; and over and above these main bases every harbour on the coast that would hold a ship could send out a privateer, so that some force in addition to the main squadrons would be required to deal with these pestilential craft. Sir Robert Walpole, speaking in the House of Commons in the early part of the following year[1], indicated the lines on which he surmised the war must proceed: "It is true," he said, "our Navy is much superior to theirs; but by our Navy alone we cannot propose to force them to a peace. We must attack them on land at some place or other, and for this purpose we must have a sufficient land force. I believe they have not at present any great number of regular troops in the West Indies; and we may prevent their sending a great fleet and army there at the same time; but we cannot prevent their sending small detachments in single ships or in half-a-dozen ships at a time, and by such means they may considerably increase their regular troops in the West Indies even before we can attack them." It will appear strange that with so clear an appreciation of the situation so little attempt should have been made to prevent the sailing either of fleets or smaller bodies of ships from the Spanish ports.

Unreadiness of the fighting forces and irresolution as to their use were among the reasons why Spain was allowed so free a hand as she was at the beginning of the war; but there were others as well. The

[1] *Parliamentary Debates*, 1740.

irresolution was to some extent created by the relations with foreign powers. A brief reference to these will therefore be made, so that the effect of the prospects of interference or assistance from the continent may be appreciated, and the extremely evanescent character of the alliances of the preceding years brought out.

From 1713 to 1731 France and England had been at peace. In 1717 they had been in actual alliance[1], and the short war of 1718–1720 had seen France, Austria and Great Britain acting together against Spain. England's attitude in this matter was dictated by her continuous policy of the preservation of the balance of power, but another potent influence was also at work—her regard for her trade; and this played no small part in weakening the ties that hitherto had bound her to Austria. The desires of the Emperor for an external commerce which he was anxious to develop from his Flemish Province, led to Austro-Spanish rapprochement which culminated in a treaty[2] in 1725. By this arrangement Spain agreed to assist Austria in the development of an overseas trade and the establishment of an East Indian trading corporation known as the Ostend Company, while Austria in return was to use her influence to obtain the restoration to Spain of Gibraltar and Minorca. Secret clauses included an attack on France, and marriages by which Austrian archduchesses were to be united with Spanish infantes and thus provide these princes with settlements in the Austrian dominions in Italy. This treaty gave rise to serious fears both in England and France. Not only trade and power were believed to be affected, but it was rumoured that a Jacobite restoration was among its provisions. Holland would be in danger, and through her, England; for the Dutch had openly announced that they would attack the Imperial ships if they should meet them in the East Indies, in which case a war would follow between the Empire and the United Provinces in which Spain would be bound to assist Austria. England could not afford to see Holland either crushed or driven into the arms of France; and, if France should go to war in defence of Holland, England could not sit by and see French squadrons attacking Spanish West Indian settlements, which would result in an increase in French strength in those parts. France, no less than England, had good reasons for not standing alone in the presence of two such powerful enemies as Spain and Austria. The result of the mutual danger was a treaty between the two powers, into which Prussia also entered[3]; and a triple alliance of England, France and Prussia confronted the dual alliance of Spain and Austria.

The moral support which Spain had thus obtained from Austria

[1] Treaty of Vienna. [2] *Ibid.* [3] Treaty of Hanover.

did not content her. She next desired active assistance in recovering Gibraltar which she attacked in 1726. But the money which was needed to induce the Emperor to participate was not forthcoming until too late owing to a blockade of Porto Bello by a British squadron under Hozier,—that terrible pacific blockade which cost so many lives. Thus Spain received no help from her ally. England likewise received none from her's, and a half-hearted struggle, hardly worthy the name of war, in which the Spanish attempt upon Gibraltar failed completely, soon came to an end.

The Austro-Spanish alliance lasted only a short time. The grouping of the powers underwent another change in 1729 in which dynastic and trading influences were supreme. Austria having rejected the proposed Austro-Spanish marriages, Elisabeth Farnese, the very masterful consort of the King of Spain, in high dudgeon carried Spain into the arms of France and England, and a treaty, in which the Emperor was obliged to take part, resulted in 1731. England was guaranteed the possession of Gibraltar, her treaty rights as regards trade were secured to her, and the Ostend Company was abolished. Spain obtained some of the concessions in Italy desired by her Queen.

From this time Anglo-French friendship had gradually grown fainter, a tendency accentuated two years later by the conclusion of the first *Pacte de Famille* between Spain and France. In this compact the former agreed—notwithstanding previous treaties—to transfer to the latter the commercial advantages conceded to England by the Treaty of Utrecht, France in return engaging to assist Spain to recover Gibraltar, to suppress the illicit trading, and provide an army of 40,000 men if required. That same year however the attention of the parties was diverted in another direction by the death of the King of Poland which brought about a war concerning his succession in which France, Spain and Sardinia were opposed to the Emperor. The British Ministry adopted an attitude of non-interference, mainly through the influence of Walpole—an attitude strongly criticised at a later date by opponents of that Ministry. Carteret, in the debate on the motion for the removal of Walpole, said: "Our joining the Emperor in the war would in all human probability have entirely cast the balance... but we remained idle spectators and by this our inaction the power of the house of Austria was diminished, the power of France increased and the whole system of Europe turned upside down." The kingdom of the two Sicilies passed at the peace in 1733 from Austria to a Spanish prince. The main effect of the war, so far as it concerned England, was a great increase of Spanish power in the Mediterranean; all that had been gained by the war of 1726 was lost.

This short survey will have shewn that while Austria entertained no friendly feelings towards Spain, she had no reason to extend any help to England, who had just been instrumental in killing at its birth her overseas trade to the East Indies, and had allowed her territories to be taken from her in the recently ended war. Holland had no cause to come into the war unless she were attacked by France; but she was bound by treaty to assist England in the event of the Protestant succession being endangered.

Of the smaller powers whose attitude affected the situation, the most important was Sardinia, whose ruler, King Charles Emmanuel, was a soldier held in high esteem by all his contemporaries. But so long as the quarrel between Spain and England was concerned with matters without the Straits of Gibraltar, the attitude of Sardinia mattered little. The northern powers similarly had even less concern in the dispute, and France only remained. Her attitude was of serious importance and of great uncertainty, and every effort was made by the British ministry to ascertain the exact relations existing between her and Spain, and whether certain rumours as to a secret treaty between them were true. As we have seen, the first family compact between the French and Spanish branches of the house of Bourbon had been secretly signed in 1733. In it France agreed to assist Spain if she were attacked by England, to obtain for her the restitution of Gibraltar and Minorca and to assist her to check the illicit trading in the West. The agreement was known to the Duke of Newcastle early in 1734, and, though the compact had lasted not much longer than the ink took to dry, it indicated the trend of a considerable body of influential opinion in France making for a close alliance between the Bourbon powers. Cardinal Fleury, the "Prime Minister" of France, was known to be averse from war. All his influence, it was rightly anticipated, would be employed in the maintenance of peace; and Newcastle hoped that if only Holland could be persuaded to throw in her lot with England the scales might be turned so definitely in England's favour that Fleury would keep out of the contest. "I sometimes flatter myself," he wrote to Horace Walpole[1], "there are strong indications of success: a little spirit in the Dutch would certainly frighten the Cardinal, and give him an excuse for not taking part with Spain, since that would bring on a general war and make the Dutch take part with us; but if our friends in Holland shew plainly nothing will engage them to act, France will then think they may then quarrel with us without endangering a general war."

[1] Duke of Newcastle to Horace Walpole, (Brit. Mus.) Add. MS. 15955.

It was however suspected that measures were on foot for a renewal of the treaty of 1733; and as the Cabinet had themselves experienced, the peaceful tendencies of a minister might not be proof against a popular outcry for war. It was therefore the obvious duty of the administration not to rely too confidently on Fleury's attitude, but to take all the steps possible to guard against the situation that might arise if he were unable to keep the reins in his own hands. The first, the most obvious, step was to prepare every ship in the yards for service, so that a force superior to that of the two powers would be available if required. As the sequel will shew, this was not done, and ministers contented themselves with gambling with the security of the nation, trusting to the pacific character of a frail old statesman 86 years of age.

Such, then, was the actual political situation when the British Government found itself faced with the necessity of deciding on some definite plan of war with Spain.

At that time the direction of all warlike measures was in the hands of the Privy Council, but in practice the business was done by a Committee of the Council, which constituted in effect a Committee of Imperial Defence. This Committee was a Committee of the Privy Council, and though the same great officers of the State who formed the Cabinet were to be found attending it, it was wholly distinct from that body, nor was attendance confined to members of the Government or Council. So far as the navy was concerned, while its representative was generally the First Commissioner, others of the Board frequently took part in the discussions; and the officers commanding the Fleet in home waters are often to be found at its deliberations. Such matters as the operations to be undertaken, the movements of the various fleets and the instructions to be given to their commanders were considered by this body[1].

The two sea-officers who in the initial stages figure most prominently in the work of preparation for, and conduct of, the war, were Sir Charles Wager, the First Lord of the Admiralty, and Sir John Norris, the Commander-in-Chief, or Admiral of the Fleet.

Sir Charles Wager was now 73 years of age. He had held the office of First Commissioner since 1733, an office held by many sea-officers since 1688[2]. In his young days he had served with Russell at Barfleur,

[1] Cf. Professor E. R. Turner in *American Historical Review*, July and October, 1913; Sir William Anson in *English Historical Review*, January and April, 1914; Mr H. V. W. Temperley in the same *Review*, No. XXVII. of 1912; *Memoirs of Court of George II*, by Lord Hervey; *Diary of Sir John Norris* (Brit. Mus.) Add. MS. 33004; Minutes of the Privy Council.

[2] Admirals Herbert, Edward Russell, Sir John Leake, Sir George Byng and Lord Berkeley.

and later was present at the taking of Gibraltar in 1704 and of Barcelona in 1705. He had made himself a rich man by the capture of a great quantity of treasure from a Spanish fleet of seventeen ships, which he boldly attacked with a squadron of three vessels only. He had commanded in the West Indies, where his conduct of affairs was marked by the success of his defence of trade and capture of prizes. He was present at the siege of Gibraltar and the blockade of Cadiz in 1726 and 1727, but he had never had the good fortune of commanding a great fleet action, and the majority of his services had been connected with squadrons rather than fleets.

Sir John Norris, the date of whose birth is uncertain[1], was apparently about 79 years old. He had been present at Barfleur, la Hogue, and at the loss of the convoy off Lagos in 1693. He took part under Sir Cloudesley Shovel at the capture of Barcelona in 1705 and the operations round Toulon in 1707. He commanded in the Mediterranean in 1710 and 1711, when he took part in the joint operations with the Archduke Charles. He had been employed in the Baltic both in naval work and diplomacy in the years between 1715 and 1727, and was appointed Admiral and Commander-in-Chief in 1734. Sir John's *Diary* contains a very full account of the meetings of the Committee of Council attended by him[2]; it gives a singularly clear picture of the method, or rather the lack of method, with which the war was directed.

It was at a meeting of the Council held on June 3rd, when Spain's failure to conform to the agreements arranged in the Convention of the Pardo was known, that the first acts of hostility were decided on. The acts of hostility were not to be acts of war but reprisals[3], blows directed against Spanish commerce in reply to the injuries Spain had inflicted upon British trade. Spanish shipping was to be attacked in its two great focal areas, Cadiz and the West Indies. With this in view the Council decided to send orders immediately to Haddock to dispose his squadron in the best manner to seize the Flota, then preparing at Cadiz, and to stop all Spanish advice-boats going to the West; and to Commodore Brown to "act hostilities against the Spaniards in the West Indies, making the interception of the galleons from Havana his

[1] Sir John Laughton in the *Dict. Nat. Biography* gives the year of his birth as 1660, with a query.

[2] It is in the British Museum Add. MS. 28132–5.

[3] "The term applied to such injurious and otherwise internationally illegal acts of a State against another as are exceptionally permitted for the purpose of compelling the latter to consent to a satisfactory settlement of a difference created by its own international delinquency." L. Oppenheim, *International Law*, vol. II. p. 34.

principal object." The defence of the kingdom was to be provided for by manning a strong squadron for home service and augmenting the land forces. The proper method of issuing letters of marque was to be gone into, in accordance with precedent.

Orders in the sense decided upon were despatched three days later in three six-rates to the Mediterranean, West Indies and Northern Colonies respectively, a fourth and a fifth-rate were sent to guard the fisheries at Newfoundland, and Sir John Norris was appointed to command the fleet at home. Thenceforward meetings of the Council were held daily to discuss the operations which were to be undertaken. The instructions to Haddock[1], dated June 6th, began with a preamble in which the unjust seizures committed by Spain, the injuries suffered by our commerce and the cruelties inflicted on our seamen were recited; and Haddock was directed, as Spain had failed to fulfil her undertaking to pay £95,000, to commit "all sorts of hostilities" against the Spaniards, seizing both ships of war and merchant vessels. In particular he was to cruise off Cadiz to try and capture the Flota fitting out for the West Indies, and also to look out for some Azogue ships expected soon to arrive, and for the galleons in case the squadron in the West Indies should miss them. As it was not improbable that these measures of reprisal might provoke the Spaniards to retaliate in the form of an attack on Minorca, he was from time to time to detach such ships as he considered necessary to prevent such an attempt being made, going himself to the island in case of urgent need, but not otherwise. Besides this he was ordered to protect trade, to station ships off Lisbon and Gibraltar for the purpose of getting intelligence of Spanish ships, and to attack the enemy's privateers; but he was directed not to weaken his own squadron to an extent that would make it inferior to any squadron that might come out from Cadiz, or from any other port of Spain to join the ships at Cadiz; which junction he was enjoined to prevent.

When it is borne in mind that Haddock's force consisted of ten ships of the line, one large frigate and eight small craft, and that the force in Cadiz so far as was known consisted of thirteen ships of the line besides small craft in unknown numbers, it will be seen that his task was sufficiently comprehensive. He had not only to keep a force off Cadiz which could engage the Spanish squadron if it came out, but also to provide ships for the other scattered services enumerated. To enable him to carry out these instructions an increase of force was obviously required.

[1] They were drawn up by the Duke of Newcastle, Lord Harrington, Henry Pelham and Sir John Norris.

The actual disposition of all the ships in sea-pay when these orders were issued was as follows:—

Rates	Plantations	Mediterranean	Home Service	Guardships
3	1	5	—	—
4	4	5	10	6
5	6	1	1	4
6	7	6	6	—
Sloops	8	1	8	—
	26	18	25	10

making a total of 79 ships, of which 36 were of the line.

On June 20th news was received from Gibraltar that two Buenos Ayres and two Azogue ships were expected to arrive at Cadiz during June. The Council at once decided to endeavour to intercept them. Sir Chaloner Ogle was ordered next day to hoist a broad pendant on board the 'Augusta,' 60, take the 'Pembroke,' 60, and 'Jersey,' 50, under his command and, as soon as he could be ready, to sail for Gibraltar with sealed orders (which were not to be opened until he reached Cape St Vincent) directing him to cruise off that Cape for the expected Spanish ships. Admiral Haddock also was warned that these ships were on their way home and informed that Ogle was being sent to intercept them. Both of these sets of orders were shewn to Lord Hardwicke, the Lord Chancellor, a statesman whose strategic insight was considerable. Hardwicke at once drew attention to the fact that the Spaniards would not neglect the obvious precaution of ordering their ships to come to some other home port than Cadiz, watched as it had been for so long, but would divert them elsewhere, probably to Coruña. In confirmation of Hardwicke's surmise information appears to have been received that some such measure had been taken, and it was settled immediately after the Lord Chancellor's remarks to send another force to watch off the northern capes of Spain. For this purpose the Council decided to employ a squadron which had been prepared for the purpose of making the opening moves against Spain in the West Indies, and now lay at Spithead, nearly ready, under the command of Admiral Edward Vernon[1]. The instructions to Chaloner Ogle were therefore not altered, and Vernon was directed to get to sea as quickly as he could and proceed to Finisterre with the object of intercepting the Spanish ships in case they should make for Coruña.

[1] 'Burford,' 70 (flag); 'Worcester,' 70; 'Strafford,' 60; 'Princess Louisa,' 60; 'Norwich,' 50.

As however it was important that he should arrive in the West Indies before the galleons should leave for Europe, which they were expected to do in October, he was told not to wait more than fourteen days off Finisterre unless he should get information that the ships were actually coming, and in any case not to wait so long as to risk missing the galleons in American waters.

Ogle was unable to get away until July 22nd in consequence of a severe gale, and even when he did sail the weather was still tempestuous; after a day or two of battling with foul winds he lost his foremast and was obliged to return to harbour. A new mast was stepped and rigged and he once more set out on the 30th and worked down to Cape St Vincent, where he found three of Haddock's squadron —the 'Ipswich,' 70, 'Edinburgh,' 60, and 'Dragon,' 60,—already cruising on the look out for the same quarry as himself.

The possibility that the Azogue ships might be met and protected at their home terminal by the Ferrol squadron caused the Admiralty to strengthen Vernon's command by four more ships[1] under Captain Coville Mayne, and with these he sailed the day after Ogle's first departure and ran into the same bad weather. Although he lost no spars he was not able to get clear of the Channel until the end of the month, the foul winds keeping him battling about the Isle of Wight until then. On the 2nd August he was out of the Channel and on the 9th he made Cape Ortegal where he cruised for the inside of a week, and then, leaving Covill Mayne the three 70-gun ships and the frigate which had been added temporarily to his squadron, with orders to cruise in those parts for another month, he bore away with the remainder of his ships towards Madeira, where he arrived on the 23rd of the month.

Mayne continued cruising with the detached squadron off Ortegal until the 1st of September when he received certain news that the Azogue ships had got into Santander a month before. This was true. Under the command of Admiral Pizarro they had sailed from Vera Cruz and made their European landfall at Cape Clear; in that part they appear to have received warning from an advice-boat sent out from Spain that the British squadron was cruising off Cadiz, whereupon Pizarro shaped course across the Bay direct for Santander where he anchored in safety on August 2nd. Mayne, having thus missed his quarry, returned to England.

The Azogue ships had good luck in their safe arrival. But for the foul winds which had delayed the departure of the two British squadrons there would have been a very fair chance of their being intercepted

[1] 'Lenox,' 70; 'Elizabeth,' 70; 'Kent,' 70, and 'Pearl,' 40.

off Ortegal, if indeed they were not met in the northern part of the Bay. Thus the first blow of reprisals in home waters had failed.

In the Mediterranean, Haddock, after refitting quietly at Mahon, had arrived at Gibraltar on April 1st on his way home in accordance with his instructions of recall. Here the orders met him rescinding those instructions, and directing him to remain at Gibraltar. He was still there in the end of June when the orders for executing reprisals reached him. He sailed within a couple of days with a strong squadron[1] to cruise in the approaches to Cadiz, with the objects of falling upon the Flota if it should put to sea, and of intercepting the homecoming Azogue ships of whose expected arrival he had received timely notice. Making his base off Cape St Mary's, that convenient spot just within Portuguese territory so often used by British squadrons for observing Cadiz, he kept a detachment cruising about Cape St Vincent, sending a constant succession of reliefs from the main body; and in this manner he was in a position to deal with either the Flota or the Azogue ships and to save his own as much as possible.

Haddock remained in this situation throughout July and the early part of August. Fresh instructions then reached him in which he was told to devote his main attention to preventing the Spaniards from using the delay in the declaration of war to concentrate their fleet or get the Flota to sea. Nothing, he was told, was to divert him from keeping a sufficient number of ships off Cadiz to frustrate either of these movements. Thus the British ministry were prepared to treat any attempt towards effecting a junction between the Cadiz and Ferrol squadrons as an act of war; but as this blockade could not be maintained indefinitely the Admiral soon received instructions for more drastic action. On August 13th the Privy Council had decided to attempt what was an actual act of war and to attack the Spanish squadrons in their own harbours[2]. His particular attention was directed to a squadron of four ships which was known to be at Carthagena under the command of M. de la Bene. The reason for this new orientation is clear. The administration, as Haddock's original instructions shew, were particularly anxious lest Spain should attack Minorca without any declaration of war, and were not averse from forestalling any such action if a favourable opportunity presented itself, by the destruction by bombardment or burning of the squadron and shipping which constituted the most serious threat to the island. The instruc-

[1] 'Somerset,' 'Berwick,' 'Edinburgh,' 'Ipswich,' 'Plymouth,' 'Dragon,' 'Canterbury,' and 'Chester.'

[2] This was agreed to by the Privy Council on August 13th, but the instructions were not sent out until September 4th—a delay of three weeks. Add. MS. 33004.

tions to attempt to destroy the Spanish squadron reached Haddock towards the end of September. He at once sent Lord Augustus Fitzroy to reconnoitre Carthagena and Barcelona—the latter being the port at which any troops destined for the enterprise would collect as they had on previous occasions—with orders to bring back a report as to the possibility of executing an attack upon either the squadron or the shipping by means of fireships and bomb-vessels. Lord Augustus, who returned in the middle of October, reported that the enterprise was impracticable in view of the strong defences of the harbours.

In the same despatch in which the burning of the shipping was recommended to Haddock's consideration, he was instructed to keep the main body of the squadron off Cadiz as long as the weather would permit, and then return to Mahon for the winter. His station at length yielded him two prizes of value, the first captures since the orders for reprisal. On September 23rd and 29th his squadron took two rich Caraccas ships whose cargoes were valued at over £200,000. This was more than double the sum of which the non-payment had led to the present situation.

In this manner the opening moves of a preparatory and protective nature were made and reprisals were carried out. Vernon had been sent with his squadron to attack Spanish trade in the most advantageous manner at one end of the trade route, at the same time protecting the British trade and settlements in that area, while Haddock's squadron at the other end held up the outgoing and intercepted the homecoming trade and protected Gibraltar and Minorca. The fleet in home waters was being fitted out as fast as the defective organisation for manning would admit, trade was carried on under convoy, and a few cruisers were sent out into the Soundings to protect shipping against attack by privateers. It now lay with the Council to determine how the coming war was to be conducted.

At the time when England issued the orders for reprisals, Spain had sixteen ships at Cadiz, of which two only, which were preparing to sail with the Flota in July, were ready. The remaining fourteen were under orders to be fitted out as soon as possible, in consequence of the threatening aspect of affairs. At Carthagena there were five ships, and at Ferrol there were from twelve to fourteen, of which four only were ready for the sea. Like England, Spain experienced great difficulties in manning her ships and was anxious to protract negociations and stave off reprisals or war as long as possible, or at any rate until the valuable Azogue ships should have arrived. She accordingly did not answer the British order for reprisals at once, but when those vessels reached Santander safely, in August, she felt herself in a position to take action. Her orders for reprisals were issued and a number of privateers got to sea with very little delay.

The plan upon which Spain intended to conduct the war consisted in a general attack upon British trade by privateers. The field was to be opened for them by forcing the British to concentrate their naval forces by threats of invasion of the British Islands and the recapture of Minorca and Gibraltar. For this purpose three armies were to be formed, one in Gallicia ostensibly to be thrown into Scotland or Ireland, one opposite Gibraltar and one in Catalonia to menace Minorca. It was further anticipated in Madrid that France would throw her lot in with Spain in accordance with the terms of the Family Compact. The number of ports the English squadrons would then have to keep under observation would demand so great a naval force that the Spaniards hoped that not enough ships would be available to deal with their privateers. They estimated that a squadron of twelve vessels would by these threats be tied to Gibraltar, and another of the same force to Mahon, so that the privateer zebecks from Majorca and Catalonia would be free to ravage the unprotected British trade[1].

The English plan consisted mainly in an attack on Spanish sea-borne commerce until information should be received as to which oversea Spanish ports were vulnerable to attack. But the idea as to how the campaign against commerce was to be organised was by no means clear in the minds of the Council; and while instructions were given to Haddock to cruise off Cadiz and blockade that port, no measures were taken to maintain a squadron off the other great arsenal at Ferrol. One only of the Spanish bases was watched; and, as Spain had hoped, an insufficient force was provided to deal with the privateers on which she so largely depended to cripple our resources. Very slowly the Council set about receiving and considering suggestions for an oversea military expedition against some part of the Spanish colonies. Although the order for reprisals was issued in June, no war plans were made or even discussed, nor were any methods taken to get troops ready (beyond the formulation in the Council of a pious opinion that it was advisable to augment the land forces) until September. On the 4th of that month the Privy Council met to consider the undertaking of some expedition to the West Indies, but dissolved without doing anything[2]. On the 10th they reassembled and heard a scheme proposed by Colonel Bladen[3] and his son-in-law, Mr Tinker, which consisted in a suggestion to attack and make a settlement in the

[1] Duro, *Armada Española*, vol. VI.
[2] Minutes of the Privy Council. Newcastle Papers, Add. MS. 33004.
[3] Colonel Bladen was uncle of Lord Hawke.

isthmus of Darien, and, holding this as a base, to seize the Spanish gold mines, which, said Mr Tinker, would be the means of carrying on a trade with the Spaniards and the opportunity of putting off great quantities of European goods. A force of 2000 men was supposed to be all that would be necessary. The Council were pleased with the notion; and, saying the scheme "deserved consideration," they referred it to Sir John Norris and Sir Charles Wager. These officers met on the 17th September and reported that the plan was feasible and could be carried out either by sending ships to Panama, or from the Eastern side by carrying the men up the Chagres River. Further consideration however caused the scheme to be laid aside, and another proposal which had been brought forward earlier[1] to send two 50-gun ships to the Philippines to intercept the Acapulco ship and assist the Portuguese to recover Salsette was examined. This developed into a proposal to attack Spain in the South Seas and as a part of the operation to capture Manila and there take the Acapulco ship. A squadron which should leave England before Christmas could reach Manila in time. The garrison was reported to be very weak—only 150 men—and it was suggested that after capture the city should be transferred to the East India Company who would then provide the permanent garrison—that a flourishing trade with China and the South Seas might result. A similar suggestion of making a permanent settlement on the coast of Chile with the same object was discussed[2] and rejected, but it was agreed that a squadron of three or four ships on the Chile coast would be able to do serious harm to Spanish trade. One further proposal remains to be mentioned. General Oglethorpe, the founder of the colony of Georgia, had recommended sending an expedition to demolish the Spanish settlement at San Augustine, and on September 25th this was agreed to. The General was to raise forces locally, ordnance and other stores were to be provided from England, and the stationed ships on the American coast were to form the necessary naval force. A 50-gun ship was at once sent to tell Oglethorpe what had been decided, and to carry the necessary instructions to the vessels scattered along the seaboard of the northern colonies.

Although the Council were able to make their decision in this small matter by the end of September they were wholly unable to do so with regard to the other and more important operations. The expedition to the Chile coast was not agreed upon until November 10th, and even then the Council could not make up their mind as to whether the Manila proposal should be carried out. They met and dissolved again many times without settling anything, preferring, it would appear

[1] On September 6th. [2] October 12th, 1739.

postponement to decision. It had been intended that Captain Anson should command the Manila expedition, and he had been recalled from sea in October—he was then cruising in the Soundings for the protection of trade—and informed that he would do so. The operations on the coast of Chile were to be undertaken by another squadron under Captain Cornewall who was to proceed thither round the Horn, and after ravaging the Spanish trade and settlements on the west coast of South America, stretch across the Pacific and join Anson at Manila. This scheme was however dropped, at the instance of Walpole who considered that it would take too many men, and that as one squadron was already going to Chile it might as well afterwards cross the Pacific and take Manila. Finally, after three months of vacillation and two months after war had been formally declared, the Council made up its mind in the direction suggested by Walpole. Anson was to take four ships round the Horn, attack the trade of Chile, attempt to capture Darien, and if necessary proceed afterwards to Manila and endeavour to intercept the Acapulco ship.

The larger question of a serious territorial attack on the Spanish possessions had meantime been discussed as well, though the manner of doing so had been equally dilatory. The Council on September 10th expressed the opinion that it was "extremely desirable" that an expedition should be made in the Spanish West Indies which should distress the Spaniards, and they asked when any number of land forces sufficient for that purpose could, with safety, be spared from the country. No answer to this elementary request seems to have been given, and although an opportunity of increasing our land forces in a simple manner was afforded, advantage was not taken of it. In September the King of Sweden had offered to hire a number of his Hessian troops to France; but Prince William of Hesse-Cassel who was to marry Princess Mary, offered 6000 troops to England. The Council advised the King to accept the offer, which would set free a number of troops for service abroad, but nothing came of it. Another month went by, and on October 12th, the day after the Council had advised the declaration of war, the subject of the large expedition which had lain dormant since September 10th was once more brought out of its pigeon-hole, and Wager and Norris were directed to consider it. This they did. "Sir Charles and I," wrote Norris, "took into consideration what Sir Robert Walpole has so earnestly desired as his Majesty's opinion and all of his Council, that some undertaking of consequence should be undertaken in the West Indies; and the Havana being the first to be wished for." The two Admirals examined all the information available about Havana and concluded that it was impossible to attack it by sea, the town being walled round and the entrance closed by a boom, but that it could be captured by an army. Its batteries mounted 152 guns and its garrison consisted of 1300 good soldiers, 5000 militia and six troops of horse of from 60 to 70 men each; the arsenals contained arms for 10,000 men. Taking these matters into consideration it was estimated that an army of from 8000 to 10,000 men would be required, who might be landed in a bay to the westward of Havana—a distance of about two miles—while the ships carried the heavy stores along the coast. The town was reported to be weakest to the westward, but with no gates in that direction, so that the attacking troops would not be in danger of a sally by the garrison. If however so many men were not available, Wager and Norris considered Cartagena the next best place to take and hold, "as the entrance of that port is narrow and may be made defensible against a stronger force; the town is likewise commodious for that purpose and, being upon the continent, if we can maintain ourselves, communication with the natives will follow, and the way to the mines [that] are now used by the Spaniards[1]." Thus Cartagena would fulfil the necessary condition of being self-supporting, and easy to hold, would open up a trade with the interior, and by its position on the flank of the trade route to Porto Bello would enable the power that held it to dominate the Spanish trade. "The Spaniards," said Norris, "would hardly venture to send their galleons to Porto Bello with us in possession of Cartagena." In suggesting the number of men that would be necessary the Admiral instanced that de Pointis took the city in 1697 with 3000 men, and proposed to send the same number, which might be supplemented by a force of 1000 local buccaneers.

When these proposals were put before the Council they caused some consternation among its members. Walpole informed the sea-officers that the idea of taking Cartagena came as a complete surprise to the Ministry, who had never had that operation in their minds; while as to Havana, he said, they had never imagined that so large an army would be required. The intention had been to send General Wade with a far smaller force than that suggested, and though he thought the lesser number proposed for Cartagena might be obtained, he did not think the 10,000 for Havana could be had[2]. To this the Admirals very properly replied that the military force was purely a soldier's question on which their opinions might be wrong, and Norris added that "the best method to avoid diversity of opinion would be a meeting with a Secretary of State, Sir Robert Walpole and whom his Majesty should think proper to be consulted, which of the expeditions should

[1] *Diary of Sir John Norris.* [2] *Diary.*

be undertaken: and Sir Charles Wager and myself being with them would answer how far the naval assistance could sustain the expedition that should be thought proper to be undertaken[1]." This proposal was not adopted, and full meetings of the Council went on without any decision being arrived at. One day it was agreed that 10,000 men could not be had; Havana was then laid aside and Cartagena considered; a few days later the Duke of Newcastle suggested that perhaps more men could be raised in America which might make the Havana enterprise possible. But when the subject became difficult it was dropped and one of the other expeditions—Manila, Panama, Chile—was brought up and toyed with. The inevitable result was that time passed and nothing was done.

While the British Ministry were thus dallying with war the Spaniards were making effective preparations. Reinforcements were being despatched from Ferrol to Cartagena and Havana, both of which were rightly considered as threatened, and privateers were putting to sea in increasing numbers daily. The Spanish armies were assembling as arranged, and the fleets were preparing, albeit slowly.

The omission on the part of the British Fleet to observe Ferrol, an omission which permitted those reinforcements to sail without hindrance was not due to forgetfulness. From the first Norris had urged that ships should be kept off Finisterre for the double purpose of intercepting troops and supplies intended for the West Indies, and as a precaution against a possible junction of the fleets of the supposed allies, France and Spain. No notice of his reiterated advice had however been taken. Sir Charles Wager appears from Norris's account to have persistently opposed this measure. Sir John's disappointment at the failure to take this obvious step is repeatedly shewn in his accounts of the Council meetings. His *Diary* for November 26th, 1739, contains the following entry, rather involved in its construction but clear in meaning: "Sir Charles [Wager] was asked if 2 Spanish men-of-war with about 4 or 5 hundred men were not sailed from Ferrol to the West Indies: he said he believed there was; and in almost all Councils I have been called to I have always proposed some ships to cruise off the Norward Capes to prevent the Spaniards putting to sea from Ferrol: the different sentiments of Sir Charles has prevented it, and it has always been my opinion that if we could not keep a squadron off that coast to prevent the ships at Ferrol coming to sea, that [they] might with those men-of-war and two or three thousand soldiers send to the West Indies, and by that means disappoint any desires we might have of making great conquests in those parts."

[1] *Diary of Sir John Norris*, October 21st, 1739.

Norris himself was strongly in favour of making Havana the main objective. His plan was to collect all the troops then in the West Indian garrisons and North America, together with those from San Augustin after that place had been captured, and assemble them at Providence, there to be joined by an army coming out from England. The whole force would then move direct to Havana. Climate, he urged, was a matter of the highest importance in determining the objective, and in this respect Havana was in every way preferable to Cartagena, being 12° further to the northward and comparatively healthy, whereas Cartagena was notoriously unhealthy. The approaches to Havana presented no great difficulties, but at Cartagena the landing was bad in the strong winds that prevail along the coast, and, in addition, the fortifications were known to have been considerably strengthened since its capture in 1697.

A decision, typical of the Duke of Newcastle, was finally arrived at on December 5th. The expedition should be sent to Jamaica, and when it arrived there a local council of officers should decide what was to be done with it. The responsibility was thus shifted from Newcastle's shoulders to those of other people. As to the command of the army, the first proposal was that it should be given to Lord Stair, a veteran of Marlborough's wars and one of the most distinguished soldiers of the time; but the King refused to consider his name when it was submitted to him, and desired the command to be given to Lord Cathcart[1], another experienced officer who had taken part in the previous war.

The Council at last, six months after they began to take steps which must infallibly lead to war, had succeeded in deciding that an expedition should be sent to the West Indies, its objective to be decided when it got there; and the question of raising troops for that expedition began to form the subject of their deliberations. It was agreed that a force should be raised in America under the command of Colonel Spotswood of Virginia; that the Governors of the colonies should be instructed to embody men, grant commissions to officers and arrange transport so as to meet the army coming from England at Jamaica; and that all the troops in the West Indian garrisons were to join the expedition. Five regiments, to be called Marines, were to be raised at home; but in truth, these regiments were Marines in name only. The essential of a Marine was and always had been that he was borne principally for manning and fighting on board the ships of the Fleet. These Marines were not to be in any way allotted to the squadron, but were to be an expeditionary force, and were given the name of

[1] *Diary of Sir John Norris*, December 14th, 1739.

Marine only because under that name it was easier to raise men, as the public believed them to be for the service of the Navy. The regiments were ordered to be assembled in the Isle of Wight, and transports for 8000 men at the rate of 1½ tons per man, victualled for six months, were ordered on the 31st December, 1739.

While these matters were under discussion the preparation of the fleet in home waters proceeded slowly. Men were the great difficulty. Although bounties of two guineas a head for able seamen and thirty shillings for ordinaries were offered, seamen were not forthcoming. It was proposed to remedy this lack in various ways. One suggestion was to withdraw the protections from impress extended to the seamen of the coastwise traffic and fisheries who numbered some 14,000 and thereby make them available for service in the fleet. Another alternative was to man the fleet largely with soldiers; while a better one, which had the support of the sea-officers of the Council, was to re-establish the Marines and to use them for the objects for which they had originally been raised of manning the fleet and providing a body of continuous service seamen[1]. Sir Robert Walpole's proposal to embody men into regiments for the West Indian expedition and call them Marines, when they were not going to form part complements of the ships, was naturally ill-received by the seamen on the Council; and though the men so raised were denominated "Marines" in spite of the protests of the Admiral of the Fleet, the intention as to their functions was subsequently modified and a proportion of them was definitely allocated to the sea-service. But while these discussions continued as to the methods in which men were to be obtained to man the fleet, the ships were lying helpless in the dockyards, the ports of Spain were insufficiently watched, and the ports of France were not watched at all.

It soon however became known that, for the present at any rate, no danger was to be expected from France. A letter from Lord Waldegrave, our Ambassador in Paris, received on October 25th, shewed that no immediate junction of the French and Spanish ships was to be apprehended, as the French ships could not be ready before the spring of the following year. In consequence Haddock was even ordered to send home six of his ships[2], a number reduced a week later to four, and eventually cancelled altogether when French preparations were again reported. For the present, a watch on Ferrol and Cadiz

[1] See Appendix on the manning question.

[2] He had had a reinforcement of six ships sent him in consequence of the expected interference of France. He was to send home six of his earlier ships when this reinforcement reached him. Minutes of Privy Council, October 25th, 1739, Add. MS. 33004.

would meet all strategical requirements; but it was imperative to hurry on the manning and fitting out of the fleet, as the French might early in the next year have twenty-eight ships of the line ready[1]. Seeing what the actual state of preparations were it is not surprising that when on October 2nd the Council met and discussed whether it were not now time to declare war, Norris strongly opposed such a precipitate step. He urged that there was not only no need to declare war, but that it would be most undesirable to do so until the naval and military forces were ready to carry out offensive operations against Spain and to protect the kingdom and its outlying possessions. At present, he pointed out, such squadrons as were abroad had instructions which entitled them to do all that lay within their powers; more they could not do. The winter was approaching in which regular sea blockades would be most difficult to maintain, and until the fleet was manned it would be impossible to support those blockades. Besides this, he argued, France could have no object in joining Spain until we actually declared war, and it would be well to be ready to meet both powers from the beginning. To exhaust our ships in a winter blockade would lead to their being unready to undertake the operations in the spring when the naval forces of both the allied powers might be ready for combined action against us. He might indeed have continued his arguments further—possibly he did—and carried them on from the unreadiness of personnel and material to the not less important matter of unreadiness of a war plan. But whatever pleas he used he only succeeded in delaying the declaration of war for a few days. Notwithstanding his protests and arguments, the decision, deferred on October 2nd, was definitely taken on October 11th, and war was formally declared by proclamation on October 19th. In this proclamation the unjust seizures made and the injuries done to our merchant ships and seamen, the interference with legitimate commerce, the claim of Spain to the right of search in other than her territorial waters were referred to. Her failure to fulfil her part of the arrangements agreed to in the Convention of the Pardo, and the apparent impossibility of obtaining either redress or any guarantee of future security were mentioned; and it was represented that since all peaceful means of settling the dispute had proved fruitless there remained to us only to endeavour to secure our rights by war.

To this communication Spain replied on November 17–28 by one couched in similar language. England's declaration of war, her pretensions, and her failure to observe treaties, left Spain, so it ran, no

[1] Eleven were preparing at Brest, five at Rochefort and twelve at Toulon.

course open but to declare war in self-defence. Relations between the two powers were broken off, and commerce between them ceased[1].

War was at last begun, and it cannot be said that it began under the most favourable auspices. The fleet was not ready, the army was not ready, and the offensive operations had not yet been determined, nor were they fully decided upon two months later. After a period extending over several years during which the relations of the two Powers had steadily tended towards a conflict, war had actually broken out before the British Administration began to consider in what manner it should be conducted. Months more passed before the Cabinet decided, and then only partially, what operations against the oversea possessions of the enemy should be undertaken and how they should be executed. Such an unreadiness shews how little the problem of war occupied the mind of the Government during the years of disturbed peace preceding 1739.

[1] The cessation of commerce meant the laying up or transfer of a very large quantity of British shipping, the volume of which may be appreciated by the fact that in the year 1737, out of 1243 French, Dutch and British ships that entered Cadiz, 183 were French, 153 Dutch and 907 were English. Duro, *Armada Española*, vol. VI.

CHAPTER III

THE OPENING OPERATIONS IN THE WEST INDIES

THE orders for reprisals, issued when Spain failed to fulfil the obligations imposed upon her by the Convention[1], reached Commodore Brown at Jamaica in July 1739. They directed him to "act hostilities" against the Spaniards in the West Indies, and accordingly he took his squadron[2] to sea early in August, and cruised with it in a solid body, first between Cape Corrientes and Cape Antonio for outgoing trade, and then between Cape Santa Maria and Havana for the trade arriving at the latter port. Two ships were detailed to see the homeward-bound British trade through the Windward Passage, and a sloop was kept cruising along the north coast of Jamaica to guard against small raids from Cuba.

Brown's information was that the Spanish ships in the West Indies were scattered. He heard there were no ships of war at Havana, but that three lay in Cartagena, two in Porto Bello and two at San Domingo; a small force under Pizarro, which had been sent to cover the trade from Porto Bello in the preceding winter, was reported to have sailed already for Spain and was in fact the force that reached Santander on August 2nd. The galleons however were collecting or collected at Havana, and upon them, as the principal objective against which reprisals could be executed, he concentrated his attention. What amounted to a pacific blockade of Havana ensued, as a consequence of which hardly a ship left that port between August and October. In the middle of October, knowing that Vernon was on his way and ought to arrive shortly, Brown carried the bulk of his squadron down to Jamaica leaving only the 'Windsor' and 'Falmouth' to watch Havana. He arrived on the 28th to find Vernon impatiently awaiting him.

Admiral Edward Vernon, whom we have already seen starting from England to cruise off Finisterre, was now fifty-five years of age. At Westminster as a boy under the famous Dr Busby he had learned Latin and Greek, and is said to have made some progress in Hebrew by the age of sixteen, when he went to Oxford. There he studied mathematics, navigation and geometry, and, under a private

1 Minutes of the Privy Council, June 3rd, 1739, B.M. Add. MS. 33004.

2 'Hampton Court,' 70; 'Windsor,' 60; 'Falmouth,' 50; 'Torrington,' 40; 'Diamond,' 40; 'Shoreham,' 20. The 'Windsor' was at that moment cruising off Hispaniola: Brown recalled her to join him as soon as possible.

tutor, fortification and gunnery. He was nearly seventeen when he entered the Navy, and his first experience of battle was at the destruction of the galleons at Vigo, which took place a month before his eighteenth birthday.

Vernon thus started his sea-life with a good grounding in the elements of the most important part of his profession, and also with a liberal education of a wider nature than that of the average sea-officer of his time. He combined broad views on varied subjects with an attention to all matters of detail connected with his profession. His writing is the formed hand of an educated man, and his letters display an insight and thoughtfulness which are not to be found in the same degree in those of the majority of his contemporaries. His early education may possibly have contributed to his defects as well as to his qualities, and it is not unnatural that while his outlook was wider than that of the greater number of the officers of the day he was affected by an impatient temper which did not permit him to suffer fools gladly. He who saw so clearly the essentials of a situation, who could pierce through superficialities and reach main principles, found himself unable to sit silent while he observed an Administration blundering in the mires created by its own lack of foresight. He could not resist the temptation, which a certain facility in expressing his opinions encouraged, of putting forward his views and criticisms with a directness which no Ministry at that time appreciated. In Parliament, where he sat for Rochester, Penrhyn and Ipswich[1], he was a frequent speaker, especially upon all subjects connected with the seamen, of whose cause he was always a pronounced and advanced advocate.

Vernon's first operations on leaving England had been concerned with the attempt to intercept Pizarro. Apart from this diversion, his instructions, dated July 16th, 1739, directed him to take command in the West Indies and there "commit all sorts of hostilities against the Spaniards in such manner as you shall judge the most proper." Further, he was to sink, burn and destroy all Spanish ships; to procure the best intelligence about the galleons at Cartagena and Porto Bello, particularly the time at which they were to sail from either port on their return voyage, and of all Spanish ships in West Indian waters; to take station and cruise or lie in the best places to intercept Spanish trade; if the Spaniards appeared to be preparing to attack South Carolina or Georgia, to send ships to intercept any squadron or flotilla sent from Havana for that purpose; and always to keep two or three

[1] Horace Walpole says he was elected at the same time for these three constituencies (vol. I. p. 93). He is shewn as Member for them in *Parliamentary Debates*.

small frigates about Jamaica for the protection of that island and its local trade. The instructions continued: "In case you shall find that the Spanish men-of-war or galleons either at Cartagena or Porto Bello lie so much exposed as that you shall judge it practicable to burn or destroy them in port, you are to attempt to do it provided it may not too much hazard the disabling of our squadron under your command from performing any other services that may be necessary." Secret instructions were added later, directing him to make it his business to procure the best intelligence as to where a descent could be made on the Spanish dominions in the West Indies or on the continent, which would be of prejudice to Spain and of advantage to England. He was to state the number of troops that would be required, and, so soon as he had ascertained these matters, to send the information home with the utmost despatch by a sloop.

From all this it will be observed that Vernon was by no means sent out, as the popular legend would have it, to capture Porto Bello; for except in so far as an attack on the shipping in the harbour is mentioned, Porto Bello is not referred to in his orders. It will also be noted that territorial attack on the Spanish possessions was contemplated, though not decided, so early as July, 1739; but while Vernon was ordered to send home prompt information as to where these possessions were most vulnerable, the Ministry took no steps whatever to be ready to act upon that information when it should be received, other than by passing a resolution in a Cabinet Council in June that His Majesty should be advised to increase his land forces[1].

From the time of leaving England Vernon had assiduously busied himself in preparing his squadron for service. His first consideration was the manner in which he would handle his command in action, and he issued an addition to the Fighting Instructions "for forming a sort of *Corps de Reserve* in case my squadron should exceed the number of the Spanish Fleet I might meet with, and which I explained more fully to them in the verbal orders I gave them upon it yesterday, having called all my Captains together to deliver them their orders, and advise with them on the execution of them[2]." The Additional Instructions ran as follows:—

"In case of meeting any squadron of the enemy's ships, whose number may be less than those of the squadron of his Majesty's ships under my command, and that I would have any of the smaller ships quit the line, I will in such case make the signal for speaking with the captain of that ship I would have quit the line: and at the same time I will put a flag, striped yellow and white, at the

[1] Cabinet Memoranda, June 3rd, 1739, Add. MS. 32993; Minutes of the Privy Council, June 3rd, 1739, Add. MS. 33004.

[2] Vernon to Duke of Newcastle, July 29th, 1739.

flagstaff at the main topmast-head, upon which the said ship or ships are to quit the line and the next ships are to close the line, for having our ships of greatest force to form a line just equal to the enemy's. And as, upon the squadrons engaging, it is not to be expected that the ships withdrawn out of the line can see or distinguish signals at such a juncture, it is therefore strictly enjoined and required of such captain or captains, who shall have their signal or signals made to withdraw out of the line, to demean themselves as a *Corps-de-réserve* to the main squadron, and to place themselves in the best situation for giving relief to any ship of the squadron that may be disabled or hardest pressed by the enemy, having in the first place regard to the ship I shall have my flag on board, as where the honour of his Majesty's flag is principally concerned. And as it is morally impossible to fix any general rule to occurrences that must be regulated from the weather and the enemy's disposition, this is left to the respective captains' judgement that shall be ordered out of the line to govern himself by as becomes an officer of prudence and resolution, and as he will answer the contrary at his peril."

This order is noteworthy. It is the first Additional Instruction; and thus the originator of the system which set the Navy free from the trammels of the Fighting Instructions was Vernon. His care was always to look as far ahead as possible and to issue instructions to govern such cases as he could foresee; but he was none the less careful to limit those instructions, and to explain their limitations, making it clear to his subordinates that he could provide only for the conduct of affairs up to a certain point, after which it fell to individual captains to act according to the circumstances of the case. He realized that signals in battle may fail, and impressed upon his captains that he could not depend upon being able to send them any instructions during the progress of an action. He provided, in fact, the major tactics to be followed, and left the minor tactics to be evolved according to the unforeseen circumstances that might arise. "It is from my knowledge of the experience of my captains," he wrote, "and my confidence in their resolution, that I have my chief reliance successfully to execute his Majesty's orders." Throughout his operations Vernon pursued this course, taking his captains into his confidence, explaining to them verbally what he wished them to do, and letting them know that he depended on them to carry out his intentions by an intelligent exercise of their own judgment. And in no case during his command did his captains fail him.

Besides this he exercised his ships' companies daily with the guns and small arms. He had, he said, found "our unfledged mariners very raw at it." This inexperience of his ships' companies was the theme of more than one of his letters. "We are under one general misfortune," he wrote, "to be sent upon service with such numbers of raw men we have to instruct in everything"; and it was upon his passage out that he expressed his opinion to the Duke of Newcastle that it would be well to turn several of the marching regiments into

Marines in order to strengthen the ships' companies with riflemen, and provide men capable of being readily turned into able seamen—an intention as regards the formation of a Marine corps that dated back to the reign of William and Mary[1], and was still prominent in the minds of the senior men.

Vernon's efforts to intercept the Azogue ships on his way out had been fruitless. After leaving Finisterre he had stood for the Canaries and thence passed on to Palma, but had failed to get any news of them at either place. He therefore sailed for Antigua which he reached on the 28th of September. From Antigua he went on to St Kitts and there detached Captain Waterhouse with three ships[2] to harry the trade off the Spanish Main from La Guayra to Puerto Cabello, and then rejoin him at Port Royal. Waterhouse on parting company sailed to La Guayra, where he saw some ships and small craft hauled up in the cod of the bay. He at once made preparations to attack them, but when he got nearer, he found the difficulties were greater than he expected. The harbour mouth was defended by two well placed forts, he had neither chart nor pilot to guide him in the local navigation, and the shifty breeze inshore increased the risks of attacking under such circumstances. The forts received him with a smart fire, and he soon found that an attempt to force his way into the bay would probably involve his squadron in losses which would not be compensated for by the destruction of a few coasting vessels. Knowing how important it was that his ships should be in a fit condition for the more important services that were to follow, he hauled off after a brisk engagement and proceeded to rejoin Vernon at Jamaica. His conduct met with the Admiral's full approval.

After detaching Waterhouse, Vernon had proceeded with the rest of the squadron to Jamaica, and anchored at Port Royal on the 12th of October. Here he found things very different from what he expected. His original intention had been to proceed direct to Havana to intercept the galleons, but he now heard that they had not even all arrived at that port. One was still at Cartagena and none were likely to be ready to sail till after Christmas. He had expected to be joined by Commodore Brown immediately on his arrival at Jamaica, and was much annoyed to find the Commodore was not there, but was still cruising with his squadron at Havana, where according to his information, there was no need for him.

Vernon's last instructions directed him to advise as to where a territorial attack would best be made against Spain. His views on this

[1] See Appendix.

[2] 'Strafford,' 60; 'Princess Louisa,' 60; 'Norwich,' 50.

question, in the light of both an earlier and later experience of land warfare in the West Indies, are so clear that they shall be quoted with some fullness. He was uncompromisingly opposed to any operations of the kind on an extended scale; but if territorial attack, with a view to ultimate possession, were intended, he considered Cuba would afford Spain the "most sensible loss," and was most capable of being retained and colonized. "But when I reflect," he wrote, "on the populousness of that island, their neighbourhood to the French at Hispaniola, who would never fail to assist them and could always speedily do it, the great expense of a transport from Britain of any number of forces into these seas, and the many unsuccessful expeditions of that kind that have been attempted by land in these seas, the best advice I can think of giving is to lay aside all thoughts of such expensive land expeditions, as all advantages may be better and cheaper procured by keeping a strong superiority at sea in these seas; by which means, let who will possess the country our Royal Master may command the wealth of it: and as such a force at all times not only serves to distress his Majesty's enemies by destroying their trade, but to protect and encourage that of his Majesty's subjects, I can never be the adviser of land expeditions especially into this country, that may drain the Royal Treasury, and, in case of a French war, disable His Majesty from keeping a superiority at sea, on which, in my apprehensions, both the security and the prosperity of the Kingdom depend[1]."

Among the proposals he was directed to consider was that, already referred to, of Mr Tinker for making a settlement at Darien with the object of developing a private trade with the Spaniards. This scheme he deprecated. Such trading could equally well be carried on from Jamaica, which was also a better base for naval operations, both from its geographical position and from the fact that it was more difficult for the enemy to gather information of intended movements from there than from any place on the mainland. "Success," said Vernon in a letter to the Duke of Newcastle of January 23rd, 1740, "depends on well-concerted enterprises of which they can have the least notice." He pointed out as an additional argument against Darien that scattered solitary settlements were only a weakness, needing garrisons from the army and detachments from the fleet to defend them. The wisdom of these remarks has received abundant confirmation since Vernon's time.

Vernon also answered that part of the questions put to him as to the force required, in an interesting manner. "My own reflections," he

[1] Vernon to the Duke of Newcastle, October 31st, 1739. Received March 13th, 1740.

wrote, "upon the almost general disappointments of past expeditions in America is this: that they were principally owing to delays in order to gather more strength in these parts, by which they were weakened more in the force they brought out within that time than any additional forces they collected amounted to: and gave the enemy all the time they could desire to strengthen themselves against them. So that, in my judgment, I should limit all expeditions to this country to be entered upon immediately on their arrival, and to be executed within the first six weeks, before their men would begin to fall sick[1]." The history of West Indian operations shews how well judged was this advice. At a rather later date the life of a battalion in the West Indies averaged two years. In the three terrible years 1793, 1794 and 1795 the services of no less than eighty thousand men were lost to the country, and at any time during those years the proportion of sick in the West Indian garrisons might be taken as fifty per cent. at the least. In reading these almost prophetic opinions of Vernon's it is not difficult[2] to appreciate his impatience at the dilatory methods of Wentworth in the subsequent operations at Cartagena and Santiago.

While Vernon considered what operations should follow, he had to determine what to do at once to distress Spain. Casting his eye round the station he saw that he could not strike any blow directly against the Spanish Navy, and his attention centred on the two nearest main ports of trade—Cartagena and Porto Bello. Trelawny, the Governor of Jamaica, who conferred with him, strongly recommended an immediate attack on Cartagena, but with the force he had, without more troops, Vernon did not consider it would be practicable. Porto Bello, however, he thought could be taken. Reports reached him that the Spaniards were moving, or intended moving, many of their ships towards it from Havana, Vera Cruz and Cartagena, thus showing that they were very anxious about its safety. The treasure had not yet reached Porto Bello, and therefore no direct blow in the shape of its capture could be effected, but an attack on the harbour promised several important results. By arriving there before the Spaniards, the British squadron might attack and destroy the fortifications and render the harbour useless as an assembling-place for trade; or it might, by being off the port when the enemy arrived, intercept his ships and sink them; or finally, if any Spanish ships were there before him, Vernon felt confident of being able to sail in and attack and destroy them at their anchors, as he had seen the galleons at Vigo attacked and de-

[1] Vernon to the Duke of Newcastle, January 23rd, 1740.

[2] Cf. Fortescue, *History of the British Army*, vol. IV. and vol. VII. Bryan Edwards, *History of the West Indies*.

stroyed in his younger days. Everything in his opinion pointed to Porto Bello as his most suitable objective, and in deciding to sail there, he acted in fact upon the principle that the best place to find the enemy's squadron is in the vicinity of what he most wishes to protect.

Having made his decision, Vernon prepared to sail as soon as possible, with or without Commodore Brown. Brown however returned to Jamaica in time on the 28th of October, his ship was watered and victualled with all despatch, and the squadron[1], consisting of the five ships Vernon had brought out from England and the 'Hampton Court' sailed for Porto Bello on the 5th November. A sixth-rate—the 'Sheerness,' 20—was detached to watch Cartagena and keep Vernon informed of any movements made in that part, especially looking out for the arrival of reinforcements from Spain.

The harbour of Porto Bello is a small bay running about east and west, a few miles to the eastward of the Colon of to-day: to the westward lies the harbour of Nombre de Dios. Both of these ports were connected with Panama by a paved road (which still exists) across the isthmus. By this road the treasure and merchandise were carried to and from Panama, except such portion as was embarked at Chagres at the season when the river of that name was full enough to permit navigation[2]; at such time the treasure was carried down the Chagres, leaving only a short land journey between Panama and the place of shipment on the river.

The entrance to Porto Bello harbour is a bare half mile across, and the land rises steeply behind it on either side. The winds inside are tricky and in the month of October are light and mainly westerly. On the north shore, with thickly wooded hills immediately behind it, stood the Iron Castle. At the head of the bay in its south-eastern corner were the Gloria and San Jeronimo Castles, protecting the town. There is bold water close inshore at the Iron Castle, so that ships could go practically alongside, but the Gloria and San Jeronimo could not be approached closer than about 400 yards.

Vernon issued his orders as to the manner in which he proposed to attack, on the day after sailing from Jamaica. The squadron, led by Commodore Brown, was to sail in close line of battle so as to pass less than a cable's length from the Iron Castle, each ship firing its broadside into the castle as she went by; from this point Brown was instructed to lay up for the Gloria Castle and anchor as near as he

[1] The line of battle was as follows: 'Hampton Court,' 70; 'Worcester,' 60; 'Norwich,' 50; 'Burford,' 70; 'Strafford,' 60; 'Princess Louisa,' 60.

[2] The present Panama Canal follows the line of the Chagres River for a long way.

could to its eastern end, leaving room for the 'Worcester' to anchor astern of him abreast the western bastion. The 'Norwich,' after passing the Iron Castle was to anchor off the fort of San Jeronimo and engage it; the 'Strafford' and 'Princess Louisa,' following the flagship, were to anchor abreast the Iron Castle and assist in its bombardment. All ships were directed to have their longboats in tow astern and their barges alongside ready to tow the longboats in with the soldiers, who would receive their directions as to landing from the Admiral. Special instructions were given to avoid hurry, confusion or waste of ammunition.

The squadron arrived near Porto Bello on November 20th, and Vernon anchored for the night some two to three leagues to windward in order to avoid being driven to leeward. At five o'clock next morning he called all his captains on board to give them final instructions. An hour later the squadron weighed, formed line of battle, and beat to windward until it could weather the Salmadinas rocks. In order to avoid the possibility of any mistake in the leading, Vernon had arranged that when the red flag was hoisted at the maintopmast-head it was to indicate that Commodore Brown was to lead whichever tack was on board. This was the first introduction of this invaluable signal which so greatly increased the flexibility of tactics. It was wanted badly when Mathews left Hyères Bay on February 10th, 1744[1].

The wind during the forenoon was between north and north-northwest. By about 2 P.M. the 'Hampton Court' was in a position to weather the Salmadinas, and the Commodore bore away, passed between the Rocks and Drake's Island, and when he opened the harbour mouth hauled his wind to stand up harbour. But now the wind came easterly. His orders to attack the Gloria Castle became impracticable. Without hesitation he disobeyed them and anchored half a cable off the Iron Castle. His prompt action received full approval. "Commodore Brown," wrote Vernon, "discharged his duty like an experienced good officer." For about half an hour the 'Hampton Court' alone was engaged with the Iron Castle, for the light wind had opened out the squadron and their progress was slow, but in that half hour the heavy fire of the Commodore's broadsides beat down much of the Spanish defences. The 'Hampton Court's' cable was then cut away by the enemy's shot and she dropped to the southward before she could bring up again, but as she did so the next two ships,

[1] On that occasion a shift of wind on leading out of harbour reversed the tacks and in consequence the whole line had to be inverted in order that the commander ordered to lead with the starboard tacks might get into his position. The meaning attributed to the signal by Vernon was a special one, the red flag—No. 3—having no signal significance when so hoisted.

'Norwich' and 'Worcester,' came in and took up their positions inshore of her. They opened fire as briskly as the leading ship had done, while Brown, seeing that the resistance would not be long, prepared for the assault which was to follow by getting his soldiers and seamen into his boats ready to push in to the shore immediately the signal to land was made.

Close behind the 'Norwich' and 'Worcester' came the flagship, which was so lucky as to pick up a large puff of wind as she rounded the point, which enabled her to luff up and anchor closer her next ahead; she dropped her anchor within about a pistol shot of the castle, hauled her broadside to bear with a spring, and opened fire. A tremendous battering of heavy guns and fusillade of small arms from the three closely placed ships was now concentrated on the castle, whose defenders were already shaken by the 'Hampton Court's' attack. Vernon very quickly saw that the resistance was broken and within a few minutes of anchoring signalled for the boats to land. Brown's boats were immediately on their way, and in less than a quarter of an hour the men were on shore, scrambling up into the lower batteries, helter skelter, driving what remained of the garrison before them. Such of the Spaniards as were able escaped, and when the attackers climbed into the upper batteries they found no more than some thirty-five of the defenders remaining alive. Before the 'Strafford' and 'Princess Louisa' got into position abreast the Iron Castle the Union flag was flying over its bastions.

Thus four ships only had got into action and had all been engaged with the Iron Castle. The rest of the plan was undone. The reason for this was that the wind, which had been at about north when the squadron stood into the harbour, went round to the eastward before the ships were in position, a shift which not only delayed the rear ships from getting into action but also prevented the three leading ships from carrying out the intended plan and moving up the harbour to engage the Gloria and San Jeronimo Castles. Brown, in his *Journal*, after describing the capture of the Iron Castle, remarks: "The wind being far easterly which obliged me to anchor as it was right down the harbour: ordered a spring on our cable and fired several shots at Gloria Castle as they did at our ships till nigh eight o'clock at night." Some of the Gloria's fire reached the ships of the squadron. The 'Burford's' foretopmast was cut through and other slight damage done, but most of the shot fell short. The ships replied, and although the range was long they dropped some shot into the castle and sunk a sloop lying close off it. Vernon soon afterwards carried the squadron a little further to the south-westward to be out of range for the night,

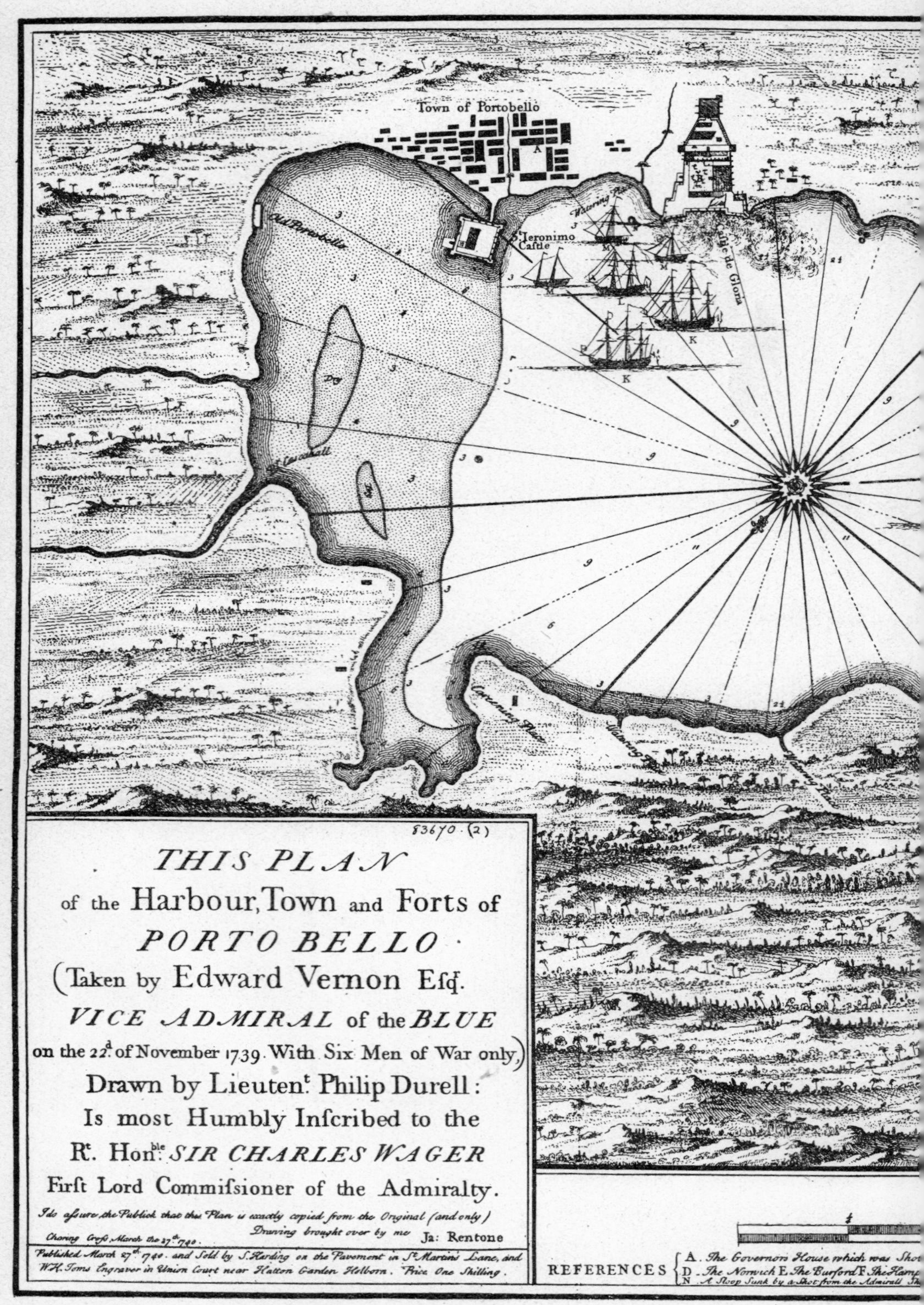
Town of Portobello
A
Old Portobello
S.t Jeronimo Castle
Watering Place
Castle de Gloria
Dry
Careening Place
Watering Place
83670.(2)
THIS PLAN
of the Harbour, Town and Forts of
PORTO BELLO
(Taken by Edward Vernon Esq.
VICE ADMIRAL of the BLUE
on the 22.d of November 1739. With Six Men of War only,)
Drawn by Lieuten.t Philip Durell:
Is most Humbly Inscribed to the
R.t Hon.ble SIR CHARLES WAGER
First Lord Commissioner of the Admiralty.
I do assure the Publick that this Plan is exactly copied from the Original (and only) Drawing brought over by me Ja: Rentone
Charing Cross, March the 27.th 1740.
Published March 27.th 1740. and Sold by S. Harding on the Pavement in S.t Martin's Lane, and W.H. Toms Engraver in Union Court near Hatton Garden Holborn. Price One Shilling.
REFERENCES
A. The Governors House which was Sho
D. The Norwich E. The Burford F. The Hamp
N. A Sloop Sunk by a Shot from the Admirall Sh

Gualiclia R.
Rio Mandaton
Dry
Dry
Id. Bona Aventura
C
F
I
P
D
E
G
I
Iron Castle
Drakes Id.
H
Sallmadinos
P. Durell delin. November 1739.
W.H. Tomo Sculpt 1740
A Scale of Two English Miles
P The Top Gallant Mast of the Norwich Shot off by one of the Cannons from the Iron Castle
ugh by one of the lower tier of Guns from the Admirals Ship the Burford B. Plantation in the Castle de Gloria. C. The Worcester Man of War
ourt G. The Strafford H. The Princess Louisa I The Tenders K Two Spanish Guarda Costas L Spanish Snow that brought over Capt. Rentone M 3 Trading Sloops
Two Boats going to land the Soldiers under the Walls of the Fort. NB The Figures on the Sands are Feet the other Fathom

and the ships ran out the necessary warps and made all possible preparations to be ready to resume the attack the first thing in the morning.

At 5 A.M. on the 22nd, the Admiral again called the captains on board and gave them instructions for the attack on the remaining castles, and an hour later the squadron began moving up harbour. Hardly had they got under way when a launch was seen coming off from the shore with a flag of truce, brought by the Governor of Porto Bello who was prepared to surrender the town upon conditions. Vernon received him, but not finding the articles proposed sufficiently to his liking, as they did not include the surrender of the vessels in harbour, he returned them, and giving the Governor until 3 P.M. to agree to the conditions which he laid down, he continued to warp his ships into position. In the afternoon the Admiral's terms were accepted. The troops were landed at once and took possession of the castles. Vernon gave the strictest orders against plundering the inhabitants, and the occupation of Porto Bello was carried out in a manner which the Spaniards admitted did honour to the Admiral's humanity and justice[1]. Vernon now set about destroying the fortifications, in order, as he told his captains, to leave the place "an open and defenceless bay." The iron guns were spiked, the brass ones and the ammunition were carried on board, and the walls of the castles were blown up, their demolition being entrusted to Captains Boscawen and Charles Knowles, who carried it out with skill and thoroughness. This work occupied three weeks, during which Vernon considered the possibility of repeating Morgan's exploit of 1671 and making a dash on Panama. The treasure from Lima was reported to be there, and the temptation to make the attempt was great, but the difficulties were considerable. The distance across the isthmus is over forty miles; the road, a paved path through thick bush where ambushes might be arranged; and cannon for attacking the walls would either have to be dragged by hand, for the squadron had no transport, or the walls would have to be carried by assault. Even if these difficulties were overcome the object might be missed, for it was not impossible that the treasure would have been shipped back to Lima. The journey would thus have been in vain, and there was the added risk that during the landing party's absence the Ferrol squadron, that ever-present danger, would have arrived and cut off their retreat. In these circumstances he decided to return to Jamaica and refit his ships, and wait to determine

[1] Principal authorities consulted for the preceding description: Admiral Vernon's Despatches and *Journal,* Commodore Brown's *Journal, Journals* of Captains of ships concerned. Letter of A. Campbell in *A Forgotten John Russell,* by M. E. Matcham.

his next move until he should have received further reports from his cruisers.

On arrival at Port Royal, the Admiral found a refit a less easy matter than he had anticipated; the stock of stores of all kinds in the dockyard had fallen very low, and no supplies had been sent out since reprisals were ordered. This neglect on the part of the authorities seriously hampered his movements; but though this fact was fully realized and was the subject of much just criticism at home, his successors suffered in a similar manner, and the operations in the West Indies were gravely prejudiced throughout the war from this cause.

In consequence of the difficulty of refitting under these conditions, he was not ready for sea again until February 25th. During this time however, he had five ships out cruising off Havana, convoying and attacking trade; and he employed his enforced stay at Port Royal by making improvements in the administration of the place. His characteristic care for the seamen shews itself throughout his despatches. It was at this time that he reported the necessity for an hospital at Port Royal, plans of which he drew out and sent to the Navy Board, shewing all the requirements of such a building in this climate, with comforts both for officers and men. He strongly recommended its being taken in hand, using a reasoning that he knew would appeal to the authorities, namely, that it would prove an economy. "It would be a great saving to you in a long war," he wrote, "and be a means of preserving many men's lives and securing many men from desertion."

While Vernon was refitting at Jamaica, a small joint expedition was in progress in Georgia. Colonel Oglethorpe having obtained permission to attack the Spanish settlement at San Augustin which threatened his colony[1], the Admiralty ordered all the ships stationed on the American coast to take part in the operations[2]. The troops were to be furnished by the garrison of Georgia, reinforced by a regiment and a troop of horse voted by the Legislature of South Carolina at a cost of £120,000.

The squadron[3] under the command of Captain Vincent Pearce was assembled by April and at once established a close blockade of San Augustin in the course of which some warm fighting took place with the local flotilla of six half-galleys and two armed launches. The land forces under Colonel Oglethorpe failed however to make any serious impression upon the Fort. Both Oglethorpe and Pearce proved them-

[1] Minutes of the Privy Council, Add. MS. 33004, September 21st, 1739.

[2] Admiralty 2.55, dated October 5th, 1739.

[3] 'Flamborough,' 20; 'Phoenix,' 20; 'Tartar,' 20; 'Hector,' 40; 'Shoreham,' 20; 'Squirrel,' 20; 'Spence' and 'Wolf,' sloops.

selves indifferent leaders; the former, though he developed the idea, was incapable of putting it into execution; the latter saw difficulties everywhere but made little effort to overcome them.

The redeeming feature of an otherwise unsatisfactory enterprise was the conduct of Colonel Vanderdussen and Captain Peter Warren of the 'Squirrel,' both of whom continually urged their superiors to energetic action, and when acting together worked in that perfect harmony which is the outcome of a full appreciation of the joint dependence of the Services. Subordinates, however, are powerless in the face of unintelligent or inactive superiors, and the small expedition, which was brought to an end by the approach of the hurricane season in July, failed solely for want of energy and initiative.

This enterprise, while in no way affecting the main course of the war, represented the sound conception of defence by forestalling attack, and illustrates the flexibility of the system of colonial defence then in vogue[1] which enabled a number of scattered ships to be rapidly assembled and formed into a useful little squadron for such local operations.

Although the defence of Georgia and South Carolina formed a portion of Vernon's responsibilities he was not called upon to make any detachment from his squadron at Jamaica to assist in the attack upon San Augustin. The ships remained at Port Royal throughout the winter, and when the refit was completed in February, the Admiral sailed to reconnoitre Cartagena. Some fire-ships and bomb-vessels had recently been sent him from England wherewith he was recommended to endeavour to attack the shipping in Cartagena—a very favourite scheme of the Duke of Newcastle, who appears to have thought the destruction of shipping in a fortified harbour by means of bomb-vessels a simple operation; Ferrol and Barcelona were among the places to which he proposed to apply this method of attack, although frequently informed by seamen that it was impracticable[2]. Vernon was under no delusions on the matter, but he desired to know what defences there were at Cartagena, and, if possible, tempt the Spanish Admiral to sea to fight him. He arrived there on March 2nd, sent the boats of the fleet away sounding, and sailed close along the coast himself examining the works from seaward. After five days' surveying and observing he ordered the bomb-vessels in with covering ships, and opened fire on the town, moving the ketches about as the enemy picked up the range. Five large ships of the line, under Don Blas

[1] See Appendix, Vol. III. "Colonial Defence."

[2] The views of Lords Keith and Barham on this matter may be noted. See *Barham Papers*, vol. III. pp. 156–162.

de Ledo, and an equal number of galleons,—a force nearly double his own,—lay in the harbour, but though he carried out these deliberate observations, and insulted the town by throwing bombs into it, he could not tempt Don Blas to sea to fight him. Though so far unsuccessful, he had by this reconnaissance in force gained much useful information. St Philip's Castle "appeared to be a regular square fort of four bastions containing 22 embrasures in the two faces, and I take it to be a fortress of upwards of 80 pieces of cannon. They seem to have raised some new works under it level with the water, and there was another fort built in the water on the opposite side of the channel." So he says in his *Journal*; and to the Duke of Newcastle he wrote that he now knew as much about the approaches as the Spaniards themselves. Besides this material information gained, the poor opinion he formed of the fighting spirit of the Spaniards was not without its influence on his attitude towards them in the later operations of the war. In the second week in March he weighed and sailed for Porto Bello. His next objective was Chagres.

Chagres, lying at the mouth of the river of that name, was of importance as a headquarters of the guarda-costas and as related previously, as a port of embarkation of treasure. The port was protected by a castle of no great strength, and this Vernon intended to destroy. Sending a few cruisers to block up the harbour, he watered his ships at Porto Bello and appeared off Chagres on March 23rd. The ships of the squadron under Captain Herbert of the 'Norwich,' and the bomb-vessels under Captain Knowles, opened a bombardment at 3 P.M. which continued until 10 o'clock at night. Next day the castle surrendered. Knowles with a party of seamen was landed to destroy the fortifications; the stonework was blown up, the woodwork burnt, and the merchandise, which was of considerable value[1], together with all the guns worth taking, were carried off.

Having thus destroyed another of the Spanish bases and set a further check on their trade, Vernon sailed on March 30th for Porto Bello and Cartagena, with the object of intercepting on his way two Spanish ships of the line which he heard were expected at Santa Fé. Lack of provisions and stores did not however permit him to remain cruising for more than a few days, and he was obliged to return to Jamaica on May 3rd, thereby missing the Spaniards who got safely into port, bringing a reinforcement of 700 soldiers for the garrison, as well as a new Governor for the town.

1 "Having now got a deal of the Nut I may the less envy Don Blas de Ledo the shell of his galleons, tho' I shall narrowly watch him for them too." Vernon to the Duke of Newcastle.

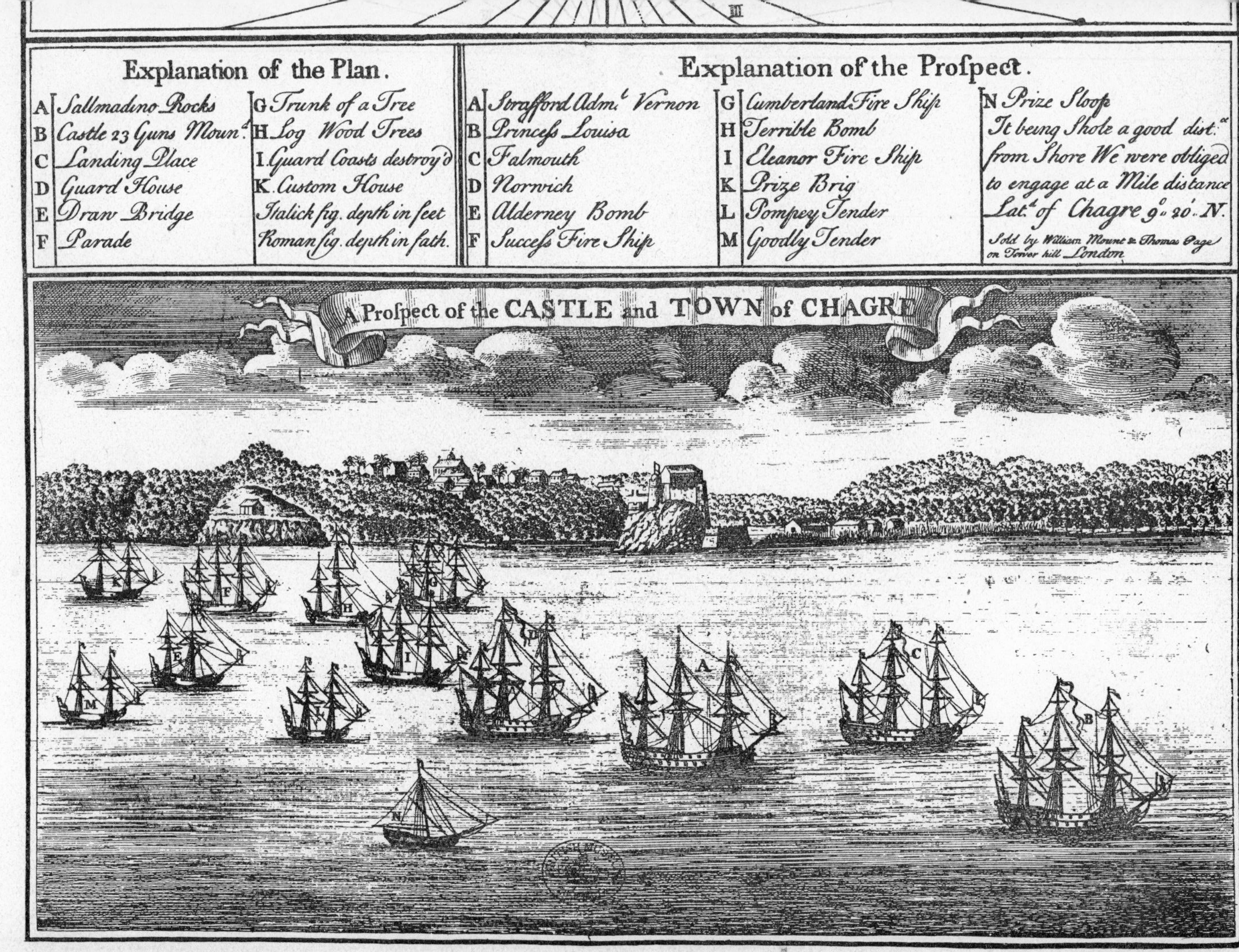
Explanation of the Plan.
A Sallmadino Rocks
B Castle 23 Guns Moun.d
C Landing Place
D Guard House
E Draw Bridge
F Parade
G Trunk of a Tree
H Log Wood Trees
I. Guard Coasts destroy'd
K. Custom House
Italick fig. depth in feet
Roman fig. depth in fath.
Explanation of the Prospect.
A Strafford Adm.l Vernon
B Princess Louisa
C Falmouth
D Norwich
E Alderney Bomb
F Success Fire Ship
G Cumberland Fire Ship
H Terrible Bomb
I Eleanor Fire Ship
K Prize Brig
L Pompey Tender
M Goodly Tender
N Prize Sloop
It being Shole a good dist.ce
from Shore We were obliged
to engage at a Mile distance
Lat.d of Chagre 9° 20'. N.
Sold by William Mount & Thomas Page
on Tower hill London
A Prospect of the CASTLE and TOWN of CHAGRE

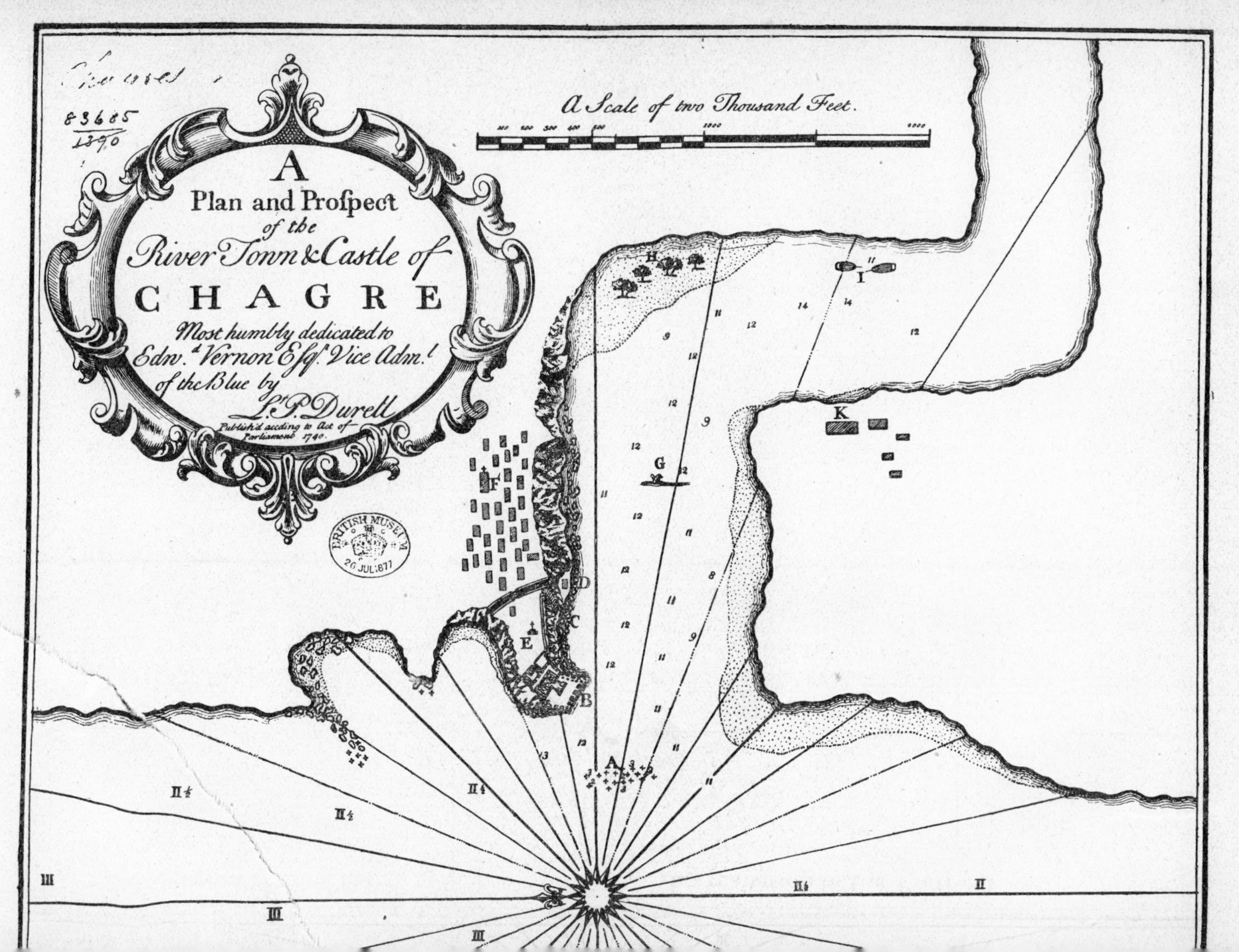
A Plan and Prospect of the River Town & Castle of CHAGRE
Most humbly dedicated to Edw.d Vernon Esq.r Vice Adm.l of the Blue by
L.t P. Durell
Publish'd accding to Act of Parliament 1740.
A Scale of two Thousand Feet.
A
B
C
D
E
F
G
H
I
K

The news of the capture of Porto Bello had reached England in the end of March. It gave the greatest gratification, and the Ministry exploited the success to the utmost, using it as a proof of their own aptitude for conducting war. How little the capture had been of their own devising the extracts from Vernon's instructions have shewn. It was wisely resolved to leave him a free hand in any further operations. "The King," wrote the Duke of Newcastle on March 26th, "does not think it proper to prescribe any particular service to be undertaken by you, but leaves it entirely to your direction to act against the Spaniards in such a manner and in such places as shall appear to you best to answer the ends proposed by his Majesty's orders to you." The compliment to Vernon's capability, implied in this sentence, was lessened by the fact that his advice on the matter of land expeditions was wholly neglected.

Though this reply of the Duke's gave Vernon a free hand, he was in some difficulty as to how to act effectively against the Spaniards. His squadron was small and he had no troops. The only places which lay within his power to attack—Porto Bello and Chagres—he had reduced. All the other ports were more strongly defended and would require the assistance of a land force. There remained the attack upon Spanish trade, which he could carry out either by spreading his ships in the channels of approach or concentrating them to blockade the principal ports. The state of his ships and his lack of stores made it difficult to maintain a blockade, and on the other hand he felt it was undesirable to scatter his forces now that war was declared and Spain might concentrate her navy and take the offensive; especially as he apprehended that France might at any moment join Spain and attack him[1]. In these circumstances he decided that the only course open to him was to collect the bulk of his squadron and await further developments.

Vernon's fears that Spain would take the offensive received apparent confirmation towards the end of May when he received a letter from Lord Tyrawley, our Ambassador at Lisbon, dated April 21st (N.S.), informing him that a squadron of nine of the line and three frigates had sailed from Cadiz under Admirals Pintado and Reggio, and was believed to be coming to the West Indies. This news was corroborated a few days later by a letter from the Duke of Newcastle, dated April 18th, which told him not only that the Cadiz squadron had sailed on the 19th March, but that the Ferrol squadron had also got away the day before, that both were believed to be coming to the West Indies, and that he was to arrange to protect Jamaica. The Duke said that

[1] Vernon to the Duke of Newcastle, May 9th, 1740.

a division of ten ships from Haddock's command in the Mediterranean would reinforce him so soon as it should be definitely known that the enemy had gone to the westward. A "most private" order of the same date showed that the Government shared Vernon's expectations that France might play some part in assisting Spain, although war should not be declared, and instructed him how he should act in such a case. He was told that if in making attacks on the Spanish ships or settlements the ships of any other nation should defend either the vessels, effects or possessions of Spain, he was not to allow them to stop him, but was to carry out his designs; and if the ships of the Flota coming from old Spain, or the galleons on their return journey, were convoyed by ships of any other nation, he was nevertheless to attack, sink, burn and destroy them. The same letter brought him the first intimation that his advice against extensive land operations had been ignored. It contained the constitution and intentions of the expeditionary force which, he was told, was shortly to sail under the command of Lord Cathcart, would consist of about 8000 troops in all, and would arrive at Port Antonio in September when Vernon was to have his squadron cleaned and ready for instant action. A body of troops was also coming from North America, which was expected to arrive before the main body from England.

Vernon's reading[1] of the situation was that the Spaniards, in sending this considerable fleet to the West, intended to cover the homeward journey of the treasure, now held up at Panama. It is noticeable that he does not refer to the possibility that the enemy might come and attack his little squadron. He believed that they would make either for Porto Bello or Chagres, the only places in the vicinity of Panama where the treasure could be embarked; and as he had destroyed the fortifications of both these places he would in such case have an opportunity to attack the enemy at a considerable advantage. Their squadrons would be crowded in the harbours, unprotected by batteries, and he proposed, if Haddock's reinforcement should reach him in time, to proceed at once to those places and fight the enemy at anchor[2]. Though his numbers would be inferior to the combined squadrons, the advantage of the attack in such a case would lie with him, and he intended to make full use of it. Until, however, the reinforcement did arrive, he would be too greatly inferior to the enemy to hope to effect any valuable service; but there was a chance that he might be able to fall in with a separated portion of the large fleet on its way out, and with this object he hastened the refit of his squadron so that

[1] Vernon to the Duke of Newcastle, June 3rd, 1740.
[2] *Ibid.*

by dint of hard work he was able to sail with six ships and a fire-ship on the 6th June. With five of these he intended to lie in wait off Cartagena for the Spanish detachment he hoped might arrive; the other two he sent to cruise between Vera Cruz and Havana to intercept the Viceroy of Mexico, who was reported to be about to sail from the former to the latter place, and whose capture, as he would command in any land operations, would be of importance. These two ships very nearly achieved their object, as they captured the Dutch vessel in which the Viceroy was travelling; he narrowly escaped by shifting into a fast privateer, but all his papers and orders, some of which gave Vernon much up-to-date information as to the progress of affairs in Europe, were taken.

The cruise off Cartagena came to an abrupt conclusion. Rotten rigging and spars sent two ships back to Jamaica within a few days; another was damaged aloft and forced to follow them about a week later, and Vernon returned in the 'Burford' on June 21st, leaving the only remaining serviceable ship, the 'Hampton Court,' to watch Cartagena. Again it was want of stores that crippled his squadron and hampered his operations; not a coil of rope had so far been sent to Port Royal since reprisals were ordered over a year before.

Another month passed without Vernon's getting any information as to the whereabouts of the Spanish squadrons; for this reason, and also on account of the very doubtful attitude of France, he decided to keep his squadron together and run no more risks of damage in cruising. Beyond sending out ships to the necessary stations for trade protection and attack—the Windward Passage, off Havana and Cartagena,—and to watch the French off Port Louis, he kept his vessels at Port Royal preparing them as far as possible for service[1].

The proposed territorial operations occupied his mind, and he did not cease to communicate his views on the subject to the Duke of Newcastle. Writing on July 25th he reiterated his feeling against extensive military operations in these unhealthy climates: "the more I consider of it," he wrote, "I think the objections the stronger against the Havana," and he explained what those objections were. The island offered no anchorage for a fleet near the town whence a descent could be made; anchorage on the open coast would be most inadvisable, especially after November when the Northers—northerly gales of great violence—set in; the nearest large anchorage was in Honda Bay, but that was very far from the objective, and a long overland march was most undesirable.

Turning from Havana and Vera Cruz to Cartagena, he expressed

[1] In letters. July 19th, 1740.

the opinion that a better chance of success lay in the latter place; but the rainy season was now in progress and would continue until November. Operations there would be impossible until the rains were over, but if the troops arrived, as the Duke said they would, in September, Vernon considered that the best immediate step to take would be to capture Santiago de Cuba. The troops could then be kept exercising there until November, when they would make straight for Cartagena where the so-called dry season would have set in. With men seasoned by this experience of local warfare and confident in themselves, the attack upon the larger town would be undertaken under the conditions most promising of success. The proposed occupation of Santiago had a further advantage. By holding this port Vernon would occupy a base interposed between the Spaniards at Havana and the French in Hispaniola, a matter of importance in the supposed event of France co-operating with Spain.

With this campaign planned in his mind, Vernon sent the 'Sheerness' in August to reconnoitre Guantanamos Bay with the view of using it as his base of operations. He intended, so soon as he heard that Cathcart had sailed from England, to carry the squadron off the West end of Hispaniola and meet him there, and thence to proceed at once in execution of his plans, falling upon Santiago by surprise. Above all he was anxious that the troops should not come to Jamaica and there "get acquainted with Captain Punch," which, as he truly said, might cost as many men as a general action. It was at this time that he issued the well-known order, for which and his waistcoat, so is history distorted, he is better known than for his real talents as an Admiral. The order is in effect one of the many evidences of Vernon's real care for his men[1].

The welcome appearance of some store-ships on the 5th of September, under escort of the 'Defiance' and 'Tilbury,' enabled him to refit his squadron; but here good fortune ended. September passed with no news of Cathcart, and on October 3rd, thinking he must surely be nearing these waters, Vernon sailed for Tiburon with his squadron to meet the expedition. He threw ships out to windward as far ahead as Cap Nicolas to get warning of its approach, and before many days

[1] The order for the mixture of water with rum, termed 'grog' after Vernon who wore a grogram waistcoat, and was known as 'Old Grog.' It runs thus, after a short preamble: "You are therefore hereby required and directed as you tender both the Spiritual and Temporal Welfare of His Majesty's Service, to take particular care that Rum be no more served in Specie to any of the Ship's Company under your Command, but that the respective daily allowance of Half-a-Pint a man for all your Officers and Ship's Company be every day mixed with the proportion of a Quart of Water to every Half-Pint of Rum...."

received some news, but not what he hoped for. From the master of a Spanish brigantine captured by the 'Tilbury' on October 12th, it was learned that she had left Ferrol in the company of a squadron of twelve ships of the line under Admiral de Torres with 2000 troops on board, which had gone to Porto Rico and sailed thence on October 6th for Cartagena. Nor was this all. The same day that the 'Tilbury' gave him this information he received a despatch from England saying that Cathcart was delayed at Portsmouth by foul winds, that the Channel squadron under Norris was windbound at Torbay, and that it was feared that the Spanish squadron had sailed from Ferrol—as it had; in which case, so soon as its destination was known, a reinforcement of ten ships would be sent him as on the previous occasion. The ten ships must however be still a long way off, while the Ferrol squadron was already here and might get between him and his base. Luckily, it had gone to Cartagena and not to Havana, and was thus to leeward of him. It had not yet joined the ships in Cuba, and was not in a position to attack the troops coming from North America. In this situation Vernon decided to carry out his attack upon Santiago with the American troops if they arrived soon enough: but if they did not, he would be obliged by want of supplies to fall back on Jamaica and replenish his fleet in order to be ready for Cathcart's arrival.

Six days later worse news reached him, which sent him back without further delay to Jamaica. A French squadron from Brest under the command of the Marquis d'Antin had anchored in Martinique. This squadron, Vernon guessed, had not come all this way "to take the air only"; he now expected that the squadrons of the two powers would unite and attack Jamaica, and he most impatiently awaited instructions as to how he was to act in view of this probability[1].

At Jamaica he received definite news from his cruising ship, the 'Strafford,' that the Spanish squadron had reached Cartagena on the 21st October and landed troops there next day, the 'Strafford' herself having narrowly escaped capture; and he decided that the first thing to be done when the promised reinforcement of ten ships should arrive was to blockade Cartagena, and, if Cathcart arrived in time, to attack Santiago as well. But neither Cathcart nor the reinforcement reached him.

In the meantime the transports from the northern colonies had begun to arrive; but they were not all assembled until the 12th December; it was a relief to Vernon that they had reached Jamaica in safety, for the situation was now worse. The 'Torrington' had

[1] Vernon to the Duke of Newcastle, October 20th, 1740.

captured a Spanish sloop and from her had acquired information, which he had given to Vernon on November 26th, that the Brest squadron, after embarking an extra 1200 troops at Martinique, had arrived at Port Louis, and had there been joined by the Toulon squadron under de Rochalart; and another of his cruisers reported that the Havana squadron was preparing to sail. These movements confirmed his opinion that the combined enemies intended to attack Jamaica. "The French collecting their forces to windward of this island makes me conjecture their views are against this island, particularly as they own they daily expect orders for a war against Britain[1]." He had ministerial authority for believing that the French would not do less than assist to protect the Spanish trade and settlements[2], and they might well be expected to do more. But whether the Spaniards were going to act offensively in conjunction with the French against the British squadron or settlements, or to content themselves with protecting their trade and carrying it home in safety, he could not tell. Until further reinforcements reached him he could only concentrate his force at Jamaica and act defensively against the superior numbers that threatened him from three directions. The causes that had led to this unhappy situation must now be traced.

[1] Vernon to the Duke of Newcastle, December 12th, 1740.
[2] See *ante* p. 54, "Most Private Letter" of April 18th, 1740.

References to the Plan of Port Bello

A. The Governor's House which was shot through by one of the lower tier of guns from the Admiral's ship the 'Burford.'
B. The Plantation in the Castle of Gloria.
C. The 'Worcester' man-of-war.
D. The 'Norwich.'
E. The 'Burford.'
F. The 'Hampton Court.'
G. The 'Strafford.'
H. The 'Princess Louisa.'
I. The tenders.
K. The Spanish Guarda-costas.
M. Trading Sloops.
N. A Sloop sunk by a shot from the Admiral's ship.
O. Two boats going to land the soldiers under the walls of the Fort.

Soundings in fathoms. Figures on sands in feet.

CHAPTER IV

BEGINNING OF THE WAR IN THE MEDITERRANEAN

On October 1st Haddock carried the bulk of the fleet from his advanced station at St Mary's to Gibraltar, for the purpose of watering and victualling. He left a detachment out to keep an eye upon the Flota and the men-of-war in the inner harbour above the Puntales; the instructions to these cruising ships were if possible to prevent the Spaniards from coming to sea, but if they should do so in superior force, the detached cruisers were to rejoin the flag with all despatch.

The disposition of the Squadron on October 1st, 1739, was as follows:

Station	Ship	Guns	Remarks
At Gibraltar	'Somerset'	80	
	'Augusta'	60	
	'Lancaster'	80	
	'Edinburgh'	70	
	'Ipswich'	70	
	'Berwick'	70	Several planks rotten
	'Pembroke'	60	Bowsprit sprung
	'Plymouth'	60	
	'Eltham'	40	Going to Lisbon and England
	'Dolphin'	20	
	'Solebay'	20	Going convoy to Mahon
	'Mercury'	8.6	Fire-ships
	'Ann' galley	8.6	
	'Duke'	8.6	
	'Salamander'	6.8	Bomb
	'Grampus'	6.10	Sloop
Off St Mary's	'Canterbury	60	
	'Dragon'	60	
	'Jersey'	60	
Off St Vincent	'Oxford'	50	
With Captain Clinton	'Gloucester'	50	Attending trade in the Straits and about Gibraltar
	'Guarland'	20	
	'Aldborough'	20	
Convoy to Alexandria	'Falkland'	50	
Convoy to Italy	'Kennington'	20	
On Italian coast	'Tyger'	50	Convoying trade. To return to England
Cruising off Lisbon	'Dursley' galley	20	
Cleaning at Lisbon	'Greyhound'	20	Then to cruise off St Vincent

The Mediterranean squadron had by now been brought up to twenty-eight sail all told. The main body was based upon Gibraltar with the observation of Cadiz as its principal object; the small ships were mostly dispersed for trade protection, endeavouring to suppress the privateers which the Spaniards were sending out in continually increasing numbers. Haddock's small craft were insufficient indeed for the purpose, and he had to supplement them by hiring vessels locally. His letters at this time shew that he expected considerable difficulties in protecting trade.

The news of the declaration of war reached Haddock on December 2nd by the 'Fox.' His instructions had been to winter at Mahon, but this he had not done, as it would have been impossible to maintain the watch on Cadiz from so distant a port. He had therefore remained at Gibraltar and tried to keep his squadron efficient with the local resources, but this had proved very difficult as there were neither sufficient stores nor facilities for refitting, and the hospital accommodation was wholly inadequate. Sickness was rife among his crews, and in his letters home he continually reiterated the urgent need of a properly equipped hospital for the fleet, succeeding at length in January of the New Year in obtaining a grant of land from the Governor for the purpose.

The arrival of a reinforcement of five clean ships[1] in the middle of January, coinciding with reports from his cruisers that the Flota shewed no sign of moving, furnished Haddock with an opportunity of giving his most disabled ships a more complete overhaul than had been possible at Gibraltar. He was however faced with the difficulty that if he should unduly weaken the squadron in the neighbourhood of Gibraltar he would be unable to frustrate any attempt the French might make to cooperate with the Spaniards in Cadiz, or any junction of the divided Spanish squadrons. Still, the need of refitting was pressing, and though he should keep all his squadron at Gibraltar, trying to clean them two or three at a time, he would still have only a patched up fleet to meet the enemy's clean ships if they made any move. The indication given by the unreadiness of the Flota to sail pointed towards the probability of no immediate action on the part of the enemy, and this, combined with the fact that even if the French did make any movement, even to the extent of trying to enter Cadiz, his instructions did not give him permission to attack them, made him decide that the risks of leaving Gibraltar were not so great as was the importance of efficiently refitting his ships. A final, and apparently determining factor, appears to have been a letter he received at this

[1] 'Prince of Orange,' 'Lyon,' 'Superbe,' 'Sunderland,' 'Warwick.'

time from General Anstruther, the Governor of Mahon, informing him that serious preparations were being made in the eastern Spanish ports for an attack upon Minorca. He therefore decided to go to Mahon.

While Haddock was making this decision his position was also being considered at home. The Council received his report as to the unreadiness of the Cadiz squadron and the Flota at the end of January; and at the same time they heard that no preparations for a military expedition were being made in Catalonia. On January 31st a Council was held, at which it was decided that the opportunity was a favourable one for Haddock to clean his ships at Gibraltar, keeping a small detachment to watch Carthagena and cover Minorca[1]. It was considered that even with such a detachment and with ships absent cleaning he would still have enough strength cruising to deal with either the French at Toulon or the Spaniards at Cadiz. "As the Spaniards could not sail from Cadiz but with easterly winds," argued Sir John Norris, "so Mr Haddock could always pass the Strait with the same winds, which would probably prevent their sailing: and should the ships at Toulon pass and join the Spaniards and their flota at Cadiz, if his strength was sufficient he could take a proper station or go to join Vice-Admiral Vernon, or other[wise] come to England as should be most proper as considering the affairs at home." It will be noted that Sir John assumed the ships could be cleaned at Gibraltar, whereas Haddock's letters point to the conclusion that they could not, owing to want of facilities, and, more particularly stores.

The Council, in accordance with Norris's opinion, sent instructions, dated February 4th[2], directing Haddock to keep five ships based on Mahon to watch Carthagena and provide against a surprise from the Catalan ports, and to cruise off Cadiz with the remainder to intercept the Flota. If the Toulon squadron should come through the Straits and go to Cadiz to form part of the Flota's escort across the Atlantic, so that it would be too strongly protected for Haddock to venture to attack it, he was to detach five ships to join Vernon and warn him of the coming of the fleet. Thus strengthened, Vernon could deal with it; but if the Toulon fleet passed the Straits and did not go to Cadiz, Haddock was to leave Ogle with ten ships for the Mediterranean and himself come to England with all the remainder of his squadron, the fear being that such a move on the part of the Toulon squadron

[1] *Diary of Sir John Norris*, January 31st, 1740.

[2] The members of the Council present who drew up these instructions were Sir Robert Walpole, Duke of Newcastle, Lord Harrington, Lord Hardwicke, Lord Wilmington, Sir Charles Wager and Sir John Norris.

would indicate an intention on the part of France to begin operations against the British Islands themselves.

Before these instructions reached him Haddock had already sailed for Mahon with six ships. He weighed from Gibraltar on February 11th, leaving Ogle there in command of a squadron consisting of the cleanest ships[1] to continue the observation of Cadiz, and proceeded up the coast to look into Carthagena on his way to Mahon. De la Bene's squadron still lay there; and he got information that considerable preparations were in progress at Barcelona, where troops were being massed and a large number of fishing boats and other small craft were collected, capable of carrying from twenty to thirty men apiece. It appeared to be the intention to use these to convey the troops across to Minorca when a fine weather opportunity presented itself, and although he did not regard these preparations with any great seriousness, he responded to them by detaching two of his ships and four small craft[2] to cruise between Minorca and the Catalan coast. The other four ships he carried to Mahon and began cleaning them.

A week after the orders of February 4th had been drawn up, a despatch was received in London from the Dutch Minister in Madrid, with a very alarming account of Spanish preparations in Catalonia for an attack on Minorca. A hundred battalions with 28 guns were said to be collected there, and the tenour of the report appeared to indicate that everything was ready for immediate action. In the same despatch the Dutch Minister reported the assembly of a number of troops, foot and horse, in Gallicia under the Duke of Ormonde for the purpose of disturbing England.

The Council at once made out instructions which were sent two days later to Haddock by the Falmouth packet, enclosing the Dutch Minister's report and directing him, if he had not already done so, to detach a sufficient force of ships under Ogle to prevent the sailing of any expedition from Catalonia towards Minorca, and to endeavour to destroy the transports inside the Mole of Barcelona or at Majorca by means of his bomb-vessel. With the remainder of the squadron, Haddock was to cruise off Cadiz to prevent the Spaniards from sending the Flota or any ships or troops to the West Indies, "which you will be particularly careful to do"; but, notwithstanding this, the safety of Minorca was, he was told, to be his "first consideration," and he might even, if he considered it necessary, take his whole force to Mahon. The contradictory nature of these instructions is to be noted: the

[1] 'Lancaster,' 'Elizabeth,' 'Lyon,' 'Prince of Orange,' 'Superbe,' 'Sunderland,' 'Tyger,' 'Warwick,' 'Greyhound,' a bomb-vessel, a sloop and a fire-ship.

[2] He had supplemented his small craft by hiring two Zebecks locally.

Admiral is enjoined to be particularly careful to prevent the Spaniards from sending troops to the West Indies, and at the same time is told that he may if necessary carry the whole Mediterranean squadron to Minorca to protect the island, in which case the road to the West Indies would be open. But as the words "first consideration" are used in relation to the protection of Minorca, it cannot be doubted that the instructions should be read as meaning that whatever western or other movements the Spaniards might make, there was to be no question that Minorca was not to be allowed to fall into their hands.

Haddock, as we have seen, had sailed on February 11th. The instructions of February 4th, directing him to keep five ships based on Mahon and to cruise off Cadiz with the remainder, arrived at Gibraltar by the 'Litchfield' and 'Assistance,' which came out in the first days of March to reinforce the squadron. They were opened by Ogle. The distribution of the ships, since Haddock had already gone to Mahon, was practically in accordance with those instructions; and beyond replying that the Spaniards were reported to have a force of fifteen completely fitted ships in Cadiz, Ogle took no action upon them. But a few days later—on March 6th—in came the Falmouth packet, which had hurried out under a press of canvas with the new instructions of February 14th, emphasising the danger in which Minorca was reported to be. Ogle was now placed in a position in which he had to decide immediately what course he should take.

The decision was not an easy one. Haddock, so far as he knew, had gone to Mahon under the impression that nothing was ready in the Catalan ports that could endanger Minorca; he would therefore have begun at once to strip and careen his ships. The information from England was confirmed by a report Ogle received at the same time from a trading vessel, which set out the news in even more circumstantial detail. Eighty battering cannon, twenty field guns, eighteen mortars, twenty-four cohorns, intrenching materials in great quantities, ammunition and all natures of military stores were at Barcelona, together with fifteen thousand troops under the Conde de Glimes; and the general impression at Barcelona was reported to be that France had agreed to join Spain as soon as the campaign should be opened in April.

Such accurate information in detail, corresponding in general so completely with the news sent him by his Government, could not be lightly treated by the officer in command. In the earlier orders the safety of Mahon had been indicated as his first consideration; he had been told that if he deemed it necessary he might carry the whole squadron there; and now both the local news and that from England pointed to the island being in immediate danger. Ogle had to consider that Haddock, with his six ships, probably already being stripped and in any case inside the harbour of Mahon, might find himself blockaded by the squadron from Carthagena long enough to allow the Spaniards to land their troops; or, if the anticipations as to French action were correct, he might be crushed by the combined French and Spanish squadrons. To Ogle it seemed that the safety or loss of Minorca in either case was a matter depending on instant action, and if he were to be any help to Haddock he must start at once. The first week in March had already gone by, and foul winds—Levanters are common in the spring—might well delay his arrival for weeks. On the other hand he had to consider his orders respecting Cadiz, where lay the Flota, and in all probability the troops that might be carried either to the West Indies or to join the force at Ferrol where the Duke of Ormonde's army was assembling, thence to make a descent on England, Scotland or Ireland. Once that squadron got to sea unlocated its possibilities of mischief were incalculable. When Haddock sailed from Mahon he had guarded against this danger by leaving Ogle to watch Cadiz, and if Ogle were now to follow him Cadiz would be left open. The orders of February 14th enjoined on the Admiral however that the importance of Minorca overrode everything. That Ogle's choice was difficult it is impossible to deny. Unfortunately the decision that he made proved not to be the right one. He decided to sail at once for Minorca, which appeared to be the place towards which there was no doubt that an expedition was being directed. Whether he brought France into his calculations is uncertain, but from the fact that he took with him only six ships it appears probable that he considered Spain alone; such a force would be superior to the Carthagena squadron, but even if combined with Haddock would be greatly inferior to the combined Toulon and Carthagena ships. So far as Cadiz was concerned, he effected a compromise by leaving a squadron of four ships under Captain Hervey in the 'Superbe' to cruise off St Vincent for the homecoming Register and Azogue vessels, which were expected soon to arrive, with instructions that if intelligence were received that either the Cadiz or Ferrol squadrons passed the Straits, Hervey was to follow and join Haddock at Minorca with the least delay. This disposition provided only for the interception of homecoming trade. Cadiz, from a military point of view, was left practically open. The squadron there was free to proceed and carry troops to any part of their own or of British oversea possessions, or to combine with their northern squadron for an attempt on the United Kingdom. They were not slow to take advantage of their opportunity.

Haddock in the meanwhile had arrived at Minorca, and had fully satisfied himself on his way thither as to the state of affairs at Carthagena and Barcelona. At the former place he saw that the squadron was lying well up the harbour, protected by batteries; the wind was then on shore, and all places in which a landing might have been practicable were protected by works; his ships were foul after twenty months cruising and he did not consider a descent possible. As to any attempt on Minorca, which he heard the Spaniards proposed to attack with 16,000 men, he wrote: "As such an embarkation must take up a very considerable time and a great number of ships and vessels, it seems to me very impracticable with the force they have at present only (*sic*) in these seas to put their designs in execution: and as I hope we have nothing to fear from other Powers in friendship with us, I shall not doubt of defeating any resolutions the Spaniards shall be able to form by themselves." It will be noticed that Haddock's feeling of security was based largely on having nothing to fear from any foreign power. It would appear from this that he was not kept informed as to the probabilities of French intervention. On October 25th, 1739, after war had been declared, a Cabinet Council had been held at which it was decided that so soon as a reinforcement reached him Haddock should be ordered to send home six ships; this decision was in consequence of letters from Lord Waldegrave[1], which indicated that no junction of the French and Spanish fleets appeared probable during the winter, and that Haddock's squadron would be sufficient to deal with any force the Spaniards might send into the Mediterranean. A week later the number of ships to be sent home was reduced to four. During November Lord Waldegrave's letters[2] shewed that the French might fit out from forty to fifty-five ships in the spring; and by the time the reinforcement reached Haddock in January, it was decided that the possibility of Spain's being joined by France was so great that it was undesirable to deprive him of any part of his force[3].

France thus entered into all the calculations of the Government; her interference was looked on as not only possible but probable. Yet Haddock was told nothing of this probability, and he was basing his movements on the supposition that no danger from Toulon was to be expected, an assumption that was clearly incorrect and one which he would not have made if the Ministry had kept him fully and constantly informed as to our foreign relations. By their own actions as regards

[1] Minutes of the Privy Council, Add. MS. 33004. Also *Diary of Sir John Norris*, October 26th, 1739.

[2] Read at Council Meeting, November 26th, 1739. *Diary of Sir John Norris*.

[3] Minutes of the Privy Council, Add. MS. 33004. See also p. 76, *post*.

Haddock's ships the Council shew that they anticipated interference; and the main line of their defence in Parliament, when attacked for their conduct of the war, was that they had not a free hand in consequence of France[1]. Yet they left their Admiral in the Mediterranean under the impression that he had nothing to fear from our neighbours.

As a matter of fact the French fleet was in a state of much less readiness than the Government supposed. From a reconnaissance of Toulon, made by Captain Pocock of the 'Aldborough' on March 23rd, Haddock learned that though there were nineteen ships of 40 guns and upwards in the harbour, three only of the whole number were ready for service. Ignorant of the danger supposed by the Government to be brewing, and satisfied by his own reconnaissance that no large French force was in a fit state to do him any harm, Haddock had no fears of an attack by France. He had made himself equally secure from Spain by the four ships he had detached to cruise on the Catalan coast[2], he knew that Ogle was keeping watch on Cadiz, and was thus with an easy mind able to refit his remaining ships at Mahon. It is possible to conceive therefore what his feelings must have been when on March 29th Ogle sailed with his squadron into the harbour, having come with all speed from Gibraltar in twelve days.

The information which Haddock had as to the situation shewed him at once that a supreme mistake had been made. Minorca, contrary to the expectations which had brought Ogle there in such haste, was in no danger. The force already under Haddock's command at Mahon was amply sufficient to deal with any embarkation the Spaniards could make from Catalonia, and the reconnaissance of Toulon had shewed that nothing was to be feared from that quarter. An unnecessarily large force had thus been drawn into the Mediterranean and Cadiz had been thrown open. The Spanish plan had indeed succeeded admirably; the troops had attracted the ships exactly as the Spaniards had hoped they would.

The only thing to be done was to send Ogle back to Cadiz at once, or as soon as he could be made ready—for he had sailed from Gibraltar without waiting to take in any of his stores, and many of his ships needed repair and provisions. A fortnight was spent in getting four ships fit to go, and on April 16th Ogle, with the 'Augusta,' 'Elizabeth,' 'Lyon' and 'Plymouth,' left Mahon to return to Cadiz as fast as was consistent with his passing down the Catalan coast in case of there being a possibility of doing any service against the squadron or the

[1] See *Parliamentary History*, vol. x., and the many debates on the war at this time.

[2] 'Oxford,' 'Guarland' and two small frigates.

shipping on his way. The repairs of three more ships were hurried forward, and Haddock calculated that with two others that would be ready soon after, Ogle would then have at least nine clean ships, or with those already off St Vincent, thirteen ships, to watch Cadiz; but he could not fail to see that in all probability Ogle would be too late to prevent the Spanish squadron from leaving the port if it wished to do so.

Several points are brought out by this incident. In the first place, the force assigned to Haddock was too weak to carry out the watch on both Cadiz and Carthagena. It was hardly sufficient, when the exigencies of reliefs are allowed for, to maintain the blockade of Cadiz. When Haddock went for his absolutely necessary refit, after twenty months cruising, the force he left with Ogle was barely equal to holding the Spanish squadron, still less to the duties of continual cruising in a long blockade of that squadron. This was a matter for which the Ministry were responsible. But, if when Haddock left, he had informed Ogle of his intention to reconnoitre Carthagena and Barcelona on his way to Mahon, Ogle would have been in no apprehension for that fortress, for he would have known that if the preparations in Catalonia were in any way advanced, Haddock would not risk laying up his ships. This he did not know; and an omission on the part of the Commander-in-Chief to inform his subordinate fully of his intentions was undoubtedly in a high degree contributory to the miscarriage. The root cause of the whole misunderstanding, however, seems more likely to have been the ministerial instructions, particularly that clause, which does not appear in those proposed by Norris, which referred to taking the whole Mediterranean squadron to Mahon.

The news that Ogle had left Gibraltar reached the Council at the beginning of April. They had previously been informed that Haddock had gone to Mahon, and the error now made was seen no less clearly by them than by Haddock. After hearing the letter read on April 2nd the Council[1], "observing that Sir Chaloner Ogle was gone to join Mr Haddock with almost all the squadron under Mr Haddock's command, whereby the Spaniards might be at liberty to send from Cadiz what ships or forces they might think proper to the West Indies, were of opinion that directions should be forthwith sent to Mr Haddock to go himself or send Sir Chaloner Ogle to lie off Cadiz with as many ships of war as can be spared...leaving all the small ships, fire ships and bombs with as many ships of the line as he may think proper

[1] Present: the Lord Steward, Lord Chamberlain, Sir Robert Walpole, Sir John Norris and the Duke of Newcastle. Minutes of the Privy Council, Add. MS. 33004.

for the defence of Minorca." Detailed instructions in this sense were despatched on April 6th. It was further pointed out—perfectly truly but somewhat unnecessarily and somewhat late, considering that the Council themselves had told Haddock he could take the whole fleet if he considered it necessary—that a strong fleet of ships of the line was not required for the defence of Minorca, as M. de la Bene had only four or five heavy ships at Barcelona; and Haddock was ordered to leave at Minorca all the small ships of his squadron, "which will be of greater use for intercepting the Spanish Embarkations than ships of a larger size," also such ships as he should think necessary to deal with de la Bene; and take all the rest to Cadiz.

The Spaniards had not let slip the opportunity that was offered them. In the third week in March the Cadiz squadron sailed[1]. A rumour to this effect reached the Council on the 10th of April. It was confirmed four days later by a letter from the Dutch Minister at Madrid which stated categorically that twelve ships had sailed from Cadiz. There was no mention of troops in the Minister's letter, but it was stated that a Spanish Governor for America was on board one of the Cadiz ships. This, combined with the probability that the Spaniards intended to crush Vernon—the news of the capture of Porto Bello had been received about three weeks previously and was known throughout Europe—indicated the West Indies as the destination of the expedition. As this would leave the squadron in Carthagena as the only Spanish naval force in the Mediterranean, it was decided that Haddock with about five ships and some small craft would be able to fulfil all purposes of defence of our Mediterranean possessions, and Ogle with ten of the line should be directed at once to sail and join Vernon. A few ships for purposes of observation were to be left off Cadiz, where it was said the Spaniards had still some ships fitting out or ready. Orders in this sense were prepared; but before they were sent fresh news arrived on the 17th. Seventeen Spanish ships had sailed from Ferrol in addition to those which had left Cadiz.

A new set of instructions was hurriedly made out, in which Haddock was told that nine sail of the line and three frigates had sailed from Cadiz on March 19–30, and eleven of the line from Ferrol on March 18–29. Their destination was believed to be the West Indies, and if the course they had taken confirmed this belief, Ogle was at once to go to Jamaica with the ten best sailing ships and join Vernon, who was being warned of his danger by a sloop despatched with the intelli-

[1] 'St Ysidoro,' 70; 'Asia,' 60; 'San Antonio,' 60; 'Andalucia,' 60; 'Real Familia,' 60; 'Nueva España,' 60; 'San Luis,' 64; 'El Fuerte,' 64; 'Galga,' 54; 'Grieg,' 24; 'Jupiter,' 22; 'Mars,' 22.

gence from England. If, on the other hand, the Cadiz ships had gone to Ferrol, Ogle was to follow them thither; and if they had shaped course for Great Britain he was to come home. If Haddock should be at Gibraltar with seven or eight sail only when these orders reached him, he was to send these to Vernon at once without waiting for reinforcements from Mahon. The rest of the squadron was to be retained for the defence of Minorca.

On April 23rd the situation took yet another turn. A letter from Madrid stated that the two Spanish squadrons had not gone to the West Indies, but were cruising to interrupt Haddock's communications, and were going to Ferrol to embark the Duke of Ormonde's army. The Duke of Newcastle now proposed suspending the instructions of the 18th, which had directed Ogle to take ten ships to Jamaica, and instead to prepare ten ships at home in case the Spaniards should after all go to the West Indies.

On April 28th information was received stating definitely that the Cadiz squadron had gone into Ferrol. Lord Hervey in his *Memoirs* gives a picture of the state of indecision into which the Duke of Newcastle was thrown by these movements of the enemy's squadrons. Describing a meeting of the Council on the 28th, he says that after two letters had been read which shewed that the Cadiz squadron had joined the Ferrol ships in their harbour, Newcastle proposed despatching the instructions to Haddock, referred to above, not to detach the ten ships to America, as he had been ordered a fortnight ago, "because," says His Grace, "you know as soon as those orders were gone we changed our minds, and thought it better to send ten ships from hence to America to reinforce Vernon, and prevent the ill effects of the Cales squadron arriving there; but as on changing our minds we forgot to change the first orders to Haddock, if we do not send soon, those orders[1] will be followed, and instead of ten ships being sent to America, twenty will go, ten from hence and ten from Haddock." Astounding as it may seem nothing however was done, and another week went by. The Council met on May 2nd, and then again on the 6th, and on that day[2] the Duke of Newcastle enquired when they should ask the King to send the counter-orders to Haddock about the ten ships, and what further orders should be sent to him and to Ogle; and read his previous orders dated April 18th with gusto. To which, Hervey says, he (Hervey) observed that counter-orders would now be no use as the orders of April 18th would already have been acted on—

[1] The orders had been sent out at once in a 60-gun ship which was to form one of Ogle's squadron for America.

[2] *Memoirs of John, Lord Hervey.*

Ogle with ten ships would have gone to Ferrol and would in all probability be overpowered; to which Newcastle replied "Yes, it is so," and bemoaned Ogle's fatal step in leaving Cadiz; but in the end no further orders were given for yet another three weeks. Who can wonder that war conducted in such a fashion is unsuccessful?

Ogle, on parting company from Haddock at Mahon, had proceeded to and cruised off Cadiz. When Haddock received the instructions of April 18th, he sent the part of them which related to ordering Ogle to the West Indies to that officer, and directed him to complete with provisions at Gibraltar at once, then look into Ferrol and, if the Spaniards had gone to the West Indies to follow them, making the best of his way to Jamaica[1]. This order reached Ogle on June 2nd. He at once dropped down to Gibraltar to complete and was about to sail on June 14th when a letter from the Lords' Justices, dated May 27th, arrived, instructing him to return with his squadron to England. So, leaving three small ships at Gibraltar for the service of the garrison, he sailed for Spithead where he arrived on July 8th. Sir John Norris with a squadron was riding there, and Ogle put himself under his orders.

The news of the sailing of the Cadiz squadron reached Haddock at Minorca early in May and confirmed the fears he had expressed when Ogle unexpectedly turned up at Mahon. "By the intelligence I have received," he wrote to the Duke of Newcastle, "the feint against Minorca was pretended only to draw off our squadrons from the coast about Cadiz, which to be sure hath too well succeeded: and the troops the Spaniards have embarked to Majorca will serve as well to defend any design they may apprehend against them (*i.e.* Majorca) as to make a descent on this island were they to find it defenceless." Haddock now remained at Mahon to ensure its protection, in accordance with his instructions to make its security his principal care. He kept some frigates cruising and busied himself refitting the remainder of his squadron[2]. Having got four ships fit for sea in June, he took them over to the Catalan coast and cruised, principally off Barcelona, to hinder any shipping from getting in or out of the harbour and to

[1] Haddock to Ogle. In letters.

[2] The state and disposition of the ships remaining with Haddock on May 7th were as follows:

'Somerset,' 80, 'Harwich,' 50, 'Aldborough,' 20...	Preparing to careen.
'Lancaster,' 80	In need of careening but kept ready for sea.
'Ipswich' (flag), 70, 'Pembroke,' 60	Careened. Ready for sea.
'Oxford,' 50, 'Dursley,' 20	Cruising between Majorca and Catalonia.
'Kennington,' 20	Cruising on Italian coast.
'Guarland,' 20	Observing Carthagena.
Two fire-ships and one bomb-vessel	Getting ready for sea.

observe the preparations being made there. He returned to Mahon at the end of July.

And now a new factor appeared upon the scene—the Toulon squadron. It had been known that the ships at Toulon were fitting out for sea. In March, as we have seen, Captain Pocock had looked in to the port and found only three ships ready; at the end of May Captain Watson, who made a reconnaissance, found this number increased to twelve. A fortnight after Haddock returned from his cruise off the Catalan coast, the 'Oxford,' Captain Russel, sighted this squadron at sea to the southward of Minorca, standing to the westward. All the outlying ships[1] on the Catalan coast at once returned to Mahon for fear of being cut off; but, although the presence of a French squadron at sea was disturbing, Haddock did not believe they meant him any ill, and on September 1st, when he had refreshed his squadron after his July cruise, he took all his ships to sea to blockade Carthagena and Barcelona, for he was expecting a convoy of storeships from England and it was essential to ensure their safety. When the convoy arrived at Mahon in the second half of October, Haddock also returned to port, and, leaving three ships to cruise off Cadiz under Captain John Byng, he awaited further developments at Mahon.

When Parliament met in November the Government came in for a storm of criticism as to the "worst conducted part of the worst conducted war that was ever carried on by this nation or any other[2]." A debate, originating in a motion of Lord Carteret's, that Haddock's instructions from the time of his sailing in 1738 up to June 24th, 1740, should be laid before the House, developed into a general attack on the whole conduct of the war. The events which had resulted from those instructions having already taken place, it was argued there could be no harm in letting the House know what the instructions were, for the enemy could now profit nothing by such information, and Parliament could judge whether the war was being conducted intelligently or otherwise. The Duke of Newcastle declined to produce the instructions. They were, he said, the expression of the plans which had been made for protecting our Mediterranean trade and possessions, and to expose them would enable the enemy to evade the measures that the country was taking, and be of great benefit to the Spaniards. To this Mr Sandys replied: "There have been, Sir, many incidents in these last two years of which examination can be of very little advantage to the Spaniards: I do not know what pernicious intelligence they can gain from an enquiry into the reasons for which

[1] 'Pembroke,' 60; 'Warwick,' 60; 'Advice,' 20; and three small craft.

[2] Lord Chesterfield, *Parliamentary History*, vol. x.

Haddock's fleet was divided, and Ogle sent to the defence of Minorca, or for which he afterwards returned." Lord Bathurst said that the only secret that he was afraid of was the secret of procuring such instructions to our Admirals as must prevent their doing their duty to their country; and Pulteney sarcastically remarked that "every man that has had opportunities of knowing the wonderful accomplishments of our Ministry, the depth of their designs, the subtility of their stratagems and the closeness of their reasoning will easily conceive it possible that they might send such orders as none but themselves could understand." The suspicion was general that Haddock's orders had either been improper, or that they were so worded that they might be misunderstood. The preceding narrative will have shewn that the Opposition were not far wrong in assuming that in this cause lay some of the seeds of the miscarriage.

The criticism on the conduct of the war in general took the line that although a whole year had gone by, no offensive action of any importance had been taken against Spain. Why, it was asked, had not any use been made of the army? Why had both the fleet and the army been used for nothing but defence? Gibraltar needed no protection; it had already shewn its impregnability. To secure the safety of Minorca a force superior to the Carthagena squadron and no more was sufficient. The United Kingdom was in no danger so long as we had a superiority at sea. If the army had been utilised oversea to attack Cadiz or Ferrol, and to harass the coasts of Spain and its northern ports, Spain would have been too much occupied in her own defence to attempt any invasion of the United Kingdom; while the advantage of destroying the Spanish naval forces in their own harbours might have resulted. The Ministry defended the policy of not employing the army,—or a portion of it, such as some 8000 or 10,000 men,—in an attack on Cadiz, by reference to previous unsuccessful Cadiz expeditions, and to the necessity of keeping troops at home in case of invasion. They could only explain the escape of the Cadiz squadron by saying that it arose through "an accidental mistake as to the orders which were sent to our Admirals[1]"—a sufficiently damaging admission. The Duke of Newcastle's unfailing following carried him, however, through the storm, and though the debate clearly brought out that the war was being most inefficiently conducted, the motion which would have served to place its management in other hands was defeated.

[1] Lord Cholmondeley's speech, *Parliamentary History*, vol. XI. p. 802.

CHAPTER V

EVENTS IN HOME WATERS, 1740

WHILE ministerial mistakes were contributing to the movements which allowed the Spanish squadron to sail from Cadiz unopposed on the 21st of March, they were similarly concerned in the sailing of the Ferrol squadron the day before. No steps had been taken to keep Ferrol either under observation or blockaded.

During the first months of the war the ships in home waters were still fitting out; and the beginning of 1740 passed by without a fleet being made ready in the Channel, in spite of the reiterated advice of Sir John Norris. He saw clearly enough the need of watching the northern Spanish ports, and was anxious from the first to get ships to sea without delay, manned with the crews of the less ready ships and soldiers of marching regiments. He continued to advocate this measure unceasingly, pointing out that a squadron off Ferrol was the first necessity, and that the step next in importance was to make ready every ship that could float, so that a fleet might be completed in the spring and assembled at Spithead in a condition to be employed against Brest if France should join Spain, an eventuality that he considered as being certain to arise.

On the 18th of January a meeting of the Council took place, at which the Duke of Newcastle, Lord Harrington, Lord Hardwicke, Lord Wilmington, Sir Charles Wager and Sir John Norris discussed the preparations to be made for the expedition to the West Indies under Cathcart. The hiring of the necessary transport, the arms and clothing to be sent to the American contingents, the instructions to Vernon as to meeting the troops, were looked into, and the action to be taken by the Mediterranean squadron in the event of the Toulon ships going to Cadiz or coming to the ports on the French Atlantic coast was considered. It was agreed that if the Toulon squadron should go to Cadiz, Haddock was to be ordered to cruise with his whole force on that coast, except such strength as he considered necessary to cover Minorca from any attempt that might be made from Carthagena; if it came to the Atlantic ports he was to sail direct for England, as it was clear that such a move would necessitate strengthening the force in the Channel and securing the kingdom from the danger of invasion. Sir Charles Wager was directed to prepare orders and bring them up for consideration, and on the 24th of the month his draft was examined by the Council. Sir Robert Walpole expressed his apprehensions that France would join Spain, and pointed out that caution was therefore necessary in our conduct of the war with the latter Power, while the Duke of Newcastle went so far as to propose the withdrawal of the whole Mediterranean squadron at once in order to strengthen the force on our own coasts. To this Norris made strong objection. His appreciation ran as follows: "It was my opinion, that to reduce our force in the Mediterranean to be inferior to the ships at Toulon and Carthagena would be the greatest disgrace to our country, and give the Spaniards an opportunity to take Mahon, which, if we once lost we could never retrieve. And without it in a French war there is no port where we could support a superior naval force against France and Spain, and must in war be the loss of all our Mediterranean trade. And as the French have about twelve men-of-war that can be fitted at any time they please, and should they attempt to sail from Toulon to Cadiz or West France, our squadron by proper care can't want intelligence of them, and keeping their ships clean by two or three at a time they will always be able to follow them and have a sufficient strength against the four Spanish ships at Carthagena. And if they find the French to stop at Cadiz and our ships [are] equal to what the French and Spaniards may have together, with intelligence of their intentions to convoy the Flota or Galleons to the West Indies, they can cruise off that coast: but if they think themselves inferior to that strength they may detach a proper strength, or all of them if proper, to join Vice-Admiral Vernon in the West Indies and by a superiority in the West Indies disappoint the intentions of France and Spain: or, as it may appear to them after they are sailed from Cadiz, they may send a part of our ships home. And as our ships may be supposed to be cleaner than the Spaniards' and they having their laden Galleons or Flota under their care, they won't separate from them to give us chase."

To put it briefly, Norris's plan was to make the Mediterranean squadron up to the strength of the French and Spanish squadrons in Toulon and Carthagena; to follow the Toulon squadron wherever it went; and to be in no fear of pursuing a superior force to the West Indies, as Vernon was there and the superiority could be reversed in those waters.

At the same time, he pointed out that over 30 per cent. of our ships of force were unfit for sea, "and therefore I was for using all methods," he writes, "for repairing or building ships, the want of which in the year 1690 when Lord Herbert Torrington (*sic*) commanded our fleet in the battle of Beachy sufficiently shews how necessary it is to have our Navy in good condition, as our country is unguarded when an enemy can be superior at sea[1]."

It was not big ships only that were wanting. The small cruisers had been allowed to fall into disrepair, and none were available for service where they were urgently required to deal with the Spanish privateers. On the 31st of January the Council wrote: "Finding that the demand for convoys and cruisers become very frequent we think it our duty to represent to your Majesty that there is not a sufficient number of ships of the 5th and 6th rates[2] to answer the several services that may be required, and do therefore humbly propose that we may be empowered to give orders for the building of five ships of 40 guns and twelve of 20 guns by contract in the merchants' yards in the room of as many of the same rates whose names are in the margin which were a part of the Navy but have been some time since worn out and sold as unserviceable or broken up for other use[3]."

Besides ships, men were lacking. A Committee on manning had made proposals which were intended to improve matters; but the problem was a large one, and so far the suggestions of the Committee had not been acted upon.

The news of the Spanish preparations both in Gallicia and Catalonia, where large camps were being formed in accordance with the Spanish war plan, was received at the same time[4] and their bearing on the situation so created was considered. The Catalonian forces, which were presumably intended to threaten Minorca, could be sufficiently guarded against by retaining in the Mediterranean a squadron equal to that at Carthagena; the assembling of so many men in Gallicia might be connected with the recent appearance of the Young Pretender at Madrid, and indicate an intention to repeat the attempt of 1719. But it was believed that the formation of the camp was more probably intended for gathering together troops for the reinforcement of Havana, whither they would be carried by the ten ships from Ferrol, a certain number having already sailed to the West Indies to strengthen the garrisons. Norris wrote bitterly in his *Diary* at this time about the neglect of his advice to station ships off Ortegal to stop these reinforcements. "Had we as we should have kept a few clean ships to cruise off the

[1] *Diary of Sir John Norris*, January 18th, 1740.

[2] *I.e.* 40- and 20-gun ships.

[3] Ad. Sec. In letters. Orders in Council, January 31st, 1740. The ships named were the 5th rates, 'Dover,' 'Folkestone,' 'Feversham,' 'Gosport,' 'Lynn'; the 6th rates, 'Rye,' 'Lyme,' 'Fox,' 'Winchelsea,' 'Lively,' 'Experiment,' 'Port Mahon,' 'Rose,' 'Biddeford,' 'Success,' 'Scarborough' and 'Bridgewater.' Thirteen fireships were also to be bought.

[4] Reports read at the Council, January 24th, 1740.

Norward Cape the Spaniards would not have ventured to sea[1]." As these precautions had been neglected, and vessels had not been stopped at the point of departure, hurried orders were sent to Vernon to intercept them off Havana—an obviously unsatisfactory measure, as it was by no means certain that Cartagena might not be their destination.

Every advice that came in from France pointed to the probability of her soon throwing in her lot with Spain. A great number of East Indiamen, capable of being armed with 60 guns, was assembling at l'Orient, an embargo on both ships and men was strictly laid in all French ports, and the greatest activity was reported at Dunkirk, where the defences, demolished under the Treaty of Utrecht, were rapidly being restored. Any interference with this clear breach of the Treaty was delicate work, as it might drive France into the arms of Spain; and our Ministry, while keeping an anxious eye on these preparations throughout the early months of 1740, felt itself unable even to protest, much less to hinder the works at Dunkirk by force. The question of forming an alliance with Prussia and Holland, and with their help attacking France, was considered and rejected[2]; but on April 18th Newcastle wrote the "most private" order to Vernon, already referred to, in which he empowered him to attack French ships interfering with his operations[3].

Thus the interference of France was fully anticipated, but at the same time it was hoped that it might be delayed, or that even if she did take a hand she might confine her action to the West Indies and observe a neutrality in Europe. The operations in the West Indies involved, in fact, a vast diplomatic gamble, the result of which depended more than anything else on the personality of the French Minister and the chance of his remaining in office. The French themselves were convinced that the intention of England was to strike at their interests in the West Indies, and thus cripple a great and growing trade in silk, laces and cloth. "France could not look on with an indifferent eye at a quarrel in which her interests were so much involved: to allow the English to destroy the Spanish settlements in America, establish herself there and take possession of their trade, was to permit the ruin of the flourishing French commerce[4]." Besides, the French believed we intended to force them into a war to destroy a growing maritime rival[5].

[1] *Diary of Sir John Norris*, January 28th, 1740.

[2] Notes of Cabinet meetings. Newcastle papers, Add. MS. 32993. Meeting of April 23rd *et seq*.

[3] Newcastle to Vernon, April 18th, 1740, Add. MS. 32693.

[4] *Les préliminaires de la Guerre de la Succession d'Autriche*. Maurice Sautai.

[5] *Ibid*.

The Duke of Newcastle took no definite line of action. He thought the French might come in, hoped they would not, expected they might, and in the end preferred to believe that they would do nothing. Writing to Lord Harrington a few months later—in July—when French naval preparations were far more advanced, and their squadrons nearly ready for the sea, he said: "As the dread of war affects the Cardinal more than any other consideration, I am apt to think he will either flatter himself that we shall miscarry in our attempt in the West Indies, and in that case their taking part will be unnecessary: or if we should succeed, that he may be able to patch up such a peace as may prevent any ill-consequence from our success in the war[1]." This view was indeed not without plausibility. The Duke had received a definite report from our Ambassador in Paris, pointing to the determination of France to take a part if we should seek to extend our possessions in the West Indies[2]. In this letter Lord Waldegrave had written that the Cardinal had said, "that as long as we did not make ourselves masters of any part of the Spanish possessions in the West Indies and did not offer at keeping them as our own, he had nothing to say to us; but if we did, as such a step could not but be a great detriment to France, and curb her trade in the West Indies, she should be forced to take a share in the war." Yet with this pronouncement in his hand, and the knowledge that it was the intention to capture Havana or Cartagena, Newcastle indulged himself in the pleasing belief that France would do nothing; and he took no measures to guard against the situation that would arise if his conjectures were incorrect.

Whatever excuse there may have been for postponing measures against France it is difficult to see any for the lethargy in dealing with Spain. No steps were taken to stop the continued activity of the Spaniards in sending troops to their West Indian possessions, although the necessity for establishing a watch on the northern part of Spain was proved still more clearly by news, which arrived on March 3rd, that another thousand troops under convoy of two men-of-war had left San Sebastian and Santander. It appears to have been impossible up till now for Norris to stir the Council into an appreciation of the military necessity of intercepting these succours, although its members were well alive to the need of conducting active offensive operations against the Spanish treasure fleets. Thus, when information was received on March 25th that two Buenos Ayres ships had sailed homeward, orders were despatched on the same day express to Ports-

[1] Duke of Newcastle to Lord Harrington, July 11th, 1740, Add. MS. 32693.

[2] Newcastle to Lord Harrington, quoting Lord Waldegrave's letter, July 4th, 1740. Newcastle Papers, Add. MS. 32693.

mouth, to send three ships[1] to sea at once under Covill Mayne to capture them.

Mayne wasted no time in getting to sea, and the events of his cruise may here be related, as they are not connected with the movements of any other part of our fleet. His squadron was increased by two more ships—the 'Rippon' and 'St Albans'—he weighed at 3 A.M. on the 29th of March with a north-easterly wind and slipped through the Needles and down Channel, picking up a fair wind after two days. On the 5th of April the 'Rippon' and 'St Albans' dropped astern, and though Mayne lowered his topsails and waited for them they did not come up again. On the 9th, being then about 300 miles south-west from the Lizard on the look-out for the Buenos Ayres ships, the 'Lenox,' 'Kent' and 'Orford' sighted a ship to the northward and gave chase; the log of the 'Lenox' contains such a graphic description of the action which followed that it is here given:

"At 10 'Orford' handed her topgallant sails, hauled up her mainsail and settled her topsails. We continued our sail till we came within 2 miles of the chase: at ½ past 11 she hauled down her French jack and hoisted a Spanish ensign, upon which we fired a shot from one of our chase guns, as soon after did the 'Orford' who was astern. About ¼ before 12 we gave her our larboard broadside on her starboard bow, which he returned with his starboard broadside, and shooting ahead of her more and brought our larboard broadside on his lee bow and gave him a second broadside, then wearing under his lee brought our starboard broadside to bear upon him and carried away his foretopmast. Then wearing again passed under his lee and gave him our larboard broadside, then passing astern tacked and came up to him and seeing him lie disabled, raked him fore and aft with a starboard broadside repeating it five times more and on coming up to fire the 7th broadside she struck her colours."

The prize was the 'Princesa,' 74, mounting however only 64 guns. She was brought to England at once by the squadron which arrived at Spithead on the 27th of April.

At the same time as the orders to Mayne were given, the Council at last awoke to the need of checking the movements of Spanish transports, and decided to send a squadron of seven of the line under Sir John Balchen to cruise off Ferrol, as well as ordering Ogle to cruise off Cadiz with the same object. The instructions to Ogle however proved useless, as the very next day the Council received his despatch announcing that he had left Cadiz to assist Haddock at Mahon in defending the island against the anticipated attack from Barcelona. Those to Balchen, although decided upon on March 25th, were not given to him until April 2nd. They directed him to sail without a moment's loss of time, with the 'Russell,' 'Boyne' and 'Grafton,' from Spithead; to pick up the 'Norfolk' at Plymouth, the 'Dunkirk' off the Start and the 'Deptford' off the Lizard; off Finisterre he would

[1] 'Lenox,' 'Kent' and 'Orford.'

find Mayne's squadron of five ships, and there he was to cruise "and to use your utmost endeavours to prevent the Spanish squadron at Ferrol from going thence or the West Indies: but if they should get out and endeavour to sail towards Great Britain or Ireland you are to follow them, and use your utmost endeavours to destroy them[1]."

Every one of these orders was too late. Ogle, as we have seen, had already left Cadiz when those to him were sent. The Ferrol squadron which was to be blockaded by Balchen had sailed on the 18th of March—a week before the Council made up its mind to send him to stop it; and the Buenos Ayres ships arrived at Santander on April 4th. The failure to oppose these movements of the enemy can only be attributed to the Council, which had been advised in ample time what steps were necessary, but had neglected to take them. "Had my continued opinion been observed," wrote Norris on March 25th, "in guarding those stations very few ships going in or out of old Spain would escape our ships."

A spell of easterly winds was holding in the Channel[2] and was as favourable to Balchen as it had already been to Mayne, enabling him to escape the unfortunate delays which gave rise at a later period to such serious results. Balchen received his orders, which were dated April 2nd and sent by express at 10 o'clock at night, on April 3rd. He had to complete his complements and pick up the 'Norfolk,' and on the 9th he left Plymouth Sound with four ships. Off Ushant he found the 'Deptford,' and with this squadron he proceeded to Coruña, where he could see that there were no Spanish vessels; but it was not so easy to get information as to the state of affairs in the well-closed harbour of Ferrol. Information, gathered from craft he met, put the force at Ferrol as five ships, but there was much uncertainty about the correctness of the reports, and he decided to remain cruising off Ferrol unless he should find out for certain the ships were sailed, or until he received other information or instructions from home.

The day after Balchen sailed a rumour reached the Council that a French squadron of twelve ships had left Brest, and that the Spanish squadron had left Cadiz with eight men-of-war and four other ships. No great uneasiness was felt, as it was expected that the latter had gone to the West Indies, where Vernon's fleet would be able to deal with them, especially as a reinforcement of two men-of-war, which were convoying some store ships, was already on its way to Jamaica. But to be on the safe side it was decided to send two more ships which,

[1] P.R.O. out letters, April 2nd, 1740.

[2] April 10th, E. by N.; 11th, E. by N.; 12th, E. by S.; 13th, E. by N.; 14th, E.N.E.; 15th, E. by N.; 16th, N.E.

Wager said, could be got ready in about ten days' time, provided men could be had to man them.

The news of the departure of the Cadiz ships was confirmed on the 14th, but the easy feelings with which the news had first been received were rudely dispelled by the additional information which came in at the same time. The Ferrol squadron was also at sea. Matters now were more serious, for if these two squadrons joined they would form a powerful fleet, while hovering in the neighbourhood was the uncertain factor of the ships from Brest. In addition therefore to the measures agreed upon for dealing with the movements of Haddock's ships, Norris proposed that Balchen should be recalled, leaving a couple of clean ships off Ferrol for observation, and that every ship that would float should at once be completed with six months' provisions. The fleet thus formed should, he said, be assembled at Spithead ready to sail wherever their services might be required[1]. For a couple of days no more news was received. A letter was written to Vernon telling him of the sailing of the Spanish squadrons and of the reinforcements which would be sent him if necessary. Three days later it was heard that some Spanish regiments were under orders to embark at Bayona. The possibility that this meant an attempt to land in Ireland was at once considered, and orders, dated April 18th, were sent to Balchen, ordering him to return to England if he found the Ferrol squadron had sailed to the West Indies, leaving a few ships to intercept the Galleons and Buenos Ayres ships.

Definite information was received on the 28th of April that the combined squadrons had undoubtedly returned to Ferrol, and now Balchen's force was evidently in danger of being crushed. The Spanish squadron was reported to number twenty, of which fifteen were ships of the line. Balchen had only seven ships at the most, for Mayne's squadron, which had never joined him, had returned with its prize on the 27th of April. The capture of the 'Princesa' had reduced the Spaniards to fourteen, but even this was double Balchen's force. There were no ships ready at home which could be despatched immediately to join him, and in consequence it was decided to recall his squadron and to employ it in defence of the trade in the Soundings and to safeguard the United Kingdom. Although as yet at war with one Power only, and that Power immeasurably weaker at sea than herself, Great Britain was drawing in her naval forces and assembling them in the Channel for defensive purposes. To such a point had a combination of inefficient administration and war direction brought

[1] *Diary of Sir John Norris.* He added, "but the want of men for manning our ships will one day be fatal to the nation."

the country which had seen the triumphs of the Elizabethans and the Commonwealth.

In accordance with this decision orders were sent to Balchen, dated May 1st, to return to Plymouth at once, leaving two ships to cruise off Scilly for the defence of trade against the privateers in the Channel mouth. Balchen meanwhile had been cruising off Ferrol with the intention of holding that station till he got definite intelligence as to whether the enemy were inside. It appears that he was not able to keep the close watch his instructions required of him, for the combined squadrons, after meeting at sea, returned in company into Ferrol on the 16th of April. Balchen heard of their arrival about a fortnight later, on the 2nd of May; and realising, as the Government had done, that their junction would make them too strong for him to deal with, he withdrew further to the northward, to the latitude of 46°, and wrote home asking for a reinforcement or for further instructions.

The orders, as we have seen, were already on their way. After despatching them on May 1st the Council received no more news for some days either of the enemy, Ogle or Balchen, but some disturbing information from France came in. On the 6th of May it was definitely reported that the French were getting twenty ships ready at Brest, to be under the command of the Marquis d'Antin. There was still a measure of uncertainty as to whether the ships that returned to Ferrol were only those that went out, or whether the Cadiz squadron formed a part of them. Norris appears to have been of the opinion that the Cadiz ships had gone west and not joined those at Ferrol, but Sir Robert Walpole spoke in favour of their having effected the junction, saying "that as the squadrons were useless so long as they were kept separate, it must in common sense be the policy of Spain to unite them as soon as she was able, and then to employ them either in an invasion of England or Ireland, in preventing Lord Cathcart's expedition to the West Indies, or in attacking Vernon or our colonies in the American waters"; and concluded by saying that if they were joined by the Brest squadron and made any attempt on the kingdom itself we appeared to have no force capable of resisting them. Such indeed was the situation.

Certain news that the combined squadrons, to the number of twenty sail in all, were in Ferrol, was received on May 19th by a letter from Lord Waldegrave. At the same time came reports concerning the camp in Gallicia, which was considered to indicate an intention to invade Great Britain. Fifteen thousand troops were assembled there, 20,000 stand of spare arms were ready, the Duke of Ormonde, that faithful adherent of the Stuart cause, was expected daily, and an embargo had been laid on the shipping and seamen in all the Gallician ports. The Carthagena squadron was reported to have passed the Straits, evidently on its way to complete the concentration of the Spanish naval forces, a squadron of twelve ships of the line was being prepared at Toulon and another of eighteen sail under d'Antin at Brest. The situation was unquestionably becoming threatening, and the available forces to meet it were but inadequate. Balchen with six or seven ships was cruising somewhere in the Bay, but nothing had been heard of Ogle for some time, and for all that was known he might have gone to the West Indies as he had been ordered to do.

The Cabinet met next day to consider the situation, and it was agreed that either an invasion of Ireland or an attack in the West Indies was intended. At last the Ministry was stirred into considering more seriously the condition of the ships in home waters. The Admiralty accounts appeared to shew there were enough ships to withstand the Spanish fleet, if they could be got together and if they could be manned. Norris, as Commander-in-Chief, was asked why matters were in such a state; to which he replied that not having any part in the administration, he had no powers to force the Admiralty to provide men. He reminded the Council that he had from the beginning recommended that twenty-five ships should be manned and kept ready as a home guard, "and the people not turned over to other services." The "application" of those ships, he said, would have prevented the Spaniards' coming to Ferrol or their ships at that port from going to sea. The Council thereupon desired him to go on their behalf to the Admiralty and elicit from the Board a report as to the state of affairs—the state of the ships in commission, what provisions they had on board and what number of men, how many tenders had been taken up and what men they had procured, and what stores and provisions there were in the yards. The Admiralty at Norris's request made their report, which was considered next day. It confirmed Walpole's opinion expressed on the 6th. There was no squadron in home waters ready to sail to oppose the Spanish fleet if it should come towards England. The Lords of the Admiralty,—Lyttelton, Poulet and Lord Vere Beauclerk—were called in and examined, but could make no suggestions as to how the fleet was to be manned. They thought that by turning over 1000 men from the less ready ships, seventeen might be put in a condition to sail. But to get these ships really fit for service 2465 men were required; while to complete eight ships and a frigate that were supposed to be ready for sea another 2200 were wanted. Unfortunately they could make no suggestion as to how these numbers were to be obtained.

After this expression of inability their Lordships withdrew, and the Council debated what steps should be taken. Walpole suggested cancelling all protections covering colliers, fishermen and outward-bound ships, which would set free 14,800 seamen; but Norris pointed out that this method would be too slow, and repeated his previous suggestion that two battalions of foot and 1800 marines should be put on board. The proposal to embark troops for service abroad was viewed with some distrust. What would happen, suggested Walpole, if an invasion took place? To which Norris replied with the simple solution that in that case they could be landed again. Indeed, if the fleet could but be manned so that it could lie off Ferrol, the danger of invasion disappeared, for the enemy would not be able to leave his harbour. In the end Norris's suggestion was adopted, and the Council decided to advise the King to embark two regiments and raise 1800 more marines, to recall Ogle, to order Balchen to cruise off the Scillies for the protection of trade, and to send two clean ships off Ferrol to obtain information of the movements of the enemy[1]; this last was the recommendation made by Norris three weeks before but not yet carried out, as, according to Wager, there had been no clean ships to send!

Before the orders ordering him to cruise in the Soundings were sent to Balchen, a despatch from him was received saying that his provisions were exhausted and he would be obliged to return. The orders were therefore altered, and he was told to victual at Plymouth and get ready to sail again at the shortest notice[2]. Balchen made the Scillies on June 1st and anchored next day in Plymouth Sound.

A concentration in home waters was thus being made at the cost of a withdrawal of the squadrons in the Bay. Ogle with ten ships had been recalled to Portsmouth, Balchen with six to Plymouth; and measures were being taken to complete a squadron out of the ships that, except for want of men, were ready for sea. Some relief was caused three days later when it was heard that the Carthagena ships had been damaged by a gale and had returned to their port.

There were now signs that an offensive policy was going to be adopted by the Spanish squadron at Ferrol. Admiral Pintado put to sea with all his force to attack Balchen. But he made his movement in so half-hearted a manner that even the Spanish Government found

[1] The regiments ordered to embark were those of Colonel Bland and Lord James Cavendish. The ships ordered to observe Ferrol were the 'Fox,' 20, and 'Dolphin,' 20. Accounts of this Council meeting are given in Lord Hervey's *Memoirs* and Sir John Norris's *Diary*. They are corroborated by the Minutes of the Privy Council in Add. MS. 33004. The figures given above as to shortage of men are those presented to the Privy Council.

[2] The orders were sent by the 'Mountagu.' She was to find Balchen "cruising n lat. 46° between Ushant and Finisterre." Out letters, May 23rd, 1740.

fault with him. They removed him from his command, and superseded him by a more energetic admiral, de Torres. At the same time the advices from Brest shewed great activity in that port. Eighteen ships were in harbour, of which nine were complete and ready for the sea, and the Marquis d'Antin who was to command the squadron had already left Paris on the 10th of June. Admiral Rochalart was simultaneously to hoist his flag at Toulon.

The fleet for service against this imposing force of potential and actual enemies was to be commanded by Sir John Norris. The exact duties it was to carry out were discussed in Council on the 11th of June. Sir John was told, to his infinite surprise, that he was to take the fleet to Ferrol, and on arrival there to hold a council and consider forcing the entrance and destroying the squadron and arsenal.

Such a wholly impracticable task was opposed strongly by the Admiral. He pointed out, to begin with, that the decision to undertake such a task as this should be made at home before the fleet sailed; and next that the undertaking was as much a military as a naval one. The method of executing the operation and the force necessary to do so should first be considered. From the purely seamanlike point of view, ships, hampered by failing winds, could not sail up that narrow and tortuous approach, shut in by high land on both sides, and strongly defended by batteries. Appealing to history, he pointed out that in all such previous expeditions it had been considered necessary to land an army to take the shore defences; and he quoted a wealth of past examples. Thus, when the Dutch attacked Chatham they first took the fort at Sheerness; when the Anglo-Dutch fleet went to attack Brest they landed their men in Camaret Bay; in the attempt on Cadiz under Rooke and Ormonde, the troops were landed at St Mary's, but in consequence of their failure to take Fort Mattagorda the attempt did not succeed; in Rooke's attack on Vigo the troops landed and took Redondella before the fleet forced their way up the harbour; and de Pointis, in his attack on Cartagena, did not attempt to force the Channel of Boca Chica, but rode outside, landed his troops and captured Boca Chica Castle before entering the harbour. In the same way, the Admiral pointed out, must an attack on Ferrol be managed. The first essentials were to decide how it was to be done and to provide a sufficient army for doing it.

These arguments so convinced the Council that they decided that the attack upon Ferrol by the fleet alone must be given up; and Norris and Wager were directed to consider what else the fleet might do. A week later a Captain Cole[1] brought a report shewing how Ferrol

[1] Who this was I am not sure; he appears to have been a military agent.

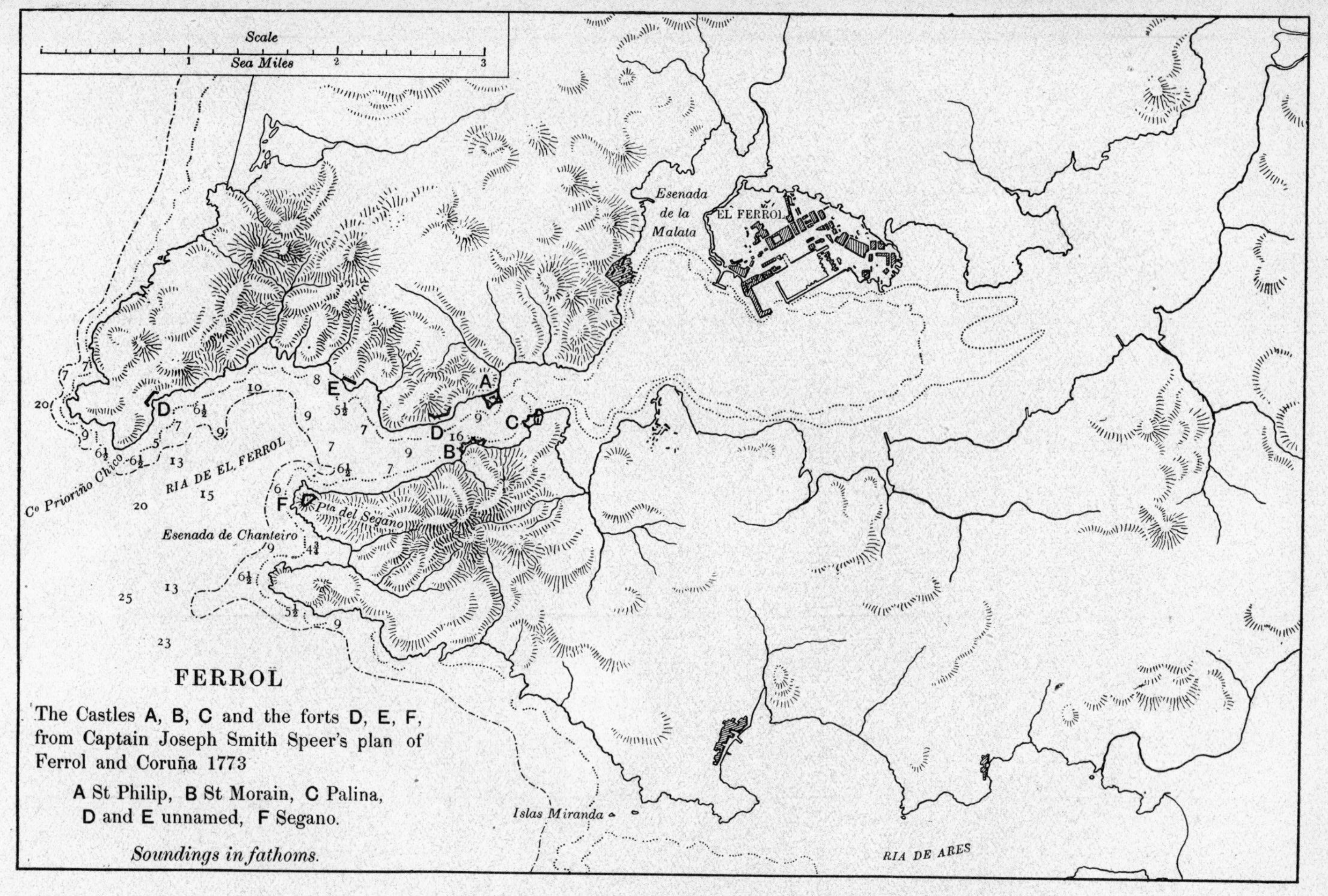

FERROL

The Castles A, B, C and the forts D, E, F, from Captain Joseph Smith Speer's plan of Ferrol and Coruña 1773

A St Philip, B St Morain, C Palina, D and E unnamed, F Segano.

Soundings in fathoms.

could be taken by a land force, and Norris at once proposed that Cathcart's army, now practically complete at Spithead, should be used to put the plan into execution. The troops were ready and so was much of the shipping; the destination of the expedition had already been published as the West Indies (which could not fail to mislead the Spaniards) and this would secure the important element of surprise. Of all means of destroying the Spanish naval power, this offered the fairest prospects of success. "If the Spanish men-of-war can be destroyed in Ferrol," wrote Norris, "the Spaniards could not be able to make any naval action for some time in this war." Norris was convinced that this was the best possible use to make of both the land and sea forces. Once the Spanish fleet was destroyed, the British army would be re-embarked and brought home again, or could proceed on its way to the West Indies, where its operations would be secured against interruption. A few ships only would then suffice to watch the remaining Spanish naval forces in their home ports, and the main body of the fleet would be free to devote its attention to France if that Power should feel inclined, after this blow to its ally, to join in the war[1].

The Duke of Newcastle would not adopt the suggestion. His idea was that the fleet could watch at one and the same time the harbours of Brest and Ferrol, and by that means cover the West Indian expedition. Writing on July 4th to a correspondent he said that the strong fleet under Norris would prevent France from interfering with Cathcart's sailing, while "Vernon will have a great strength with him and as long as the Spaniards are locked up in Ferrol, he can't want more. I heartily wish we could burn their ships in Ferrol. Sir John Norris won't hear of it without land forces and we cannot spare any at this time except we would have entirely defeated Lord Cathcart's expedition, which we all think would have been destruction."

Doubtless the Duke did "heartily wish" the Spanish fleet in Ferrol could be burnt, but unfortunately he and his colleagues declined to provide the means by which this wish could be gratified. Instead of being so employed, the troops were to be sent to destruction in another manner at the hands of an inexperienced officer and a cruel climate.

The main fleet was at length in a way to be ready for sea, the manning difficulty being overcome by the embarkation of the soldiers and marines, and Norris received his orders to take command on

[1] Pitt had the same idea of attacking Ferrol in 1804 and sent Sir John Moore to examine the defences and report on the feasibility of taking it with 18,000 men. Cf. *Diary of Sir John Moore*, by General Maurice.

June 20th. The instructions[1], dated the day before, June 19th, 1740, ran as follows[2]:

"Upon receiving these instructions you are to repair immediately to Portsmouth and take his Majesty's ships mentioned in the margin under your command; and you are to proceed with them to the coast of Gallicia, and there to cruise or to take such other station as you shall think most proper for the execution of these your instructions; and you shall also take under your command such other ships as shall be sent to you or shall afterwards be directed to join you.

When you are arrived at your station you are to endeavour to get what intelligence you can, whether the Spanish ships are still in Ferrol: and if you shall find that they are remaining there you are to cruise on that coast in order to keep them in, in case they should attempt to come out. And you are to employ the ships that are or shall be under your command in such manner as you shall think may most distress and annoy the enemy, and be most for his Majesty's service.

If you should receive certain intelligence that the Spanish fleet, or any part of them, are sailed from Ferrol you are in that case to endeavour to discover which way they are gone; and if you shall find they are coming towards Great Britain, or Ireland, you are to follow them with your whole fleet if you shall judge it best and endeavour to take, sink, burn and otherwise destroy them.

But if you should find that the Spanish fleet, or any part of them, are gone to the West Indies or towards Cadiz or into the Mediterranean, you are then to detach such a number of ships as you shall judge necessary to reinforce the squadrons his Majesty may have in those parts and to make them equal or superior to the strength the Spaniards may be sending thither.

In case you shall meet with Sir Chaloner Ogle you are to take his Majesty's ships, that he has with him, under your command, and dispose of them as you shall think best for his Majesty's service. But as soon as you shall be joined by Sir Chaloner Ogle you are to transmit an immediate account of it and of the number and condition of the ships he shall have with him.

You are to protect the trade of his Majesty's service as far as is consistent with the services directed by these instructions; and you are to transmit constant accounts of your proceedings with such intelligence as you shall be able to procure of the motions and designs of the Spaniards, and of everything that may relate to his Majesty's service, to one of his Majesty's principal Secretaries of State, with whom you shall correspond, or to the Secretary to the Lords Justices; and you are to follow such further orders and directions as shall be sent to you by one of his Majesty's said Principal Secretaries of State, or by the Secretary to the Lords Justices."

The fleet[3] which Norris was to command was to consist of twenty ships of the line, three frigates, three fireships and a hospital ship. On paper it looks sufficiently formidable, but even if it had consisted of the ships named in the list it would clearly have been inadequate to carry out the duty the Duke of Newcastle contemplated, and at

[1] Instructions to Sir John Norris, June 19th, 1740, S.P. Dom. Naval, 1740.

[2] These instructions are signed by Lords Hardwicke and Wilmington, Dukes of Dorset, Richmond, Devonshire, Montague and Newcastle, Lords Pembroke and Ilay, Sir Robert Walpole and Sir Charles Wager.

[3] 'Victory,' 100; 'Princess Amelia,' 80; 'Princess Carolina,' 80; 'Boyne,' 80; 'Shrewsbury,' 80; 'Cumberland,' 80; 'Chichester,' 80; 'Torbay,' 80; 'Cambridge,' 80; 'Russell,' 80; 'Norfolk,' 80; 'Grafton,' 70; 'Lenox,' 70; 'Kent,' 70; 'Orford,' 70; 'Suffolk,' 70; 'Prince Frederick,' 70; 'Dunkirk,' 60; 'Deptford,' 60; 'Weymouth,' 60; 'Winchelsea,' 20; 'Fox,' 20; 'Phaeton,' 20; 'Firebrand,' 'Etna,' and 'Blaze,' fireships; and 'Princess Royal,' hospital ship.

the same time watch the ports of Brest and Ferrol. There were about twenty Spanish ships, of which fourteen or fifteen were ships of force, lying in Ferrol, and the French had another eighteen in Brest, of which latter at least nine were ready for the sea. To prevent either of these squadrons from interfering with Cathcart's expedition it would be necessary to watch each port with a force at least equal to the number in that port, or to escort the expedition with a squadron equal in strength to the French and Spanish fleets combined. The latter would be the more economical use of force, but on the other hand it would be open to the objection that while the army's departure would be protected, the country would be left open to attack. Besides, how far should the expedition be carried to sea? The customary practice was to escort a convoy about 100 leagues out, after which it was in such open water that it was considered safe till it arrived at its destination. But what if the enemy should send their conjunct fleets into the Caribbean Sea and appear before Jamaica, as the probable starting-point of any expedition against the Spanish territories, and there await the coming of the army over sea? No real security could be given from that danger without escorting the transports the whole way.

The alternative method of blockade, while possessing the advantage of preventing the enemy's squadrons in Brest and Ferrol from uniting, from sailing unobserved, or from making an attempt on the British islands with troops in Gallicia, had the disadvantage of requiring a very great force to put it into execution. No method is so expensive in ships as close blockade. To maintain a squadron cruising off an enemy's port which shall at all times be at least equal to the blockaded squadron, a surplus number for the purposes of relief is essential. To watch Brest in the summer months this surplus might be as low as twenty-five per cent.; and at least the same proportion, but more probably a higher one, would be required for Ferrol. The total number of ships in the two harbours was not less than twenty-six, at a low estimate, so that thirty-two ships at the smallest computation would be required to maintain blockades on the two ports. If Cathcart's expedition were going to sail at once, so that the blockade would only be temporary until the convoy was clear, a lesser number might suffice, but the delays consequent on foul winds had to be taken into consideration when a fleet of transports of the magnitude of that in question was concerned. A hundred and sixty transports could not beat down channel in company against a south-wester, and weeks might go by without the fleet being able to weigh from St Helens. This was shewn in 1740 when from July 9th until September 13th, out of 67 days there were only 12 in which the wind came free enough to fetch down Channel[1].

Norris left London for Portsmouth to take command on the 22nd of June, under the impression that his ships would be awaiting him. He hoisted his flag on board the 'Victory' on the 24th, and found that by no means all the squadron was ready; and as neither the regiments nor the marines had yet arrived, such ships as were at Spithead were 1197 men short of complement. Knowing the importance of getting to sea at the earliest possible moment, Norris wrote that he would sail as soon as he had fifteen ships ready, this being the number he estimated as being in Ferrol, though he recognised that it was possible there were more.

On the 5th of July the Duke of Cumberland, who was about to begin a sea-career, joined the 'Victory'; on the 7th the Admiral reviewed the troops of Cathcart's army in the Isle of Wight; and on the 9th, no more ships having yet joined, he wrote that sooner than wait he would put to sea with fourteen ships. Ogle had just arrived from St Mary's with his squadron[2], but it was 851 short of complement and had 621 sick on board whom he had to land before he could do anything; otherwise the squadron was capable of going to sea again, and Norris prepared to sail, asking that marines might be sent out after him in the victuallers to complete his crews.

Next day, July 9th, Norris received a letter from the Duke of Newcastle, urging him to get full information about the state of the ships at Brest, and telling him that if they should join the Spaniards, he was to act so as "to disappoint the views of the united fleets," but particularly to take care that Cathcart with the fleet and transports went safely to the West Indies, and to prevent any attempt on the British islands.

In consequence of these directions Norris sent the 'Winchelsea,' 20, Captain Mostyn, to cruise off Ushant. As Maurepas had lately complained that the English men-of-war cruised in an offensive manner off Brest, Norris told Mostyn to explain, if asked, that he was looking out for Spanish privateers until Cathcart and his troops were safely at sea. Mostyn was to remain off Brest as long as the squadron there remained in harbour, and when they sailed to bring the Admiral information of their movements. Replying to the Duke of Newcastle in acknowledgment of the receipt of his orders, Norris said that he took them to mean that if the French tried to enter Ferrol he was

[1] Commissioners Book, Portsmouth Dockyard.

[2] 'Augusta,' 60; 'Elizabeth,' 70; 'Lyon,' 60; 'Prince of Orange,' 70; 'Superbe,' 60; 'Litchfield,' 50; 'Jersey,' 60; 'Assistance,' 50; 'Falkland,' 50.

to treat such a movement as an unfriendly act and would prevent it; but at the same time he pointed out that while he was off Ferrol blockading the Spaniards, there would be nothing to prevent d'Antin from attacking Cathcart's expedition without any declaration of war. "I confess," he said, "I do not see that it is in my power to prevent it." In reply to this, a letter drafted by Hardwicke, Walpole and Wager was sent to him, which was intended to clear up the situation. "It is not his Majesty's intention," it ran, "to begin hostilities against France unless the conduct of the French squadron should make it unavoidable by shewing an indispensable resolution to attempt to join the Spanish fleet, which can only be with a view to protect and defend the King's enemies against his Majesty's arms.... Upon the first intelligence you shall receive from any of your cruisers of the French squadron putting to sea and coming towards Ferrol you should endeavour to put yourself between that port and them, and dispose your squadron so as to make it difficult for them to go into Ferrol without either using force against you, or you removing from before that port, which you will refuse to do though demanded, and declare to the Commander of the French squadron that though his Majesty is firmly resolved on his part to preserve the most perfect friendship with the Most Christian King, yet that you cannot suffer any ships of force belonging to any power whatever to go at this juncture into Ferrol as long as the Spanish squadron shall continue there, and the place be blocked up by his Majesty's fleet, since that can be for no other purpose but to protect and defend the King's enemies from his Majesty's just resentment." This letter gave Norris a free hand to prevent the French from joining the enemy in Ferrol.

The escort of the transports across the Atlantic was to consist of a small squadron of three ships and two small frigates[1] under the command of Captain Gascoigne, whose orders for this duty were dated July 10th—the day after Norris had written pointing out the danger from Brest. On that same day Balchen, who had completed the six ships now under his command with water and victuals, arrived at Spithead. Ogle had arrived on the 8th, and thus the fleet was now brought up to a total of twenty-six[2] ships. As this gave Norris a stronger force than he needed to deal with the Ferrol squadron, he detached Balchen with four[3] to strengthen the escort and see the expedition

[1] 'Buckingham,' 70; 'Rippon,' 60; 'York,' 60; 'Experiment,' 24; 'Seahorse,' 20.

[2] Thirteen of those ordered under Norris, seven of Ogle's and six of Balchen's ships.

[3] 'Russell,' 80; 'Norfolk,' 80; 'Cumberland,' 80; and 'Prince Frederick,' 70.

100 leagues into the sea. The Commander-in-Chief was now waiting only for a favourable wind to get away from Spithead.

On July 13th the wind came into the north-west by west and Norris prepared to sail. He had with him a vast convoy of over 160 sail which he was ordered to escort clear of Brest, and a leading wind was necessary to carry this fleet down channel. At 9 A.M. next day the breeze came further to the northward, and he weighed; but the fair wind did not hold. It veered to west by south and west, and was soon blowing a fresh gale, but in spite of this he managed to get as far as Exmouth. During the night of the 16th, when the fleet was tacking, his flagship the 'Victory,' was fouled by the 'Lyon' who came on board her, carried away her heads and bowsprit and did other damage, losing her own foretopmast in the collision. Putting the fleet into Torbay, Norris carried the 'Victory' back to Bembridge and shifted his flag into the 'Boyne,' rejoining the fleet at Torbay on the 22nd. That day the wind again came fair from the northward and the squadron got as far as the Start; but a southerly gale came up, the weather turned thick and bad, and Norris, finding it impossible to tack down channel with his great fleet, which had by now been increased by several other merchant vessels seeking protection, was obliged to return to Torbay, into which anchorage he thought himself lucky to arrive without loss. As he lay there wind-bound, with the gale blowing strong between west and south, he learned on the 29th that d'Antin, with seventeen sail of the line and three frigates, had been lying in Brest road ready to sail at an hour's notice. He might already have gone by the time the news reached the Admiral; but calms and fogs now followed the recent gales, and Norris could do nothing beyond transmitting the intelligence to the Duke of Newcastle.

On receiving the news of the impending departure of the Brest squadron the Admiralty decided to strengthen the escort for Cathcart's expedition. Gascoigne's squadron was increased to five ships and four small vessels, and until it was clear of danger it was to be accompanied by the squadron which was bound to South America under Anson, and also by six ships under Sir John Balchen, who was to be in command of the whole force until 150 leagues into the sea[1]. The expedition

		Large ships of over 40 guns	Small ships
[1] Balchen's squadron	'Russell,' 'Cumberland,' 'Prince Frederick,' 'Princess Amelia,' 'Lyon,' 'Grafton,' 'Augusta'	7	
Anson's squadron	'Centurion,' 'Gloucester,' 'Severne,' 'Pearl'	4	
	'Wager,' 'Trial'		2
Gascoigne's squadron	'Buckingham,' 'York,' 'Mountagu,' 'Assistance,' 'Litchfield'	5	
	'Seahorse,' 'Strombolo,' 'Vulcan,' 'Pr. Royal'		4
		16	6

would thus have an escort of sixteen large and six small vessels to protect it against the Brest squadron. Gascoigne's instructions were to provision his squadron for six months, be ready to leave at immediate notice, and, on receipt of orders from Balchen, to sail with the rest of the convoy until it was clear of the danger area. He was then to part company, make the best of his way to Montserrat or St Kitts, water and take in anything required, embark the regiments from Antigua and the Leeward Islands, and go with the least delay to Port Royal where he would come under Vernon's orders. Anson's instructions were to place himself under Balchen, continue with the expedition till Balchen left it, and then carry out his own orders. The whole of these orders were dated July 24th, 1740.

The bad south-westerly weather which had delayed Norris's start continued and detained him at Torbay. His impatience and anxiety were increased when two of his cruising ships off Ferrol brought him the news that thirteen ships lay there ready to sail, all of from 60 to 78 guns, and that another three of the same size lay in Santander. As his main fleet could not get away he resolved to attempt an attack upon the lesser Biscay ports with some of his frigates. He had been told by the Duke of Newcastle on July 19th that fifty-six English prizes lay in San Sebastian; he therefore detached the 'Newcastle,' 50, 'Dolphin' and 'Fox,' 20's, to cruise off that part of the Gallician coast; and in informing the Duke that he had made this detachment he asked if some bomb-vessels could be sent as well to endeavour to bombard the ports. None however were available, all the bomb-vessels being in the West Indies or the Mediterranean.

The Parliamentary effect of carrying out some military operation against these ports was obvious and appealed irresistibly to the Duke of Newcastle. Directly he received Norris's letter saying he had detached the three cruisers, the Ferrol squadron was forgotten, and the Duke sent down orders (dated August 12th) directing the main fleet to attack San Sebastian, for which purpose two more regiments, Whetham's and Handasyde's, were being at once ordered to join the Admiral. Any landing operations, said the Duke, were to be under the command of Colonel Bland, and the object was to destroy the local arsenals and shipping. Bland, who was ordered to obey all orders given him by Norris—a rare case of a naval Commander-in-Chief in a combined operation—replied that he would do so cheerfully "as Sir John's known abilities in all military operations are beyond dispute."

Sir John's military abilities shewed him two things very clearly; one, that September was very late in the year to begin landing operations on the iron-bound coast of Gallicia; and another that the proper duty of the fleet was to get to sea as quickly as possible and lie off Ferrol, in order to prevent the squadron there from sailing to the West Indies; or, better, to intercept it if it should put to sea. Every day's delay caused by waiting for the embarkation of the regiments for such a secondary enterprise as attacking the lesser Gallician ports was increasing the chance that the Ferrol squadron would sail. Cathcart's expedition was already embarked on board the transports at St Helens, and the danger to which it would be exposed if the Spaniards got to sea was incalculable.

Before the winds had allowed the unfortunate Commander-in-Chief to get away with his unwieldy mass of ships, the news reached England that the Spaniards were leaving Ferrol. A message came from Ostend on August 14th, saying that a vessel of that port had met sixteen sail of Spanish men-of-war 30 miles off the Burlings on the 31st of July; they were coming from Ferrol and steering to the west by south. There could be little doubt of the truth of this report, as it was confirmed at once by news from other craft.

The departure of Cathcart's expedition was at once deferred until the escort had been strengthened. Norris—who was still lying windbound in Torbay[1]—was ordered to readjust the fleets, sending Chaloner Ogle with seven ships[2] to join the convoy and escort it to the West Indies, while Balchen, whom Norris had left at Spithead, was to rejoin the main force. By this arrangement the expedition would be escorted the whole way by twelve of the line, all of which would then reinforce Vernon and give him a superiority in case the combined Spanish fleet had sailed direct to the West Indies.

Worse news was to follow. On August 31st Mostyn, who for the past six weeks had been cruising off Brest to watch the movements of the Brest squadron, returned with information gathered from a Dutch ship on the 27th that the French had been sighted at sea on the 27th of August standing to the westward. Much as Norris must have longed to get to sea on receipt of this news, he was still rendered helpless by foul or light winds, and it was not until September 4th that he was able to weigh with the wind at east by south. His hopes of getting in touch with the French were short-lived, for two days later he was once more anchoring in Torbay, driven back by a severe westerly gale.

Here the Lord Justices transmitted to him a letter of Lord

[1] The winds this fortnight were: 14th, W.S.W.; 15th, S.W. by W.; 16th, S.W. by W.; 17th, S.W. by W.; 18th, S.; 19th, W. by S.; 20th, S.W.; 21st, S.W. by S.; 22nd, E. by N.; 23rd, N.N.E.; 24th, S. by W.; 25th, S.W.; 26th, S. by W.; 27th, W. by S.; 28th, S.S.W.

[2] Two of 80 guns, three of 70 and two of 60.

Waldegrave's, received on September 4th, which made the situation, bad enough already, far worse. Not only did it confirm the sailing of the Brest squadron on August 22nd, but it stated definitely that the other French squadron under Rochalart had also sailed on August 15th: "and," their Lordships continued, "there being reason to believe that both those squadrons as well as the Spanish ships that sailed from Ferrol are gone to the West Indies...you are to remain at Torbay with the fleet under your command until you shall have their Excellencies' further directions." The proposed operations on the Spanish coast now assumed their proper proportions and were dropped; the regiments embarked for the operations were ordered to be landed at once[1].

Fresh instructions followed next day. Since the Spaniards had now left Ferrol, the necessity for blockading that port had disappeared. Another six ships[2] were therefore to be added to the escort for Cathcart. But, curiously enough, although the troops for the expedition against the northern coast of Spain had already been ordered to be landed, the project was revived. Norris was ordered to carry the ships which would now remain with him to the north of Gallicia "to pursue such other parts of your instructions as remain practicable." Anson, without further waiting, was to proceed on his voyage, already long overdue from constant delays and procrastinations, and the trade, which had encumbered Norris's sailing, was ordered to proceed with an escort of three ships only.

The ships which would remain with Norris when he had strengthened Ogle's squadron numbered twelve, the escorting fleet numbered thirty-three large and eight small ships; but the ships of the enemy that were now loose on the ocean amounted in all to thirty-nine sail. What their intention might be could only be guessed at, but the probability was that a rendezvous had been arranged for them in the West Indies, and the whole of the squadrons would there act in conjunction against the British expedition.

The order to Norris of the 5th of September about attacking the northern coasts of Spain, which was rendered peculiarly impossible by that of the preceding day ordering the regiments to be landed, was cancelled a few days later, and Norris was told[3] on the 8th to return to Portsmouth, victual the whole fleet and take it to the West Indies after the enemy. He weighed from Torbay on the 12th, and arrived

[1] Lords Justices to Sir John Norris, September 4th, 1740.

[2] 'Russell,' 80; 'Cumberland,' 80; 'Prince Frederick,' 70; 'Princess Amelia,' 80; 'Lyon,' 60; and 'Grafton,' 60.

[3] Duke of Newcastle to Norris, September 8th, saying that it appeared the Brest, Toulon and French squadrons numbering 39 sail had gone to the West Indies.

at Spithead on the 13th. There he found orders awaiting him to the effect that Ogle was to take command of all ships at Spithead and escort Cathcart to the West Indies, whilst he himself was directed to come ashore. Norris struck his flag next day and went to London, after, as he said "a campaign of ten weeks with continual bad weather and contrary winds."

A week later (September 20th) Sir John Norris was again attending the meetings of the Council. On this day the Duke of Newcastle had an interesting document to communicate to the members, in the shape of a copy of a circular that the King of France was addressing to Foreign Courts, explaining his reason for sending his squadrons to the West Indies. In this document it was clearly stated that the object was to prevent Great Britain from making any conquests in those parts, and that there was no intention on the part of France to attack the possessions of this country. This information was of the same colour as that which had been received in July, when "101"[1] informed Lord Waldegrave that if we made acquisitions in the West Indies, France could not remain inactive. In the two months that had passed since his report came in, France and Spain were reported to have drawn closer together and a more active policy was to be anticipated. Newcastle had therefore written urgently to Lord Waldegrave to take all possible steps to discover whether a Franco-Spanish Treaty had been actually signed, but this question still remained unsolved[2].

On the announcement at the Council meeting that the French squadrons had gone to the West, Walpole remarked "that it was like to break out into a new sort of war"; and Norris asked "if this war was to be supposed to be only England against Spain and France: which Sir Robert nor any of the company said otherwise." If we were to have France and Spain against us, with no European complications on their side, so that both could devote the whole of their money to a naval war, Norris thought they would certainly be too strong for us. "I told Sir Robert," he says, "I thought the best way to embarrass France was to endeavour to get four score thousand men into Flanders without reckoning on the Dutch that would then be obliged to come in: that as France and Spain were now joined, the Emperor could not be secure of his hereditary dominions without the help of us and the Northern Powers: and if he could see in case he engaged in a war that we would not leave him, upon a satisfaction stipulated for his security he must certainly come into it: and were I in Sir Robert

[1] M. de Bussy is alluded to as "101" in the correspondence.
[2] Letters from Lord Waldegrave, B.M. Add. MS. 32802.

Walpole's place I would by March have an army of 80 thousand men in Flanders and the Emperor in Naples: [this] would be the greatest hope of success against France[1]." As an outcome of this, Walpole told Norris a couple of days later that measures were being taken to form an alliance with the Emperor. On October 7th a full Council meeting was held, at which the advisability of declaring war with France, and the formation of a grand alliance against her and Spain were considered. The Duke of Newcastle's notes run thus:

"Considered: Whether to declare war against France for sending their squadrons to the West Indies avowedly to act against his Majesty's, and for the repairing of the works at Dunkirk contrary to the Treaty of Utrecht and the Triple Alliance.

"If there was a neutrality in Europe only with France we might be obliged to be at the same expenses at home for our own security: it being not safe to depend upon the faith of that neutrality: in which case France would be at liberty to carry on their trade without being molested, which if war was declared they could not do: and it is apprehended their trade would suffer much more from us than ours would do from them, considering that we are at present at war with Spain and must for that reason be necessarily obliged to have convoys for our trade in those seas."

The gist of this note is that we should be better off with the active hostility of France than with her precarious neutrality.

The grand alliance proposed was to consist of England, the Emperor, the Czarina, Prussia, Poland, the States General, the Landgrave of Hesse and such other princes of the Empire as could be induced to join. The Emperor, upon reciprocal engagements and proper conditions with England, was to be assisted to recover Naples and Sicily; the Czarina was to use her good offices to obtain the duchies of Berg and Julier for the King of Prussia; and the minor states were to obtain proportional advantages[2]. Whatever decision might have been come to in this matter was however rendered nugatory by the death of the most important partner in the proposed coalition. On the 20th of October the Emperor died. A new grouping of the Powers was the result, very different from that proposed by the Privy Council; and the course of the Anglo-Spanish War was to be deflected into new channels.

When this news reached the Council, their attention was still occupied by the question of the probability of success of the West Indian expedition. In the middle of October they heard that four of Rochalart's squadron had already returned to Toulon, and four of d'Antin's to Brest on the 2nd of October, thus reducing the French

[1] *Diary of Sir John Norris*, September 22nd, 1740. Cf. Newcastle's views on Policy in letter to Hardwicke, September 2nd, 1749, *Life of Hardwicke*, vol. II. p. 23.

[2] Minutes of the Privy Council, October 7th, 1740, Add. MS. 32993.

squadrons abroad to a total of nineteen ships; but in addition to these, six more ships were fitting for the sea in Brest. So far as the information at the disposal of the Council went, there was a possibility of being faced in the West Indies by a total of thirty-nine, or, including two additional ships believed to be with d'Antin, forty-one, sail[1].

The fleet which was eventually to go out with Ogle consisted of twenty-five sail, to which Vernon's ten would be added when it reached the Caribbean. Norris's belief was that the enemy would unite and attack Vernon; in which case the result would depend largely upon which fleet had the wind. With the weather-gage he believed Vernon could deal with them, but if the enemy had the wind he considered he would be weak. He foresaw that the season being late, Vernon would probably be constrained to attack Cartagena rather than Havana on account of the strong northerly winds which would make operations on the north coast of Cuba impossible. Threatened, therefore, as the Spanish squadron at Cartagena would probably feel itself, Norris considered it probable that it would not remain in harbour, but would attempt to join the fleet coming out from Europe, thus establishing a slight superiority over the forces under Vernon.

Meanwhile Ogle was still at St Helens. The revictualling of his ships, which had been using up their provisions since June, had been begun early in September. The question of keeping this great fleet and army supplied with food and water was a very important one, and though the crews were still far from complete, it was decided that as the troops were on board it was better the fleet should sail short of complement than remain any longer at St Helens consuming its supplies at anchor. Accordingly on the 18th of October the wind, coming into the east by south, gave Ogle the opportunity he desired. He weighed with the whole fleet, but only to be driven back by a south-wester the following day, nor was it till the 26th that another shift to north-east allowed him to get away. The wind held northerly for another day and enabled him to clear the Channel before it went back to the westward; then he ran into strong westerly gales which scattered his squadron and transports. Luckily both the French and Spanish squadrons were well ahead, and the quarry offered by Ogle's

[1] Made up as follows:

From Toulon 12 had sailed and 4 returned	8
From Brest 15 had sailed and 4 returned	11
From Ferrol 14 had sailed	14
There were at Cartagena (in America)	6
	39
Two ships possibly with d'Antin	2
	41

storm-driven vessels, now sailing singly and unprotected, was not within their reach. The scattered ships found their way in safety across the Atlantic and gradually rejoined at the rendezvous, Prince Rupert's Bay, where they were all reassembled by December 23rd.

Greatly to the disappointment of the Spaniards the enemy squadrons did not effect a junction. The Ferrol squadron, as we have already seen, after calling at Porto Rico went to Cartagena and landed some troops; but fearing that a British squadron would fall upon it, sailed again as quickly as it could for Havana. The French squadrons proceeded to Martinique. Their effect upon the operations in the West Indies was to be as marked as it had been upon the movements of the ships in home waters.

Before concluding the operations at home in this year the expedition under Commodore Anson must be referred to, as although it had been first proposed so early in the war as October, 1739, it was not until September, 1740, that it sailed from England, and the discussions and delays which preceded its departure are an example of the dilatory and inefficient conduct of the war by the Administration.

Originating, as has been seen, in a proposal to attack Manila, which was brought up in the Council in the middle of October, only a few days before war was about to be declared, the scheme was under discussion—if indeed the term "discussion" may be used for a series of desultory conversations—for over two months. On November 1st Anson, who had been chosen for the command of the expedition, was ordered to attend the Admiralty for orders; but November passed without any decision being made. In the middle of December the Manila part of the scheme was abandoned, Walpole considering that it would take too many men, and orders were given for Anson to command the expedition destined to annoy Spanish trade in the South Seas.

Instructions were drawn up by Wager on the 28th of December and discussed; they were agreed upon on the 8th of January and were dated the 31st of that month. Their terms were that Anson was to proceed with the squadron[1] to the South Seas and distress the Spaniards by sea and land. He was to attack any town or other places practicable of assault, endeavouring to get the Indians to side against the Spaniards. A council of war was to consider whether Callao should be attacked, and if it were decided not to do so, or if the attack were made and miscarried, he was to go on to Panama, looking into all the ports between Lima and Panama and capturing shipping. On arrival at

[1] 'Centurion,' 60; 'Gloucester,' 50; 'Severne,' 50; 'Pearl,' 48; 'Wager,' 28; 'Trial,' 8.

Panama he was to get into communication overland with the West Indies squadron, and if it were considered practicable by the commanders of the joint forces, some of the troops in the West Indies were to be landed at Porto Bello to attack Panama, both squadrons cooperating from the sea.

This done, his subsequent movements were to be at his own discretion. He was told he might go to Acapulco, the American port of arrival of the Philippine trade, and endeavour to take the treasure ships as they arrived then return home by the Cape or the Horn as he desired, leaving, if he considered it necessary, two ships in the South Seas to protect trade and cover any places taken.

In an enterprise of this kind swiftness of execution, secrecy and good organisation are essential to full success. None of these was present. Discussed in October, 1739, decided on in December, and ordered at the end of January, 1740, the expedition did not sail till September, 1740,—exactly eleven months after the first proposals were made in the Council.

Although the expedition had the primary military object of attack upon the enemy's interests in the South Sea, there was a suspicion, from the fact that cargo was put on board and two agents lately in the employment of the South Sea Company were appointed to trade, that there were the seeds of a commercial venture in it. Sir John Norris wrote of this: "It was my opinion that instead of 20 tons of merchandise it might have been better to have carried that quantity of rice or other provisions, to prevent the calumny that may arise from the opposers of the Administration that this expedition is for the advantage of a private trade more than to annoy the enemy: and in my opinion, all the warlike expeditions of the Crown should be free from that censure, that the public may be satisfied that all expeditions are purely for their nation's good." Even if every possible step to preserve secrecy as to the objects of the squadron were taken, it would have been impossible to prevent the news from leaking out when the commercial element was introduced. Long before the squadron was ready to sail the Spaniards had received information of its proposed destination and were preparing a superior squadron, under Admiral Pizarro, to forestall it[1].

In addition to the handicap thus given to the enterprise by its plans being known to the enemy, the organisation for equipping it was so bad that the regiments put on board were composed of invalids and old worn-out men, entirely incapable of the arduous service

[1] 'Asia,' 64; 'Guipuscoa,' 74; 'Hermiona,' 54; 'Esperanza,' 50; 'San Esteban,' 40; and a patache. A battalion of 300 infantry was embarked.

demanded of them. It is indeed impossible to imagine worse conditions than those under which this expedition finally sailed from England.

In June, 1740, the squadron was at length considered ready. On June 19th orders were sent to sail at once, but owing to the threatening news from Brest it was detained to form part of the escort to Cathcart's expedition, which was to have sailed in July. The movements of the French and Spanish squadrons which delayed the departure of the West Indian expedition kept Anson also at Spithead, and it was not until September, when the decision to escort Cathcart with the whole fleet was arrived at, that Anson was directed to sail alone[1].

The Spaniards being sufficiently well informed of his movements and destination were able to dispatch their squadron ahead of him, and while Anson anchored at Santa Catalina on the coast of Brazil on December 21st, Pizarro arrived at the River Plate on January 5th. Anson sailed again on January 18th, and Pizarro having already heard of his arrival hurried to sea also on January 22nd without even awaiting the embarkation of fresh provisions. On their way to the Horn the squadrons were so near to one another that one of Anson's ships, the 'Pearl,' becoming separated from her consorts, actually sighted and was nearly taken by the Spaniards.

Terrible weather was experienced in the south. One only of the Spanish squadron, the 'Esperanza,' got round to the coast of Chile, and shipwreck and scurvy took their toll of the remainder. The British squadron, though hard hit, fared better. The 'Severne'—on board of which was the future great Lord Howe—and the 'Pearl' parted company off the Horn, and the 'Wager' was wrecked; but the 'Centurion,' 'Gloucester' and 'Trial' at last reached their rendezvous at Juan Fernandez in June and July, 1741, having passed through three months of hardships only comparable to those experienced by Drake in his great voyage. Wind, weather and the fatal scurvy had played their part. More than 600 men were dead.

After refreshing at Juan Fernandez, Anson sailed up the coast, snapping up prizes as he went. He stormed and captured Paita and sank the shipping in the harbour: but the projected attack upon Panama was not made, for the Commodore, from information of the situation in the West Indies, concluded that no troops would be available for Panama. He therefore put into execution that part of his instructions which gave him discretion to proceed to Acapulco, hoping there to secure a treasure-ship he knew was coming from the

[1] Orders of September 5th and September 11th, 1740. Out letters.

Philippines. But he was too late; the treasure-ship was safely in harbour before he arrived off the port.

Anson replenished on the coast and sailed on the 28th of April, 1742, for China. On the way across the 'Gloucester' was abandoned and burnt, the ship being no longer sea-worthy and the crew so reduced by sickness that they were too few to work the ship. The 'Trial' had already been destroyed, and the 'Centurion' alone proceeded grimly on her way, the scurvy destroying men daily. In August she reached the Ladrone Islands and refreshed at Tinian, where two months were spent in building up the shattered health of the crew, and thence she sailed for the Canton River and anchored off Macao in the end of November. Here she remained, refitting, all the winter; and on the 15th of April, 1743, she weighed and sailed for the Philippines, Anson's intention being to endeavour to capture the Manila galleon. Arriving off Espirito Santo on the 31st of May he cruised for three weeks, and was rewarded on the 20th of June by the appearance of the long-hoped-for treasure-ship, the 'Nuestra Señora de Caovadonga.' After a smart action of an hour-and-a-half the ship was taken, and putting her under the command of Lieutenant de Saumarez, Anson stood away once more for Macao which he reached on the 12th of July. Here, after spending some months in making arrangements, he sold the prize, and on October 15th, 1743, sailed for England, rounding the Cape of Good Hope in March, 1744.

On the 15th of June, 1744, he anchored at Spithead, having providentially passed through a French fleet in the soundings in a thick fog.

The voyage must always rank as one of the most wonderful exhibitions of dogged resolution of all time. As an operation of war its effect was negligible; but for all that the voyage has an interest of its own from a strategic point of view; it illustrates the conservative tendency of naval thought. Both in its principal object and in its execution it betrays itself as a link with the Elizabethan idea of warfare. The resemblance to Drake's great voyage, even to the details of the taking of Paita, is too remarkable for one to forbear connecting the one with the other, and tracing the influence of 1577 on the thought of the eighteenth century. But it was the last of its kind; a new conception of war had already grown up, and the dissipation of naval strength in predatory voyages was to be relegated to the past.

CHAPTER VI

THE EXPEDITION TO CARTAGENA, SANTIAGO AND PANAMA

As the preceding narrative has shewn, the decision to send an expedition to the West Indies had no connexion with the capture of Porto Bello. The enterprise was determined on before that place was attacked, and Cathcart's troops were assembling in the Isle of Wight before the news reached England that it had been taken. The actual decision was reached in December, 1739. Transports for 8000 troops were ordered, the command was to be in the hands of Lord Cathcart, and meetings of the Council were held, at which he was present, to discuss the details of the matter.

It was decided that so soon as the five regiments miscalled Marines should have been raised, the English part of the army should sail for Montserrat. There Colonel Daly's regiment was to be embarked and the army would thence go to Jamaica. The troops from the northern colonies under Colonel Spotswood were to be assembled at Port Antonio, then the principal careening port in Jamaica, as soon as they could be transported thither. Vernon was ordered to meet the transports at Donna Maria Bay, in the West end of Hispaniola, with his squadron, and the whole force was to sail in company for Havana. The first intention was that the expedition should sail in March, and transports were ordered to be at Portsmouth during that month; but as by sailing then, the army would arrive in the West Indies during the hurricane season, and, for the further very good reason that the troops were not ready, it was determined to defer the sailing till July and thus bring its arrival to September.

Vernon's first letter to the Duke of Newcastle, dated October 31st in which he strongly advised against West Indian operations on shore on a large scale, was received on March 14th; but whether the advice therein given was communicated to the Council is not certain. The letter does not form a part of his usual correspondence, written in duplicate by his secretary, but is a separate letter, written in his own hand and marked "very private." The Duke of Newcastle's memoranda of Cabinet meetings contain no indication that he let the other members of the Council know Vernon's opinion; and Sir John Norris in his *Diary*, which very fully relates all the discussions which took place, makes no mention of this matter. As far as negative evidence goes it is by no means improbable that Vernon's opinions never got beyond the Duke.

In any case, preparations continued. By the end of July the troops were embarked. It has been shewn that the initial idea was to escort the army with five ships under Captain Gascoigne, strengthened by Anson's squadron and covered from interference by that under Norris; that foul winds blocked Norris in Torbay and prevented him from getting away to watch the western ports of Spain and France; and that, in consequence, while both army and fleet were wind-bound in their anchorages the actual enemy in Ferrol and the presumptive one in Brest put to sea from their respective ports unchallenged. The covering force was then no longer required, a larger escort became necessary, and the former was converted into the latter.

Command of the sea in the area to be used is regarded as an essential preliminary to the transport of an oversea army. There was no established command in this case. A force of about 8000 men was to be carried across the Atlantic, escorted by a squadron of twenty-five sail of the line, in the presence of hostile fleets whose numbers amounted to about forty of the line, whose whereabouts and destination were unknown. It can hardly be denied that the movement was a bold one, unless the enemy were thought so contemptible that his forces could be disregarded. This was far from being the case, and Ogle cannot but have been anxious for the security of his expedition. The destination of the army was as well known to the enemy as to ourselves for no attempt at secrecy had been made, and, as in the case of Anson's squadron, both France and Spain were fully aware of whither it was going. This carelessness, or worse, compares very unfavourably with Cromwell's procedure when he had a similar enterprise in hand. By him the secret of his Hispaniola expedition was most jealously guarded. No one ever knew against what part of the world it was directed, and no one knew better than he the advantages of simulation and dissimulation "to lay asleep opposition, and to surprise. For where a man's intentions are published, it is an alarum to call up all that are against them[1]." The Ministers of a later date had a less clear appreciation of the importance of secrecy in war[2].

Owing to the various causes that have already been described, the expedition instead of sailing in July did not leave St Helens until October 26th. As Sir Chaloner Ogle's great fleet worked down Channel,

[1] Bacon, *Essays*, "Of Simulation and Dissimulation."

[2] Mr Fortescue gives many examples in later wars. His comments in *History of the British Army*, vol. IV. p. 102 are very just.

additional items of information as to the general situation filtered in as they were picked up from passing merchant ships. The squadrons from Brest, Toulon and Ferrol were reported all to be to the westward; and while one account said they were going in company to capture Jamaica, another had it that it was their intention to lay in wait for the expedition and attack it. Thirty sail of large ships had been seen in company on the 11th of October, so that evidently some parts of the squadrons had joined, and it appeared by no means improbable that the allies would endeavour to intercept the British fleet.

No interference however took place. In spite of encountering a severe gale which scattered many of Ogle's ships, the transports and squadron arrived at Dominica within a few days of each other, and when all were collected one ship only, the 'Cumberland,' was missing. She, having been dismasted in the gale, had made for Lisbon where she refitted and subsequently joined the fleet off Hispaniola.

At Dominica an event befell which influenced the whole course of the later events. Lord Cathcart was seized by an internal complaint and, after a brief illness, died. The command of the expedition thereupon devolved on Brigadier-General Wentworth. "Lord Cathcart is dead," wrote a letter-writer, "and General Wentworth commands the forces, which gives great concern as he was never yet in any service, but he is certainly a very sensible man." Something more, however, than "a very sensible man" who had never seen service was needed for an undertaking of such magnitude.

On December 27th, the transports having all rejoined, the fleet weighed and sailed for Jamaica. The voyage was not interrupted by the enemy, but a first sight of the French was obtained. On the morning of January 7th, when the fleet was about six leagues to the southward of Cape Tiburon, and therefore in the neighbourhood of the French ports in the western end of Hispaniola, four strange ships of war were sighted. Ogle detached six of his squadron[1] under the command of Lord Aubrey Beauclerk to examine them. No colours were shewn by the strangers until three in the afternoon, when French ensigns were hoisted, but as this was no certain evidence of their nationality Lord Aubrey continued his chase, and eventually overhauled them at about 10 o'clock at night. The 'Weymouth,' Captain Charles Knowles, was ordered to speak with whichever ship she could come up with, and closing to within half-pistol shot, her interpreter hailed one of the ships and asked what they were. The question was

[1] 'Prince Frederick,' 70; 'Orford,' 70; 'Lyon,' 60; 'Weymouth,' 60; 'Rippon,' 60, and 'Dunkirk,' 60. The French were 'Ardent,' 64; 'Mercure,' 54; 'Diamant,' 50; 'Parfaite,' 44, under the Chevalier d'Épinay.

met by a counter-question of the same nature, to which Knowles replied that they were English men-of-war. "And we are French men-of-war, and what is it you want?" replied the stranger. Knowles replied that he must speak with them. The French—for such they were—then asked if war were yet declared, and were told that it had not been when the squadron left England.

While this conversation was passing, Lord Aubrey was similarly hailing another of the ships. He appears to have received no answer, and, suspecting them to be Spaniards, he fired a shot across the bows of the ship he was speaking, following it soon after by another as the first induced no reply. To this the chase replied by a broadside, and a hot engagement immediately began between the three leading British ships and the four Frenchmen. After about an hour's random fighting Knowles, who was separated from his antagonist, went on board the 'Prince Frederick' and advised that the fight should be stopped, "as we were in a wrong cause," but his representations were not acted upon and scattered fighting continued until about 4.30 in the morning, the other British ships taking part as they came up. The wind being variable and light the ships became much separated and the British ships were never all in action together. The 'Rippon' was never engaged at all, the 'York' fired two or three broadsides only, while in the confusion of the fight the 'Dunkirk' fired into the 'Orford.'

At daylight the French were seen lying to about a mile off, preparing to renew the engagement, but after a consultation had been held by Beauclerk, at which Knowles reiterated his opinion that the ships were French, it was agreed to send over a flag of truce to ask who they were, and why no answer to the hail had been given. The French commander replied to the flag with the information that they were French men-of-war bound from Petit Guave to Port Louis, and that they had answered to that effect the night before; then, after somewhat restrained mutual compliments, the squadrons separated. The incident gave no clue to the intentions of the French except in so far as it tended to shew that the French had not any instructions to begin hostilities. In the British fleet the skirmish was looked upon as a blunder. "What is said of the affair here," wrote a correspondent to the Duke of Montagu, "is that we had done too much or too little": a description which fairly represents the situation as it appeared to the men on the spot[1].

[1] Accounts of this engagement are in Vernon's despatch, Lord Elibank's narrative, the Journals of the ships taking part, a letter of Sam. Speed to the Duke of Montagu in Montagu Papers, Hist. Man. Com. Report: and of the French view in Lacour Gayet, *La marine militaire de la France sous Louis XV*.

The British detachment, after repairing such damage as it had suffered aloft, made sail for Jamaica where it rejoined the main body, whose arrival there on January 7th had filled Vernon with chagrin and dismay.

As late as December 26th Vernon had hoped to be able to meet the expedition to windward, and had kept cruisers off Cape Tiburon to give him early notice of Cathcart's arrival. His wishes to do so were not governed solely by the need for avoiding the influence of "Mr Punch" at Jamaica; the arrival of the French squadrons at Port Louis had accentuated the importance of not coming to leeward. So soon as he knew that their junction had been effected at Port Louis he saw that a new situation had been created. He at once wrote to Cathcart and Ogle, desiring them to anchor the fleet between Donna Maria Bay and Cape Tiburon where he could hasten to join them directly he heard of their arrival. His reasons for this will best be given in his own words: "The Brest and Toulon squadrons having joined and having posted themselves just to windward of us at Port Louis, and brought with them 1800 men raised at Martinique, I cannot imagine to be with any other view than immediately to attack this island whenever we should set out on any expedition to attempt anything on any part of Spanish territories. And as thus posted they will be masters of this island, and all our trade, whenever we should move from hence to leave it exposed to them, I cannot but judge it to be absolutely necessary for his Majesty's service that these auxiliary forces of the Spaniards should be first secured before it can be safe for us to attempt anything else; and fear, without it the whole event of this expedition will be rendered fruitless[1]." If the fleet and army were to come to leeward, and need watering at Jamaica, "I think," he wrote, "your arrival here with so large a fleet of transports would be the fatal Rock for this expedition to split on, thro' delays and the many other fatal consequences that would result from it. Your Lordship has experienced the difficulty of getting out of Channel with a large fleet of transports with a fair wind, and may easily imagine the greater difficulty there will be to beat up to windward with them with a contrary wind, which must be the case here. And besides that uncertainty, I fear a month or six weeks would be lost before they could be got into the sea again, if they wanted to water here: and this six weeks is the flower of time for expecting any service from new comers into these climates[2]." Unfortunately this letter never

[1] Vernon to Lord Cathcart, December 26th, 1740, S.P. Dom. Naval, 85.
[2] *Ibid.* S.P. Dom. Naval, 90.

reached the out-coming expedition, which therefore made its way to Jamaica, as already related, anchoring there on January 7th.

A meeting was held as soon as possible to discuss the operations to be undertaken. Vernon, Ogle, Wentworth, Guise and Governor Trelawny were present. They agreed at once that the only action possible was that suggested by Vernon against the French at Port Louis. There was the most complete harmony between the officers of the two services; in the Admiral's letters of this time and for some time forward there are frequent references to the excellent relations which existed between them.

The fleet, as Vernon had feared, needed watering before it could sail again. This considerable labour was at once begun, and proceeded with such despatch that it was completed by January 21st, well within Vernon's estimate of the time required. The first division of ten ships under Ogle sailed next day, the second division under Commodore Lestock followed two days later, and the Commander-in-Chief's division began working out on the 26th, followed by the transports on the 27th. By the 28th of January the whole fleet, consisting of twenty-nine sail of the line[1] (including two 50-gun ships), a 40-gun ship, twenty-three corvettes, bomb-vessels and tenders, a fireship, a brigantine as Admiral's tender, together with eighty-five sail of transports had got to sea and was starting on its way towards Cape Tiburon, to find and destroy the French squadrons and then be free for the attack upon the Spanish possessions.

On the same day that the first division sailed, Vernon detached the 'Wolf' sloop, Captain Dandridge[2], to observe the French at Port Louis. Dandridge arrived off this port on January 30th, looked into the harbour, and wrote as follows in his log: "1 P.M. Saw nineteen sail of ships, one whereof had a large white flag at his maintopmast head, another with a white broad pendant; their colours were all hoisted, etc., awnings spread, at the same time the flag on the fort and that on the look-out were hoisted. It being very hazy under the land, that we might better view them hauled the mainsail up and backed the maintopsail; judging ourselves about five miles from Port Louis Castle and being much embayed, at 2 P.M. out reefs and worked to windward." Having got this information, Dandridge bore away for

[1] Vernon had 30 of the line, but the 'Augusta' took the ground in leaving harbour, owing to the parting of a warp, and was obliged to return for repair, having beat off her rudder.

[2] Dandridge was an officer who for some years past had been a planter in America, but came to sea again when war broke out, when he was given command of the 'Wolf,' then employed upon the coast of America. He was married to a sister of George Washington.

Cape Tiburon and continued cruising in that part until February 8th when the fleet arrived. He then carried his news to the Admiral.

Vernon at once called a council of war which decided to attack and destroy the French fleet. The troops were first to be disembarked to take the land defences, the fleet was to attack the forts and the ships at anchor in the harbour. The decision to take this extremely decisive step is particularly interesting in view of the instructions issued to the French commander to protect the Spanish settlements, instructions which were in full accordance with the reply given to the question of our Ambassador in Paris as to the intentions of the Cardinal regarding the French ships fitting out in their ports[1]. A sentence, in a letter from Maurepas to d'Antin found on board a prize, put the matter very clearly: "L'objet capital de sa Majesté et celui de votre destination, est toujours de mettre à couvert les colonies espagnols, et à plus forte raison les nôtres, de toute entreprise de la part des Anglais. Vous ne devez point perdre cet objet de vue, et sa Majesté attend que vous employerez tous les moyens possibles pour rompre leurs desseins, soit séparément ou conjointement avec les espagnols[2]." The whole question lay in whether the French or British should take the initiative; the council of war decided that it should be the British.

This decision having been made, everything was at once prepared to put it into execution. The fleet worked close inshore to land the troops and by the 12th of February all the ships were in position. The 'Spence,' sloop, Captain Laws, was then sent in to get further information as to the position of the French squadron. She rejoined with the news that sixteen sail of men-of-war lay at anchor within. But some contradictory reports having then been received from some vessels and boats which had been sent in to sound the channels, Vernon sent the 'Spence' in a second time. Laws returned with the distressing information that he had been deceived by the haze and that the vessels he had seen were merchants only. To obtain confirmation of this news Vernon sent Knowles ashore with a message to the Governor. Shortly afterwards a French officer came out with a letter

[1] See *ante*, chap. v. p. 77.

[2] Vernon to Duke of Newcastle, enclosing the intercepted letter. So great was the exasperation caused in Spain by the failure of the French squadrons to support the Spaniards in the West Indies that it was reported that the Queen of Spain was ready to make peace in order to pay out France for her behaviour. *Vide* Mr Thompson's letters in June, 1741, S.P. Foreign, France, 1741.

The situation in which Vernon found himself may be compared with that which Admiral Alexieff anticipated might arise in the East when the Anglo-Japanese Treaty was concluded. "La flotte anglaise surveillerait les vaisseaux de notre escadre et génerait nos operations en menaçant d'ouvrir les hostilités au moment qui lui plairait." *Russian General Staff History of the Russo-Japanese War*, French edition, vol. I. pp. 272, 273.

of civility from M. de Larnage, offering the hospitalities of the port and volunteering the information that d'Antin's fleet had sailed for Europe a month before.

The French had sailed on January 27th. Not only had the 'Spence' been deceived, but Dandridge in the 'Wolf' had made a similar mistake on January 30th when he thought he saw the squadron of men-of-war[1]. In hazy weather he had made his examination from about five miles from the Castle, inside which the squadron would be lying, a distance in such circumstances that was too great to ascertain the particulars of the ships with that exactitude which a reconnaissance demands.

Thus it was not until February 13th that Vernon and his colleagues learned that the French had sailed eighteen days earlier, before even his whole fleet had been clear of Port Royal. The supreme importance of early information of any movements of the French fleet makes it desirable to trace why it was that they were able to get away from a place a bare 180 miles to windward of Jamaica without the news of their departure reaching the British Admiral within forty-eight hours at the outside. If Vernon could have had two cruisers off Port Louis with the usual instructions, there is no reason why the news of d'Antin's sailing should not have reached him by the 29th of January, before his whole fleet was away.

The reason why he had no cruisers off Port Louis was that owing to his having so few he had been unable to keep them clean, and he could not risk a foul ship close off an enemy's port. "I have no cruisers clean enough at present," he had written on January 5th, "to trust off Port Louis." To make up for this he had stationed his cruisers in the safer area off Cape Tiburon[2], and there he had had them cruising up to January 26th. But it so happened that at the critical moment there were no cruisers even in that part. "As I find a period of four days between the 26th and 30th of January that I had no one to watch the Marquis's motions in, I cannot be certain which way he may move in that time." The accidents of the sea had removed the watching cruisers on those days, and during their absence the French sailed unobserved. It is perhaps idle to speculate what would have happened if immediate information had been brought to Vernon of their departure; how soon he could have learned that d'Antin's destination was France cannot be said, but there can be little doubt that he would have known of it soon enough to enable the expedition to arrive at

[1] A letter (S.P. Dom. Naval, 1741) confirms the sailing of Rochalart on February 7th (N.S.) from French sources. Captain Rentone, who went to Petit Guave, brought back the news that d'Antin had sailed "about the 26th of January" (February 6th, N.S.).

[2] See *ante* p. 105.

Cartagena some weeks earlier than it did. Dandridge's incorrect report again was a cause of loss of time. If on the 30th this officer had found that the French fleet was not in Port Louis the information might have reached Vernon a few days sooner than it did, and the four days spent in getting the fleet round from Tiburon to Isle de Vache would have been saved. Dandridge has been saddled with the blame for the whole of the loss of time caused by coming to windward; but taking all things into consideration it is doubtful whether more than a week was lost through his mistake. In judging him we must remember not only the circumstances of pomp and procedure observed by him and his officers, confirming the opinion that the ships they saw were men-of-war, but also that Captain Laws made a similar error. Thus, accurate observation was evidently difficult. The incident serves as a warning to remind officers of the imperative necessity of making absolutely sure, and of their duty, as expressed by Admiral Patton, of going sufficiently near to form a clear and accurate judgment of the size and force of any ships seen[1].

A second council of war then sat to discuss the altered situation, which decided that before proceeding further it was essential to get more news of the French, and find out whither they had gone when they left Port Louis. Frigates were sent to Petit Guave and Leogane with that object and the fleet was moved round to Irois and Donna Maria Bays, where wood and water could be obtained, there to await the return of the cruising ships. In those bays the soldiers were landed and employed in cutting wood and making fascines for the forthcoming siege operations, the seamen meanwhile filling up the water casks, four weeks already having passed since leaving Jamaica.

The 'Squirrel,' Captain Warren, which had gone to Cartagena from Jamaica, rejoined the squadron on February 23rd and brought the report that de Torres with fourteen ships had sailed on January 31st, and was believed to have gone to Havana; only three sail of the line and six galleons were said to have remained at Cartagena. From Petit Guave came the news that only seven sail of French men-of-war lay there. Where d'Antin had gone was however still absolutely unknown. He might, as the French officer had said, have returned to Europe; but it was equally probable that this was merely misinformation, and that he had really gone to Havana to join de Torres. Havana was the nearest spot at which any body of the enemy of sufficient strength to dispute Vernon's operations could be; much time had been lost already and further delays were dangerous. It was therefore de-

[1] Cf. Mostyn's mistake off Brest March 18, 1747; Linois and Dance; Dewa's reconnaisance of the Russian squadron, Feb. 9, 1904; and other similar cases.

cided to take the risk of the two squadrons having joined, and to move down to Cartagena at once. This uncertainty as to the whereabouts of the French squadron must be fully appreciated in considering the further operations[1].

By this time the chances of success had been seriously prejudiced. A combination of circumstances, some avoidable and some unavoidable, had set a severe check on the progress of the expedition. The delay in sailing from England, which could have been avoided if proper precautions to watch the ports of the enemy had been taken at an earlier date, was the first and principal cause; Vernon's operations were then hampered by the presence of the French squadrons in the West Indies. Owing to their appearance he took the expedition to windward to Port Louis; in consequence the troops, instead of arriving at their destination by the end of January, fresh and ready for the work before them, spent another month on board the crowded transports and did not reach Cartagena until the beginning of March. The loss of this month was not only of supreme importance in a region where climatic conditions have to be so carefully studied, but may also have altered the whole course of the campaign. If Vernon had sailed direct for Cartagena there is a strong possibility that he might have met de Torres' squadron at sea. The result of an engagement between a fleet of twenty-nine ships and one of fourteen could hardly be doubtful. It is even possible that he would have arrived off Cartagena before de Torres sailed, in which case the entire Spanish squadron would have fallen into his hands so soon as the harbour mouth had been forced.

That neither of these things happened was through no fault of Vernon. The responsibility lay at home where the proper covering for the oversea operations had not been provided. Instead of being able to carry his expedition straight to its destination Vernon had to go out of his way to deal with the French, and had also lain exposed to a blow from Spain—a blow that did not fall only because the Spanish Admiral failed to execute the well-conceived instructions he had been given by his Government. These instructions

[1] The following is a summary of the movements of the French (all in O.S.):

Aug. 14 Rochalart with 12 ships of the line sailed from Toulon;
Aug. 21 D'Antin with 14 of the line and 5 frigates left Brest; detached 4 ships under Roquefeuil to cruise on Spanish coast;
Oct. 10 D'Antin arrived Martinique. Embarked about 1500 troops;
Oct. 27 D'Antin arrived Port Louis, Hispaniola;
Dec. 7 Rochalart with 8 ships joined d'Antin;
Dec. 28 Roquefeuil with 4 ships joined d'Antin;
Jan. 27 French sailed for Europe, leaving about 7 sail under Roquefeuil at Petit Guave.

directed de Torres to attack Vernon whilst he was still in inferior force before Ogle joined him; or, if Vernon retired to Jamaica, to blockade him there. Vernon did retire to Jamaica, as the Spanish orders anticipated, and a great opportunity was then open to de Torres. He lay with a considerably superior force between Vernon's squadron and the reinforcements that were coming to him from England, and might have moved with troops from Cartagena immediately on Port Royal and by a rapid blow captured both the squadron and the port itself, the defences of which were weak. He might have cruised to intercept the transports which were on their way, unprotected, from the North American colonies. He did neither: and at length hearing in January that d'Antin, whose help he had hoped for, was returning to Europe, he hurried to Havana and remained there to defend it, hoping at least that de Roquefeuil with the small squadron left him by d'Antin would join him—a hope doomed to disappointment[1]. Vernon therefore remained unmolested and the transports arrived without loss.

In accordance with the decision of the council of war to make Cartagena the first objective, the 'Wolf' was despatched to England to inform the Government. The fleet sailed on February 25th. It stood down to leeward and came to an anchor on March 4th in Plaza Grande, the roadstead off Cartagena. The small ships were sent in at once towards the northern end of the town as though a landing there were intended, while the 'Weymouth,' 'Dunkirk,' 'Experiment' and 'Spence,' sloop, passed close along and examined the shore from Boca Grande to Fort San Philip. They found only one small fascine battery of six embrasures on that stretch of coast, but the heavy swell on the beach near the town, rendered a disembarkation in that part impracticable, and the result of the three days[2] examination of the shore led to a decision to get the fleet inside as soon as possible. This involved an attack on the batteries guarding the Boca Chica. From the plan it will be clear that the prevailing wind being east by north to east-north-easterly the passage could not be rushed by ships under sail so long as the shore forts and castles covering it were in the hands of the enemy. Besides these forts, a boom was in place across the channel, covered by the guns of four Spanish ships of the line.

On March 6th the method of attack was decided on. Three 80-gun ships—the 'Norfolk,' 'Shrewsbury' and 'Russell'—were to move close

[1] De Torres' orders, and a letter from him expressing his intentions, were found on board a Spanish prize and sent home by Vernon.

[2] The fleet was anchored by the afternoon of March 5th. The bombardment preparatory to landing began at 9 A.M. on the 9th.

in and bombard Forts St Iago and St Philip. The 'Princess Amelia' and 'Litchfield' were to engage the battery of Chamba, the bomb-vessels at the same time throwing their shells into Fort St Louis which was outside the battering range of the ships' guns. When the forts close to the shore should be silenced the troops were to land and take Fort St Louis by assault; while in order to occupy the attention of the garrison of Cartagena itself and prevent them from coming to the assistance of the defences of the Boca Chica, Lestock's division was to remain off the town and make a feint of landing there.

Vernon thereupon drew up his instructions. In these he clearly explained the situation, saying that it was intended to attack Cartagena vigorously by land and sea. The first thing to be done was therefore to secure Boca Chica Castle and the forts covering the entrance in order to block up the town effectually and secure a safe anchorage for the transports; the landing place was to be the small bay between St Iago and St Philip—the point, he said, where de Pointis had landed. His instructions then proceeded to describe the forts to the northward of the entrance, and to insist that what was particularly required was to engage all the batteries as closely as possible.

Thus far his memorandum was in the nature of a general survey of the situation, giving broad outlines as to the opposition he expected and the methods by which this opposition should be overcome. He then continued: "Having thus informed and instructed you according to the best intelligence I have received, and furnished you with pilots of the best abilities and experience I could procure, I rely on your judgement and resolution for the due execution of my orders giving such additional orders as you shall find to be necessary from the motions and dispositions of the enemy and other events that may arise in the vigourous execution of these orders." To Chaloner Ogle he further wrote: "And the better to secure the success of your enterprise you are to give orders to every respective Captain of your division not to suffer any imprudent or hasty firing from their ships, which only serves to embolden an enemy instead of discouraging them; but to give strict orders not to suffer any gun to be fired from any of the decks till the officers appointed to command on each respective battery has seen to the pointing each gun he is appointed to have the inspection over, and directed the firing of it, so that all possible care may be used to secure the success of this first attempt on which the success of the whole so much depends; and they are to endeavour to persuade and convince their men of the folly and imprudence of hasty firing, which serves only to encourage their enemy and expose themselves. And you are likewise in your orders in writing to assign

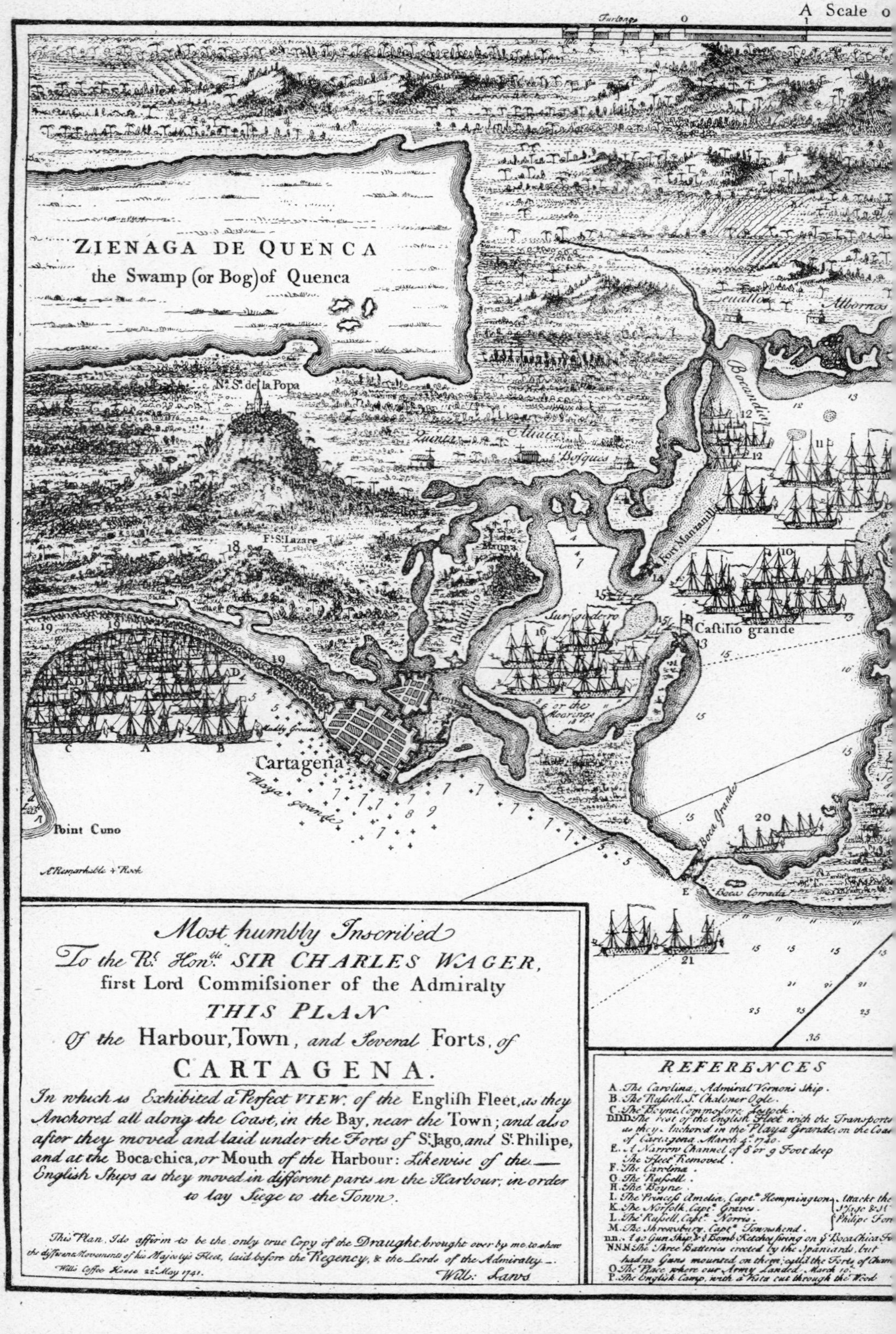

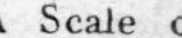

Furlongs 0 1

ZIENAGA DE QUENCA
the Swamp (or Bog) of Quenca

N.ª S.ª de la Popa

Zuinta

Alhaia

Bosques

F.t S.t Lazare

Bocandilla

Fort Manzanillo

Castillo grande

Surgidero

or the Moorings

Cartagena

Playa grande

Point Cuno

A Remarkable + Rock

Boca Grande

Boca Corrada

Albornos

Most humbly Inscribed

To the R.t Hon.ble SIR CHARLES WAGER,

first Lord Commissioner of the Admiralty

THIS PLAN

Of the Harbour, Town, *and Several* Forts, *of*

CARTAGENA.

In which is Exhibited a Perfect VIEW, *of the* English Fleet, *as they Anchored all along the Coast, in the* Bay, *near the* Town; *and also after they moved and laid under the Forts of* S.t Jago, *and* S.t Philipe, *and at the* Boca-chica, *or* Mouth *of the* Harbour: *Likewise of the English Ships as they moved in different parts in the Harbour, in order to lay Siege to the Town.*

This Plan, I do affirm to be the only true Copy of the Draught brought over by me to show the different Movements of his Majesty's Fleet, laid before the Regency, & the Lords of the Admiralty.

Wills Coffee House 22.d May 1741.

Will: Laws

REFERENCES

A. *The Carolina, Admiral Vernon's Ship.*
B. *The Russell, S.r Chaloner Ogle.*
C. *The Boyne, Commodore Lestock.*
D.D.D. *The rest of the English Fleet with the Transports as they Anchored in the Playa Grande, on the Coas[t] of Cartagena March 4.th 1740.*
E. *A Narrow Channel of 8 or 9 Foot deep The Fleet Removed.*
F. *The Carolina.*
G. *The Russell.*
H. *The Boyne.*
I. *The Princess Amelia, Capt.n Hemmington.*
K. *The Norfolk, Capt.n Graves.*
L. *The Russell, Capt.n Norris.*
M. *The Shrewsbury, Capt.n Townshend.*
} *Attacke the S.t Jago & S.t Philipe For[t]*
n.n. *1 40 Gun Ship & 2 Bomb Ketches firing on y.e Bocachica Fo[rt]*
N.N.N. *The Three Batteries erected by the Spaniards, but had no Guns mounted on them; call'd the Forts of Cham[…]*
O. *The Place where our Army Landed, March 10.th*
P. *The English Camp, with a Vista cut through the Wood*

…e 20 Gun Battery raised by our Army. to play …ainst the Boca Chica Fort. w.ch they Stormed in y.e night 25.th March
… Forts of S.t Jago 8: S.t Philipe 10 Guns, mounted on …n. Attackt the 9.th of March.
…nglish Bomb Battery between the two Forts.
…l Large Thick Woods from our Camp to y.e Boca Chica Fort.
… Boca Chica Fort mounted with 63 Guns. Storm'd y.e 25.th
…n Blass's Ship the Galicia taken by the English. in …ich were the 2 Captains that were brought to England.
…wo of the Spanish Men of War Sunk. & another Set … Fire by themselves.
… S.t Josephs Fort mounted with 16 Guns.
… Boom laid cross the mouth of the Harbour held by Anch.rs
…e Enemys 15 Gun Fascine Battery on y.e Barradera side.
… Enemys unseen 5 Gun Fascine Battery under which …r Men Landed.
… Large Number of Boats full of the Seamen going through …ods to be landed. Headed by Capt.n Laws w.th the Admirals …ision. Capt.n Boscawen, with S.r Chaloner Ogle's and …t.n Coates. w.th the Comodores, to Attack the two Batteries …hich they destroy'd on the 26.th March.
…e Spanish Sloop that was to Supply the 2 Batteries with Ammunition, burnt by our Seamen.

5.5. The Spence Sloop sent to find out Harbourings for the Ships in case they should be drove away from the Mouth of the Harbour & also for the Boats.

6.6. Two Fascine Batteries raised by the Enemy at the Entrance of the Passa Cavallos.

7 The Admirals Ship the Carolina, Anchoring in the Harbour, with some others with him. March the 26.th

8 A Watering Place, where lay Capt.n Perry Maine in y.e Worcester.

9 A Serpentine Passage for Boats. through which Don Blass made his Escape in a large Boat, with several other Boats following.

10. The Admirals Ship moved further into the Harbour near the Castilio Grande.

11. S.r Chaloner Ogles Ship.

12. Transports.

13 The Castilio Grande mounted with 60 Guns, which Surrendred without firing one Shot, on which was hoisted the English Colours. Mar. 31.st

14. The Manzanilla Fort mounted with 18 Guns. but made no defence.

1515. Two Spanish Men of War, & six Galleons sunk on each side of the Passage to the Moorings

16 Five English Men of War at Anchor, to lay Siege to the Town. The Orford L.d Augustus Fitzroy. the Burford Capt.n Griffin, Capt.n Lawrence & Capt. …

17 A French Merchant Ship Burning. April y.e 1.st

18 Fort Lazare.

191919. The Spaniards — going away from the Town. April 2.d

20 Don Blass's Ship & another lying before the narrow Channel in the Harbour.

21 The Lyon and the Burford lying near the — Narrow Channel.

N.B. The Lyon lost her mast by being drove out to Sea when She had the Generals aboard going to view the Fortifications on the Terra Bomba, and was lost for near a day, the Spence Sloop went after her, & brought them back to their Respective Ships.

22. Comodore Lestock with the Transports

to each particular captain the post he is to take, and the order he is to execute, that no one may have the least pretence to plead ignorance of your orders, which you are to enjoin the due execution of, at their utmost peril[1]."

The clearness with which Vernon's orders are drawn up is admirable. The general plan of attack is made clear, the parts the different bodies have to play are clearly set out to their commanders. There is nothing rigid except that the ships will proceed to certain places with a certain object in view, and the essential flexibility is attained by an ample decentralisation of command. No attempt is made to predict all that may happen or to provide for every eventuality that may arise. The commanders, unfettered by hampering instructions, are trusted to use their own judgment and to act as unforeseen circumstances may direct.

On March 9th, all preparations having been completed and the necessary information as to depth of water and other matters obtained, the five ships selected for attacking the batteries moved in. They anchored as close to the shore as possible and opened a devastating fire with all their tiers upon the batteries. In less than two hours the Spanish gunners were driven from their guns, the ships, except the 'Shrewsbury,' suffering very small losses. That ship, whose cable was cut by an unlucky shot in the forenoon, drove close in to the harbour's mouth before she could be brought up, and received the whole fire of the heavy inner forts and of the Spanish ships which were moored inside the boom; and it was not until after dark that she could be warped out of range, having lost over sixty men.

By noon the shore batteries were all silenced. The order was then given to land the troops, and the grenadier companies to the number of 500 men were ashore by 2 P.M. on Terra Bomba, and secured themselves. Disembarkation continued during that and next day, and by the evening of the 10th the whole army was on shore. No advance however was made. The 11th was spent in landing tents and forming a camp, the seamen working without intermission in getting the artillery and stores on to the beach, most of the time in a heavy surf.

This dilatory manner of beginning the movement against Fort Louis, whereby two days were occupied in doing nothing, was observed by Vernon with extreme uneasiness. Well acquainted with the climate and not less acquainted with the character of the enemy and the art of war, he foresaw that a continuance of these methods would spell ruin to the undertaking. He and Ogle therefore wrote a joint letter to Wentworth suggesting that an immediate advance through the

[1] Vernon's report to Duke of Newcastle and Vernon to Chaloner Ogle. S.P. Dom. Naval, 90.

woods to the inner side of the harbour, would, by isolating the castle of St Louis by land, serve greatly to lessen the resistance of that fortress. They further pointed out that if the troops lay about in the sun a general sickness would be the result.

Wentworth did not adopt these suggestions but continued to form his camp. Guards were placed to protect it, and the work of raising batteries to attack the fort was begun. A mortar battery was ready by the 13th, but the heavy gun battery was not finished until the 22nd. Although the island where the troops were encamped was separated by several miles of sea from Cartagena Wentworth entertained constant fears of an attack and placed large guards on all sides of the camp for its protection. This, besides harassing the troops unnecessarily, took them from services in which they were required, and a shortage of men was felt. Vernon was therefore applied to to lend his marines. The Admiral declined to do so. His fleet was lying in an exposed anchorage and might at any time have to put to sea, when all the ships' companies would be needed on board; and, for another and more important reason, the French and Spanish squadrons were at large, and as intercepted letters shewed that they were acting in conjunction the topsails of their combined fleet might at any moment appear above the horizon[1]. Vernon could not risk being suddenly attacked from seaward by an equal or superior force with a large proportion of his complements on shore[2]. Even in fine weather re-embarkation of a number of men would take time, which might prejudice his tactical position. The unsettled weather, however, was already making boat work difficult; a night attack from the sea upon the Baradera battery had to be postponed for this reason on the 18th, but was executed by Captain Watson on the 19th in a brilliant manner, the battery being boarded and set on fire.

On March 21st another council of war was held, at which the military representatives urged that the ships should attack the castles of St Louis and St Joseph by bombardment. These castles were far

[1] Vernon to the Duke of Newcastle, March 17th, 1741.

[2] When Sir Cloudesley Shovel landed his men at Lord Peterborough's request for the storming of the castle of Monjuich in 1705, the circumstances were wholly different. The French fleet was located in Toulon where Shovel's cruisers were watching it. The news of its sailing was immediately to be communicated to the Admiral, who would have time to re-embark his men before the enemy's squadron was upon him, and that they should be re-embarked in such a case was an essential condition upon which he agreed to land them. In Vernon's case it was not known where the enemy were, nor their strength. It was impossible so to command the approaches with cruisers as to ensure adequate notice of the enemy's approach; and if the enemy appeared on the horizon it would be too late to begin embarking and getting his large fleet under way and formed in line of battle.

more formidable works than St Iago, St Philip and Chamba. Vernon and Ogle reluctantly agreed to make the attempt, though, as they set out in writing, it was against their judgment as seamen to risk the ships in battering castles of such strength. The 'Boyne,' 'Prince Frederick,' 'Hampton Court,' 'Tilbury' and 'Suffolk' were placed under Commodore Lestock's orders for this service, with most strict injunctions that, in order to prevent confusion, he was to give the captains positive orders "not to have their men to the guns till the ship be safely anchored where she will have your orders to post herself for battery."

On the 23rd the ships moved in and attacked St Louis Castle and the battery. The depth of water did not permit the ships to get closer in than 700 yards from St Louis and 900 yards from St Joseph's. At such a range the ships were at a great disadvantage. "'Tis most certain," wrote Lord Elibank, "that where a ship can come within musket-shot of a fort there is no withstanding her. The constant fire from three tier of guns, joined to that of the small arms from the poop and tops, make it impossible for an enemy to stand to their guns, and indeed such a fire is irresistible. But it is quite otherwise where a ship attacks at a distance; for besides that it is impossible to take aim from a ship so well as from a battery, every shot that hits any part of a ship has its effect. The sides of a ship are so far from covering the men that the splinters do more execution than the ball itself, and every man on board is more exposed than if he had nothing to cover him."

It was in such circumstances as these that the ships attempted to batter the castles. For two days a gallant attempt was kept up, and then, with their ammunition expended, the 'Boyne,' 'Prince Frederick' and 'Hampton Court' severely damaged, Captain Lord Aubrey Beauclerk and a large number of men killed, they were ordered to withdraw. No effect had been produced on the castle and the squadron was diminished by the disablement of the ships.

A second assault had now to be made on the Baradera battery, which the Spaniards had succeeded in repairing after the previous attack on the 19th. Watson was sent in again on the afternoon of the 24th, and this time having daylight to work in, not only made a thorough business of the battery, but afterwards hauled his boats across the narrow spit of land behind it, and pulled into the harbour, where he captured and burnt a sloop which had served as ammunition carrier for the battery. This assault was even more brilliant than the preceding one.

In spite however of the evidence given by the destruction of the

Baradera, that a resolute assault would drive the enemy from his positions, Wentworth would not attempt to carry Fort St Louis. Within two days of the completion of his heavy battery on Bomba Island several of the guns of the castle had been dismounted, and a breach had been made on the third day—the 25th. Vernon wrote on the 23rd suggesting that as the castle had then been well battered for twenty-four hours it might be taken by assault; and next day he wrote again, saying: "The longer you delay the attack, it will be the harder work for you." On the morning of the 25th the naval council again wrote, urging an energetic attack: "Diffidence of troops," they wrote, "we fear tends only to discourage them; and in our opinion you have numbers sufficient for finishing the attack of such a paltry fort with vigour, that has no outworks." Further, they expressed the opinion that long distance battering would never do any good, as the enemy would keep them in play till sickness destroyed the army. "As we are best acquainted with this intemperate climate," they wrote, "we think it our duty...to advise your pursuing more vigorous measures as most conducible to the preservation of your mens' lives from the ravaging sickness."

Whether the naval officers were right in thus giving their unasked for opinions to the General as to the best way of conducting a siege may be questioned. Their duty was to assist in any operation in which the ships and men could be of use; but in offering views upon a purely military concern they went beyond their province. It may well be that Wentworth chafed under these letters, and in the manner of many a weak man, obstinately took the opposite course. The excuse for the Admirals is that they had long experience of the climate and of the Spaniard in those parts, and knew that once sickness set in more men would die in a day than would be lost in a direct assault on the walls. Besides this their large fleet was lying in an open roadstead, its ground tackle was being cut to pieces and the need for getting the ships into the shelter of the harbour was an urgent one. For these reasons their impatience was great and must be allowed for[1]. But neither Vernon nor any other seaman would have tolerated interference from a military officer in a corresponding naval operation, and it is natural that Wentworth should have resented the attempts of the seamen to dictate the manner in which he should conduct his business. Probably however the Admiral's opinions could have been proffered in a more tactful form, and friction might have been avoided if this had been done. But it is greatly to be doubted whether it were really possible for two men of such different temperaments as Vernon

[1] Compare the case of Hood at Capri in 1793.

and Wentworth to work harmoniously in company. In truth, it was a misfortune that they came to be associated[1].

Up to this point however the friction had not become acute, and in reply to Vernon's letter of the 25th, Wentworth wrote to say that a sufficient breach having been made in the walls of the castle he would assault it. Whether or no Vernon had been right in making the suggestion, the result justified his views.

On receiving Wentworth's letter the Admiral at once ordered the bomb-vessels to be ready to support the assault by a bombardment of St Joseph's Castle. A party of seamen under Knowles, who had with him Captains Watson, Cotes, Dennis, Cleland and Brodrick was also ordered to make a diversion on the Baradera side to draw the Spaniards to that part. When all the preparations were completed the grenadiers advanced against the castle. No sooner was their approach seen than the garrison hung out a white flag and beat the "chamade" for surrender. But the flag not being made out, nor the "chamade" understood by the British officers, the advance and firing continued, and the garrison fearing that this indicated that no quarter would be given, incontinently fled, so that the castle fell into the hands of the army without trouble and with the loss of one man only. The misunderstanding about the "chamade" was however unfortunate, and it caused the escape of the 500 men of the garrison, who got away to swell the ranks of the defenders of Cartagena city. That the fort was in no condition to withstand assault is shewn by the words of an officer who took part in its capture. "It was surprising," he wrote, "to reflect upon their having kept this place so long, for besides the breach in the walls the embrasures were all knockt down and of 90 cannon only two remained fit for service, with one iron mortar of vast diameter[2]."

While the troops were assaulting St Louis Castle, Knowles landed his party of seamen and soldiers at the Baradera. Seeing the panic which was taking place at the castle he immediately manned his boats, pulled into the harbour along the southern shore, and with his boats' crews stormed St Joseph's Castle, all unbreached as it was. Having taken this work by about 10 P.M. he rowed to the 'Gallicia,'

[1] The reason for the great failure at St Domingo in 1654 was the impossibility that Penn and Venables should work together, and Cromwell, great man that he was, knew where the fault lay and unhesitatingly laid on himself the blame for having allowed those two officers to be sent on a joint enterprise.

[2] An account of Admiral Vernon's attempt upon Cartagena in the West Indies, Add. MS. 3970; see also Narrative of Lord Elibank in Hardwicke Papers, Add. MS. 35898; *Journal* of Captain Knowles (P.R.O.); Naval Chronicle; and Vernon's letters to the Duke of Newcastle; besides the various published discussions.

the Spanish flagship, which had been deserted by all but sixty men and fell an easy prize. Knowles then cut the boom and the cables securing it; the entrance to the harbour was now open except for the wrecks of the 'San Carlos' and 'Africa' which the Spaniards had deserted and sunk in the main channel. Of the remaining men-of-war the 'San Philip' was burnt, but the 'Conquistador' and 'Dragon' together with some other shipping lay out of reach in the carenage off the town.

Next day—the 26th—the Admiral began moving his fleet into harbour. The sunken vessels had to be shifted and the whole fleet and transports had to be warped in through the narrow channel. The labour was great, but by the evening of the 27th the whole of the ships were berthed inside. It was none too soon, for the weather was tempestuous, the holding-ground bad and ships' cables were badly cut.

Once inside Vernon wasted no time in pressing his advantage. The 'Burford' and 'Orford' worked up to within gunshot of Castillo Grande on the evening of the 26th, and the 'Gallicia' was converted by the carpenters of the fleet into a floating battery to bombard it. Knowles was sent in the 'Weymouth,' with the cruiser sloop, to destroy the batteries at Passo Cavallos and seize the hulks there as a first step towards isolating the town. These batteries were demolished by the 28th. Sixteen cannon were nailed up, and Knowles rejoined the fleet in the upper part of the bay.

When he had anchored the fleet in security Vernon felt justified, as well he might do, in writing a triumphant despatch, which he sent home at once by Captain Laws. The ease with which the Baradera battery, St Louis and particularly St Joseph's Castles had fallen, and the abandonment by the Spaniards of four ships of the line without an attempt to defend them, gave him confidence that the enemy would not stand if they were pressed vigorously. The capture of the town should therefore follow quickly.

The news of the imminent fall of Cartagena ran like wildfire through Europe. Vienna, St Petersburg, Turin and the Hague received it with rejoicing, Paris and Madrid with acute depression, and Europe suddenly turned from its own affairs to those of the New World. Cardinal Fleury foresaw that the French trade of over sixty million livres annual value would be lost, and that all his efforts to keep France out of the war must fail. "He has the unhappiness of seeing that the conquest which the English have just made, places them in a condition to become masters of the American trade and to carry further weight in the great affairs of Europe; and that if he wishes to oppose her in it he must come into a general war, which he greatly dreads[1]."

Preparations for the new landing began on March 30th, when a council of war decided to put the troops ashore on the east side of the harbour and isolate the town by a cordon across the neck of land joining the lake to the bay, running behind La Popa Hill. The Spaniards at the same time proceeded to block the approaches to the town by sinking eight galleons, all the shipping in the harbour, and their last two 64-gun ships in the main channel. While this was being done they evacuated Castillo Grande, the large fortress mounting 60 guns which commanded the approaches. Captain Knowles, whose eye missed nothing, observed the stores being removed. He at once pointed this out to Ogle, who ordered him in to attack the fortress. Knowles weighed immediately, laid his ship alongside the fort and opened a fire which was not returned. The garrison had abandoned it.

The failure to retain this strong work besides giving further evidence of the quality of the opposition which any determined attack would receive, opened the way to the town, made the removal of the hulks sunk by the Spaniards an easier matter, and rendered it possible to land the troops closer than had been intended. A day's hard work sufficed to clear the fairway. By April 2nd the bomb-vessels were in position to open fire on the town, and the 'Weymouth' cruiser and eight fire-ships were warped in to cover the landing by scaling the bushes with their fire. On the night of the 5th the disembarkation was begun at Texar de Gracias, three miles from Madre La Popa. No serious opposition was met and by noon on the 6th it was completed.

Everything now depended upon rapid and determined action. But the General was unable to relax the strict rules of his art to meet the conditions of a combined operation, and again time was wasted in forming camps and in consultations. Letter-writing began again with vigour but no advance was made. In vain Vernon and Ogle on that day reminded Wentworth of the approach of the rains, which once they had begun, would not allow further operations. "As every day's experience," they wrote, "has shewn the Spaniards are an enemy that cannot stand being vigorously pushed we cannot but advise you against slow proceedings as what may prove of greatest detriment to your forces, it being plain the enemy are infinitely better provided with engineers than you[2], and will have the advantage

[1] Chambrier to Frederic II, June 5th, 1741. *Les préliminaires de la Guerre de la Succession d'Autriche*, M. Sautai, pp. 361, 362. Cf. corroborating this Mr Thompson to Duke of Newcastle, S.P. Foreign France, 1741.

[2] Mr Moor, the principal engineer, had been killed in the operations round St Louis Castle.

of you in everything depending on carrying on works of that kind."

The military council of war had however decided to march to La Quinta and there encamp, and thither they went led by General Blakeney. They passed through a wood in which a few of the enemy were posted, with a loss of only one man killed; and coming to a clearing where a road crossed the bush path and a large house commanded the approaches leading to the city, found a detachment of about 500 Spaniards drawn up. As soon as an attack could be developed on the position these also gave way and retreated pell mell for the town. Now was the moment for a dash! The enemy, wholly demoralized, were on the run, the road was open for the city gates, and there were those present who thought that a rapid pursuit would have carried the British troops into the city with the fleeing Spaniards[1]. But a fatal caution, a fear of ambushes and stratagems, and a lack of appreciation of the total want of moral in the forces opposed to him, weighed strongly with the General. Instead of following up his success he recalled Colonel Grant from his pursuit, and proceeded to encamp and post guards for his own defence. A council of war was held to decide how to capture the hill on which the convent of Madre La Popa stands. But while the council was deliberating the question was solved for them. A party of "marauding American soldiers," with a most reprehensible disregard of the proprieties of war, climbed the hill themselves and occupied it without the slightest opposition.

The only remaining outwork was the fort of San Lazar. This was a small square building mounting six guns on each face, the walls of which were about fifteen to twenty feet high. The western face is approached by a fairly gentle slope which was covered by the guns of the town. The approach to the southern face is very steep and inaccessible, and that to the eastern is also broken and steep. The northern face, although narrowed, presented the best line of approach as it is led up to by an easy slope, but troops ascending it were enfiladed by the guns on the eastern bastions of the town[2]. Although however the fort was a sufficiently strong little work it was commanded by a hill not more than 300 yards from it, the ascent to which was somewhat steep but not impracticable. A battery mounted on this hill would have knocked the fort to pieces in a few hours.

[1] Lord Elibank's narrative; also Add. MS. 3970. Lord Hervey's *Journal* says: "'Twas the opinion of most of the generalls that had we pursued the enemy in their retreat we should with very little trouble have gained San Lazar." Lord Elibank expressed the view we should have gained the town itself.

[2] It is to be noted that the bearings given by Beatson in his description of the town are wrong. He has turned the place round through eight points to the right.

Road to Cartagena — The original fort — Hill on which guns were to be mounted by engineers

FORT ST LAZAR FROM THE NORTH

Two whole days went by during which the General neither advanced to seize the fort by assault nor took steps to raise a battery on the hill. Vernon urged an assault at once. Wentworth considered the fort must first be reduced by battering, and requested that the squadron might bombard it—a wholly impracticable suggestion in view of the range. Vernon replied by reminding Wentworth that when de Pointis took Cartagena he did not wait for a breach, but recognising the danger of the climate, rushed the foot of the walls and scaled them; and he suggested that if the foot of the walls were reached they might be mined and blown up. So paltry a fort, said he, needed no battering, but if the General was of the opinion that a battery was necessary, the fleet would provide the guns and get it ready so soon as the engineers should have selected the position in which they wanted it raised. The engineers however could see nothing but difficulties in getting the battery erected on the commanding hill. Mr Armstrong, now the principal engineer, gave as his opinion that to get the battery in place would take so many men and so much time that in the circumstances it would be impracticable, for the rains were now beginning and the mosquitoes were already at work. Sickness among the troops had increased terribly, and each hour's delay was adding to the quota of the victims. The engineers also confirmed Vernon's opinion that the walls were not too high to be scaled, adding that there was no ditch and that the approach was not difficult. From what point they had made their reconnaissance cannot be said; but while the slow advance of the army had been made the Spaniards had busied themselves digging entrenchments outside the walls, so that, in the opinion of an officer[1], the outworks were now stronger than the fort itself.

Urged by Vernon to go on "sword in hand[2]" and the place would fall, advised by his engineers that the walls could be carried by assault and that a battery could not be raised, Wentworth, after a heated discussion at the military council in which Blakeney and Wolfe strongly took the opposite view, decided to assault the fort at daylight on the morning of April 9th. Fifteen hundred troops were ordered for the attack, the remainder—some 500—being kept as guards to the camp. The main assault under Guise was to be made on the eastern—the steeper of the two possible faces,—and another under Colonel Grant on the northern face. At 3 A.M. the advance began. The troops carried woolpacks and scaling-ladders and advanced as silently as possible, led by a locally obtained guide. Colonel Wynyard, who led one column, particularly requested that Colonel Blane, who had made a recon-

[1] Colonel Burrard, Add. MS. 34207.

[2] Letter of 8th of April, Vernon to Wentworth.

naissance two days before, might accompany his column as guide, but Wentworth refused this, "bidding him follow the guides he had appointed[1]." On the eastern side the enemy was ready and received the attack with a hot fire at twenty paces, and the troops, instead of rushing the entrenchments with fixed bayonets, advanced slowly, carrying out "street firing" and losing heavily. On the northern face no better result was obtained. No sooner was the alarm given by the outguards than the guns in the town joined in the defence with a flanking fire. In a description written by Colonel Burrard[2], he says, "We received a continual fire of their cannon from the town and fort and their batteries, which swept off many of our men being quite exposed to their shot, and when we drew near enough for them to make use of their muskets their fort and batteries seemed one continuous light. The men behaved with the utmost resolution but 'twas our misfortune to attempt an impossibility. 'Tis true we got up to their breastworks and drove them from their trenches but what could we do when we came up to the fort we found it surrounded by a very deep trench and the walls of the fort too high by ten feet for our ladders, and we in return firing against their stone walls." A one-sided battle in which Colonel Grant fell, mortally wounded, continued for over two hours, after which the attack was abandoned and the troops withdrew, having lost about 600 men and 43 officers. The 500 men in camp were not sent to make a demonstration on the southern face which might have assisted the assault, but remained behind, an unused reserve. No feint had been made against any other part, and Grant, in the agonies of death, exclaimed that the General ought to hang the guide and the King ought to hang the General. According to Captain Watson, who commanded the naval force that took part in the attack and met the Spanish officers when burying the dead afterwards, the Spaniards fully expected the fort to be taken and said that it might have been "if other methods had been pursued." The squadron was unable to give any help in the attack as a bombardment of the town at long range could not have assisted the assault on the hill; it would not have served to withdraw any of the fire from the eastern walls which caused such losses to the troops ascending the northern face; and no battering at the southern face, which was the only one the ships' guns could reach, could have had any effect on the action proceeding at the outwork.

This repulse at San Lazar had a most depressing effect on the troops, and not less so on the leaders. On April 10th another council

[1] Lord Elibank's narrative.
[2] Letters of Col. Burrard, Add. MS. 34207.

of war was held by the military commanders at which it was agreed that the forces now remaining were insufficient to provide guards for the camp, much less to raise and work batteries against the fort; and unless the fleet could arrange to provide men not only to get the guns up but also to man and work the batteries the whole enterprise had better come to an end. A very acrimonious correspondence followed, ending with a letter from Vernon saying that the sea-officers could give no opinion as to where the batteries should be placed, but if the General would say where he wanted them, the seamen should not only raise and fight them, but storm the breach as well; and if it was desired to isolate the town and the General could not spare troops or feared being cut off, seamen should also be landed to do this; but the last danger was not a real one for he had given instructions for the 'Dunkirk' and a sloop to support the outlying party on its calling for help.

On receiving this letter Wentworth proposed a council of land and sea-officers, which sat on the 14th of April. At this meeting the General represented that he had now only 3500 men left out of the 8000 with whom the attempt had been begun; these were dying daily and it would take at least a fortnight to raise the batteries to bombard San Lazar during which time sickness would still further reduce the force. After a heated debate the decision was made to abandon the enterprise and re-embark the army. Orders to this effect were therefore given, and the 'Gallicia,' fitted with protective lockers of sand round her batteries and manned by 300 volunteers, was sent in at 5 A.M. to moor as close alongside the main walls of the town as possible. The difficulty of warping a ship close to the shore batteries under a heavy fire, combined with a defective knowledge of the soundings, prevented her from being placed with exactitude[1]. She maintained nevertheless a hot action for several hours in which she lost one-fifth of her crew. Then, in a sinking condition, she was abandoned after a gallant but too unequal fight. The exact reasons for sending her on this fatal service are not easy to determine. It is clear that it had been contemplated to use her to cover the embarkation, as the report of the naval council of war of three days earlier shews. She was to be supported by the bomb-ketches, but these vessels had expended all their ammunition. Vernon, in a letter to the Duke of Newcastle, says that the 'Gallicia' was sent in "to satisfy gainsayers," meaning, perhaps, to prove to the General by an ocular demonstration

[1] The criticism in one of the contemporary attacks upon Vernon, that the 'Gallicia' could have gone closer in since galleons could moor alongside, leaves out of account the different circumstances in which they reached that position.

that the fleet was not able to do more in the capture of fortresses than it had done. But it is difficult to see why he should think this necessary after the ample evidence of March 23rd, when to satisfy Wentworth he had made a similar attack against St Louis. If his object were merely to stifle criticism it was one unworthy of him and quite uncalled for.

Whilst this engagement was proceeding the remains of the army were embarked and as soon as the transports were warped out of the harbour they sailed for Jamaica. The fleet, before following them, destroyed all the captured shipping, carried off such stores and masts as would be of service, and blew up all the forts that had been taken.

It may be questioned why, having gained the Boca Chica and possessed themselves of the harbour the commanders of the expedition did not think it worth while to retain those dominating points. The Council in London had previously considered the retention of Cartagena as a permanent possession with the object of proceeding thence to seize the mines in the interior, but the place itself would have been too expensive a possession. It would have saddled the army with a large permanent garrison requiring complete renewal every two years, and the navy with the provision of a squadron to attend upon the garrison. These objections applied with less force to the castles at the entrance. They could have been held with a much smaller force and their retention would have placed in our hands a tremendous weapon against Spanish trade. By holding them and keeping an observation upon the Spanish naval forces in the west, the trade of Cartagena would have been stopped as effectually as that of London was stopped while the Dutch rode outside the Thames. Not a ship could have passed in or out, and as the shipping of the harbour had been destroyed, troops from the city could not have retaken the forts on the island of Tierra Bomba. A squadron operating from the bay could have had the trade of the coast at its mercy.

Such at least was the view Sir John Norris was quick to take when the news of the failure of the expedition reached London. The retention of the harbour mouth he said "could have prevented the Spaniards the use of the coast and have been a means to enable the Government to treat with Spain towards a peace: which being abandoned takes from us the advantages we might have had in treating with them; for [if] we could have kept that port the Spaniards could not have got any effects from the kingdom of Peru by the West Indies. And by taking the castle of Vera Cruz they would likewise be debarred the use of the kingdom of Mexico. That must have brought us the advantage of a good peace and commerce with them." The wise old Admiral shews herein the clearness of his statesmanship and his strategy. His words form a confirming comment on the dictum of de Crissé that the object of war is peace.

In considering what their next move should be after the failure of the attempt on Cartagena, it will not be just to assume that the desirability of garrisoning the castles and retaining what they held was overlooked by the commanders. Lord Elibank, in his account of the expedition, refers to the idea, saying that the occupation of Boca Chica would be as good as holding Cartagena. It is probable that with the troops dying, and the harbour becoming daily more unhealthy as the rainy season approached, it was deemed impossible to leave either ships or men in the place with any hopes whatever of their surviving[1]. Hosier's losses at Porto Bello had not yet been forgotten, and this blockade of Cartagena—for such it would have amounted to—would have been but a repetition of Hosier's terrible pacific blockade of the Bastimentos. At all events the decision to abandon the place was taken, and the castles having been blown up and all stores of any value embarked, Vernon sailed on March 6th followed next day by Ogle, and on the 9th by Lestock with their respective divisions. After a beat to windward to examine the French harbours the Admiral returned to Port Royal on the 19th. No signs of the French squadrons were seen.

Meetings of the naval and military commanders and the Governor of Jamaica were at once held to discuss further operations. Intercepted despatches had disclosed that the defences of Havana had been greatly strengthened and the garrison increased, so that no attempt against it was practicable with the forces available. Trelawny put forward the favourite Jamaican idea of an attack upon Panama but the other officers considered this undesirable. After several days' discussion it was decided on May 26th to attempt to capture Santiago. This place, as Vernon had pointed out in an earlier letter to the Duke of Newcastle, lay between the main base of the French in Hispaniola and that of the Spaniards in Cuba. If France should come into the war its possession would thus be of high value to us. It was moreover an important privateer base on the flank of the main channel of outward trade to Jamaica. Finally, there was the question of an ultimate conquest of Cuba which was in the minds of the Ministry though Vernon himself doubted its possibility. Though the forces at the disposal of the General were wholly inadequate to invade Cuba without considerable reinforcement the occupation of Santiago could be effected by them and a *pied à terre*

[1] Even the delay of the few days which were spent in demolishing the castles cost a great many lives (Lord Elibank's Narrative).

secured which would be of service if more comprehensive operations should be ordered later.

The strategy of making the attack upon Santiago has been commented on in such adverse terms that it deserves consideration. The criticism[1] is based upon the argument that the conquest of Cuba was the chief object in view, and therefore "sane strategy" would have dictated firstly the annihilation or neutralisation of that formidable "potential fleet" at Havana and secondly the dealing of a blow at the heart instead of at the extreme end of the island.

If the conquest of Cuba had been the chief object, and if the military resources had been adequate to undertake it, there is much to be said for this view. But neither of these conditions was present. The commanders carefully considered that question and rejected it as impossible, but knowing that the Ministry contemplated sending out reinforcements and that the capture was greatly desired by the Cabinet, they decided to utilise the time at their disposal by undertaking the lesser operation. In view of these actual facts the sweeping criticism falls to the ground, unless it should be said that even in an attack upon Santiago the proper station of the fleet was one of observation of Havana. Vernon however had orders, dated September 25th, 1740, to send back to England as soon as possible all ships beyond those necessary for local superiority. In his cruise to windward after leaving Cartagena he had been able to satisfy himself that the French had now certainly returned to Europe, and as the Spaniards, according to report, had only nineteen ships of the line in West Indian waters, he considered it essential to act upon those orders and to detach his surplus eleven ships to England; this he made ready at once to do, placing them under Lestock's command and sending with them the homeward-bound trade. The remaining squadron would not have been sufficient to furnish the necessary escort to an expedition and maintain a blockade of Havana, considering its distance from the base and the prevailing winds; considerations which make it clear that Vernon was not so deficient in strategical insight as his critic implies.

No offensive operations could be begun until the fleet had been refitted and replenished. As soon as the ships were ready, Lestock's detachment sailed for England, and on June 30th Vernon, with the remainder and the transports, sailed from Jamaica for Guantanamos Bay where they arrived on July 18th.

After a reconnaisance of Santiago a council of war sat on July 20th to decide the method of attack. Captain Rentone who had made the observations reported that the high land, the failing breezes inshore

[1] *History of the Royal Navy*, Laird Clowes, vol. II. p. 77.

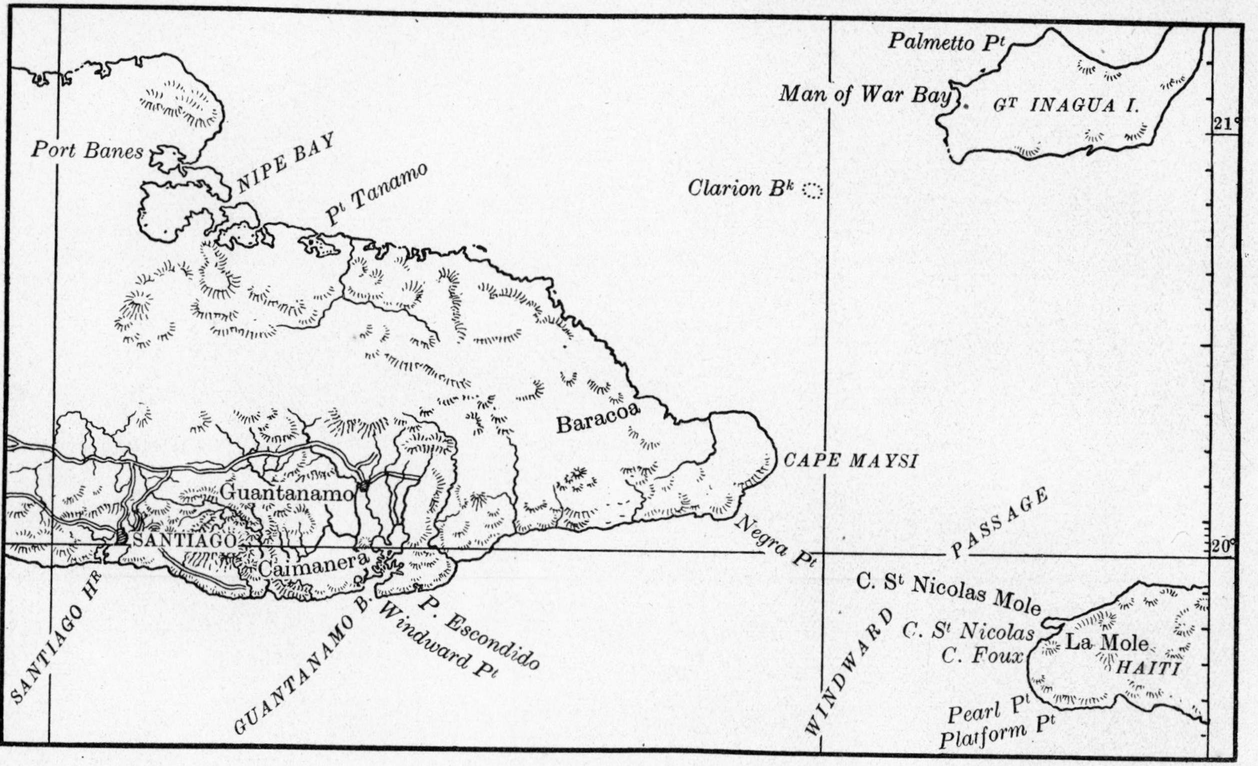

GUANTANAMO BAY

and the strong forts covering the narrow entrance made a sea-attack impossible, and Vernon with his own experience of attacking castles, concurred in this view, after having personally made an examination of the entrance. The Council thereupon agreed that the attack must be made by land[1]. It was therefore determined to land the army at Guantanamos Bay, march to the heights overlooking the town, and assault the defences from that direction. It was further agreed that when this had been successfully accomplished Santiago should be held and future movements must depend upon the arrival and strength of the reinforcements which were expected to be coming from England.

The troops were therefore landed, and an advance was begun against the village of Catalina, but ceased abruptly before reaching that point. The same hesitations which had marked the military operations at Cartagena were repeated, and with them the campaign of letter writing began. Vernon and Ogle wrote a joint and strongly worded protest to the effect that the service was not being conducted with zeal. Wentworth replied that the squadron ought to have forced the mouth of the harbour—an operation agreed to be impossible by the general council of war which included himself. Although protesting that the advance on Catalina was impracticable, he nevertheless resumed it, and arrived there without encountering the smallest resistance. On this success Vernon wrote an encouraging and friendly letter, complimenting him upon his success, urging a further rapid advance and expressing the opinion that the only enemy to be feared was delay. He promised further that directly the troops arrived above the Morro he would cooperate off the harbour's mouth with the fleet; but he declined to land more than a comparatively small number of his marines for the same reason as he had refused to do so off Boca Chica: the Havana squadron might still have to be engaged.

Wentworth now saw nothing but difficulties. The road was long, the enemy might be industrious and resolute, though of industry or resolution they had not yet given a sign. The burden of his reply was that there might be opposition to his march and that if there were, nothing could be done. Again Vernon and Ogle wrote, urging that the danger was surely small and that a little vigour and determination would overcome it; but they wrote in vain. For over a month the only campaign which was conducted was one on paper, in which the General argued that it was quite impossible to do that for which he had come. Yet during all this time small parties, wholly unmolested, were going out in all directions, bringing in cattle as they

[1] Cf. Norris's views on this general question as expressed in the discussion in Council to attempt Ferrol.

pleased, and meeting resistance nowhere. Vernon in desperation went round again to Santiago on September 2nd to see whether he could not force the harbour mouth, but the narrow entrance and the uncertain breezes inshore, in which the ships would lie at the mercy of the batteries, convinced him that such an attempt would be useless.

September passed without anything further being done. The operations had dwindled down to an occupation of Guantanamos Bay, and all efforts to stir Wentworth into a more energetic policy failed. The men fell sick with appalling rapidity, and more than half were down with agues and fevers by the end of the month; fifty-one died in the last week of the month and twice as many in the following week. "Our inactive situation is very melancholy as well as useless," wrote a correspondent. "Our men are very sickly and die fast, more from want of necessaries than the inclemencies of the climate, I fear. Some die from their own excesses in drink[1]." So the army dwindled away, dying in camp from its own immobility.

To a man of Vernon's temperament such inaction was maddening, and it may well be imagined that he expressed his feelings with little restraint, till personal communications between the commanders became impossible. At the end of September the Admiral wrote to the General saying that in future all communication between them had better be made in writing. But no representations, whether verbal or written, made any difference, and October passed as September had done, the list of sick and dead steadily increasing with each week, until some companies which had embarked at Jamaica seventy strong could muster only six men.

The fleet suffered less than the army, for Vernon, seeing that the Spaniards were as inert as his colleague and that no danger was to be feared from them, sent his ships cruising. His instructions had enjoined him to attack Spanish trade and protect our own. Keeping only a small body at Guantanamos to attend upon the army and protect it against attack by privateers, he dispersed the squadron on six cruising stations for that purpose in the main lines of trade[2]. This

[1] Sam. Speed to Duke of Montagu. Montagu Papers, Hist. Man. Com. Report.

[2] The stations were as follows:

(i) To windward of la Hacha, to intercept ships outward bound from Spain to Cartagena or Porto Bello;

(ii) Between Cape Corrientes and Grand Camanes, for ships from Cartagena, Porto Bello or the Caraccas going to Vera Cruz or Havana;

(iii) On the north side of Cuba to intercept ships going to Havana by the old Bahama Channel;

(iv) To windward of Cape François to protect British trade coming from North America;

(v) Off Cape Bacca to protect trade passing along the south side of Hispaniola;

(vi) Off Santiago.

dispersion had its dangers; in the face of an energetic enemy it would have been impossible. But Vernon rightly gauged that his enemy would be inactive, and with a squadron only equal in numbers to that at Havana, he at the same time covered the military operations and protected and attacked trade. Herein lies one of the many differences in character between Vernon and Wentworth. The former, after experience of his enemy's behaviour, drew conclusions as to what he was likely to do and acted accordingly, adopting measures which were not risky because he knew that the enemy would not take advantage of the weakness of his dispositions. The latter never appeared to get the measure of the enemy's character.

The demands for ships in home waters in the late summer of 1741, owing to the difficulties of keeping the Mediterranean squadron up to a strength sufficient for the operations under Haddock rendered it necessary still further to reduce Vernon's squadron. Orders, dated August 17th, reached him late in October, directing him to send home eleven unsheathed ships that they might be refitted and made ready for the spring campaign. He had shortly before made a detachment of five, having learned that the Spanish squadron at Havana had been reduced to sixteen ships. This made a great drain upon his strength, but he proceeded at once to make four more ships[1] ready, which was the most he felt he could spare, reducing however their crews to bare sailing complements in order to keep up the strength of his remaining ships. This detachment reduced his squadron to twelve ships whose duties were numerous. De Torres with about sixteen was still at Havana, the Spaniards and the French were reported to be preparing ships at Cadiz and Toulon which might be coming his way, and the army had to be covered. The protection of British trade moreover had latterly become increasingly difficult. The Spanish privateers, driven by Vernon's cruising ships from the favourable areas like the Windward Passage and the track south of Hispaniola, had extended their operations further north and were even meeting ships as far away as lat. 30°, to the southward of Bermuda, entailing a far greater effort upon the British cruisers. Spread over a wider area the privateers were more difficult to deal with by cruising methods, and the only satisfactory manner of securing the trade was by convoying it through the whole of the danger zone. The smaller ships—sloops and lesser craft—were scattered in the channels used by the trade, the more powerful ships were employed in convoys, and the bulk of the ships of the line was massed in a squadron to cover the operations of the army. The defeat of this squadron, Vernon

[1] 'Orford,' 70; 'Prince of Orange,' 70; 'Suffolk,' 70, and 'Prince Frederick,' 70.

remarked[1], would overthrow all the other objects; for the ring would then be broken and the whole organisation would fall to the ground—a very good example on a small scale of the complementary duties of ships of the line and cruisers.

The further reduction in his squadron led to a council of war being held on October 31st to review the situation. Attacks upon Havana, Cartagena and Panama were all once more discussed and rejected. Havana was too strong—as it had always been—Cartagena had already repulsed an attack by a force stronger and in better health than the army then available, and Panama was so far to leeward of Jamaica that if a French war broke out that island might be in danger. It was therefore decided to remain at Guantanamos and await the arrival of reinforcements in sufficient numbers to allow of an attack on Santiago. The decision was an unfortunate one. How many more troops were expected is not stated, but apparently not more than 3000. If the original force, of which about 1500 men were now out of action, had been considered inadequate, the extra number would not counterbalance the increase in strength of the defences at which the Spaniards had been labouring for three months.

Thus for another three weeks a deplorable inactivity continued; it was brought to an end by the alarming increase of illness during November. No less than 2260 men were down with fever on the 24th of the month, and each day shewed a rising sick rate. It was therefore decided to abandon the expedition, and the troops after occupying the ground round Guantanamos for four months were re-embarked and carried back to Jamaica. Vernon, bursting with rage at the miserable conduct of affairs, asked permission of the Duke of Newcastle to return to England as he desired "no longer to be conjoined to a gentleman whose opinions I have experienced to be more changeable than the Moon."

In spite of the disappointing results of their previous conferences, another council of war was held on arrival at Jamaica to consider a fresh enterprise. Trelawny again suggested Panama and received the support of a naval lieutenant called Lowther—a gentleman until lately a pirate, but to whom a commission had been given for services which he had rendered to the fleet. Lowther knew the isthmus of Panama well and considered it perfectly practicable to carry artillery up the Chagres River as high as Cruces, whence a good road and open country led to Panama. This was the old treasure route used in the season when the river carried water enough for navigation. It avoided the long and difficult land transport of cannon across from Porto Bello

[1] In letters. October 31st, 1741.

by the paved treasure path through the bush, and, from the nature of the surroundings of the river, an attack upon the boats would be practically impossible. The troops could land at Porto Bello and march by the road, unencumbered by heavy baggage. The distance was about forty-five miles. The scheme appeared feasible to the Council, and they decided to make the attempt. Lowther was sent at once to Porto Bello in the 'Triton' sloop to reconnoitre and return with his report as soon as possible. The ships were prepared for sea and the army for further service, Lowther having laid stress on the necessity that everything should be ready for a start immediately he returned with his report, in order that the expedition might be carried through before the rains began. The rainy season at the isthmus of Panama is something of a misleading term: it rains there nearly all the year, but more persistently in that season than at other times.

On the 15th of January the expected reinforcement consisting of 3000 men—rather more than had been lost at Santiago—arrived from England. A fortnight later the squadron was in a condition to sail. The troops however were not yet ready, for the requisite negro transport had not been obtained. The employment of negroes in any capacity other than in the plantations was often a very difficult matter to arrange, owing to the opposition of the planters who resented the slaves being taken away from earning their master's fortunes. The gentlemen of the West Indies, in whose interests so many lives of soldiers and seamen were sacrificed, and so much money spent, gave but a poor assistance to the Mother Country. The merchants supplied the enemy with stores to enable him to continue his depredations, the shipowners seduced the seamen from the king's ships to man their privateers, and the planters put obstacles in the way of the employment of negroes, vehemently opposing the formation of black regiments which would have saved the lives of thousands of British soldiers.

On this occasion their unwillingness to co-operate added another to the many difficulties of the expedition. The months slipped by. On March 2nd Vernon wrote and reminded Wentworth that time was everything; delay would spell ruin. He suggested that the expedition should get away at once without waiting to complete the number of negroes, but the General said he could not do this. The army would not be ready, he said, until the 6th, nor, if he sailed at once, could he land until the negro transport arrived.

Next day Vernon received information that a Spanish squadron was reported to be on its way to Cartagena carrying troops. Leaving Ogle with the remainder of the ships to convoy the army, he got to sea with the 'Boyne,' 'Mountagu,' 'Worcester,' 'Defiance' and two small craft and stood over to La Guayra in the hopes of intercepting them, with instructions to Ogle to join him off Cartagena. He cruised on and off Playa Grande, Cartagena and the coast to windward, seeing nothing of the Spaniards, and getting more impatient each day, until the 25th of March, when the transports (from Jamaica) and their escort came in sight. The whole force at once bore up for Porto Bello and arrived there on the 28th. As usual Vernon had prepared his orders in advance giving full instructions as to how the squadron was to approach the harbour, to anchor, and to begin the operation of landing. After anchoring a naval council met and decided to send boats up the Cascajal River at once and cut off the communications between Porto Bello and Panama. This was about to be done when Vernon received the astonishing request from Trelawny for the use of a ship to take him back to Jamaica! The expedition had been abandoned before a soldier's foot had been put on shore. With the troops ready to land, with news that Anson was in the vicinity of Panama, with Lowther's report that the garrison consisted of but 450 men and that the place could certainly be taken, a military council of war decided not to make any attempt. The reasons for this surprising decision were twofold. It was said that this weakly garrisoned place could not be taken with less than 3000 men, and, owing to sickness on the voyage, the force now amounted to only 2032, and that as the rainy season was so close it would be undesirable to make the attempt. Both these reasons may have had some justification, but Wentworth before leaving Jamaica when reminded by Ogle that the season was getting late had replied that he anticipated no difficulty from the rain. Now, however, he anticipated every difficulty and used it as an argument to support the conclusion that the enterprise was impracticable. As far as the numbers were concerned Panama was a weakly defended place by land, its garrison was small, and even two thousand men would seem to have a good chance of success against it. In any case the reasons for abandoning the attack were of a kind which, even had they been sound, should—and could—have been advanced sooner. It was too late to make these discoveries only at the moment when, after three months preparation, the expedition arrived at the port of disembarkation. "More changeable than the moon" seems indeed a not inappropriate description of the character of Wentworth.

As the General had come to this decision there was nothing to do but to return. The last of the convoys sailed for Jamaica on April 9th and Vernon followed on the 14th with the two flagships, two 70's, four 60's and three small craft. He first beat up to Cartagena to see

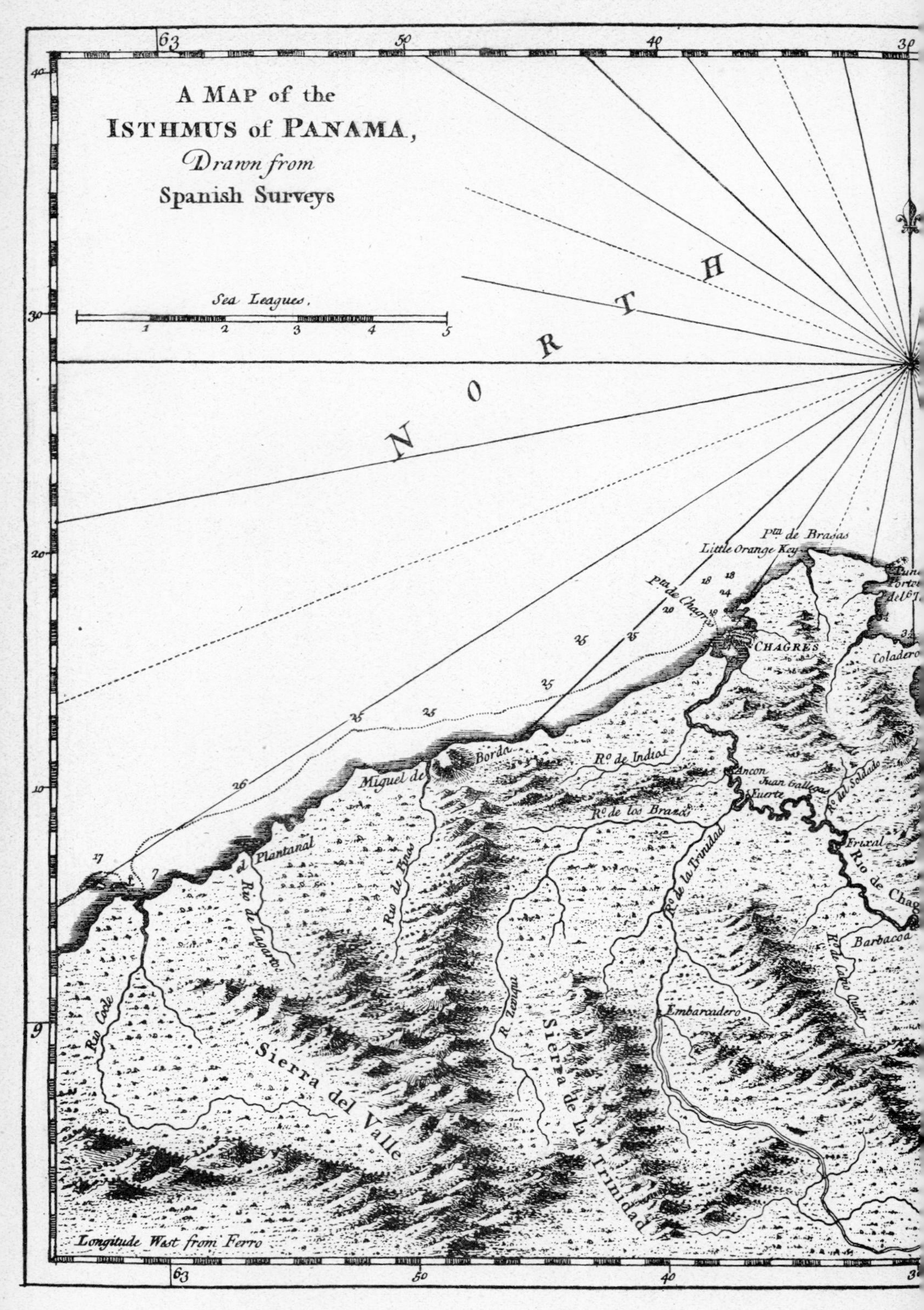

A MAP of the
ISTHMUS of PANAMA,
Drawn from
Spanish Surveys
Sea Leagues.
NORTH
Pta. de Brasas
Little Orange Key
Pta. de Chagre
CHAGRES
Coladero
Borda
Miguel de
Ro. de Indios
Ancon
Juan Gallegas
Fuerte
Ro. de los Brazos
Ro. del Soldado
Frixal
Rio de Chag
Plantanal
el Rio de Lagartos
Rio de Brias
Ro. de la Trinidad
Barbacoa
Ro. de Caño Quebr
R. Zevigua
Embarcadero
Rio Code
Sierra del Valle
Sierra de la Trinidad
Longitude West from Ferro

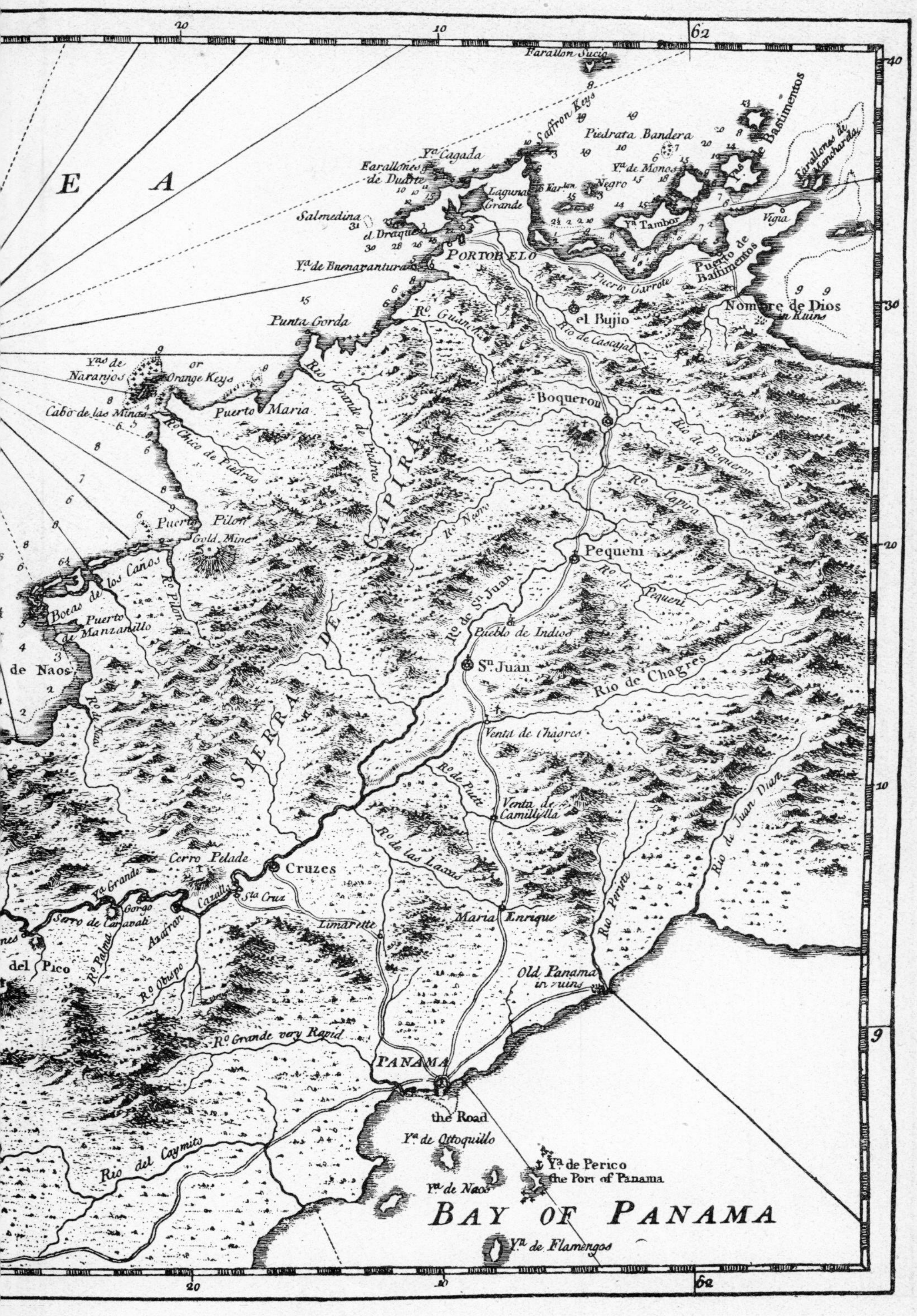

E A
Farallon Sucio
Saffron Keys
Piedrata Bandera
Ys.de Bastimentos
Farallones de Manchardo
Ya. Cagada
Farallones de Duarte
Laguna Grande
Ya. de Monos
Negro
Salmedina
el Draque
Ya. Tambor
Vigia
PORTOBELO
Ya. de Buenaventura
Puerto Garrote
Puerto de Bastimentos
Nombre de Dios in Ruins
Punta Gorda
Ro. Guanchs
el Bujio
Rio de Cascajal
Yas. de Naranjos or Orange Keys
Puerto Maria
Cabo de las Minas
Rio Grande de Piedras
Boqueron
Rio de Boqueron
Ro. Chico de Piedras
Ro. Capira
Puerto Pilon
Gold Mine
Ro. Negro
Pequeni
Ro. de Pequeni
Bocas de los Caños
Ro. Pilon
Ro. de Sn. Juan
Puerto de Manzanillo
Pueblo de Indios
de Naos
Sn. Juan
Rio de Chagres
SIERRA DE CAPIRA
Venta de Chagres
Ro. de Putt
Venta de Camillylla
Rio de Juan Dias
Cerro Pelade
Cruzes
Ro. de las Lazas
Ya. Grande
Gorgo
Serro de Caravali
Cazalla
Sta. Cruz
Limarette
Maria Enrique
Rio Perite
Ro. Palma
Azafran
del Pico
Ro. Obispo
Old Panama in ruins
Ro. Grande very Rapid
PANAMA
the Road
Ya. de Ottoquillo
Rio del Caymito
Ya. de Perico
the Port of Panama
Ya. de Naos
BAY OF PANAMA
Ya. de Flamengos
20
10
62
40
30
20
10
9

if anything were passing in that part, and then stood up to Jamaica, fetching the western end of the island at Blewfields where he landed on the 12th of May and returned by land to Port Royal.

Councils of war again met to discuss the situation and any further operations. To Vernon's mind the attitude of France had again become a most disquieting feature. Intelligence from the Mediterranean shewed that France was adopting an attitude in those waters similar to that which she had adopted in the West Indies, and he inferred that her active participation in the war must soon follow. This he proposed to anticipate by taking the army to Léogane, the French station in the west end of Hispaniola, and capturing it. The proposal was not adopted, and finally all that this great armament effected was to seize and garrison the little island of Ruatan, off the coast of Honduras, with the object of securing it as a base from which to protect and attack trade.

Henceforward trade defence and attack formed the principal object in the West Indies. Detachments from the squadron had gradually reduced it to eight sail of the line. The Spanish squadron at Havana rarely fell below fourteen, but varied in strength according to the convoys. Both squadrons occupied themselves with the defence of their own trade in their own way, and, in the end of 1742 both Vernon and Wentworth were recalled, and they returned to England.

Vernon's return may be said to mark the termination of the policy of conjoint naval and military operations in the West Indies. Though proposals for further territorial attacks on a smaller scale were made at a later date, they were none of them of the magnitude of those of 1740 and 1741, and were rather concerned with the immediate defence of trade than with any great strategical object of bringing the enemies to a peace. Perhaps the termination of the policy may be said to be dated with the accession of Carteret to power, the last act of Walpole's administration being the despatch of the reinforcement of 3000 men at the end of 1741.

It is the fashion to attribute the failures in the West Indies to Vernon, and to speak of him in a contemptuous and disparaging manner. His capture of Porto Bello is treated as an operation of no importance, and the failure at Cartagena is put down to his overbearing and arrogant attitude towards his colleague. He is summed up as a boasting creature of no solid qualities, though in reality the boasting attached to his name was none of his doing, but was the outcome of the spirit of the time. His success at Porto Bello was made much of, not by him, but by the Ministry, who hoped to derive credit for their conduct of the war from it. The foolish mob believed the Ministry and made a hero of Vernon for an action which in its practical execution was of no very great difficulty. What should be borne in mind in relation to the taking of Porto Bello is Vernon's attitude towards the operation. He had spoken of it as a place that could easily be taken, when other men believed it to be impregnable. When the opportunity came Vernon attacked it as he had said he would, in a manner which was believed to be the incarnation of rashness; but Vernon saw no rashness in the attempt. He believed that if he could get close enough he could destroy the castles and take them, and he did so. He believed this without knowing how very weak the place actually was—as the despatch of de la Vega shews it to have been; it is this accurate judgment and resolute execution more than the absolute operation which entitles him to credit.

Vernon is described by a contemporary[1] as "Mr Vernon that provident great Admiral who never suffered any useful precaution to escape him." It is impossible to read Vernon's despatches, his orders and his instructions, without concurring in this description and seeing that he was a careful, competent and resolute commander. The repulse at Cartagena was the result of a series of causes, the first link in the chain of which was the incompetent Administration at home. Every canon of the art of war was broken by the Ministry. War, which was rendered nearly certain when Newcastle played a double game and rescinded the order to recall the Mediterranean squadron on March 6th, 1739, became quite certain when Spain failed to fulfil her obligations on May 25th. Yet, while the Ministry pursued a policy which was nearly certain to lead to war, and when it became evident that war would be the outcome, they did nothing towards making the necessary preparations for the result they were courting. It was not until over six months from May that a decision was come to as to the plan of war that was going to be pursued, and, when this decision was reached the news of it was known in Madrid as soon as in Whitehall.

Following upon this, the expedition was prepared in a leisurely way. Transports were not ordered till December. Owing largely to the unreadiness of the fleet, but also to the manner of employing it, the Spanish ports were not watched, and reinforcements to the garrisons of Cartagena, Havana and Vera Cruz sailed from Spain without let or hindrance. Walpole spoke truly enough when he said that single ships or even small squadrons could not be prevented from sailing; but no attempt worthy of the name was made to prevent them, nor were the measures taken such as would hamper the movements of whole squadrons or fleets. At a time in which Vernon had under his

[1] Probably the writer was Lestock.

command a force of twelve ships, mostly crippled from want of stores—a failure of supply for which the Administration was responsible—a Spanish squadron of seventeen sail and two French squadrons making twenty-two sail were permitted to put to sea and to proceed unhindered to act as their Governments might have ordered them. It was no thanks to the foresight or strategy of the Ministry that Vernon was not destroyed before ever Ogle and his reinforcement saw the coast of San Domingo, nor indeed that that reinforcement and army ever arrived there. If the policy of France had been directed by men who appreciated better than Fleury the true interests of their country, or if the Spanish Admiral had intelligently executed the orders given him, they would never have done so. Vernon recognised the position more correctly, as men are apt to do when they themselves are in the position of danger. He saw that the French squadrons formed a bulwark against his contemplated operations, and inferring with justice that Monsieur d'Antin "was not come to the West Indies to take the air," as soon as he had his fleet together he proceeded against that detachment of the enemy—the French—whose whereabouts he knew of, with the definite intention of destroying it. What lay in his power to remedy the deficiencies of the strategy of the Government, Vernon did, at the risk of a very remarkable stretch of his instructions.

In estimating the blame of the failure one must further consider that, besides the delay of a year in sending the expedition, the troops of which it was composed were largely raw men. The Ministry had in their power, notwithstanding the low state to which the army had been reduced, to send regular troops of seasoned men; but this they did not do on account of France, the Jacobites and the fear of invasion. "If we had no disaffected party among ourselves," said the Duke of Newcastle, "or if we had at the beginning of the war no enemy but Spain, we might perhaps have ventured to have sent a few of our regular troops for attacking Spain in the West Indies, before we had replaced them by new levies: but neither of these was the case...if the Spaniards had found means to land 4 or 5000 regular troops in any part of Great Britain or Ireland, at a time when we had not a sufficient number of regular troops for its defence, the invaders would have been joined by such a number of the disaffected as would have made it very difficult for us to support our Government at home, and consequently utterly impossible for us to attack the enemy, or even to defend our own dominions abroad[1]."

[1] *Parliamentary History*, vol. XI. p. 711 *et seq.* Debate in the Lords on a Motion for Admiral Vernon's Instructions.

Having thus done nothing to reduce the difficulties of a most arduous undertaking, the Government despatched it at a time which left a very narrow margin to allow for climatic conditions. They made the force unnecessarily large and thereby delayed its departure. Fewer men sent earlier would have done the business. Indeed, if 3000 troops under an able commander had been sent at the beginning of the war, it is well within the bounds of possibility that Vernon, as he said he could, might have taken Cartagena. There still remains however the undoubted fact that the best was not made of the bad situation, and that in spite of the politicians Cartagena might still have been taken. For this Vernon is commonly held responsible, and the failure is put down to his brutal insolence to Wentworth, his boisterous and peevish manners. Even incidents so remote from tactical or strategical considerations as his catching turtle for the ships' companies and not for the army are employed as arguments to prove his share in the failure. But no boisterous manners or brutal insolence on the part of the Admiral could have been the cause of Wentworth's pitching his camp where the enemy's shell fell into it, of his assaulting St Louis Castle too late, or of his making no proper arrangements for the attack on St Lazar. All these were matters in which Vernon, whatever he might think and whatever he might say, had no part.

That Vernon used every method from advice to action to expedite the undertaking admits of no question. Indeed, the fault to be found with him is that he offered too much of the former; but for all that, what he offered was good. It was for the General to accept or reject the advice. He chose to reject it at St Louis and to proceed against the castle by the slow methods of Low Country warfare, whereby his men became saturated with fever; he accepted it at St Lazar but made ineffectual arrangements. If success had crowned the undertaking the honour would have been his. So also must failure lie at his door.

That harmonious co-operation between naval and military commanders is essential to success in a conjunct operation is an axiom needing no elaboration, but it is doubtful whether harmony were possible between two men so fundamentally different as Vernon and Wentworth. If it were shewn that Vernon in any case held back and failed to render assistance when it lay in his power he would deserve great blame: but that is a wholly different thing from saying that his manners were the cause of the failure.

These conclusions might safely be drawn from Cartagena only, did it stand alone. But it does not. At Santiago and Panama there were the same indecision and lack of initiative in the military commander. What Wentworth was at Santiago, so he was at Cartagena: and we have only to read the despatches, the letters of officers who took part, and the reports of the councils of war to see clearly whom, of the officers on the spot, to blame. Had the Administration at home been in the hands of a Chatham and the military direction in the hands of a Peterborough, Wolfe, "No-flints" Grey, Abercrombie, Auchmuty, Moore, or any of the brilliant soldiers whose names illuminate our record of amphibious warfare, we never should have heard a word about Vernon's pride or incompatibility of temper, and the actual operations in the West Indies in 1741 and 1742 would form a chapter we should read with pride.

CHAPTER VII

THE BEGINNING OF THE WAR OF THE AUSTRIAN SUCCESSION

Events in Home Waters 1741

THE West Indian expedition of which the outcome has just been described was well upon its way towards the theatre of its operations when Parliament met on November 18th, 1740. Threatening as the attitude of France had been—she had followed up at the time of its departure her uncompromising declarations of opposition by the actual step of despatching two considerable squadrons to enforce them—there had yet existed a hope that an alliance might be arranged in Europe which would deflect her energies into other channels, more favourable to the employment of British sea power. This hope however had been dashed to the ground by the death of the Emperor Charles VI on October 20th. In place of the grouping of powers, with defined objects in view, which Walpole had desired to create, an unknown and precarious situation faced England. The King's speech in the House of Lords on this occasion reflected the anxiety with which Ministers viewed the European situation. "The great and unhappy event of the death of the late Emperor," so it ran, "opens a new scene in the affairs of Europe, in which all the principal Powers may be immediately or consequentially concerned. It is impossible to determine what turn the policy, interest or ambition of the several courts may lead them to take in this critical conjuncture. It shall be my care strictly to observe and attend to their motions, and to adhere to the engagements I am under to the maintaining of the balance of power and the liberties of Europe: and in concert with such Powers as are under the same obligations or equally concerned to preserve the public safety and tranquillity, to act such a part as may best contribute to avert the imminent dangers that may threaten them[1]."

These fears that the "interest or ambition" of the several courts might be productive of complications were quickly realised. Claimants for the whole or for parts of the Hapsburg dominions sprang up on every side. Among those who came forward to wrest her heritage from the new Queen Maria Theresa were the heads of many states

[1] *Parliamentary Debates*, 1740.

which had agreed to guarantee her succession. Their demands became henceforth a dominant factor in British naval policy.

Spain had never been satisfied with the terms of the Treaty of Utrecht by which she had lost, besides Gibraltar and Minorca, her territories in northern Italy. Sicily had been ceded to Savoy; Naples, Sardinia, Mantua and Milan fell to Austria. In 1714 King Philip of Spain had married the Princess Elizabeth Farnese, heiress to the Duchy of Parma and claimant by virtue of her descent from the Medici, to the Duchy of Tuscany, and smarting under the recent losses, the able Italian Cardinal Alberoni was bent on using the claim as a lever to restore the Spanish power. Time, however, that essential factor both in war and statesmanship, was denied him. Hurried by his masterful Queen the Cardinal's hand was forced in 1718 into a premature effort to recover Sicily and Sardinia. A quadruple alliance of England, Austria, France and the United Provinces, all parties to the Treaty of Utrecht, brought an end to this attempt; and after a two years' war the Spaniards were ejected from both Sicily and Sardinia, the former of which was transferred at the peace to Austria and the latter to Savoy, whose reigning Duke thenceforward took the title of King of Sardinia.

The war of the Polish succession saw a further readjustment. The Grand Duke of Parma having died in 1731, the succession to the Duchy passed to Don Carlos, son of the King of Spain and Elizabeth Farnese. On the marriage of Maria Theresa, heiress to the Emperor, with Francis of Lorraine, yet another redistribution of territory took place. Louis XV objected to the increase of the Empire which would occur through the addition of Lorraine, and that duchy was in consequence ceded to France, the Duke receiving Tuscany and Parma in exchange, while Don Carlos was given the Kingdom of Naples. The Queen of Spain thus saw the territories to which she laid particular claim forcibly torn from her son, and transferred to the House of Austria. Herein lay seeds of further trouble.

The two sons of Leopold I were without male issue, and the Emperor had therefore made special provision that the daughters of the elder, Joseph, who were married to the Archduke Charles Albert of Bavaria and the Electoral Prince of Saxony, should have precedence over those of the younger, Charles. Joseph died in 1711. His brother, on succeeding to the throne, at once began to make arrangements for the succession of his own daughter in disregard of his father's wishes. Having passed a secret law which transferred the precedence to her, he proceeded steadily to obtain from the Estates of the Empire and the Powers of Europe an assent to her rights. After years of diplomatic bargaining, in the course of which he was obliged to make substantial concessions, he obtained the guarantee, known as the Pragmatic Sanction, for his daughter's succession, from all the estates and Powers except Bavaria and the Palatinate. Among the concessions was the transfer of Parma, Placentia and Guastalla to Don Carlos, an agreement which was abrogated in the Treaty of Vienna by the placing of Don Carlos as related above, on the throne of Naples.

Charles had however neglected the measure essential to secure that the treaties should be observed. He had an insufficient army to enforce them.

The Archduke of Bavaria, by virtue of his marriage with the elder daughter of Leopold I, claimed the Imperial crown itself, in spite of the fact that his wife had renounced her own title to it. Spain demanded the Italian Duchies, which the Queen desired as an establishment for her son, the infante Don Philip. Minor claims were made by other powers: but the height of iniquity was reached by King Frederick of Prussia who concealing his actions with protestations of recognition and offers of military help, invaded Silesia in December, sending at the same time a message to Vienna that if the Queen would cede that province to him he would assist to maintain her claims to the remainder of her dominions. Maria Theresa indignantly repudiated the suggestion; but she was hampered by her father's neglect of military measures. The Prussian army rapidly overran Silesia; its capital, Breslau, fell into Frederick's hands.

The Prussian example was quickly followed. Bavaria and Spain prepared to support their claims by force of arms, and the grouping of the Powers began. Although France had been one of the guarantors of the succession, and her Prime Minister admitted that the Elector of Bavaria had no claim whatever to the Imperial Dominions[1], she began negociating with Bavaria, Spain and Prussia with the view of placing the Elector of Bavaria upon the Imperial throne, assisting Prussia to secure Silesia and Spain to obtain territories in Italy. The aim of this policy is evident. Not only would France's great rival, Austria, be weakened, but the Emperor having obtained his crown through the good offices of France would develop into a friend and an ally.

Maria Theresa appealed to the Powers who had given their word

[1] "If the pretensions of the Elector of Bavaria had some foundation, and if it had been possible to find in the dismemberment of the heritage of the Emperor, some opening of which advantage could be taken in favour of the most serene Infante......but...it is clear by the will of Ferdinand Ist that the House of Bavaria has not any right to the Austrian succession." Fleury to Philip V, Nov. 24th (N.S.) 1740. *Les Préliminaires de la Guerre de la Succession d'Autriche*, Sautai.

to recognise her claims, but without success. Among others she applied to England for the 12,000 troops promised by that Power[1]. England however was already deeply involved in her struggle with Spain, the bulk of her army was on the Atlantic, and such as remained could not be spared out of the kingdom when at any moment European affairs might take a turn which would bring France into the conflict against her.

As events turned out the war did not immediately become general, nor did France take any further steps which threatened England. The operations against Spain were therefore for the time unaffected, and no alterations were made in the dispositions of the British squadrons or the instructions to their commanders. Although the situation in the West Indies was admittedly dangerous, and there was considerable uncertainty as to how it might develop, it was not looked upon with any grave anxiety even when, at the end of January, the fact was definitely established that the two French squadrons had joined, and, reinforced by some troops from Martinique, lay at Port Louis in Hispaniola. They might be intending to attack Jamaica, as Vernon suggested in a letter written when he learned of their arrival in that part; but in the opinion of Sir John Norris, given at a Council meeting, their choice of this station was in accordance with the intentions with which, according to our information, they had been despatched. "As Port Louis is towards the west end of Hispaniola and near the Windward Passage, and consequently to windward of all S. America they may have taken that station to intimidate our people from attempting anything on the Spanish settlements[2]." There was every reason to believe, from our information from Paris, that Vernon would not be interfered with by the French until he made a move against some Spanish port. Vernon could well be depended upon to exercise his judgment wisely according to the situation and not to expose his expedition to the risk of destruction at sea. It was always possible that the French and Spaniards might act independently of each other, and if they did so the British force could cope with either; but even if they joined and proceeded to attack Vernon, Norris considered that he would have a fair chance against them in spite of his inferior numbers as he could strengthen the complements of his ships so greatly by means of the troops of the expeditionary army. The Council thus felt that no reinforcements need be sent to the West Indies.

[1] Her letter was discussed in the Cabinet meeting of January 15th, 1741.

[2] *Diary of Sir John Norris*, January 29th, 1741. Describing Council meeting discussing letters received from Vernon. Present: the Lord Chancellor, Duke of Newcastle, Duke of Devonshire, Lord Harrington, Sir Robert Walpole, Sir Charles Wager and Sir John Norris.

At home however matters were less satisfactory. It was reported in the early days of January that the French had taken ten or twelve sail of their East India ships, each mounting some 50 to 60 guns, into the Royal service, and that ten ships were fitting out at Ferrol besides some galleons which were being armed as men-of-war. To oppose these there was no British force ready. There were about nine sail of the line that might be fitted out, but none were manned, and without some other stronger authority to raise men than the Admiralty possessed Sir Charles Wager said he saw no possibility of providing crews for them. "It requires the utmost diligence," wrote Norris on hearing this, "to do everything in our service to get a fleet in condition superior to the naval force of those two kingdoms or else we shall not get well out of this war."

The first step was taken a fortnight later, on February 1st, when a strict embargo was laid on all shipping and it was announced that no merchant vessels would be allowed to sail until the fleet was manned. A Bill for the registration of seamen, the terms of which compelled them to serve in the navy if called upon, was drafted by Wager and Norris and submitted to Parliament. It called forth a vigorous debate. Its promoters urged the undeniable need of manning the fleet and the danger to which the Kingdom would be exposed if the ships could not be prepared. Its opponents, among whom was Pitt, denounced it as an encroachment upon liberty and an injustice to one particular class of men, in that they alone of all others should be selected for compulsion. The Bill was rejected by a large majority. Thus, between Parliament's opposition to take measures of either compulsion or concession and the seamen's refusal to come forward and serve, trade was paralyzed, the fleet was impotent and the Kingdom exposed to the enemy. The want of some means of rapidly expanding the personnel of the fleet was a factor which must not be lost sight of in considering the operations of this war. On this occasion its results were very far reaching. The delays in fitting out the fleet affected the whole of the operations of this year, and reacted upon the subsequent campaigns in every theatre.

A means which had not been used did however exist and had been suggested by Norris. Marines could have been raised for the sea-service at an earlier date, and the manning of the fleet made, as it should have been, their first duty. In opposing the Bill for compulsory service of seamen Sir John Barnard, among many others, drew attention to this: "The Marines that have been raised too lately to be of any service," he said, "might with the same ease have been levied sooner: they might have been dispersed in proper proportions among the crews of our men-of-war, where, by instruction and example, the business of a common sailor might have been quickly learned, and our merchants might still have had a sufficient number of sailors to enable them to carry on their business[1]."

The embargo lasted from February 1st till April 14th. On March 28th the merchants petitioned for its removal, but their petition was dismissed in Parliament by 166 votes to 95. The Admiralty then offered to remove the embargo if the merchants would guarantee to contribute a proportion of their crews to man the men-of-war, and in the end an arrangement was made by which the merchants bound themselves to carry landsmen as one-third of their crew and to supply one man in every four to the King's ships. By this means the Mercantile Marine was made to serve as an agency for the provision of men.

The need for hastening the preparation of the fleet was accentuated in the middle of March when it was learned that d'Antin's squadron was on its way home, a report which evoked a great outcry in France where the commander was severely censured for abandoning the West Indies and leaving the British forces at liberty to act as they chose[2]. In view of the strong feelings which were reported to exist as to his return and this repeated declarations of Cardinal Fleury that France would oppose any British attempts, it was felt that some important reason must exist for this movement, connected in all probability with the European situation; and this view was accentuated by a declaration of the Cardinal that he did not consider France bound by the Pragmatic Sanction[3]. The efforts to get a fleet ready in the Channel redoubled. But although the embargo and the agreement with the merchants was now producing men, the crews were coming in but slowly, and when the French squadrons returned to their home ports in the middle of April[4] there was still no force ready to deal with them. As it turned out, the return of these squadrons could not immediately affect the situation. It was soon learned that no sinister purpose underlay their changed plans. Illness had decimated the crews of whom over 2000 were dead, and the ships were so foul that it would be some time before they could again be ready for service. One cause for immediate anxiety was thus removed, and though reports soon arrived which stated that France was working with the utmost expedition to refit the ships

[1] *Parliamentary Debates*, 1741. See also Norris's proposals. Appendix I. vol. I.

[2] S. P. Foreign, France. All the information from France shews how much the squadron had been relied upon to prevent the British from increasing their possessions and engrossing the trade of that part of the world.

[3] Mr Thompson to Duke of Newcastle, April $\frac{3}{14}$, S. P. Foreign, France.

[4] Rochalart with seven ships reached Toulon on April $\frac{2}{13}$. The remainder arrived at Brest on April $\frac{7}{18}$.

and intended to put out a fleet of 50 sail, it was known that so great a result could not be quickly obtained.

The news of the capture of the forts and harbour of Cartagena reached London on May 17th and sent up the spirits of the Administration beyond words. Captain Laws of the 'Spence' sloop brought Vernon's despatches and attended at a meeting of the Council at the Cockpit, at which he described the operations to the members of the Council. This opened up a new situation. With Cartagena taken, as the despatches provided good reason to hope that it would be, it would no longer be necessary to keep so large a naval force in the West Indian seas. The French had all, or nearly all, returned, and it was at the same time reported that Don Roderigo de Torres had sailed for Spain from Havana with twelve sail. In view of this Norris recommended that some of Vernon's force should at once be recalled, and that 2000 troops should be despatched to garrison Cartagena and enable further attacks to be made on the Spaniards. The Council however rejected this advice, twice proffered[1], and decided to wait until Vernon's success was complete. The Commander-in-Chief received this decision with grave forebodings, since he had no sufficient squadron in readiness at home if the French should come into the war: "It is highly necessary," he wrote, "all the force of our navy should assemble at Spithead, as France and Spain are doing all they can to get their naval force in condition for the sea[2]."

Before the news of the capture of the approaches to Cartagena had been received our Ambassador in Paris sent over the information that at last France and Spain had arrived at an agreement[3]. At the same time another most disquieting piece of information came in. The British squadron which had been watching Cadiz had been blown off in a gale, and the Spanish squadron had seized the opportunity and sailed to Ferrol where it had joined the other division. Combined with the activity at Brest these reports gave rise to serious apprehensions. A hot press was ordered on June 2nd, and Norris received instructions on the 11th to repair to Spithead with the utmost despatch and take command of the fleet, the ships of which were scattered in the various ports of the Kingdom[4].

[1] At the Council meetings of May 19th and May 27th.
[2] *Diary of Sir John Norris*, May 27th, 1741.
[3] Mr Thompson to Duke of Newcastle, May 20th, N.S. (May 9th O.S.)
[4] 'Victory,' 100; 'St George,' 90; 'Cambridge,' 80; 'Bedford,' 70; 'Buckingham,' 70; 'Kingston,' 60; 'Assistance,' 50 ... At Spithead
'Nassau,' 70 ... ... At Portsmouth
'Royal George,' 90; 'Royal Sovereign,' 90; 'Duke,' 90; 'Marlborough,' 90; 'Essex,' 70 ... ... At the Nore
'Elizabeth,' 64; 'Ruby,' 50 ... ... At Plymouth
'Lenox,' 70 ... ... In the Downs

A few days later another factor entered into the situation. The Havana squadron of seventeen sail under Admiral de Torres, bringing the treasure from Vera Cruz, was definitely reported to be on its way home, and our Ambassador in Paris sent the information that so scarce was money now in Spain that the court of Madrid were most anxiously awaiting the arrival of this squadron. So much were the Spaniards in need of ready money that the expedition preparing at Barcelona was at a standstill for want of it. When the financial condition of Spain at this time and her entire dependence upon her West Indian fleets for ready money are taken into consideration, the importance attached by our Ministers to intercepting the treasure will be appreciated. It was not a mere piratical attack for the sake of gain; it was a means of preventing Spain from being able to carry on the war[1].

New instructions to Sir John Norris, dated June 18th, 1741, were issued. They ran as follows:

"Whereas we have received advice that a squadron of Spanish ships has passed from Cadiz to Ferrol and since put to sea again from Ferrol; and whereas there is reason to suppose that ten or twelve Spanish ships of war lately gone from Cartagena to the Havana may be soon expected in some of the ports of Old Spain; and whereas we have also accounts that ten French men-of-war are now at Brest ready to put to sea, and that they may be strengthened by more ships now in the port of Brest. We have thought it for his Majesty's service to order you with the ships named in the margin[2] or with such of them as shall be ready and such others as may join you, to proceed forthwith to Cape Finisterre and to continue cruising between that Cape and the mouth of the Channel. And you are during your said cruise to commit all manner of hostilities against the Spaniards, and to take, sink, burn or otherwise destroy all Spanish ships and vessels that you shall meet. And particularly you are carefully to look out for the Spanish squadrons which is supposed to be coming from the Havana to Old Spain, and may probably be intended to put into Ferrol, and to use your utmost endeavour to intercept and take or to sink, burn or otherwise destroy the ships belonging to the said squadron.

2. And you are to distress and annoy the Spaniards in the best manner you are able either in their ports or on their coasts. And whereas it would be of great importance to his Majesty's service that the Spanish ships of war or privateers which may be in the port or harbour of San Sebastian, or in any other of their ports in the Bay of Biscay, or in Gallicia, should be destroyed, you are (in case you shall find it practicable) to attempt it, either by going thither yourself with your squadron, or by detaching such a number of ships as you shall think proper for that purpose. And you are to detach cruising ships to intercept and take the Spanish privateers (and especially those from San Sebastian) or any other Spanish ships: and to procure what intelligence you can of the motions of the enemy. And you are in the best manner you are able to protect the trade and

[1] Cf. letters of Mr Thompson of June 14th, 23rd and 30th, all emphasising the urgent Spanish need of money at this moment. S. P. Foreign, France, 1741.

[2] 'Victory,' 100; 'Royal George,' 90; 'Royal Sovereign,' 90; 'St George,' 90; 'Duke,' 90; 'Marlborough,' 90; 'Cambridge,' 80; 'Bedford,' 70; 'Buckingham,' 70; 'Nassau,' 70; 'Lenox,' 70; 'Essex,' 70; 'Elizabeth,' 64; 'Rupert,' 60; 'Kingston,' 60; 'Assistance,' 50; 'Ruby,' 50; 'Argyle,' 50; 'Newcastle,' 50; 'Bridgewater,' 20; 'Success,' 20. Bomb-vessels, 'Thunder,' 'Blast,' 'Carcass,' 'Lightning.' Fireships, 'Scipio,' 'Blaze.' Hospital ship, 'Sutherland.'

commerce of these kingdoms, and particularly the homeward and outward bound merchant ships.

3. If you shall have an account that the French squadron now at Brest (of which you will constantly get the best intelligence you can as well with regard to their number as their motions) should be gone into the Mediterranean, you are, in that case, to detach from the squadron under your command such a reinforcement to Admiral Haddock as you shall judge proper, and at the same time to send him the best accounts you can procure as well with respect to the motions of the French as of the Spanish squadron. But if you should find that the squadron from Brest should be come towards the Channel, or shall have reason from your intelligence to believe that the said squadron is preparing so to do, you are in that case, so to dispose the squadron under your command as to be able to follow them immediately, and carefully to watch and observe their motions. And if they shall commit any hostility against any of his Majesty's ships, or on the coast, you are to oppose them with your squadron and to use your utmost endeavours to take, sink, burn or otherwise destroy them.

4. You are to keep a constant correspondence, as opportunity shall offer, with Rear Admiral Haddock and to send him from time to time the best intelligence you shall be able to procure of the motions of the Spaniards, in order the better to enable him to perform the services on which he is employed: and there will be herewith put into your hands, for your information, copies of the orders that have been lately sent to Mr Haddock, as also a list of the ships which are at present under his command.

5. You are to continue cruising two months from the time of your sailing unless you shall find it necessary in consequence of these instructions to return sooner into the Channel, or shall receive directions for that purpose. And you are to transmit constant accounts of your proceedings, with such intelligence as you shall be able to procure of the motions and designs of the Spaniards, and of the French ships at Brest, and of everything that may relate to his Majesty's service to one of his Majesty's principal Secretaries of State, with whom you shall constantly correspond; or to the Secretary to the Lords Justices. And you are to follow such farther orders and directions as shall be sent to you by one of his Majesty's said principal Secretaries of State, or by the Secretary to the Lords Justices[1]."

In obedience to these instructions Norris went down to Portsmouth to take command of the fleet. Only nine ships had arrived and these were short of complement, but some marines from the Thames and two regiments of foot—Jeffrey's and Powlett's—were daily expected, and also some nine ships from the westward.

While Norris lay at Spithead, impatiently awaiting his ships and men, news reached London that France had defined her attitude and had determined to assist the Elector of Bavaria with 30,000 men[2]. Her entry into the sea operations in Europe might therefore follow at any moment, and, what was of still greater importance, she had no further fears for her position in the West Indies for it now was known that the assault upon Cartagena had failed. This news the Duke of

[1] Signed by Lord Wilmington (President of the Council), Lord Hervey, Dukes of Dorset, Grafton, Bolton, Montagu and Newcastle: Earl of Pembroke, Sir Robert Walpole and Sir Charles Wager. These instructions, particularly in the wording relating to the protection of trade, should be compared with those of the preceding June.

[2] Mr Thompson to Duke of Newcastle, July 1 (N.S.) 1741, S. P. Foreign, France.

Newcastle at once sent off to Norris, and it is interesting to see how readily the advice of the Admiral was sought although it was so little acted upon. The Duke asked his opinion as to how these two events of the "highest importance" should now affect us. He was clearly anxious lest the sailing of the fleet to Finisterre should leave the Kingdom exposed. Norris replied that there was no need for uneasiness on this point, since the French could not dare to attack us with our Fleet at sea and its whereabouts unknown to them. There could indeed be no greater deterrent to any move by sea on the part of France than the existence of an unlocated fleet of uncertain strength. As to the West Indies, Norris replied that he had insufficient information as to the general situation to offer an opinion[1].

The next day—June 27th—the regiments and some more ships having arrived, which brought his squadron up to sixteen heavy ships[2], Norris sailed. He detached the 'Ruby' to Brest to obtain information as to the state of the squadron there, with instructions to watch if the French ships were getting to sea and, if so, to find out what course, either to the British coast or the Mediterranean, they were making; and, having determined it to bring him the news to his rendezvous.

A few days of foul wind delayed the squadron in the Channel. In the interval a French brig from Cadiz was boarded from which it was learned that eighteen large Spanish ships had been in that harbour when she left, all ready to sail at a moment's notice to meet, so it was reported, the squadron that was coming from Havana. Anxious to ascertain how soon de Torres was expected, and whether in a northern or a southern port of Spain, Norris at once detached two frigates to Oporto to get the latest news, and pressed all sail to arrive as early as possible at the rendezvous he had appointed eight leagues north of Sisargas. This he reached on the 8th of July. Another French ship was intercepted which informed him of the return of the Spanish squadrons to Cadiz. They were said to have left Ferrol on May 27th.

Still uncertain as to whither de Torres was going, for he could place no implicit reliance on these neutrals' reports, the Admiral remained cruising off Sisargas, spreading his squadron in a formation very similar to that used by Anson at a later stage of the war. After a week one of his frigates from Oporto rejoined him and corroborated the departure of the Spaniards from the Gallician ports, but brought no

[1] Norris to Duke of Newcastle, June 26th, 1741, S. P. Dom. Naval.

[2] 'Victory,' 'Royal George,' 'Royal Sovereign,' 'St George,' 'Duke,' 'Cambridge,' 'Elizabeth,' 'Essex,' 'Nassau,' 'Buckingham,' 'Bedford,' 'Lenox,' 'Argyle,' 'Assistance,' 'Kingston,' 'Ruby'; 'Gosport,' 40; 'Blaze' and 'Scipio' fireships. The 'Marlborough' also arrived but was not ready to sail and remained at Spithead.

news as to their probable destination, and it was not until he had been in this area for three weeks that he received news of de Torres. On July 28th his second frigate returned from Oporto with the information from the Consul that the Havana squadron had not been able to sail at all. The ships were in such bad state, they were so short of complement and stores and in such a condition of sickness—they had lost 4000 men from this cause—that they had been unable to put to sea. The Consul further informed him that except for a very few ships fitting out there was no Spanish force in the northern ports, but that the joint Spanish fleet was now in Cadiz, watched by Haddock with the whole Mediterranean squadron.

There was now no object in continuing to cruise off Finisterre, nor was it within the scope of his instructions to join Haddock in his blockade off Cadiz, even if his supply of provisions had been sufficient to enable him to do so. There still remained the possibility of some operations against the northern privateer bases, whither early in the cruise he had sent the 'Argyle,' which ship had captured and burnt several Spanish craft. He now detached the 'Nassau,' 'Kingston,' 'Assistance' and 'Rupert' to cruise for a month off Santander, San Sebastian and Sisargas, under the orders of Captain Medley, to operate against the privateers, with instructions that if some bomb-vessels which the Admiralty had promised should arrive he was to try to bombard and destroy San Sebastian, the most notorious and troublesome of those ports. Having made this disposition, Norris revictualled the detached ships from the remainder, and carried his squadron back to England where he arrived on August 23rd. He was followed about a month later by Medley who had made some captures but had not been able to deal with San Sebastian as the bomb-vessels did not arrive.

This two months' cruise of Norris's was most violently criticised. It was stated—in complete ignorance of what his instructions were—that he had gone out with no orders and had done nothing[1]. Yet his instructions were clear enough and had a definite object. It was moreover no fault of the Admiral's that his squadron had not sailed in time to intercept the Spaniards before they left Ferrol for the south, nor that his principal objective, the Havana squadron, did not present itself for capture.

During Norris's absence fresh information concerning the intentions of the French and Spaniards had reached the Government. These advices, which were regarded as trustworthy[2], stated that the Brest

[1] *Vide* the merchants' complaints as to lack of protection for trade.

[2] The Duke of Newcastle, in informing Norris on August 7th, described the information as being "certain."

and Toulon squadrons were intended to unite, and in conjunction with the Spaniards, convoy a combined Franco-Spanish army into Italy. To meet this situation the Channel squadron, reinforced by three more ships, was to watch Brest[1]. If the French went south, Norris, though he was not to attack them, since war had not been declared, was to follow them, join Haddock, and prevent the Brest and Toulon squadrons, either together or separately, from joining the Cadiz fleet. These instructions missed Norris; but they are important in view of the Duke of Newcastle's statement, made later in the year in defence of the measures taken by the Government, that on Haddock lay the blame for the unopposed sailing of the Spanish expedition from Barcelona. Nothing could be clearer than these instructions. No station off Barcelona could prevent the junction of the Cadiz and Brest squadrons, and these orders shew that Haddock was expected to keep his eye upon Cadiz. Yet the Duke gave the House to believe that Haddock had no authority in his instructions for observing Cadiz, and that he ought to have been off Barcelona[2].

Norris had a short time for refitting. On September 4th he was ordered again to take command of his nineteen ships[3], and on the 10th to sail to Finisterre. The reason for this return to his recent station was that fresh reports had just been received that de Torres had at last left Havana with the Vera Cruz treasure, and in consequence Norris was to work to the westward of the Cape regulating his cruise so as to return to England in the latter end of October. His instructions ended: "Whereas intelligence has been received that at the beginning of July last the intention of the French Court was that the Brest and Toulon squadrons should join and in conjunction with the Spaniards convoy the French and Spanish troops to Italy: if the French squadron at Brest should put to sea and sail to the southward you are then to follow them with all your ships and to endeavour to prevent the Brest and Toulon squadrons, either separately or jointly, from joining the Spaniards, provided the season of the year shall not be so far advanced as to endanger your not being able to return home with your squadron this winter: in which case you are not to proceed farther than the station above directed."

Norris, who had gone to London on his return, remained until September 16th, in order to attend, at the Duke of Newcastle's especial

[1] The French squadron was reported to consist of nine heavy ships: 'Superbe,' 74; 'Neptune,' 74; 'St Philippe,' 74; 'Mars,' 66; 'St Michel,' 66; 'Éclatant,' 66; 'Auguste,' 54; 'Griffon,' 54; 'Apollon,' 54; and 'Neréide,' 26.

[2] This is dealt with in the next chapter.

[3] The original sixteen and the reinforcement of three: the latter were at Plymouth but not yet ready.

request, a Council meeting on the 15th. This was held to discuss a grave report from Paris stating that France had decided on war with England and intended to send expeditions to Scotland and Ireland. As the Brest squadron consisted of nine ships, nine of Norris's were detailed at Spithead to observe them, and Norris with the remaining ten was ordered to proceed to intercept de Torres with the Havana fleet. It appears to have been considered that the weakness of the Spanish seventeen was such that Norris's squadron of ten would be sufficient to deal with them.

This alteration made, the Admiral repaired to Portsmouth next day and prepared to sail; but owing to difficulties of obtaining provisions he was not able to get away until the 1st of October. In the interval pressing letters were being received from Haddock at Gibraltar representing the weakness of his force in face of the fleet that was now preparing at Cadiz. A reinforcement of four ships under Captain Cornewall[1] had been ordered to go to join him on September 4th, but did not actually sail for over five weeks; and when Norris returned on November 7th after cruising for a month off Finisterre without seeing anything of the Havana squadron, he found an urgent letter from London awaiting him. The Toulon squadron had been sighted at sea, the Spaniards at Cadiz, fourteen strong, were preparing to sail. Cornewall's reinforcement would now be insufficient, for the French were reported to have a number equal to the Spaniards. Norris was therefore ordered to detach another five[2] sail to Gibraltar without a moment's loss of time to strengthen Haddock.

The season for cruising to the westward was now past. The great ships remaining were ordered to their ports in accordance with custom, Norris hauled down his flag and returned to London, and a disposition was made of the lesser ships to protect trade during the winter months, using the following stations:

Cruising in the Bay of Biscay	'Rupert,' 60; 'Newcastle,' 50; 'Argyle,' 50; 'Port Mahon,' 24
Between Waterford and Cape Clear ...	'Dolphin,' 24
In Bristol Channel	'Ruby,' 50
Between Milford and Lundy	'Shark,' sloop
,, Start and Isle of Wight	'Carcass,' bomb-vessel
,, Downs and Portsmouth	'Scipio,' fireship
30 to 40 leagues W. and W.S.W. from Scilly	'Lynn,' 40; 'Lyme,' 20
Between Scilly and Lizard	'Biddeford,' 20
,, Ushant and Scilly	'Bridgewater,' 20.

[1] 'Bedford,' 70; 'Elizabeth,' 64; 'Marlborough,' 90; 'Essex,' 70.

[2] Two of 90 guns, one of 80, one of 70, one of 60. Duke of Newcastle to Norris, November 7th, 1741, S. P. Dom. Naval.

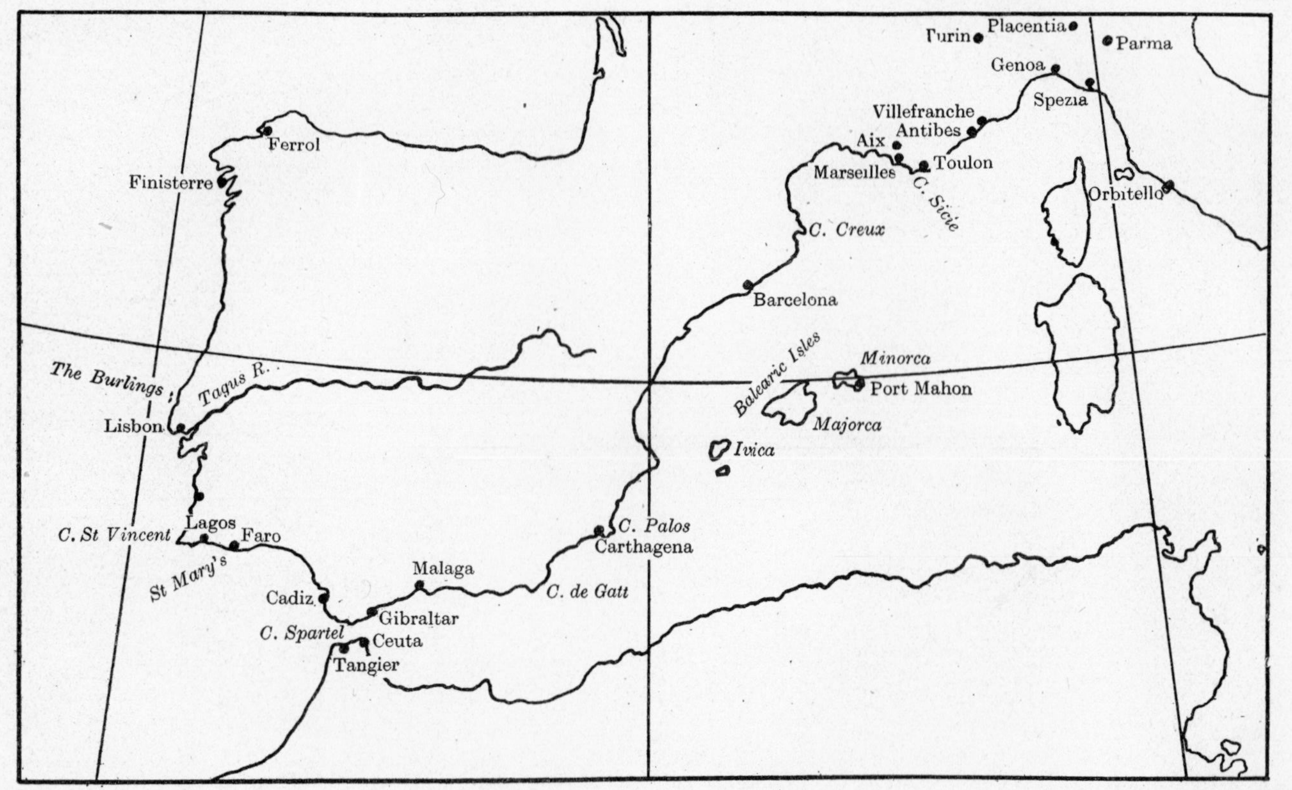

THE WESTERN MEDITERRANEAN

CHAPTER VIII

OPERATIONS IN THE MEDITERRANEAN, 1741

ADMIRAL HADDOCK, when he returned to Port Mahon in October 1740, left a small squadron[1] of observation of two heavy ships and a fire-ship off Cadiz under Captain John Byng. The duties of this detachment were to intercept single ships entering or leaving the harbour, and to keep the Admiral informed of the movements of such Spanish ships as remained at Cadiz after the departure of the Spanish squadrons to the West Indies. These consisted of a small number of partly ready men-of-war proper, and the vessels of the Flota which, unable to sail with cargoes, were being fitted as fighting ships. All the advices transmitted by our Consul at Faro pointed to the fact that the Spaniards intended in no way to slacken their attempts to hamper the British operations in the West Indies. These reports caused Byng some apprehension. Before he had been long on his station he wrote urging his need of a reinforcement. "I imagine," he said, "as the thoughts of Sir John Norris coming this way is over, they may take heart and come from above the Puntales: nay, I do not see what should hinder their coming quite out and cruising off the Straits mouth. We have nothing this side to prevent them." Byng's fatal habit of seeing the worst side of things is illustrated in this letter, the tone of which is like that of his letters from the Hyères Islands at a later period of the war, and of his celebrated letter from Gibraltar in 1755. The news of the Spanish preparations was certainly ominous, but it was as yet unconfirmed rumour only, and until some more certain advices should be received there was no need for despondency.

Haddock, who had ten ships at Mahon, did not consider it desirable to weaken his force in order to reinforce Byng. He had heard that four of the twelve French ships which had sailed to the West Indies with Rochalart were reported to have returned to Toulon, and the fitting out of other ships was at the same time said to be in progress. How many ships were ready, or what the intentions of France were, Haddock did not know, but in the unsettled political atmosphere he judged it inadvisable to weaken his own force to an extent which might render it inferior to the Toulon squadron.

Two months of comparative inaction followed, during which the reports of the Spanish preparations at Cadiz continued. On December

[1] 'Sunderland,' 60; 'Plymouth,' 60, and 'Duke,' fireship.

16th a despatch was received in London from our Consul at Faro, Mr Cayley, stating that a force of men-of-war and galleons which would carry reinforcements and supplies for the Spanish garrisons was then nearly ready to sail to the West Indies. The importance of intercepting these reinforcements was strongly felt by the Privy Council, and instructions were therefore sent to Haddock directing him to detach three or four ships to reinforce Byng[1], with orders that vessels of all nations whatsoever carrying supplies inwards or outwards for the Spaniards were to be arrested. The Admiral was ordered to remain at Mahon with the rest of the squadron and look after the defence of Minorca. He was also told to take steps to get the best possible information as to the truth of a rumour which was current to the effect that the Spaniards intended to send a considerable body of troops into Italy. The intentions as to the route the troops would take were, he was told, uncertain; they might sail from Barcelona, but it was also possible that they would be permitted to march through France and embark at Antibes, as they did in the previous war. Whatever they should do, Haddock was to make their destruction the principal object of the ships he still had in company, bombarding them in Barcelona if it were practicable, or attacking them at sea when they sailed either from a French or Spanish harbour.

Haddock's battle squadron consisted of ten ships of the line. Two were off Cadiz with Byng, and by these orders this detachment was to be made up to at least five. He would therefore be left with five ships at Mahon. Against this the Spaniards had four or five under M. de la Bene at Carthagena and the French at least four, possibly more, at Toulon. If any such move as the Council outlined should be intended it was well within the bounds of possibility that these squadrons would unite, since the whole of France's recent conduct had shewn that she might join Spain. The Council were not blind to this fact, for in a letter of the same date as these instructions, Haddock was ordered to be especially watchful of all that passed at Toulon. It is true that no reinforcements were sent him to enable him to take any measures which his watchfulness might discover to be necessary; but the account already given of the naval unreadiness at home has shewn that it would not have been possible for the Government at that moment to back up their comprehensive orders to Haddock with any increase of his forces.

In accordance with these instructions Haddock detached Captain William Martin to Cadiz with the 'Ipswich' and 'Pembroke.' He had

[1] Official correspondence of Admiral Haddock, December 18th, 1740. Egmont MSS. Add. MS. 2529.

shortly before sent the 'Oxford' to strengthen Byng, so that the squadron thus would be brought up to five ships[1]. Martin was to take over the command, with instructions[2] to lie off Cadiz, or in such station as the weather permitted, and stop all vessels of all nations going into or leaving Cadiz with men, provisions or warlike stores. If the Cadiz squadron should try to pass into the Mediterranean with superior force in order to effect a junction with the ships at Carthagena or Toulon, or to attack Gibraltar or Minorca, Martin was to detach a fast ship at once to inform Haddock, and *if absolutely necessary*[3] to bring his whole squadron to join the Admiral. The possibility that the Spaniards could bring out a superior force was disclosed in an intercepted letter from Spain which stated that the squadron then preparing in Cadiz consisted of seven large men-of-war and seven armed ships of the Flota[4]. Haddock was thus in the unpleasant situation of having his fleet, already a weak one, split into two parts which could not support each other.

However, although the Council could not know it, the French had for the present no intention of attacking British ships in European waters. Fleury was prepared to interfere in the West Indies if French interests were likely to be prejudiced, but relations at home need not be immediately affected by this. The four ships at Toulon were actually fitting for West Indian service. They were to be under the command of M. de Caylus, to whom Maurepas wrote, "Vous êtes destiné pour les Îles du Vent: les opérations que vous aurez à y faire dépendront de la situation où vous trouverez les choses[5]." He was told to steer for Gibraltar, avoiding as far as possible meeting any British ships, as well as anything else that might delay his passage.

On February 12th Caylus fell in with three of Martin's squadron[6] in the Straits. A slight brush between the British and French ships took place, but the mistake was discovered before much damage was done. Though it resulted in nothing, the episode shewed how highly charged was the atmosphere, and how small a spark was needed to set the nations definitely in a blaze. Although shots were exchanged the affair created no stir, and was not even officially reported. The Captains of the 'Ipswich' and 'Oxford' took a very light view of it,

[1] 'Ipswich,' 70; 'Pembroke,' 60; 'Sunderland,' 60; 'Plymouth,' 60; 'Oxford,' 50; and 'Kennington,' 20; 'Guarland,' 20; 'Duke,' fireship.

[2] Haddock to Martin, January 24th, 1740. Haddock In letters.

[3] The underlining is Haddock's.

[4] 'Real,' 114; 'Sta Ysabel,' 80; 'San Fernando,' 62; 'Sta Teresa,' 62; 'Paloma,' 52; 'Fama,' 46; 'Xavier,' 46. The merchant ships, of lighter build than the men-of-war, mounted from 54 to 62 guns. Egmont MSS. Add. MS. 2528.

[5] Lady du Cane's MS., *Hist. Man. Comm. Report.*

[6] 'Ipswich,' 'Oxford,' 'Sunderland.'

and alluded to it only in a passing manner in their Journals. Thus, Martin says: "at 8 A.M. saw four sail to the S.W. made sail and gave chase after them.... 6 P.M. spoke with our chase, they proving to be three French men-of-war and a merchant ship, the 'Borée,' 60 guns, commanded by the Chevalier Caylus, one of 40 guns and the other of 20, came from Toulon[1]." Byng in the 'Sunderland' described it at greater length.

Haddock, who remained at Mahon with the remnant of his force, had now four large ships and four small actually ready, and two ships refitting[2]. Five small ships were cruising and employed upon convoy work, but these were wholly insufficient to enable him effectually to defend trade, keep a watch upon Carthagena and Barcelona, and observe the area between the Balearic Islands and the Catalan coast. As a result the Spaniards were able to withdraw all their troops—some four to five thousand men—from Majorca without the loss of a man, and British trade on the Italian coast suffered appreciable losses at the hands of the enemy's privateers. The shortage of small craft to protect trade was seriously felt.

In February Captain Watson of the 'Guarland' gathered some information as to the state of affairs at Barcelona. Preparations for a military expedition seemed now to be in full swing, no less than ten to twelve thousand troops being ready for embarkation though as yet there was insufficient transport for them. At the same time news from Leghorn indicated that the Austrian territories in Lombardy were threatened from the direction of Naples—whose King, Don Carlos, was a son of the Queen of Spain—where an embargo had been laid on all shipping and a great military expedition was reported to be in preparation with Parma and Placentia as its objective. The rumours which had reached the Council in London were evidently well-founded.

Haddock's position was unenviable at this time. It was not merely in the fewness of his ships that his difficulties lay, but also in the want of men for such ships as he had. His crews had been greatly reduced by sickness, no drafts to replace his losses had been received for several months, and no local maritime resources existed on which he could

[1] Captain's Journal of 'Ipswich,' April 12th, 1741.

[2] Haddock's force at this date consisted of:

Large ships	'Somerset,' 80; 'Lancaster,' 80; 'Warwick,' 60; 'Dragon,' 60; 'Advice,' 40—with Haddock
	'Ipswich,' 70; 'Pembroke,' 60; 'Sunderland,' 60; 'Plymouth,' 60; 'Oxford,' 50—with Martin
Small vessels	'Dursley' galley, 20; 'Aldborough,' 20; 'Salamander,' 6.8; 'Ann,' 8.6; 'Mercury,' 8.6—with Haddock
	'Kennington,' 20; 'Guarland,' 20; 'Duke,' 8.6—with Martin

The 'Guarland' rejoined Haddock in January.

draw to any great extent. He therefore requested permission from the Council to embark soldiers from the garrison of Port Mahon[1]. This was granted and the Governor was directed to put four or five hundred troops on board the squadron whenever the Admiral should ask for them[2].

All through March and the early part of April Spanish troops continued to pour into Barcelona. Haddock kept all the light vessels he could constantly relieving each other in the watch upon the Catalan coast, while his ships of the line lay in Mahon ready to proceed to sea if the expedition were reported to have sailed. At length on April 21st definite news came in. On that day Captain Curtis Barnett, the senior officer on the coast, returned to Mahon reporting that the ships of the Carthagena squadron had their yards across and sails bent and were evidently preparing to put to sea. As the transports in Barcelona were still far too few to carry any considerable body of troops, Haddock inferred from this news that an attack upon trade or some expected victualling ships was intended, and prepared to sail for Carthagena.

On May 30th, when he was about to leave, the 'Dursley' galley arrived at Mahon bringing the victuallers under her escort. Besides the victuallers she brought news, and bad news. The Spanish squadron in Cadiz had put to sea and was gone none knew whither. Martin's squadron had been drawn away from the port through chasing some French ships which had attempted to enter the Bay; a westerly wind carried him well to the eastward, and through the Straits; and before the ensuing levanter enabled him to regain his station the Spaniards had taken advantage of it and sailed; they had last been seen standing to the west-south-westward.

The object of the Spanish squadron in putting to sea could only be conjectured. Martin's instructions anticipated that the Spaniards might send reinforcements and supplies to the West Indies, or come into the Mediterranean to join the Carthagena squadron. Captain Lee of the 'Pembroke,' one of the blockading ships, who became separated from Martin in the gale, when he heard that the enemy was at sea assumed that they had gone to the West Indies as their course indicated. On his own initiative—that initiative which officers used so freely in the past—he at once detached the 'Kennington,' 20, to warn Vernon at Jamaica, where she arrived on May 15th.

Haddock did not draw the same conclusion as Lee as to the object of the Cadiz squadron, but for all that he fully approved the Captain

[1] Haddock to Duke of Newcastle, March 18th, 1741.

[2] This function of oversea garrisons was frequently made use of in the wars of the eighteenth century. It deserves attention to-day, in relation to both naval and military training.

of the Pembroke's action in sending the frigate to warn Vernon "in which," he wrote to the Admiralty, "I presume their Lordships will think he did right." His own view was the Spaniards would devote their attention to European waters, and that this movement was made either with the intention of destroying Martin's squadron or of intercepting a second and more important convoy which was known to be on its way to Mahon[1]. There was the further possibility that a junction with the Carthagena squadron was intended, in order to overwhelm Haddock and force the passage of the troops, now assembled at Barcelona, across the sea to Italy.

Whichever of these might be the object of the Spaniards, it was essential for Haddock to get to sea as soon as he could, either to intercept the Cadiz ships before they reached Carthagena, or to reinforce Martin and protect the convoy. But his position was complicated by the arrival at Mahon of a most valuable fleet of nine sail of Turkey merchants. Not to afford convoy to these, in the presence of a superior squadron that might be holding the Strait's mouth, would expose him to the severest censure. Protection of trade was one of the most important of his charges, and although sailing in company with a fleet of laggard merchants might delay his passage, he considered it was his duty to convoy them even though it should involve the risk of missing the Spanish squadron. He therefore sailed with the Turkey fleet on May 5th, steering towards Cape Palos.

Next day he received reassuring news about the Spaniards. The 'Port Mahon,' sloop, joined him at midnight bringing letters from Martin and Lee, informing him that the Cadiz squadron had returned to harbour. They were eight sail strong, and their sally had been made to escort some outward-bound merchant ships clear of the British squadron—the common function of a squadron which occupies a terminal point of giving a reinforcing local escort. Haddock, on getting this news, called a council of war at which it was decided "to protect with this squadron the Levant trade, which is very considerable, through the Straits; and [I] shall then repair off of Cadiz to give a reinforcement to the ships there." The news of the return of the Cadiz squadron was most comforting. It implied that Martin was safe and the West Indies unthreatened. But there still remained the outward-bound convoy, exposed to a sally of the Cadiz squadron; and Haddock was very anxious to get into position to cover it.

Westerly winds seriously delayed his passage towards Gibraltar;

[1] The difficulty and danger of the convoy work will be noticed. Convoys had to pass through a stretch of water with strong enemy squadrons, incompletely covered, on the flank of their track.

ten days beating against them only brought the squadron as far as Cape Palos. Then all his hopeful dreams were swept away. The 'Guarland's' prize met him with the news that the Spaniards had left Cadiz a second time on April 30th, nine sail strong with orders to destroy either Martin or the outward-bound convoy. The 'Guarland's' prize had left Gibraltar with the news on May 4th, had been to Mahon to find Haddock and inform him, and since then had been working back to the Spanish coast in search of him. The preparations at Carthagena may have been a feint to detain Haddock in the Mediterranean.

The foul winds still held, and an anxious ten days passed before Haddock came in sight of Gibraltar. Martin's squadron proved to be safe and in harbour; as soon as the Admiral appeared off the Bay it put to sea to join him, bringing out also a great number of merchant ships, bound to many parts, who had put into the Bay for protection when the news got abroad that the Spaniards were at sea. At seven in the evening the whole fleet with its great convoy of over eighty vessels made sail to the westward. Haddock now intended to carry this trade at least twenty leagues to seaward of Cape St Vincent and then to seek the Spanish squadron[1].

His fears for the outward bound convoy with which his supplies were coming were no less than for Martin and the Levant trade, and his anxiety for its safety was increased by the news he received. On the following day the 'Dragon' intercepted a French ship and learned from her that the Cadiz squadron had done none of the things anticipated by the Admiral. It had gone direct to Ferrol, and had been seen by the Frenchman standing into that harbour on the 11th of the month, carrying with it some English prizes. This was indeed a great blow. The Cadiz and Ferrol squadrons were now united and apparently the convoy, or some part of it, had fallen into their hands. In the low state of the Mediterranean squadron's supplies the loss of these victualling and store ships would be most serious.

The convoy had however in reality escaped, having either been missed by the Spaniards between Lisbon and Finisterre or not having reached as far south as Ferrol when the Spaniards arrived there. The prompt action of our Minister at Lisbon on this occasion, although it did not actually save the convoy, deserves notice. Directly Lord Tyrawley heard of the departure of the Cadiz squadron he sent out

[1] His squadron at this time consisted of 'Somerset' and 'Lancaster,' 80; 'Ipswich,' 70; 'Sunderland,' 'Pembroke,' 'Warwick,' 'Plymouth,' 60; 'Oxford,' 'Guernsey,' 'Salisbury,' 50; 'Winchelsea,' 24; 'Guarland,' 20; 'Ann,' galley; 'Duke' and 'Mercury,' fireships; 'Salamander,' bomb, and three zebecks. The 'St Albans' and 'Lark' were sent with the direct homeward-bound trade and the 'Aldborough' with the trade to Lisbon.

the 'Fly' sloop from the Tagus to meet the approaching merchantmen and warn them of the danger. Escorted by five ships[1] only, the convoy arrived near the Tagus on May 13th—two days after the Spaniards had reached Ferrol—and was intercepted by the sloop. Captain Oliphant, who commanded the escort, at once ordered all his ships into the river and before dark they were anchored in safety.

No news of the movements of the convoy reached Haddock. Since his first consideration on leaving Gibraltar was the safety of the four-score merchants he had with him, he stretched to the westward of St Vincent until the 31st of May and then, being far enough out to detach them on their way alone, he began to fall back to St Vincent to cruise there with the object of intercepting the Spaniards if they returned to the south from Ferrol. He had only begun this movement when he received a report that the enemy had already returned to Cadiz. If this were true it was indeed disappointing beyond measure. The nearest place for intelligence was Lagos; thither he therefore proceeded at once to see if our Consul could confirm or add to this report. But Cayley had only heard of the arrival of the squadron at Ferrol, though he was able to give the Admiral the news of the safe arrival of the outward-bound convoy at Lisbon. As it was probable that if the Spaniards had returned Cayley would have heard of it, Haddock considered it most likely that they were still at Ferrol, and he therefore sent the Portugal trade, which he had detained till now on account of the danger, to Lisbon under escort of the 'Aldborough.' By her Captain he sent a letter to Lord Tyrawley desiring that the convoy should sail for Gibraltar at once and that he would inform the senior officer that the squadron would meet it off St Vincent.

The convoy however had sailed already. Tyrawley heard of the enemy's presence at Ferrol about May 25th and at once gave the news to the senior officer of the convoy. The 'Fox,' which had been lying in the Tagus, sailed immediately to inform the Admiral or whoever was in command at Gibraltar; the convoy sailed next day, and making a good passage arrived at Gibraltar on the 7th of June. The 'Fox,' being off the Burlings on the 28th, sighted the Spanish squadron of twelve stout ships, standing to the southward. She followed them until the evening to make sure of their course, and having satisfied herself that they were not bound to the West Indies, she hastened to Gibraltar where she arrived on the 2nd of June. A consultation of the Captains was immediately held at which it was decided to sail

[1] 'Panther,' 50; 'Falkland,' 50; 'Colchester,' 54; 'Tyger,' 50 and 'Deal Castle,' 20. A part was bound to Port Mahon and the remainder to St Helena and India.

as soon as possible and look into Cadiz and then take what news they would have gathered to Haddock off St Vincent.

The frigates sailed next day. They looked into Cadiz Bay and saw the masts of the Spaniards at anchor there: then, spreading to cover as much water as possible, they hastened independently towards St Vincent to find Haddock and give him the news. They reached him on June 8th, and "it was by them," wrote Haddock, "that I received the first certain accounts of the return of the Spanish squadron to Cadiz."

How the enemy had returned unobserved is clear. On the 31st, when they passed St Vincent, Haddock had just reached the westerly point to which he had been steering in order to secure the homeward bound ships, and the enemy passed between him and the Cape. The whole episode is a singularly interesting one, in which the risks run by convoys when incompletely covered are well illustrated; and in considering the propriety of Haddock's movements, the current doctrines of trade protection and the absence of information must be given their due weight. The convoy had experienced extraordinarily good fortune. If it had been a little earlier it might have met the Cadiz squadron before it reached Lisbon. If the news of the arrival of the Cadiz squadron at Ferrol had reached Tyrawley a little sooner he might have sent out the convoy into the very arms of the enemy.

At length Haddock had some certain news to act upon. Besides the twelve ships which had returned from Ferrol there were five or more apparently ready for the sea. There were thus at least seventeen ships concentrated at Cadiz, to which he could oppose twelve only. So far as he could see, this squadron might be intended to go to the West Indies, where Cartagena was being besieged[1] by the British expedition, or it might be going into the Mediterranean to escort the army collected at Barcelona into Italy. The latter was the more probable, but the former could not be left out of account. The junction of these seventeen sail with the squadron at Havana, the strength of which Haddock believed to be between twelve and seventeen sail, would furnish a fleet equal to that under Vernon and taking into consideration the losses which the West Indian squadron might have suffered it was within the bounds of possibility that the Spaniards might be the superior force. Although the invasion of Italy loomed large, the siege of Cartagena at that moment loomed larger. The capture of that city would influence the whole course of politics on the continent, and however greatly Haddock was concerned with affairs in Europe he could by no means dismiss those distant operations from his mind.

[1] The news of the forcing of the harbour mouth had reached England on May 17th, but was not yet known to Haddock.

He decided therefore to cruise to the westward, where he could intercept the enemy if they went to the West Indies, or follow them quickly if they went into the Mediterranean. "As we may expect, I presume, some reinforcements soon," he wrote on June 19th, "I shall continue cruising near Cape St Vincent, St Mary's or sometimes to the southward, unless for want of provisions or anything extraordinary the squadron should be obliged to proceed to Gibraltar: and their Lordships will be pleased perfectly to judge how incumbent it is on me to keep our twelve ships entirely together." None could be spared, that is to say, to watch Barcelona and Carthagena. If the expedition to Italy were to be intercepted it was imperative that he should have more ships for the constant observation of these ports.

As he soon found it impossible to keep all his squadron cruising, he made Lagos his headquarters and kept three or four ships out watching Cadiz, relieving them as frequently as possible, that none of his ships should become unduly short of provisions or water; and continued so doing throughout the remainder of June and July.

On July 25th the squadron of observation [1] was under the command of Captain Curtis Barnett, an officer of whom more will be heard during this war. On the morning of that day when he was about thirty miles to the westward of Cape Spartel, three strange sail were sighted to the east-north-eastward. Barnett's ships were separated, the 'Feversham' being to the southward in chase of a vessel, but Barnett and the two others made sail at once to close the strangers to whom they were close enough by noon to make them out to be two large ships and a frigate standing for the Straits of Gibraltar. The three British ships chased all the afternoon and gradually drew up dropping the 'Mary' galley, a slow sailer, astern as they did so. As the 'Dragon' and 'Folkestone' overhauled the chase French colours were shewn on board them. Barnett was suspicious that these were false, since a French ship should have had no reason for not bringing to. He therefore continued the pursuit, himself putting Dutch colours abroad. Towards midnight he overhauled them, and coming close to the second ship on her port side, hailed her, asking who she was and whence she came. The stranger replied that they were all French ships from Martinique. Barnett, disbelieving this, desired them to bring to in order to allow him to board them. The accounts of the subsequent conversations written by Barnett and de Caylus—for he it was who commanded the strange squadron [2]—differ somewhat, as might be expected. Barnett's

[1] 'Dragon,' 60; 'Feversham,' 40; 'Folkestone,' 40; 'Mary,' galley, 20.

[2] British ships: 'Dragon,' 60; 'Folkestone,' 40. French ships: 'Borée,' 62; 'Aquilon,' 46; 'Flore,' 26. The 'Borée' was the leading ship, then 'Aquilon,' 'Flore' in the rear.

story is that he told them he was an English man-of-war and must speak with them, and they replied that they were King's ships and would stop for nobody; that they were going their course, and Barnett might do as he liked. To which, said Barnett, "I told them if they were French men-of-war I was very far from intending to offer any insult or indignity: that they had no reason to make any difficulties in the affair, being at peace with all Europe." The French captain declined to shorten sail, telling Barnett he could go ahead and get his information from the Commandant in the ship ahead. "I then told them I asked as a favour what I was in a condition to compel them to: and that if they obliged me to do it they were answerable for the consequences: and therefore if they were French I conjured them to prevent the mischief that might happen. But all my entreaties had no effect; their answers growing more pert as I appeared unwilling to use anything but words to bring them to reason." Ranging ahead therefore, he fired two or three shots. The foreigner promptly replied with a broadside[1]. According to de Caylus, when Barnett ranged up alongside the 'Aquilon,' commanded by M. de Pardaillan, he roughly ordered "Heave to, Heave to, we are British ships of war." On being told the name of the French Commander and his ship, the English Commander replied that his name was Barkley, and that he commanded the 'Dragon': and once more ordered the 'Aquilon' to heave to. The request, continued Caylus, was refused, and Barnett was referred to the Commander of the squadron. "The impatient and very insolent Englishman then shouted 'Stop, or I will stop you,' to which no reply was given; and he repeated 'If you are French, bring to, or I shall treat you as an enemy.'" M. de Pardaillan replied that this annoyed him, and that the English Captain had only to speak to the Commodore; adding, "we are French men-of-war." To which the Englishman replied "You are not French at all. You are —— Spaniards." This "polite expression," said Caylus, was followed by a shot which passed between the 'Aquilon's' masts. Upon this M. de Pardaillan asked "Are we at war? If you fire another shot I will give you my whole broadside in the belly." The Englishman fired three more shots, and M. de Pardaillan was as good as his word and let fly his broadside[2].

Whichever account more nearly approximates to the truth—and both are probably true, differing only in the point of view of the

[1] Beatson, *Naval and Military Memoirs*. A full account of this is given copied from Barnett's letter: a copy of Barnett's letter is in Haddock's despatch of August 3rd. The Captain's Journal of 'Dragon' has the same account.

[2] Guérin, *Histoire Maritime de la France*; *Hist. Man. Comm. Report*, vol. x.; Lady du Cane's papers.

writers—it is perfectly clear that the French Captain provoked Barnett to engage. Barnett was fully within his rights in insisting on making sure of the nationality of the strangers; indeed, it was his duty so to do. It would be idle to pretend that in such a situation an officer should be satisfied with a mere statement that the vessels were French—a Spanish Register ship could have given that answer equally well.

A running fight followed. Barnett engaged the second ship which he had been hailing, the 'Folkestone' the frigate in the rear. Both ships bore away to the southward slightly, the 'Aquilon' more than the 'Flore,' and Caylus in the 'Borée' backed astern and was able to bring his after guns to bear on the 'Folkestone' and his forward guns on the 'Dragon.' In this situation the action lasted about an hour. Both the British ships were considerably cut about aloft by the fire of the three Frenchmen and were obliged to lie to to knot and splice. The French took this opportunity to make sail away from them, and when the 'Feversham' came up about four in the morning the 'Folkestone' and 'Dragon' were sufficiently refitted aloft to continue the pursuit. Daylight shewed the French going away large before the westerly breeze with all sail set, but shortly afterwards Caylus brought to and fired a gun to leeward as a signal to speak. Barnett then came up and sent a flag-of-truce on board, and mutual explanations followed, in which Barnett explained to Caylus that the whole incident would have been avoided if it had not been for the obstinacy and insolence of the Captain of the 'Aquilon.' The squadrons then parted company peaceably. Pardaillan and twenty-five men were reported killed; the 'Borée' lost a few; the 'Dragon' had four killed and fourteen wounded; the 'Folkestone' seven killed and eight wounded. Caylus wrote a despatch in which he ingeniously made it appear that his three ships had engaged four English of superior force and had beaten off their attack, and this, joined with a certain amount of airy gasconade, gained him great credit. Maurepas, the Minister of Marine, wrote to him in a highly appreciative manner about "le combat que vous avez rendu à l'entrée du détroit contre quatre vaisseaux anglais qui ont attaqué votre escadre." The fact that only two British ships were in action was neatly passed over.

Like the skirmish between Caylus and Martin on his voyage out, the incident had no significance beyond shewing how the wind was blowing, in that French commanders should be prepared to invite complications in this manner. The feeling of hostility against England was driving France into a war with her, for which on the surface there was no immediate cause or quarrel. The real feeling lay deeper and is found expressed in a letter written to Caylus by a friend of his,

M. de Remond. This writer said: "France will never be able to enjoy any peace on earth, or return to a flourishing condition until she has curbed and enfeebled the English despotism on the water." This sentence, so curiously modern, in reality sums up the national feeling. France felt that her development was in some way being checked, and she attributed the check to her greatest trade rival, England[1].

It was not only with France that friction was arising. Haddock also experienced difficulties with other neutrals in carrying out his orders to arrest ships of all nations bringing stores into Cadiz. Dutch ships carrying masts and naval stores were taken by his cruisers and strong protests from the Dutch Ministers followed. A Venetian ship was chased by Captain Watson into Villa Nova Road and taken by him actually in the anchorage. This action was protested against by the Portuguese Governor, in reply to whom Watson invoked the old doctrine that the jurisdiction of a country extended so far as a gun would carry and no further. "I do not comprehend," said he, "any neutral port to be a safeguard to enemies' ships when they are out of the protection of the fortifications." The matter was quietly smoothed over,—as was Boscawen's even more marked disregard of neutrality on a later occasion,—and nothing further was heard of it. But protests from the Dutch against interference with their shipping, which were more serious in view of our relations with Holland, continued to embarrass the Admirals and the Ministry throughout the war.

Haddock's difficulties did not end with the disputes with the neutral traders. The constant cruising, notwithstanding the use of St Mary's as a base, was wearing out his crews; in September they were falling sick in such numbers that he found it necessary to carry the squadron back to Gibraltar where he sent over 300 men to the hospital; many others lay in their hammocks on board for want of accommodation on shore. There was however some hope of an improvement, for the Council at last were sending him a reinforcement. On September 4th orders were given for four ships[2] under Captain Cornewall to be detached from home waters to join him. The preparations at Barcelona, which led to this tardy step, were interpreted in London as threatening Minorca, and Haddock was directed[3] to take the necessary measures to protect the island if he should have reason to suspect that the Spanish armament were directed against it. There was however no modification of his earlier instructions to blockade Cadiz where the main Spanish fleet of seventeen sail still lay. Yet it was palpably impossible for him

[1] The above quotations from de Caylus' letters are taken from Lady du Cane's MS., *Hist. Man. Comm. Report*, vol. x. p. 287.
[2] 'Bedford,' 'Elizabeth,' 'Marlborough,' 'Essex.'
[3] Lords Justices to Haddock, September 15th, 1741.

to observe two places over 600 miles apart with a squadron inferior even to that of the enemy in one of them. In view of the strength of de la Bene's squadron the least number of ships that he could have detached to watch Barcelona would have been four. This would have left him with nine ships, and those sickly and undermanned, to blockade a fresh and completely equipped fleet of seventeen sail and provide the necessary reliefs. To make such a division of his squadron would have been madness. He must, as he had said in July, keep all his force together. The question was, which port should he leave open? The escape of which enemy squadron would produce the more serious results? The Cadiz squadron was a concrete and certain fact. The sailing of the Barcelona expedition, though probable, was less certain; and, if it were intended to take place, there was every likelihood that the Cadiz squadron would enter the Mediterranean to escort it. Haddock therefore steadily kept his eyes upon Cadiz, nursing his ships as much as possible so that all might be available to dispute the passage of the Straits or follow the enemy whatever might be his objective. He remained at Gibraltar where fresh water and provisions, sick quarters and stores were available, keeping, as hitherto, a squadron of observation off Cadiz, and awaiting impatiently the arrival of the reinforcement for which he had pointed out the necessity in July.

At the end of September Captain Barnett, who commanded the squadron of observation, saw the Spaniards crossing their yards and bending sail. Their appearance shewed him so unmistakeably that they were coming to sea, that he dropped down to Tangier lest an easterly wind which might bring them out should find him cut off from his main body. Haddock, on getting this news, recalled Barnett's force to Gibraltar in order that the whole squadron should be assembled and ready to move together if the enemy entered the Straits[1].

Not only were the Spaniards nearly ready, but the French at Toulon were in a similar condition; and rumour added that the Brest squadron was coming to join them. This intelligence Haddock reported to the Government on October 3rd. Meanwhile fresh advices continued to pour in from his correspondents in Italy and France. The army at Barcelona was reported to be all but ready for an expedition the destination of which was kept most secret; some said Italy, some Minorca. Various estimates placed its strength at 10,000 20,000 or even 36,000 troops. The Toulon squadron was to be its escort. Finally on November 1st came news which confirmed the seriousness of the situation and the truth of the last-mentioned report; the Toulon squadron had sailed on October 11th to escort the expedition.

[1] In letters. October 14th, 1741.

This news, which was brought by the 'Dursley' galley, Captain Hughes, from Genoa, had been long in coming owing to bad weather with south-westerly gales which prevented the 'Dursley's' sailing and delayed her passage. But Hughes was able to corroborate by his own testimony the truth of the report, for on October 30th he fell in with the whole Toulon squadron, thirteen ships strong, off Cape de Gatt standing under an easy sail apparently going towards Gibraltar. Hughes closed the French and watched them for some time; but they made no effort to interfere with him and he proceeded to Gibraltar without hindrance from them.

When Haddock received this news he concluded that the French intended to join or be joined by the Cadiz squadron; he would then be faced by a fleet of no less than thirty sail. Whichever enemy squadron he should separately engage, a tough fight was to be looked for, which would leave him, even if victorious, in no condition to oppose the second fleet of the enemy.

In the meanwhile his letter of October 3rd had reached the Government. In consequence of his representations a further reinforcement[1] was now ordered to be sent to him in addition to the four that had already sailed under Cornewall. This made a total of nine when all should have joined him, but it would still leave him in an inferiority to the Allies. The need for more vigorous measures than these was quickly made evident. Four days later came the news that the Spanish army, consisting of between thirteen and fourteen thousand men, embarked on board 220 transports escorted by the Carthagena squadron, had sailed from Barcelona.

This news, though it provoked a storm of excitement and indignation in England, did not draw from the Government any decided action, such as an increase in the reinforcement, or a hastening of its departure. They seem to have accepted the strange belief, so often prevalent in public affairs, that once an order has been given the thing is accomplished. On this occasion they wrote in very measured tones, saying that as they were not certain how Haddock would have disposed the squadron, "considering the situation of the French squadron and the embarkation at Barcelona" they could not send him "any positive or absolute rules from hence for your conduct which must be governed by the motions of the enemy. Such a reinforcement is sent you as may it is hoped enable you to execute any services that may be performed by your squadron." If the troops from Barcelona should have been landed in Italy, and the Spanish squadron or transports have returned

[1] Instructions of November 7th, Sir John Norris to detach five ships, two of 90 guns and three of 60 and above.

to the Catalan ports, or gone into a Mediterranean harbour where they could not be attacked "all you can do is to prevent a second embarkation." In any event he was to try to destroy the Spanish transports either at sea, or in their own or Italian ports.

It was not "positive or absolute" or any other rules that Haddock needed. It was ships he wanted. He had thirteen of 40 guns and above; the Government believed he had four more, but these had not yet reached him. The second reinforcement of five sail was still at Spithead. According to the rumour upon which the Council was acting the combined fleet of the Allies might consist of anything from twenty-one to forty-three sail[1]. Thus they were leaving Haddock with seventeen sail, which might be increased to twenty-two when the ships which were still at Spithead joined him, to meet any of these possible combinations, and at the same time ensure the interception of the army at sea.

Ample information had been received as to the French attitude, yet at this moment, when their squadrons were ready, their demeanour hostile to us, and their armies acting against those of Queen Maria Theresa on the continent, the total reinforcement which the Government sent Haddock would give him a bare superiority of one ship over the force of Spain alone.

Not only was the reinforcement too small; it was also too late. At the very date on which the advisory set of instructions were being written the Barcelona expedition had already sailed and the Cadiz squadron was at sea on its way to join the squadron from Toulon. By the time the instructions reached Haddock the crisis was over. The squadrons had joined and were about to cover the passage of a second and a larger army into Italy.

The intentions governing the movements of the French in October are now clear. The Toulon squadron stood down to Cape de Gatt and lay there, acting as a covering force to the first expedition which was escorted by the Carthagena squadron. If Haddock had received the news that this first expedition was about to sail and had thought proper to proceed to intercept it, he would have found this squadron in his path. He would have been warned by the French Commander that any interference with the convoy would be met with force, and would have been opposed by seventeen ships from Toulon and Carthagena; for as soon as the army was ready to sail the French went to Carthagena, joined the squadron, the joint fleet went on up to Barcelona, picked up the transports and the whole fleet and expedition sailed on

[1] At a maximum, 43: Brest 9, Toulon 13, Cadiz 17, Carthagena 4; or without the Brest, 34: Toulon 13, Cadiz 17, Carthagena 4; or without the French, 21: Cadiz 17, Carthagena 4.

November 3rd for Orbitello. There they landed the first instalment of the Spanish invasion.

It was not until November 8th that Haddock received his first news of the junction of the Toulon and Carthagena squadrons. The 'Winchelsea,' which had been watching Carthagena, learned of this from a prize and also of their subsequent arrival in company at Barcelona. The sailing of the expedition had not been witnessed, and the 'Winchelsea' returned to Gibraltar with the bare but important news of the arrival of the combined squadron at Barcelona. When this reached Haddock a strong levanter had been blowing for some days, of which the enemy would probably have availed themselves if they had intended to pass the Straits into the Atlantic. He therefore inferred that the Toulon squadron was not coming to Cadiz, as he had supposed from Hughes' report of a week earlier, but that a junction between the Cadiz and Toulon squadrons would be made inside the Mediterranean. The Cadiz squadron would in that case be the next to move, and early intelligence of its motions would furnish him with the best clue to his own behaviour. He therefore sent the 'Winchelsea' to sea again at once to go to Cadiz and get information. His expectations were fully realized: she returned on November 13th bringing the news that the Spaniards had already sailed on the 4th.

Still there was no sign of the promised reinforcement under Cornewall. The first report Haddock had of its approach was brought by a schooner, one of a convoy coming out under Cornewall's escort, which hastened into Gibraltar Bay on the 19th with the news that the reinforcement itself had been intercepted by the Spanish squadron about 30 leagues south of St Vincent. This craft, by her good sailing on a wind, had managed to beat round the flank of the enemy and get past them, but there was no indication as to what was the fate of the reinforcing squadron.

Cornewall and his convoy indeed came within an ace of never reaching Gibraltar. Leaving England on October 11th—over five weeks after their orders for sailing—with a large convoy of the trade for Portugal and the Mediterranean, they ran into a violent gale on September 30th in which the 'Marlborough' lost company with the remainder. The three other ships and the convoy reached a position about 35 leagues to the southward of Cape St Vincent on November 13th. About midnight, while beating for the Straits against the levanter, Cornewall who wore his broad pendant on board the 'Bedford' sighted the lights of a fleet to windward. At daylight he made out the ships to be a Spanish fleet. The enemy at once made sail and came rapidly down towards him before the wind. Cornewall put his helm up and made all possible sail to the westward, pursued by the enemy who so gained upon him that by ten o'clock their leading ships had come up with the rearmost of the convoy, the first of which, a vessel with a valuable cargo of naval stores badly wanted at Gibraltar, was captured. As the breeze freshened Cornewall and three others of the convoy began to draw away, but one of them, the schooner already referred to, finding that the enemy gained on him with the wind aft, hauled his wind and succeeded in getting round the enemy and reaching Gibraltar. The Spaniards continued to chase Cornewall under a press of sail. "I never saw so great a cloud of sail," wrote Cornewall in his Journal, "but in point of seamanship[1] they behaved just like themselves, for they never attempted to spread to cut us off if we shifted our course, but kept in a body." When dark fell the 'Elizabeth' had dropped astern and Cornewall, though he brought to and shewed lights, was not rejoined by her or the convoy.

Knowing now that the enemy was at sea Cornewall was in some doubt as to what he should do. His instructions had directed him to call at Lisbon for intelligence of the enemy from the Consul "and if he shall advise you of a superior strength of the enemy being at sea in those parts, you are to go into the bay of Wales and stay there till you hear of their departure. But if you receive no intelligence from him of the enemy's being in your way, you are to proceed and join Rear Admiral Haddock who is cruising near Cape St Vincent, St Mary's and sometimes to the southward towards the Barbary coast[2]."

The enemy had proved to be in his way in superior force, and the fact that they were in that part shewed that Haddock was elsewhere, probably at Gibraltar. Cornewall did not consider it possible to force his way past the large squadron of whose good sailing qualities he had received some evidence the day before; and he therefore considered that he would be interpreting his instructions correctly by returning to the Tagus. For this he was subsequently court-martialled and convicted of an error in judgment, the Court considering that he should first have made an effort to join the Admiral at Gibraltar.

The experience of the 'Elizabeth,' Captain Lingen, with the convoy shews that such an effort would have been dangerous. He remained about the approaches to the Straits, beating towards the gut for several days and on the 23rd, being then near Spartel, once more sighted the Spanish fleet, also beating for the Strait's mouth. Lingen still held on, but next day was pursued by three of the enemy's squadron, and expecting

[1] This use of the word 'seamanship' to embrace more than the actual handling of a ship is frequently used at this time.

[2] Out letters. Orders and Instructions, September 4th, 1741.

that the Spanish main body might now be in Tangier or Ceuta and that if he entered the Straits he might run into them and lose all his store ships, he bore up and like Cornewall returned to Lisbon where he arrived on the 5th of December. The 'Essex,' which had been separated from the squadron when they first met the Spaniards, acted in a similar manner; the 'Marlborough,' on the other hand, although not very distant from the remainder of the squadron came through the Straits without seeing anything of the enemy and anchored at Gibraltar on November 21st. From the schooner's account of what she had seen, and the knowledge of Cornewall's instructions given by the Captain of the 'Marlborough,' Haddock guessed that the remainder would have retired to Lisbon and that his promised reinforcement was still a long way from joining him. He sent orders to Lisbon for them to come on to Gibraltar at once, and proceeded to repair the 'Marlborough,' whose damages in the six weeks' tempestuous passage were very extensive.

Although it was evident to Haddock that the Spanish squadron was at sea, and that it intended to join the French inside the Mediterranean, he did not sail at once. The 'Marlborough,' a 90-gun ship, was not in a condition to leave, and though the whole of the carpenters of the fleet were put to work on her, it was a week before she could be tightened up and made fit. Three days later—on the morning of the 24th—his cruisers in the Straits brought him in news that the Spaniards had passed through the Straits the night before.

Still Haddock decided not to move until the 'Marlborough' was ready to accompany him. On December 1st a privateer brought him news that the Spaniards were at anchor off Malaga. The repairs to the 'Marlborough' were completed that night[1], and at daylight next morning Haddock sailed with his thirteen ships[2] in search of the seventeen of the enemy. "I shall proceed," he had written, "in search of the Spanish squadron in order to attack them provided they are not joined by the French squadron which has been cruising a considerable time off Cape de Gatt[3]."

It is open to discussion whether Haddock should not have risked an engagement with a superior force, and put to sea to bring the Spanish fleet to action before it could join the French. It must be recalled that the first knowledge he had that the enemy had sailed from Cadiz on

[1] Journal of 'Marlborough.'

[2] 'Marlborough,' 90; 'Lancaster,' 80; 'Somerset,' 80; 'Ipswich,' 70; 'Pembroke,' 60; 'Warwick,' 60; 'Dragon,' 60; 'Plymouth,' 60; 'Guernsey,' 50; 'Dartmouth,' 50; 'Oxford,' 50; 'Salisbury,' 50; 'Panther,' 50; 'Folkestone,' 40; 'Feversham,' 40; 'Ann,' galley, 8; 'Duke,' fireship; 'Mercury,' fireship and 'Guarland's' prize, zebeck.

[3] Haddock to the Duke of Newcastle, November 25th, 1741.

November 4th was on the 13th. He then had with him twelve ships of the line to sixteen or seventeen (so his information went) of the Cadiz squadron. He was expecting a reinforcement of four large ships daily. The action he took was to send a cruiser to Cadiz to bring him further news, keeping his squadron in harbour where he could best make sure of being joined by the reinforcement which would give him approximately an equality with the Spaniards.

No general action had yet been fought with the Spaniards during the war, and the English had not yet established that feeling of superiority which in later times served them so well. Yet, as soon as the 'Marlborough' was ready, and it became obvious to Haddock that he must give up hopes of being joined by the remaining ships of his reinforcement, he sailed with thirteen ships in pursuit of the Spanish seventeen.

A greater man might have taken the risk of sailing earlier without the 'Marlborough'; but let anyone who thinks Haddock's conduct deserving of censure put himself in the Admiral's place, consider all the circumstances, and decide what he would have done.

Malaga Bay was drawn blank and Haddock stood on towards Cape Palos. At 3 P.M. on the 6th of December the 'Roebuck,' which was scouting ahead, made the signal to seeing a fleet, which soon became visible from the mastheads of the squadron, bearing about east. The Admiral at once crowded sail and steered in pursuit, but the wind was very light and he closed little during the night. Next morning sixteen sail were visible from the masthead at daylight. The wind was south-east by east and the enemy bore east by north and were going large to the westward of north, evidently for Carthagena. At last Haddock had his evasive enemy well in sight with every probability of being able to cut him off and bring him to action before he could gain the shelter of another port. The ships were all cleared for action, every stitch of canvas was set, and hopes ran high that the enemy would soon be brought to action.

About 9 A.M. a midshipman who was at the masthead of the 'Dragon' saw another four or five sail ahead. He came down from aloft and informed Barnett, who at that time was going round the decks seeing everything clear. When Barnett reached the poop after completing his rounds he called to the mastheadman and asked if he saw any more ships ahead; he was told that seven were now in sight. A lieutenant went aloft, and returned confirming the news. Barnett at once made the signal for seeing a fleet and altered course to steer for them as the Sailing Instructions enjoined, so as to point them out to the Admiral. The Spaniards about the same time bore away more to the westward; by 10 o'clock the strange ships were visible from the poop.

Haddock continued in chase of the Spaniards till about noon by which time the strangers could be clearly made out. It was the French squadron consisting of eleven ships. Haddock with his thirteen sail of the line was in presence of twenty-eight sail of the enemy.

The relative positions of the three squadrons can now be seen. The French bore north, about fifteen miles distant and were standing towards Haddock. The Spaniards bore east-north-easterly and were about nine miles distant, steering to meet the French. The wind was about east-south-east. Whether Haddock should attempt to attack the Spaniards, cutting them off before they should be able to join the French was now the question he had to decide. There was little doubt that the neutrality of the latter could not be depended on, "not being able," as Barnett says in his *Journal*, "to account for their having cruised near six weeks off Cape de Gat at this season of year without supposing that it was in order to join the Spaniards and defend them, if not jointly to attack us."

Haddock called a council of war of his eight senior captains which decided that in view of the great superiority of the enemy it would be dangerous to continue the pursuit, and that the best course would be to keep to windward of the enemy and not to allow him to get between the British squadron and any reinforcements that might be coming[1].

For the next four days Haddock continued cruising in the neighbourhood of Cape de Gatt with easterly winds. On the 11th the wind came westerly and drove him over to the Balearic Islands, and next morning he again sighted the conjunct fleet, now numbering twenty-seven sail and standing to the north-eastward under easy sail. They were to windward of the British squadron, but although it lay in their power to bear down upon Haddock they made no attempt to do so. From their abstention Haddock inferred that the French intended leaving him alone provided he did not attack the Spaniards. "I conclude," he wrote, "that the French in the present conjuncture will forbear hostilities, at present at least, but on condition we should offer to attack the common enemy under their protection." Arguing at the same time that it was now beyond the power of his squadron to prevent the expedition, guarded by so superior a force, from sailing, he steered for Minorca there to await further instructions or, better, a reinforcement. He anchored at Port Mahon on December 17th. The enemy, content with having prevented him from attacking, proceeded to Barcelona where they arrived on December 24th. The army was

[1] Decision of council of war. In letters. Haddock, December 15th, 1741.

ready to embark, and ten days later the fleet with 52 large transports under convoy sailed to the eastward with the intention of landing the troops at Spezia; the passage occupied nearly seven weeks owing to strong north-easterly gales, and the combined fleet then returned to the harbour of Toulon.

Haddock was right in supposing that the French would only act defensively. The instructions to M. de Court who commanded their squadron directed him to support the passage of the Spanish troops "sans cependant unir vos vaisseaux à ceux d'Espagne. Au surplus, vous garderez dans l'entretenu le croisière d'Yvice à Majorque." If the British squadron should follow the Spaniards into the Mediterranean in order to fight them—a contingency that apparently was considered improbable—de Court was instructed to inform Haddock that he had neither orders nor intentions to attack him himself; but if Haddock should attempt to attack the Cadiz squadron, the French would assist the Spaniards to defend themselves[1].

Putting aside any question of whether the policy of the French was the one best calculated to achieve their ends it must be admitted that they had handled the situation very cleverly. While maintaining peace with England which they particularly desired to do, they had the whole time hampered our operations keeping us in uncertainty as to what they were going to do. Their demonstration of activity at Brest had tied up the British ships in home waters until it was too late to reinforce Haddock; by effecting a junction with the Carthagena squadron they had secured that whichever way Haddock turned he found a force of seventeen ships against his thirteen. They had supported their ally without breaking with his enemy, and enabled him to do what he could not do alone, effect the passage of his army into Italy by sea; while at the same time their own commerce was not endangered by a war with England. They had thus succeeded in the Mediterranean as they had partly succeeded in the West Indies, in spoiling the whole of our campaign; and without breaking the peace had obtained a very considerable part of the advantages of war. The part omitted was however of supreme importance. They had missed the opportunity of destroying a British squadron, and the communications of their expedition were henceforth insecure.

A storm of indignation burst out in England when it was learned that for the third time the Mediterranean squadron had failed to prevent a junction of enemy squadrons and the success of enemy plans. Twice

[1] Newcastle papers, Add. MS. 32802. A copy of de Court's orders; ending with the information that de Court must be on his guard as Norris with ten sail was coming to reinforce Haddock.

the Cadiz squadron had sailed unhindered and joined the squadron at Ferrol, and now an even more important junction with the French, culminating in an invasion of Italy which it was our particular province to prevent, had been permitted under the very nose of the British Admiral. It is not to be wondered that a general idea took root that Haddock's forbearing to engage the enemy in the Straits was due to restraining instructions from the Government, who were openly accused, as modern expression would put it, of being pro-Spanish. One pamphleteer, writing no less than sixteen years after the event—shewing how persistently this view was held—said: "What were the motives of sending such orders does not become me to say; whatever they were, they were such as could not be made public, and therefore to justify so extraordinary and unexpected behaviour the friends of the Admiral and the Ministry urged the importance of the fleet—the ill-consequences that would happen to the nation if it should be destroyed—the necessity there was of taking care of the King's ships—and many such arguments; as if men-of-war were fitted out, armed and manned so well but for no other reason but only to make a fine figure and keep out of harm's way for fear their gildings and carved work should be damaged[1]." The same idea was current in France where it was believed that Haddock had allowed the Cadiz squadron to pass the Straits under instructions from home, given with the object of forcing the King of Sardinia into taking a definite stand on the side of England and Austria[2]. Charles Emanuel had so far taken neither side but was inclining slightly towards England. If he could be made to feel the danger he was in from the two Bourbon Powers he might, so ran the argument, be induced in self-defence to declare himself. The junction of the French and Spanish squadrons and the landing of a Spanish army were thus permitted in order to open his eyes to his danger.

It has already been seen that no such orders as those supposed were given. The last word in the matter rests in a letter written by the Duke of Newcastle on November 26th, when the news arrived that the Spaniards had sailed from Cadiz on the 4th, and it was assumed that they would proceed to the Mediterranean, "in which case his Majesty does not doubt that pursuant to his repeated orders you will have fallen upon them[3]."

It is not difficult to see that the principal cause of the failure to prevent the invasion of Italy by sea was the weakness of the squadron in the Mediterranean, owing to which it had been impossible for the Admiral to watch both Carthagena and Cadiz in sufficient force. The

[1] *Three Letters relating to the Navy, Gibraltar and Port Mahon*, London, 1757.
[2] Pajol, *Guerres sous Louis XV*. vol. III. p. 7.
[3] Duke of Newcastle to Haddock, November 26th, 1741, S. P. Dom. Naval.

least that could have been done would have been to maintain Haddock's squadron at a strength equal to that of the Spaniards, with a margin for ships absent re-fitting; the most would have been to bring his strength up to that of the combined Powers. It is difficult, in view of the numerous references to the probability of French intervention, to avoid the conclusion that the Government was to blame for not adequately strengthening the Mediterranean fleet.

When the news of the sailing of the first expedition from Barcelona reached London, the Ministry were violently attacked. Newcastle sheltered himself by throwing the blame of the whole miscarriage upon Haddock. Speaking in the House of Lords on December 4th, he said that a reinforcement of five ships had been sent to the Mediterranean in order that the squadron might be able to oppose the designs of the Spaniards, *even though the French should lend their assistance*. The House was thus intended to believe that such a reinforcement was of sufficient strength to deal with even the combined fleet, and had been sent in time to enable it to oppose the sailing of the expedition. Neither of these suggestions was true.

The Duke went on to say that Haddock was stationed before Barcelona in order to block up the Spanish expedition. "Why he departed from that port, or upon what motives of policy or maxims of war he suffered the Spaniards to prosecute their schemes, he only is able to inform us[1]." For a shameless mis-statement, a baseless and cowardly attack upon an absent Commander, unable to defend himself and expose the truth, this must surely have few equals. Haddock was not stationed before Barcelona. His instructions made Cadiz the most important point in his strategy, and his force was insufficient to watch even that one port effectively, far more to watch both. But apart from questions of force the Duke's reply conveyed to its hearers the belief that the Ministry had sent Haddock to blockade Barcelona and that he had failed in that duty, shewing either a lack of conduct or of courage in not preventing the expedition from sailing. Walpole, in private at least, was more honest. Horace Walpole, writing the day before the Duke's speech said: "You ask me about Admiral Haddock... he had discretionary orders to act as he should judge proper from his notices. He has been keeping the Spanish fleet at Cales. Sir Robert says, if he had let that go out, to prevent the embarkation, the Tories would have complained and said he had favoured the Spanish trade under the pretence of hindering an expedition that was never designed[2]."

For us the point of living interest is whether Haddock by any

[1] *Parliamentary History*, vol. XII. p. 267.

[2] Horace Walpole to Horace Mann, December 3rd, 1741.

means in his power could have stopped the enemy's army at sea. His force consisted as we have seen of thirteen ships, some frigates and some light craft. The enemy had twenty-seven large ships and frigates, with which to protect a convoy of about fifty-two sail of transports. The chances of a successful attack on the transports in an engagement may be estimated. We may compare Kempenfelt's attack on de Guichen's convoy on December 12th, 1781, in which that brilliant Commander snatched nineteen prizes from the enemy under the noses of a superior force[1], or Cotes's attack on the convoy on March 7th, 1748. But the odds in neither case were so great as those against Haddock, nor would a defeat in either case have entailed such serious consequences.

In whatever way the blame should be apportioned, the fact remained that the expedition from Barcelona had got clear away to Italy and that its sailing gave the war a new character which materially changed the objects of the Mediterranean squadron. Up to this time the squadron had three successive principal objects. At the beginning of the war, when the offensive was restricted to an attack on trade, its objective was the ships leaving or returning to Cadiz, and as a defensive function the protection of Minorca. As the operations in the West Indies extended and developed into a territorial attack of considerable magnitude the Mediterranean squadron became in effect a portion of the forces operating in the West Indies, covering that attack from interference from Old Spain; at the same time it acted defensively as before in protecting Minorca. Then, when the invasion of Italy resulted from the Franco-Spanish compact of May 1741, and the forces at Barcelona instead of being aimed at Minorca were aimed at the Italian coast, the squadron became a portion of the Allied forces engaged in the protection of Lombardy. The maintenance of the balance of power, that fundamental axiom of British policy of the day, could only be attained by a strong support of the Queen of Hungary, and consequently Haddock's orders of 26th of November laid the greatest stress on the destruction of embarkations sailing for Italy and the prevention of "any attempt making by the Spaniards upon the dominions of the Queen of Hungary, the Grand Duke or their Allies."

With this new orientation now fully developed, Haddock on his arrival at Mahon set to work to refit his ships while waiting for the reinforcement. On January 1st it arrived at Gibraltar under the command of Commodore Lestock[2], whence it sailed, after four days

[1] Kempenfelt, 13 ships, 4 frigates; de Guichen, 21 ships, 6 frigates; Cotes, 4 ships and a 24-gun frigate; Spaniards, 9 ships. Cotes took 5 prizes.

[2] 'Neptune,' 90; 'Barfleur,' 90; 'Lenox,' 70; 'Nassau,' 70; 'Royal Oak,' 70; 'Winchester,' 50; 'Romney,' 50, and 'Sutherland,' hospital ship. All these ships arrived very sickly, *e.g.* 'Neptune,' 250 sick and had buried 54 on the passage out.

for watering and refreshing, for Mahon and anchored in the harbour there on January 27th. The original ships of the squadron were still under repair when it arrived. Five months cruising, without much opportunity or material for repair work, had reduced the ships to a very poor condition. Haddock himself was worn out. The anxieties through which he had passed had proved too much for him. He felt very deeply the situation to which he had been brought, and complained bitterly at having been left so long without reinforcement.

The ill-health of the chief Commander reflected itself in inaction of the ships; during the first three months of the year[1], the fleet remained at Mahon. No cruisers were sent out on the coast of Italy, nor were any steps taken to interfere seriously with the transport of troops and stores which the enemy was pouring into the Italian ports. At length, on March 20th, Haddock informed Lestock that he was now too ill to take any further part in the command, and directed the Commodore to call a council of war to consider what should be done. The council, which consisted of Lestock and twenty-four captains, reported that the first and immediate necessity was to send out cruisers to get some clear information as to what the enemy was doing. This report was given to Haddock, but some days passed without his being able to deal with it; and in the meantime the 'Folkestone,' which had been at Genoa and Marseilles, arrived in Mahon harbour on the 26th of March with the information that the Infante Don Philip himself had arrived at Aix and was daily expected at Marseilles. Thence he would proceed to Antibes, where he would embark for Italy in French and Neapolitan galleys, escorted by the Spanish squadron of which twelve ships were then ready, lying in the inner harbour of Toulon. The French ships were reported as unready. When this news reached Lestock he wrote to Haddock and pointed out that it was now clear that a squadron should proceed without delay to the coast of Provence; he proposed that a detached squadron of twelve ships should at once be made up to lie off Toulon and deal with the twelve Spanish ships if they should try to put to sea.

Haddock however was doubtful. He could not decide whether such a squadron would do all that would be required of it. He called another council to deliberate on the proposal, directing it to consider what force was needed, to pay due regard to the safety of a convoy expected from England, and to the possibility that such a squadron might find itself cut off from the main body. There was indeed no reason why the whole fleet should not proceed to the Riviera and so be in a position to confront the combined fleet of the Allies, if by any

[1] 1742.

chance the French should get their ships ready. Twenty-four sail were now at Mahon, their complements were strengthened by 500 men from the garrison, and this fleet would have been able to deal with any that the enemy could put to sea. As to the out-coming convoy, it was clear that the Spaniards were busy with bigger game than convoys. They were engaged in the very operation that his instructions directed him to oppose. This was not a moment to centre on the defence of store ships, nor, with the force at Haddock's disposal, need he consider anything except how to prevent the transport of troops into Italy. His attitude can only be attributed to the complete nervous breakdown from which there is no doubt he was suffering at this time[1]. It is to be regretted that he could not have been relieved sooner from his duties. It was not until March 30th that Lestock took over the command.

The Council met and recommended that the whole fleet should put to sea as soon as possible, and that in order to save time the best sailing small ships and frigates should go at once in advance to intercept the transports. Captain Forbes of the 'Guernsey' was ordered to sail that day with a small cruiser squadron[2], with instructions to cruise between Marseilles and Villefranche, particularly watching Antibes, and to prevent "the transporting of Spanish troops or utensils of war from them [Marseilles and Toulon] or any other Spanish or French ports towards Italy, or any galley with Spanish troops or effects in them." Forbes sailed on April 7th, and Lestock with the main body consisting of twenty-one large ships, a 20-gun frigate and five small craft[3] followed on the 12th for the Riviera where he arrived on the 17th.

For a few days Lestock kept the squadron together, and cruised in company watching Toulon, and sending out single ships to chase when any craft were sighted. Several Spanish coasting craft with provisions and stores were taken in the first few days. A large number of tartans and settees—about thirty—were chased by the 'Rupert' on the 17th but by spreading all except two of them escaped. French vessels engaged on the Spanish service were captured and carried inshore where

[1] Dr Lidderdale to Haddock's son, April 17th, 1742: "Nothing could so much contribute to his recovery as a total recess from business of all kinds.... I have all along advised him to proceed to England...it will be necessary that you prevail on him to begin his journey without loss of time, etc."

[2] Lestock's fleet consisted of: 'Neptune,' 90; 'Barfleur,' 90; 'Marlborough,' 90; 'Lancaster,' 80; 'Somerset,' 80; 'Ipswich,' 70; 'Bedford,' 70; 'Royal Oak,' 70; 'Buckingham,' 70; 'Lenox,' 70; 'Essex,' 70; 'Nassau,' 70; 'Warwick,' 60; 'Dragon,' 60; 'Pembroke,' 60; 'Rupert,' 60; 'Plymouth,' 60; 'Kingston,' 60; 'Dartmouth,' 50; 'Salisbury,' 50; 'Romney,' 50; 'Guarland,' 20, and five small vessels.

[3] 'Guernsey,' 50; 'Oxford,' 50; 'Panther,' 50; 'Folkestone,' 40; 'Winchelsea,' 24, and a zebeck.

they were burnt, so that the French might know what would be the fate of any ships of theirs captured while serving the Spaniards.

The numbers of small craft to be dealt with was soon found to call for a greater dispersal of the fleet, and Lestock therefore made up squadrons, composed of two or three big ships and a frigate, to cruise on different parts of the coast. Thus, on the 19th of April the 'Dragon,' 60, 'Dartmouth,' 50, and 'Romney,' 50, were sent off on a cruise to watch Marseilles. On the same day the 'Pembroke,' 60, 'Kingston,' 60, and 'Ann,' 20, went off Cape Creux with orders to stretch along the coast as far as Barcelona. On the 22nd the 'Ipswich,' 70, 'Lenox,' 70, 'Nassau,' 70, and 'Duke' (fireship) were detached to cruise to the south-eastward of Cape Sicie, stretching as far as 30 leagues out. On the 28th the 'Buckingham,' 70, 'Warwick,' 60, 'Essex,' 70, and 'Mercury' (fire-ship) were sent to cruise off Cape Sicie and to the westward. Lestock kept the remainder of his ships together, with his 50-gun frigates thrown out to within signal distance or employed to carry instructions to the outlying squadrons. With his forces thus disposed he kept his eye principally upon Antibes, as it was the place where the Spanish troops were gathering. So long as he was there the transports could not sail unless the combined fleet should come out from Toulon to drive him off and clear a passage, and this was exactly what he wished it to do. But so long as it chose to remain in harbour Lestock commanded the situation, and military help could not be sent by sea to join the forces in Lombardy. The effect of this blockade soon made itself felt. Those in Turin who inclined to favour the Spanish cause saw that matters were not so simple as had at first appeared, and Mann, our Minister at the Piedmontese capital, observed a drooping in their spirits since the squadron had established itself upon the coast and stopped the passage of the Spanish troops. "Their barks," he wrote, "continually fall into Mr Lestock's hands and they see 'tis impossible to pass."

One thing, however, Lestock badly needed—a base. He sent small craft along the coast to examine all the anchorages for a good one, "which," he said, "if we cannot find we must keep at sea or go to the eastward of Villa Frank as wind and weather will permit." For the present he made use of Villefranche, and thither he carried the bulk of his ships. In this way he carried on till May 13th, when he recalled his cruisers and gathered his fleet together to meet the new Commander-in-Chief, Admiral Mathews, who was expected soon to arrive from England.

CHAPTER IX

EVENTS IN EUROPE AND HOME WATERS, 1742—1743

THE spring of 1742 saw the European war in the full tide of its progress. The invasion of Silesia by the King of Prussia had marked the beginning of the struggle which was to develop into the War of the Austrian Succession. The rapid successes of Prussia, and the clear demonstration she gave of her importance as a military Power, dissolved such doubts as France had entertained as to what should be her attitude in the contest, and in March 1741 she had sent Marshal Belleisle as a special Ambassador to Frederick to arrange an alliance and to persuade the Electors to support the Bavarian claimant against Maria Theresa. At the same time she made ready her army to act as an auxiliary to the forces of the Elector of Bavaria.

The battle of Mollwitz in April 1741 confirmed the expediency of the choice made by France; and Queen Maria Theresa soon found herself attacked in Silesia by Prussia, and on the Danube by Bavaria and France, while another French army threatened her on the Lower Rhine. In September 1741 the Franco-Bavarian army had swept all before it and Vienna itself was in danger. Austria then, to avoid greater losses, at the instigation of the British Minister, concluded with Frederick the secret convention of Klein Schnellendorff, by the terms of which Lower Silesia was ceded to Prussia. The army which had been opposing Frederick was thereby set free to protect the capital, and at the same time 10,000 troops were recalled from the Austrian possessions in Italy to assist in the defence; but neither of these measures was effected in time to save Prague, which fell to an assault of the Franco-Bavarian army in November 1741.

So far England had done nothing directly to maintain the Pragmatic Sanction. By the terms of her agreement with the late Emperor she was bound to furnish an army of 12,000 men to support Maria Theresa, but with the whole of her army deeply engaged in the Spanish war this was impossible; and when the French move on the Lower Rhine in September became a serious threat to Hanover, King George, whose heart was in his electorate, felt obliged to agree to England's neutrality. Spain, on the other hand, had forces to spare from her large army to take a share in the spoliation; and it was with Austrian affairs in this deplorable state that the Spaniards passed their troops by sea from Barcelona into Northern Italy, protected from British attack by the combined squadrons from Toulon and Cadiz. The causes which made this invasion by sea possible have already been seen. No unusual pressure was exercised to prepare ships to reinforce Haddock, and it appears that England had not yet sufficiently realized that now, since the object of the war had developed from a purely commercial one into an endeavour to maintain the balance of power, the focus of operations must henceforth lie in Europe.

The Ministry had survived the attack made upon them at the end of 1740, but the case against them in the winter of 1741–2 was too strong. Austria had been abandoned for the sake of Hanover, the Spaniards had sent an army into Italy in the face of the British squadron, the operations in the West Indies had been a complete failure. The conduct of the war by the Ministry was criticised from every point of view—criticism which it fully deserved. But to this were added charges of a political nature, based largely on dislike of Walpole and an intense desire to drive him from office. Corruption, mismanagement, his assumption of the hitherto unheard of office of Prime Minister were charged against him; and after a series of debates of exceptional acerbity he resigned in February 1742 and retired to the Lords with the title of Earl of Orford. Pulteney and Carteret, who had been his most vehement and determined critics on the subject of the war, were admitted to the Cabinet. Sir Charles Wager, who had not come off scathless, resigned the office of First Commissioner of the Admiralty and a general shuffle took place.

The First Commissionership was offered to the Duke of Montagu, a nobleman whom Horace Walpole has described as being "very diffident of himself." The Duke refused the offer "as being a commission of sea-affairs in which he was wholly unacquainted[1]"; and it was then offered to Lord Winchelsea who, with equal lack of experience in sea affairs but less diffidence, accepted it. Sir John Norris was invited to take the second place at the Board, but indignantly refused. "I told Mr Gibbon," he writes, "that I was concerned after our long friendship that he should bring me such a message, having so long been the first officer of the Fleet." He considered it impossible that he could sit at the Board in a subordinate position, a Board "that had in all the time of this formerly (*sic*) had a seaman at the head of it, and was very right to be so." Just at this moment, while the filling of the commission was still undecided, letters came in from Haddock asking that he might be relieved in the command. Lord Carteret at once offered the Mediterranean to Norris, who replied that he would accept on condition he was given the first place at the Admiralty. "If," he

[1] *Diary of Sir John Norris*, Add. MS. 28135.

wrote, "it should be his Majesty's pleasure that I should undertake that command, and where many eminent services might be expected, I hope I might be made First Commissioner.... To be able to execute the service that was in view I thought it absolutely necessary that I should be First Commissioner of the Admiralty, and then settling what was necessary to support the service I should immediately endeavour to put myself at the head of that service in the Mediterranean[1]."

Finding Carteret obdurate, Norris petitioned the King in the following terms:

> "May it please your Majesty,
>
> I am sure your Majesty knows very well that ever since you have been in this Kingdom the chief direction of sea affairs has been in the hands of a seaman. I once flattered myself your Majesty did me the honour to think me capable of it, and I am sure all those who now have the principal part in your Majesty's business did formerly think and have often declared I was. Since it is now thought otherwise I must look upon it as a strong admonition that I am grown too old for my business, and therefore I come to beg your Majesty's permission to retire."

His application to retire was not granted; the King had too high an opinion of the valuable advice he could give. Norris therefore requested, and was granted, permission to remain on shore; but no mark of favour for his long services was given to him, and he no longer took a part in the Cabinet discussions. The Admiral of the Fleet, he said, should either be first of the Commission or have some mark of his Majesty's favour to support his command; and without such a consideration "I can neither be of the Cabinet or in those private councils where the affairs of the Navy are consulted and the intention of their operations considered." And so Norris remained in private life, and the Navy was mismanaged until another sea-officer was appointed to the Board who not only had a mind of great power which had applied itself to the study of the higher parts of his profession, but also wealth and influence to carry his ideas into execution.

The change in the Cabinet induced a change in England's share in the war. The new Ministry, headed by Carteret, favoured a policy of military co-operation on the continent to give direct assistance to Austria, and consequently in May 1742 a British army of about 16,000 men, together with a Hanoverian force, were sent to Flanders. The West Indian expeditions necessarily relapsed to a secondary place, and the squadron in those waters was reduced to a bare equality, or

[1] *Diary of Sir John Norris*. The holding of such a dual appointment had occurred before. Lord Berkeley in 1719 had, while First Commissioner, commanded a squadron in the Channel; and Sir George Byng, while a Commissioner, commanded the Mediterranean squadron 1718–20 as also E. Russell when First Commissioner.

less, with that of Spain. The Mediterranean squadron was at last reinforced in order to support the Queen of Hungary against France and Spain; and in home waters, where no enemy immediately threatened, the operations were centred round the protection of British and attack upon Spanish trade. The gradual development in the system of trade protection in home waters therefore claims attention.

The Soundings—that is, the approach to the Channel—was the all-important area to control, but in the early months of the war with Spain very few ships were employed there, not more than two ships at a time being appointed[1]. Complaints of lack of protection soon began to be made. As early as January 1740 the merchants trading to Portugal represented how greatly their fleets were suffering from the privateers; to which the Admiralty could only regretfully reply that they were fitting out ships as quickly as they could but that there was great difficulty in getting ready "so great a number as have been deemed necessary on account of the war with Spain[2]." A ship of 20 guns and a sloop were however detached to cruise on the Portuguese coast, particularly off Lisbon. Shortly after, the same question was brought up in Parliament, where the lack of small vessels to protect trade was pointed out. Sir John Barnard complained that instead of building 20-gun ships, "the only ships that can most effectually curb the Spanish privateers," we had paid all our attention to equipping ships of the line; to which Sir Charles Wager admitted that 20-gun ships were of great value but that it took time to construct them in the numbers required, and those we had "were not sufficient to supply all the services the circumstances of the war required." Many had been found unfit for sea, not having been kept in order in the preceding years of peace; others were being bought from private persons, or built in private yards; but none could be ready at once.

The Spanish privateers in the meantime were cruising in the very heart of the Channel, and the remonstrances of the merchants as their losses increased grew louder month by month. In May 1740 the West India merchants presented a petition for more protection, in con-

[1] The following ships were quoted by the Admiralty as being so employed at the end of 1739:

	Received orders		Returned
'Deptford,' 60	12 Oct.	To cruise in the Sounding for a month	11 Nov.
'Centurion,' 60	13 Oct.		9 Nov.
'Panther,' 50	17 Nov.		24 Dec.
'Advice,' 50	20 Nov.		20 Dec.
'Deptford,' 60	15 Dec.		28 Jan.
'Winchester,' 50	20 Dec.		29 Dec. (damaged).

[2] Out letters to Secretary of State, 368.

sequence of which the Duke of Newcastle gave an order to the Admiralty that "a sufficient number of ships" was to be stationed as necessary to protect trade. The weakness of the protection that had been given is illustrated by the answer the Admiralty gave to this order: that one 50-gun ship had been cruising in the Soundings since March, and that in accordance with the order another 50-gun ship and a sloop had now been sent to cruise off the Cornish coast, where some privateers had been reported in the merchants' complaint. Their Lordships "heartily wished," they said, that they could comply with all services, "but the great and unusual sickness that rages in the fleet, the difficulty of getting seamen, and the several orders your Grace has sent us from his Majesty to provide a number of ships for other services, puts us under a disability of answering the expectations of the merchants in the way we should be glad to do[1]."

Meanwhile the number of captures steadily increased. Over 100 vessels at the least were lost during the following year—1741—of which no fewer than 71 were captured in the Channel and Bay[2] and carried into Spanish Biscay ports, notwithstanding the fact that there was a considerable squadron of ships of the line in commission in the Channel during that year, and that the number of small craft had been increased. Dissatisfaction consequently increased, and towards the end of the year a great petition, signed by 214 of the merchants of London, was addressed to the King, praying that orders might be given to the Admiralty to provide better protection for the trade. The petition set forth, firstly, that upwards of 300 ships had been taken by the enemy since the beginning of the war, and these mostly in the Channel and Soundings; secondly, that this would have been in a great measure prevented if a few of his Majesty's small ships had been properly stationed from the beginning of the war, and their commanders had done their duty; and thirdly, that the trade to the North American Colonies had suffered greatly from the privateers, principally due to a want of proper care on the part of the commanders of the ships stationed in those parts.

In reply to this indictment the Admiralty prepared a lengthy memorandum, dated November 28th, 1741, in which they gave lists of all the ships that had been employed cruising for the protection of trade since the war began. It is to be observed that they shewed in their return every squadron that had cruised in the Bay, including those under Norris and Balchen. They stated that convoy had always

[1] Out letters to Secretary of State, 22nd May, 1740.

[2] *Lloyd's List*, for 1741, "Reports of vessels captured." The merchants of London however claimed that over 300 captures had been made.

been furnished when asked for, and said that fourteen outward and twenty-one homeward convoys had sailed to and from Portugal; eleven and ten to and from the Mediterranean; six and eleven to and from the West Indies; four to North America and three from thence homeward. They pointed out that to furnish convoy was one thing, but to obtain obedience to the commanders of the convoy was another. "Nothing is more frequent," wrote the Admiralty, "than the complaints from the commanders of convoys of the obstinacy or folly of several masters of merchant ships who refuse to obey their signals or directions for the better keeping company together; but disregarding all order and government desert their convoys from impatience of getting sooner into Port." Several reports from commanders of convoys were quoted to shew how common this behaviour was, and how many losses had resulted from it. "If the trade could be brought under regulation," they wrote, "as was practised in the late wars, when those concerned in the same branches of commerce advised together, and conformed to the rules agreed upon between them and the Government, for sending out their ships at times settled and fixed for the departure of their respective convoys, fewer convoys would have sufficed for all the purposes of our foreign trade, than have been employed in this war on that service; but the greatest part of our trade is at present under no sort of order or method, which we presume proceeds from the great increase of the practice of insuring ships, beyond what was known formerly: which not only makes Traders more adventurous in sending their ships to sea, without convoys, but makes them less concerned to fit them out in a defensible manner to resist an enemy. There was an Order in Council made in the Dutch War in 1672 to oblige masters of merchant ships to stay with their convoys and to provide themselves with arms and ammunition for their defence[1]."

The order in Council, at the re-establishment of which the Admiralty so broadly hinted, was one of the 4th December, 1672. It ran thus:

"His Majesty having taken into his consideration of what ill-consequence and loss it is as well to the whole kingdom as to the Persons particularly concerned, that Merchant ships going out on foreign voyages in time of War, are not sufficiently provided with Guns, Fire-arms, and other Necessaries for their Defence against the Enemy, as also that such Ships are found frequently to forsake their Convoys and the rest of their Company, by which means it often happens that they fall into the hands of the Enemy. It was this day ordered by his Majesty in Council, that all Masters of Vessels going out on any Foreign Voyage as aforesaid shall, before they be cleared at the Custom House, or permitted to sail out of any Port of this Kingdom on their respective Voyages, give good Security to the Commissioners and Officers of his Majesty's Customs that they will not separate or depart from such Men-of-war as shall be by his Majesty appointed for their Convoy, nor from the rest of their Company, but

[1] In *Admiralty Miscellaneous*, vol. 340.

that they will keep together during such their Voyage and mutually assist and defend each other against any Enemy, in case they shall happen to be attacked, and that to this End they will take care their respective Ships and Vessels shall be well provided with Muskets, small Shot, Hand Granadoes, and other sorts of Ammunition and Military Provisions according to the proportion of the men they carry. And of this his Majesty's pleasure the Commissioners and Officers of his Majesty's Customs and all others whom it may concern are to take notice, and have due regard thereto accordingly."

This system had been in use under the Commonwealth Government, who in 1653 had made convoy compulsory on the east coast of England[1]. Penalties other than pecuniary were added later. In 1689 it was enacted that "if any merchant ship shall wilfully leave the convoy to come earlier to market, if they are taken by Turks or Moors they shall never be redeemed by any public Treaty or Contribution[2]." Compulsory convoy was enforced to the westward and southward during Tourville's deep-sea cruise in 1691, but was gradually relaxed during Queen Anne's reign by a series of orders which permitted ships to sail without convoy provided they were armed in their own defence. It was to the policy of 1672 that the Admiralty evidently desired to return, a policy of grouping the various sections of the trade in convoys which would sail at regular dates, and in which obedience and some measure of self-protection and co-operation should be enforced by civil law.

This however was by no means the view of the merchants, as can well be understood. Trade requires freedom and the removal of restrictions, and their object was to obtain such protection as would allow their ships to sail so soon as they were ready, without the delays incident to collecting large fleets of traders.

It is clear that there was much to be said on both sides, and the views of neither the merchants nor the Admiralty can be lightly dismissed. Overseas trade was a matter of such importance that, as the first paragraph of the Order in Council of 1672 shews, reciprocal obligations were clearly considered to exist between the merchants and the State. It was the duty of the merchants, by arming and sailing in company, to do all that was possible to protect themselves; it was the duty of the State to give protection, without payment, by means of ships of war[3]. But the whole question was further complicated by the manning difficulty; and the problems of the protection of trade, the protection of the colonies, and the manning of the fleet are so inter-

[1] Oppenheim, *Administration of the Royal Navy*, p. 313. It was extended to whole coast at the end of the First Dutch War, *ibid.* p. 342.

[2] *Admiralty Records.*

[3] A notorious case in the last war, known as "Captain Kerr's Case," had led to the enunciation in clear terms of the illegality of the act of taking convoy money.

woven and interdependent that it is not possible wholly to dissociate one from the other. As a general proposition it may be said that the attitude of the Admiralty expressed the broader and more national view. They realized fully the importance of trade, but they were able to weigh its importance fairly in comparison with the other military needs of the war. If too much weight were given to one factor in the problem, other factors must suffer, and the paramount object which the Admiralty always kept in view was that of having a strong force to oppose the main fleets of the enemy. It is true that they did not always take measures to have that force ready at the right place and at the right time; but the doctrine was so well appreciated, so fully absorbed, that from the time of the Dutch wars onward, it was never wholly lost sight of, and England's avoidance of the heresies which affected the navies of France and Spain at this period proved her salvation. While France or Spain confined the employment of their fleets to the defensive operation of the protection of trade, and the King of France drew revenues from French merchants for escorting their ships, England used her navy to her utmost as an offensive military force, acting in conjunction with the armies of her allies, supporting her oversea military expeditions, attacking her enemies wherever they could be found, and at the same time affording such protection to trade beyond that given by the offensive operations, as the exigencies of those operations permitted.

The Admiralty's defence was transmitted to the King, and his decision—or, to be more correct, that of the Privy Council—confirmed this doctrine. The King's reply to the merchants' petition was dated the 31st of December 1741. In it the Lords Commissioners of the Admiralty were ordered to take a proper care that a sufficient number of his Majesty's ships of war be employed to cruise in the Soundings, at or near the approaches to the Channel and in other stations to protect the trade, "this service to be duly and constantly performed as far as may be consistent with the necessary services and operations of war."

This message however by no means contented the merchants. They returned to the charge at once, and in January 1742 another petition was presented, this time by the Lord Mayor and Aldermen of the City of London. Among other things it represented "that at a time when a feeble enemy holds our naval power in derision, and the conduct and distribution of our ships of war are the subject of universal censure," heavy losses were being suffered from the privateers of Spain. Commercial interests, said the petitioners, were disregarded, and those ships which they might reasonably expect "would have been employed in protecting our trade have not contributed either thereto or to the interest or honour of the nation, and that we have seen a powerful and well provided fleet remaining inactive in our ports, or more ingloriously putting to sea without the appearance of any enterprise in view or even the possibility of meeting an enemy worthy of its attention, whilst our trading vessels have been daily exposed in the British Channel and Soundings to the Privateers of a place so inconsiderable as San Sebastian."

This repetition of the complaint was not without its effect. In the following month the Duke of Newcastle gave orders for the disposition of certain ships for trade protection; orders which, although not so far reaching as the merchants desired, gave them some satisfaction and encouraged them to ask for more. These orders laid down that ten ships of the fourth, fifth and sixth rates[1] were immediately to be sent out to cruise in the Channel and Soundings, off Ushant and Cape Clear, and in the Bay of Biscay; and that at least the same number was to be constantly employed upon the protection of trade. Inter alia, a 20-gun ship and a sloop were to be kept cruising off Lisbon, and the same force off Oporto, to protect trade along the coast of Portugal; the captains of these vessels were constantly to consult with the Consuls and keep themselves informed of sailings and other relevant matters; the ships were to be cleaned at Gibraltar, and when possible, at Lisbon.

To this order the Admiralty were able to reply that fifteen ships were already so employed[2]. These ships were stationed as follows:

Between mouth of Channel and Cape Clear	'Bridgewater,' 20; 'Spy' sloop, 8.12
Between Cape Ortegal and Cape Pinas	'Leopard,' 50; 'Dolphin,' 20; 'Port Mahon,' 24
30 to 50 leagues west of Scilly, and as far as Cape Clear	'Newcastle,' 50; 'Tartar,' 20
80 leagues west of Scilly	'Biddeford,' 20
Between Ushant and 50 leagues S.W. of it	'Deal Castle,' 20; 'Hound' sloop, 8.12
In Bristol Channel	'Ruby,' 50
Between Milford and Lundy Island	'Shark' sloop, 8.12
Between Portland and Land's End	'Deptford's' prize, 8.12; 'Success' sloop, 8.6
Convoy between Downs and Portsmouth	'Scipio,' 8.8.

The discontent of the commercial community was too intense to be assuaged by such replies as this. As long as their losses continued, it gave traders little satisfaction to know that this or that number of vessels was employed, and petitions still rained in from representatives of commerce, finally culminating on March 4th in a Resolution in the House of Commons to the following effect:

(1) That notwithstanding the repeated applications of the Merchants for cruisers to be properly stationed for the protection of the trade of this nation

[1] *I.e.* 60-, 50-, 40- and 20-gun ships.
[2] Out letters to Secretary of State, 19th February, 1742.

from the privateers of the enemy, the due and necessary care has not been taken to keep a proper number of his Majesty's ships employed upon that service more especially in and near the Channel and Soundings: for the want of which many ships have been taken by the enemy, some of them of considerable value, to the great loss of many of his Majesty's subjects, the great advantage and encouragement of the enemy, and the dishonour of this nation.

(2) That the detention of the fleet of merchant ships, bound to Portugal, for near twelve months, by the refusal of protections for some time, and the delay of convoys afterwards, gave our rivals in trade an opportunity of introducing new species of their woollen manufactures into Portugal, to the great detriment of this Kingdom.

This resolution led to a Bill being brought forward on the 20th May[1], by the terms of which it was proposed that, between November 1st and December 1st of each year the Admiralty should nominate a sufficient number of vessels to act as cruisers and convoys between England and Cape Finisterre during the succeeding twelve months. These ships were to be earmarked solely for the service of protecting outgoing and homecoming trade in that area, and ships for convoy of trade to distant parts were not to be taken from their number. They were only to be available for the line of battle in case of "great necessity" and even then not beyond Cape Finisterre. A special Commissioner was to be appointed to superintend everything connected with them. If any ships came into harbour for refit this officer was to see that they refitted as quickly as possible and were sent to sea again at once. Rigorous orders for the captains of convoys were proposed, and a close watch was to be kept on the proceedings of the ships, to ensure that they cruised constantly and with diligence. Finally, each ship was to be cleaned at least three times a year, if not oftener.

Remarkable as may appear this intrusion of the legislature into the sphere of the naval executive, the Bill was framed upon the lines of two previous Acts. The first of these, passed in 1695, provided that over and above the ships of war for the line of battle, 43[2] ships were to be employed to cruise in proper stations to protect homecoming and outward trade; but in case of great necessity they might be employed in the line of battle. The second one, dated 1708, was to the same effect though the provisions were rather more extended. The merchants in that war had put forward a series of complaints of insufficient convoys, delays and consequent loss of markets through having to wait for convoy, the want of cruisers in the Channel and Soundings, and the arbitrary proceedings of the King's ships in the matter of impressment. To remedy these grievances this Act provided that "over and above the ships of war for the line of battle and for convoys to

[1] "An Act for the better protecting and securing of the Trade and Navigation of this Kingdom in times of War," *Parliamentary Debates*, 1742.

[2] Viz.: 4 of the 3rd rate, 16 of the 4th, 13 of the 5th, and 10 of the 6th.

distant parts at least 43[1] ships of war be employed as cruisers on proper stations," of which at least nine were to cruise on the N.E. coast of England and three on the N.W. coast. As in the Bill of 1742, these ships could only be employed in the line of battle on this side of Finisterre.

Although the Bill of 1742 was a repetition of that of 1708, except that it did not specify the exact number of ships, it was not carried in Parliament. Lord Winchelsea opposed it with legitimate reasoning on behalf of the Admiralty, shewing that the Board would be fettered in their disposition of ships for other purposes of war and declaring that trade must take its share in common with other interests. The practical result of such a Bill is evident. It would create a second navy, independent of the main force[2]; and the Admiralty, to whom this proposal had been made in the previous year, replied to the King in their memorandum that "we can not take it upon ourselves nor advise your Majesty to bring such an increase of expense upon the public as the creation of so many new employments and other charges" as the execution of such a project would entail. The agitation however bore fruit, as the Admiralty Lists shew. By July the fifteen ships of February had increased to twenty-five, and a more diligent conduct and greater care are to be traced in the Orders and Instructions at this time. The disposition of the cruisers employed on the protection of trade in July was as follows:

Between Ushant and Isle of Wight	'Stirling Castle,' 70
From Lizard to Scilly	'Launceston,' 40
From Dieppe to La Hogue	'Kinsale,' 40
Off Ostend and Dunkirk	'Hastings,' 40
Convoying troops to Flanders	'Liverpool,' 40
Off Belleisle	'Seaford,' 20
Orkneys and Shetlands	'Tartar,' 20
Convoying trade to Elsinore	'Gibraltar,' 20
Cruising in North Sea	'Lyme,' 20
Between St Malo and Isle de Bass	'Success,' 8.6
Isle of Wight to Portland	'Deptford's' prize, 8.10
Ostend to Calais	'Neptune,' 8.10.

Besides these there were twelve other small craft between Beachy Head and Yarmouth, convoying trade in the North Sea, and following up privateers.

This was still far from the ideal of 1708. Only one 3rd-rate and four 5th-rates are included in the force and the number is still far short of the 43 granted at the earlier time. There is no force specially

[1] Viz.: 6 ships of the 3rd rate (70- to 80-gun ships), 20 ships of the 4th rate (60- and 50-gun ships), 13 ships of the 5th rate (40-gun ships) and 4 ships of the 6th rate (20-gun ships).

[2] Cf. the Dutch Directors' ships.

appointed to the north coast of Spain, and it was from the privateers which issued from that part that our trade suffered. But although San Sebastian, Santander and the other ports in North Spain were the principal bases of the privateering industry, the French harbours were also used by the Spanish craft both for shelter and for disposing of their prizes. Information that this was being done appears to have reached England, but there is nothing to shew that any diplomatic action was taken. Small frigates or sloops were sent instead to watch the ports reported to be in the use of the enemy and possibly, an occasional French ship suffered. The instructions to the commanders of vessels so employed gave a fair latitude to them to go beyond their stations in certain circumstances. Thus, a captain ordered "to proceed to sea with H.M. Sloop under your command and cruise between Point Barfleur and Cape la Hogue," in quest of certain privateers reported to be infesting the ports of Cherbourg, la Hogue, Conquet and Barfleur, was also told that "you are at liberty to cruise on any other station where you shall have good intelligence or a probability of meeting the enemy's ships, taking care to return to the above mentioned station when the service for which you left it is performed or that there are no longer hopes of meeting with the enemy, according to the intelligence which had been given to you[1]."

Thus the year 1742 saw a marked increase in the care taken to protect sea-borne commerce since 1739; but for all that the losses were still considerable, and the number of ships employed in cruising was further augmented in 1743. The Straits of Gibraltar, through which a constant volume of trade with the States of Italy and the East was always going, was a peculiarly favourable spot for Spain, who could put out vessels of all sizes, from 24-gun privateers down to row-boats, to attack the passing British merchantmen. In consequence of this the Admiralty sent four small ships[2] expressly for the protection of trade in the Gut. The instructions to the captains of these vessels ran as follows: "You are to put yourself under the command of Captain Crookshanks of the Lowestoffe or the eldest captain of his Majesty's ships that may be cruising about the Straits' mouth, being your senior officer, and follow his directions until you receive orders to the contrary from Vice-Admiral Mathews to whose squadron you are to esteem yourself to belong, and to follow such orders as he shall send you[3]." As a matter of fact it was only in name that these ships were a part of Mathews's squadron, for the Vice-Admiral was specially

[1] Instructions to Captain Elliott, 'Granado' sloop, September 24th, 1742.
[2] 'Lowestoft,' 20; 'Solebay,' 20; 'Saltash' and 'Shark,' 8.12.
[3] Orders and Instructions, March 7th, 1747.

informed that they were placed in the Straits for the protection of trade, and he was powerless to move them. They were within the limits of his command, which extended as far west as St Vincent, but beyond that of discipline he had no powers over them. The Admiralty later in the year endeavoured to make out that they had met Mathews's requests for small ships by appointing these vessels; but this was equivalent to saying that a ship could be in two places at once; for it was on the coasts of Italy and not in the Straits of Gibraltar, that Mathews was wanting small frigates.

Measures were also taken early in this year to deal with the privateers of the Biscay ports. In March the 'Hampshire,' 50, was sent to cruise between Finisterre and Ortegal to protect ships making their landfall at the N.W. Cape, and the 'Biddeford,' 20, 'Bridgewater,' 20, 'Lyme,' 20, and 'Loo' were ordered[1] to cruise between Bilboa and St Jean de Luz, "we having intelligence of large privateers of the enemy being at sea: looking frequently into the ports within your station and using your utmost endeavours to intercept the privateers or other ships of the enemy, and to take or destroy them[2]."

Three Caraccas ships being reported to be coming to San Sebastian, the 'Sutherland,' 70, Captain Pocock, and 'Leopard,' 44, Captain Lord Forrester, were sent to strengthen this squadron for three weeks[3]; and a few light vessels with a backbone of ships were kept cruising in this station till well into the latter part of the summer[4].

The increased number of cruisers and vessels employed in the defence of trade in 1743 and 1744 is shewn best by the accompanying table. Although this slightly anticipates events, it carries the system up to a point at which a still more marked increase took place, and a separate squadron, the Western squadron, was initiated, whose function in the first instance was purely the protection of trade.

Offensive operations against Spanish trade were at the same time in progress; but few Spanish ships were taken in 1742 owing to the

[1] Orders of March 9th, 17th and 30th. 'Loo' was added 8th April.

[2] The clause as to extending the cruise beyond the limits of the station formed a part of the instructions, in terms similar to those already quoted.

[3] Instructions of April 8th and 9th.

[4] 7th June. 'Hampshire' and 'Augusta' to St Jean de Luz to join 'Sutherland,' etc., already cruising there. Intercept five or six Caraccas ships and attack privateers.

30th June. 'Prince Frederick,' 70, Captain Barnett, to cruise from Cape Finisterre to Cape Machichaca for protection of trade. To "have a particular attention to prevent any ships or privateers of the enemy from coming into or going out of the Groyne or Ferrol."

1st July. 'Lyme,' 20 and 'Dolphin,' 20, to the same station under Barnett's orders.

8th July. 'Hampshire' to St Jean de Luz so soon as she is once more ready.

small number of enemy ships at sea. The squadron in the West Indies, still in considerable strength, cruised on the trade routes, and severe British attacks were also made early in 1743 against the ports on the Caraccas coast[1]. These twin measures of passive cruising and an active offensive kept some of the trade within its harbours.

Convoys and cruisers.

Year	Month	Rates							Remarks
		3	4	5	6	Sloops	Smaller vessels	Total	
1743	March	—	3	5	9	4	—	21	
	April	—	3	4	7	6	—	20	
	May	1	10	5	13	7	6	42	11 of these taking King to Holland
	June	1	9	5	11	8	—	34	
	July	3	13	5	8	10	—	41	'Centurion,' first heard of at Canton, included
	Aug.	3	10	5	11	7	1	37	
	Sept.	3	8	4	11	10	1	37	
	Oct.	—	4	3	5	9	—	21	
	Nov.	2	9	4	6	9	—	30	
	Dec.	3	8	4	6	7	—	28	
1744	Jan.	3	7	4	9	7	—	30	
	Feb.	2	4	5	10	10	—	31	4 ships watching Brest included
	March	—	2	3	6	5	—	16	Threat of invasion; all ships assembled in Downs. War declared with France
	April	2	9	8	5	5	—	29	
	May	—	3	5	8	5	—	21	
	June	2	4	4	10	7	—	27	
	July	2	3	6	10	10	3	34	
	Aug.	—	4	7	11	12	6	40	
	Sept.	—	3	5	10	12	6	36	
	Oct.	—	4	6	10	10	6	36	
	Nov.	4	3	9	10	12	6	44	
	Dec.	7	7	10	8	9	6	47	

The effect of the increased numbers of cruisers employed on trade protection cannot be stated with accuracy, as Lloyd's lists, except that for 1741, are missing up to 1749, having been burnt in the fire of 1838. The year 1741 shews 71 British ships taken by the Spaniards. Beatson gives no figures for that year and does not differentiate between the various parts of European waters: he shews 109 as having been taken in Europe in 1742, 136 in 1743 and 84 in 1744.

[1] See *post* chapter XII.

In 1743 the Spanish trade began to sail once more and we have seen that heavy ships were sent off Ortegal and San Sebastian to intercept it. Although these ships were an addition to the force of smaller vessels that was cruising there with the purely defensive object of suppressing the privateers, they were not needed for that purpose and belong more properly to the category of ships employed in the attack of trade.

Two other small divisions concerned with trade attack were sent out in April 1743, the 'Monmouth,' 70, and 'Medway,' 60, under Captain Windham, and the 'Dreadnought,' 60, and 'Deptford,' 60, under Captain Boscawen; the former to cruise off the Canaries and the latter off the Azores. Information had been received that several Spanish ships were on their way home from the West Indies to Spain. Windham's instructions directed him to station one of his ships between Cape Gear and Lancerotto and the other off Teneriffe and Grand Canary; but these stations were not rigidly imposed, for the instructions continued "or in case you shall find that other stations about the said islands will more effectually answer the aforementioned purposes of your cruising, you are to station the said ships accordingly. But if you shall at any time receive such advices of the strength of the enemy as shall make you think it advisable to keep both ships together you are at liberty to do so, and annoy the enemy by land or sea as shall be thought proper, taking care to divide them again to the different stations when you shall judge it necessary no longer to keep them together." If Windham heard that de Torres had sailed for Spain he was to inform the three other captains[1], and consult together as to how they should act, and where it were best to waylay him. But if de Torres when met with should prove too strong to be attacked with prudence "You are nevertheless not to fail to attend him in his passage to Spain and endeavour to lay hold of any favourable opportunities that may happen of cutting off such of his ships as may be lame sailors, or which by any accident may separate from the main body of the squadron." The squadrons were to remain out as long as their provisions would last and then return to Spartel, range along the Spanish and Portuguese coasts as far as Lisbon and bring home the trade from that port. The instructions to Boscawen were of the same tenour, but gave the cruising stations of his two ships as St Mary's and Flores in the Azores.

These divisions sailed on April 25th, 1745, escorting 67 sail of merchant ships. The Spanish homeward-bound trade from Havana however did not sail. Windham's division attacked and destroyed

[1] *I.e.* Medway and Boscawen's division.

the fortifications at Santa Cruz in Gomera Island on May 20th, and took a richly-laden outward-bound ship, a privateer, and three other small craft. The 'Deptford' took a ship from Caraccas. Both divisions returned to England in July.

In the end of June another small division under Captain John Byng, consisting of the 'Captain,' 70, 'Jersey,' 60, 'Biddeford,' 20, was sent to cruise off Belleisle and the Garonne for six weeks, also for the purposes of attacking trade, but did no great service; and in October a similar small squadron under Captain Barnett, 'Prince Frederick,' 70, 'Jersey,' 60, and 'Leopard,' 44, was sent to cruise "off Cape Cantin and thence 50 to 60 leagues to the N.W." Byng, when he returned in September was sent out again with three ships, the 'Captain,' 70, 'Antelope,' 50, and 'Hampshire,' 50, to cruise 18 to 20 leagues west by south of Cape Ortegal.

To sum up the main proceedings of the ships in home waters in 1743: a force of small vessels, occasionally supplemented by ships of the line was employed upon the protection of trade by cruising in certain stations and by direct attack upon the privateers in the neighbourhood of their bases; and small divisions of two or three heavy ships were sent out to cruise to intercept Spanish trade at the principal landfalls—the Canaries, the Azores, the approaches to the Straits of Gibraltar and the northern capes of Spain.

But while the principal duty which fell to the Navy in home waters during the years 1742 and 1743 was concerned with the defence and attack of trade, an eye was kept on the French Atlantic ports and any activity in them produced its effect in England. Towards the end of 1742 the Brest squadron was reported to be fitting out, and rumours that France was about to declare war disturbed the Admiralty at home as well as the Commander-in-Chief in the Mediterranean. Admiral Stewart, who commanded at Portsmouth, was at the same time ordered to complete all the ships there[1] to four months provisions, and informed that the ships at Spithead were to be kept in instant readiness to sail. The suspected intentions of France are illustrated in the instructions sent to the 'Seaford' early in November, at which time a second frigate, the 'Biddeford,' went to reinforce him. These instructions ran: "If you shall discover any considerable squadron of men of war coming out of Brest or any other port of France you are to come away immediately with the 'Seaford' to the first port in

[1] 'St George,' 90; 'Sandwich,' 90; 'Duke,' 90; 'Shrewsbury,' 80; 'Princess Amelia,' 80; 'Princessa,' 70; 'Monmouth,' 70; 'Orford,' 70; 'Stirling Castle,' 70; 'Dreadnought,' 60; 'Hampshire,' 50; 'Lynn,' 40; 'Diamond,' 40; 'Roebuck,' 40; 'Hastings,' 40; 'Scipio' and 'Aetna,' fireships. Orders and Instructions, October 19th, 1742.

England you can reach, and send a particular account of their number to this office by express, and direct Captain Laton in the 'Biddeford' to follow them into the sea, and if they steer their course into the Mediterranean to make the best of his way to Port Mahon or where else you shall hear Vice-Admiral Mathews to be, and inform him of it."

If no intelligence of moment were found at Brest, Rochefort was to be examined and all possible information obtained as to the ships of war in that port; after which the 'Seaford' was to return off Brest and watch the proceedings of the ships there, sending in accounts from time to time.

The winter of 1742 however passed quietly and no move was made from Brest. In April 1743 rumours were again current that France was about to declare war. The British forces which had been sent to Flanders in May 1742, but had done nothing during that year, were at this moment making the move which culminated in Dettingen, and two frigates were again sent to watch the French port, and to learn whether any men-of-war had lately put to sea from thence, and if so whither bound. As the French were now reported to have a squadron ready or nearly ready at Brest, it was proposed to fit out a force in the Channel, and Norris was sent for by the King and asked to take command. The Admiral of the Fleet reminded the King of the circumstances in which he had asked leave to retire in the previous year, but the King repeated his desire, and further gave Sir John permission to express his opinion generally upon naval affairs. This Norris at once did. The first thing, he said, in view of the armament now preparing at Brest, was to assemble a strong force at Spithead: for, if the French should come over with their fleet to St Helens as they might suddenly do "we have not sufficient strength at that place in readiness to oppose, and that would prevent the junction of other [squadrons] and put the country in great consternation: and our squadrons lying in their road near Toulon might be an inducement for them to do it if they found we were not in readiness to receive them[1]." How correctly the old Admiral appreciated the possible action of France was proved by subsequent events.

Norris further told the King that he did not believe we had above ten ships of war at Spithead in a condition for action. The King said that this could not be so, for he had been shewn a list of no less than thirty sail that would soon be ready for service; to which the Admiral bluntly replied that he did not believe the report—a disbelief which was amply justified later. The King thereon directed him to put down in writing what he thought should be done. In accordance with this

[1] *Diary of Sir John Norris.*

order Norris submitted the following question to the Duke of Newcastle, on behalf of the King. "If the squadron at Brest, which according to Lord Waldegrave consists of 35 sail, of which 22 are from 78 to 60 guns, should come into the Channel and place themselves at St Helens, what force is there provided at present to drive them away or even to look them in the face?"

This direct question was put before the Council at its next meeting on April 25th. Lord Winchelsea, in reply on behalf of the Admiralty, read a report from Brest which stated that ten ships were ready, but the remainder were not as yet in a condition for sea, some still being in need of repairs. Reassured by this the Cabinet took no further steps. Nothing was done even to keep a squadron superior to that of the French ready for immediate service. The English fleet remained scattered at the three home ports and, as the preceding narrative has shewn, further broken up into small divisions to attack trade. Norris was thus appointed to a phantom command. His flagship was at the Nore, unready for sea. Some ships were at Spithead, others off the Canary Islands, others at Plymouth, Chatham and the Nore. To crown all, when he asked the Admiralty for a list of the ships in commission, with their stations and muster, so that he could form some idea of the force he would have under his command, it was refused him! Yet at this moment England's own policy was leading straight to war with France. An army under the British King in person was marching against the French in the Palatinate, and a British fleet was lying outside the principal French naval port. It was not to be expected that France would submit tamely to such treatment; nor did her manner of behaving shew her to be unresentful of the British action.

It is certain that when the failures of this war are under consideration the share borne by an Administration which behaves in such a manner must be given full weight.

SAVOY
MILAN
Milan
DAUPHINE
FRANCE
PIEDMONT
LOMBARDY
MANTUA
PARMA
Parma
Placentia
Turin
Modena
MODENA
Coni
Genoa
GENOA
Savona
Vado
Spezia
Massa
LUCCA
Col di Tenda
C. delle Melle
Oneglia
Var R.
Villefranche
Nice
PROVENCE
Marseilles
Toulon
San Tropez
GULF OF LYONS
Iles d'Hieres
Leghorn
Florence
TUSCAN
Elba
CORSICA
Str. of Bonifacio
SARDINIA
Marseilles
Toulon

THE

C E
A D R I A T I C S E A
Ravenna
Forli
Rimini
La Cattolica
Pesaro
Fano
Sinigaglia
Ancona
STATES
OF THE
CHURCH
Foligno
Spoleto
Tiber R.
Rome
N A P L E S
Naples
Brindisi
Var R.
Monaco
Mentone
Nice
S. Soupires B.
Villefranche
Antibes
C. Garoupe
I. Ste Marguerite
C. Roux
San Tropez

)AST

CHAPTER X

REINFORCEMENT OF THE MEDITERRANEAN COMMAND WITH THE DEVELOPMENT OF THE WAR IN ITALY, 1742

The Mediterranean under Mathews, 1742

Admiral Thomas Mathews, when he was appointed to relieve Admiral Haddock, was an officer just over 65 years of age. He had been in the Navy since 1690, and is believed to have served in the battles of Beachy Head and Barfleur[1]. He had commanded ships from 1703 till the peace of Ryswick. In Sir George Byng's expedition to Sicily in 1718 he was captain of the 'Kent,' serving with distinction at the battle of Passaro, and he appears to have possessed the confidence of that distinguished officer, his Commander-in-Chief. For two years he commanded squadrons in the East Indies operating against the pirates, and in 1724 he came ashore and settled down to develop his estate in Wales. In 1736 he was made Commissioner at Chatham, and held that civil appointment up till 1742 when he was sent to the Mediterranean Fleet.

During the time Mathews was Commissioner at Chatham Captain Lestock had been senior officer in the Medway. The acquaintance had not impressed Mathews favourably with the qualifications of his future second in command. "I took the liberty of giving your Grace," he wrote to the Duke of Newcastle on January 3rd, 1744, "my opinion with regard to Mr Lestock before I left England. I did the same to Lord Winchelsea and Lord Carteret," adding, that he need therefore say no more than that Lestock was a cripple and unable to sustain the fatigue which would be involved by an action or the command of the squadron. A campaign in which the senior officer from the beginning entertains this opinion of his principal colleague, is one of which the promises of complete success are not very great.

The naval operations in the Mediterranean in the year 1742 were subordinate entirely to the military operations in the north and middle of Italy. The instructions on which Mathews was to act were not issued by the Admiralty but by the Secretary of State. These will be given at some length as without them it is impossible to appreciate the share of the fleet in the continental war.

[1] *Dictionary of National Biography.*

In the preamble the Admiral was told that his principal objects were to destroy the Spanish ships and embarkations—that is, oversea expeditions,—and the combined fleets of Spain and France wherever they could be met with; and to assist, protect and defend the States and Dominions in Italy belonging to the Queen of Hungary and the Great Duke[1], his Majesty's allies. The instructions continued:

"It must in great measure be left to your discretion how and where to employ your squadron the most effectually for these purposes; his Majesty has however ordered me in a particular manner to recommend to you the procuring constant intelligence of the motions and designs of the French and Spanish Fleets; the want of doing which may possibly have been the occasion of the unfortunate accidents that have already happened; and you will from thence be able to judge whether it will be most advisable for you to attend upon the Spanish and French Fleets (now said to be in the harbour of Toulon) with your whole squadron; or whether you may not (as occasion shall offer) detach part of it to destroy any embarkations that may be at any time carrying on from Barcelona, or to intercept what may be coming from Antibes, where, it is said, the Spanish cavalry, or even some of their infantry too, are to embark; or to go directly with your whole squadron or send part of it to the coast of Italy.

As soon as you shall arrive on the coast of Italy it is His Majesty's pleasure that you should take the first opportunity of acquainting Mr Villettes, the King's Minister at Turin, with it, who will be with the King of Sardinia at the Army; and you will also take some way of informing the General, who shall command the Queen of Hungary's troops in Italy, of your arrival on that coast, and that you are ready to concert with the General that shall command the Queen of Hungary's troops in Italy, and with such person as shall be appointed by the King of Sardinia, in what manner His Majesty's Fleet may be the best employed for the service of the Common Cause:—viz. the protecting or defending the States and Dominions of His Majesty's Allies and the disappointing and defeating the designs of the Spaniards in Italy, and of such powers as may join with them; and if you and the General of the Queen of Hungary's troops and the person appointed by the King of Sardinia shall be of opinion that His Majesty's Fleet can be most usefully employed in making an attempt upon Naples in order to make a diversion of the Neapolitan troops now joined with the Spaniards and acting against the Queen of Hungary, it is His Majesty's pleasure that in that case you should do it: and in order thereto you will take care to be provided from the Admiralty with Bomb Vessels and other necessaries for the execution of such design, without however letting it be known that you have any particular service or place in view.

As His Majesty has always at heart the care and protection of the Trade of his subjects, and as there is a very considerable one constantly carrying on in the Mediterranean and through the Straits, it is the King's Pleasure that you should give the utmost attention to the security of it: and you will take care to execute that part of the directions sent to Mr Haddock by which he is ordered to have a particular attention to the security of the persons and effects of His Majesty's subjects at Leghorn during the continuance of the present troubles in Italy....

If contrary to expectation the Spanish or French squadrons should separately or jointly repass the Straits in order to go to Cadiz or to proceed on any other expedition; and if by that means no naval force or only one much inferior to yours will be left in the Mediterranean, you are in that case to employ his Majesty's squadron under your command in such manner as you may think most for his Majesty's service and for the destruction of the Maritime force of the enemy, by pursuing or following the Spanish fleet, or any other fleet that may be joined

[1] *I.e.* the Duke of Tuscany, husband of Queen Maria Theresa.

with them, wherever they go, taking care however to leave constantly on the coast of Italy such a force as may be sufficient to oppose any naval strength that can be brought against it there and for the defence of the Dominions of his Majesty's Allies in Italy and for the security and protection of the trade of his Majesty's subjects[1]."

These instructions obviously left untouched a most delicate part of the Admiral's mission, and before leaving England Mathews very naturally asked how he was to act in relation to the French. Was he to attack the French and Spanish ships in Toulon harbour if he should find it practicable? And also was he to destroy any French ships coming from Brest and going into Toulon to join the fleet in that port? In reply, the Duke of Newcastle told him, in the presence of Lord Winchelsea and Lord Carteret, that if he found he could effectually attack the combined fleet in Toulon he should do so, and that he should also attack and destroy any number of French ships that he might meet going into any harbour in which the Spanish squadron lay[2]. Further, he was to act in a similar manner towards all Neapolitan ships he should find assisting the Spaniards or acting against the Queen of Hungary. These instructions may be compared with those issued to Sir John Norris, concerning the attitude he was to assume towards French vessels attempting to enter Ferrol in 1740. Notwithstanding the declared neutrality of France, the British Government had now firmly made up its mind to prevent by force any attempt on the part of the French and Spanish squadrons to effect a junction which would place them in a favourable position in which to begin hostilities.

These instructions left nothing to be desired in clearness, decision or elasticity, but the squadron with which they were to be put into execution was less satisfactory. It consisted in June 1742 of twenty-one ships of the line[3], nine 50-gun ships, two of 40, and eleven sloops, bomb-vessels, fireships and an hospital ship, these small craft mounting from 20 to 8 guns. Thus Mathews had altogether 30 ships which he could put in the line of battle, although the 50-gun ships were not considered as regular ships of the line, and are always spoken of separately by the Admirals.

The force that lay in Toulon harbour was superior to this. Seventeen sail of Spanish ships, of which twelve were of the line—60 guns and

[1] The close analogy between the strategy expressed in these instructions and that of the Great War deserves attention.

[2] Newcastle Papers, Add. MS. 32993. These instructions are similar to those given to Nelson when he left for Toulon in 1803: "...however desirable it may be to avoid any measure of hostility against that country [Spain], you are not to suffer any squadron of Spanish ships of war to enter a French port or to form a junction with any squadron of ships or vessels of that, or the Batavian Republic."

[3] Four of 90 guns, four of 80, eight of 70 and five of 60.

upwards—had sailed into the Mediterranean from Cadiz. These had been joined by a French squadron of fifteen heavy ships, of which twelve were of the line. Mathews, therefore, so far as he knew, had to deal with a combined fleet of thirty-two ships of force, of which at least twenty-four were of the line, lying in Toulon harbour. In addition there was the squadron in Carthagena under de la Bene consisting of at least four ships. Over and above these heavy ships there was a considerable force of frigates and smaller craft.

When the position is considered it is evident that the task in front of Mathews was sufficiently formidable. A squadron probably superior, and certainly equal to his own lay in a strongly defended harbour. In the face of this he had to blockade a stretch of coast from Carthagena to Naples; to prevent succours and supplies from getting into the Neapolitan ports; to protect the trade in the Mediterranean and Straits' mouth; and also to detach vessels on any service that the common cause might require, such as the protection of the Austrian, and the attack on the Spanish-Neapolitan, sea communications in the Adriatic. If the enemy brought their whole combined fleet to a state of readiness, Mathews would of necessity require to concentrate every ship of force that was under his command to oppose them; yet while maintaining the blockade he must be able to detach ships to refit and clean at proper intervals. For this he had no margin of reserve allowed. In a paper of 1757 the Board of Admiralty expressed the opinion that a margin of 25 per cent. was necessary for a blockading squadron off Brest, in order to provide sufficiently for the reliefs, refits and cleaning[1], while at a later date an even higher allowance is to be found: "Calculating...upon making up the squadron to 20 ships of the line, upon 12 ships of the line being constantly at sea while the remainder may necessarily be in port for the purpose of repair and refreshing their crews[2]." On this estimate, in order always to be ready to engage the combined French and Spanish squadrons Mathews would require no less than thirty-two sail of the line; though this proportion might be modified by the difference between the Atlantic weather and that of the Gulf of Lyons. As has already been seen, so far from his having anything approaching this number he had only twenty-one sail of the line or, if his 50-gun ships were included he had thirty,—but none of the enemy's twenty-four referred to were of less than 60 guns. The force which would then be available for the cruising and convoy services would be two 40-gun ships and eleven

[1] *The loss of Minorca.* Navy Records Society.

[2] *Blockade of Brest*, vol. I. pp. 174, 175, N.R.S. See also *Barham Papers*, vol. II.; N.R.S. vol. XXXVIII. p. 402, where 32 sail of the line are allowed for a squadron of 24 sail off Brest.

small craft, one of which was a hospital ship; and let it not be lost sight of that these services were those for which the naval force was being maintained in the Mediterranean. It was the direct action of the British cruising ships in exercising command of the intervening waters which was preventing the conquest of Lombardy by the Spaniards or the destruction of British trade in the inland sea.

Thus, this force, even if it had been in the highest trim, would have been less than adequate; but, in fact, its state when Mathews took command was deplorable. Owing to the shortness at which Haddock had been kept, a proportion of his ships—considerably more than 25 per cent.—had not been out of the water for over two years and were in consequence foul, slow, and in need of extensive repair. This was a point on which Mathews could not be silent: "Your Grace will give me leave to say it's not possible for an officer to do the service His Majesty may reasonably expect from him except he is properly supported. I am greatly apprehensive from what I know of the condition of His Majesty's squadron now in the Mediterranean and the very few ships at present designed to reinforce it, that I shall not be able to answer His Majesty's expectations[1]."

In June 1742 the squadron was disposed as follows:

At Villefranche	'Namur,' 90; 'Royal Oak,' 70; 'Romney,' 50; 'Sutherland,' H.S.
Cruising between Marseilles and the east end of Hyères Island under Lestock	'Neptune,' 'Barfleur,' 'Marlborough' (90); 'Lancaster,' 'Princess Caroline,' 'Somerset,' 'Russell' (80); 'Bedford,' 'Essex,' 'Nassau,' 'Ipswich,' 'Hampton Court' (70); 'Plymouth' (60)
Up the Adriatic	'Pembroke,' 60; 'Warwick,' 60; 'Winchelsea,' 20
Between Leghorn, Corsica and Elba	'Rupert,' 60; 'Panther,' 50; 'Winchester,' 50
Between Cape Delle Melle, Corsica and Spezia	'Guernsey,' 50; 'Mary,' galley, 40; 'Guarland's' prize, 8
In San Soupires Bay	'Salisbury,' 50; 'Mercury,' fireship, 20
Between Villefranche and Cape Garoupe (watching Antibes closely)	'Kingston,' 50; 'Oxford,' 50; 'Ann,' galley, 8; 'Duke,' fireship, 20
Off Monaco	'Spence,' 8
Between Mentone and Cape Delle Melle	'Guarland,' 20
Between Barcelona and Majorca	'Rochester,' 50
At Mahon careening	'Folkestone,' 40; 'Buckingham,' 70; 'Dursley,' galley, 20

[1] Mathews to the Duke of Newcastle, March 24th, 1742, S.P. Dom. Naval, P.R.O.

Cruising on Languedoc coast	'Lenox,' 70*
Convoying transports with provisions from Mahon	'Dragon,' 60*
Cruising off St Vincent and Trafalgar	'Dartmouth,' 50
Proceeding with despatches	'Salamander,' bomb

* These two ships formed part of Lestock's squadron, making it up to fifteen sail, a squadron considered sufficient to meet the Spaniards if they should come out alone.

This disposition of the squadron enabled it to control the sea-communications of the Spanish armies, whose situation in the middle of the year was far less happy than it had been when they passed uninterruptedly into Italy.

The preliminary movements of the Spanish forces had all been made with success. The first body of troops, consisting of twenty battalions and seven squadrons of horse under M. de Montémar had disembarked at Orbitello in November. At the same time a Neapolitan army of 12,000 men under the Duke of Castropignano, marching through the Papal States by permission of the Pope, had arrived at Spoleto, where Montémar joined it in January. This combined Bourbon army then moved to the north-eastward across Italy and reached the neighbourhood of Faenza in March. In the meantime the second convoy of sixteen battalions under M. de Casteljar, having flouted Haddock, arrived at Spezia on January 20th. Demanding and receiving permission from the Grand Duke, this army marched through Tuscany, and on February 22nd the good people of Florence had the curious experience of seeing the army of the enemies of their ruler's wife passing with his permission under the walls of his capital.

From Florence Casteljar's troops moved up to join the forces which had preceded them, and by the middle of March an army of over 30,000 men was assembled at Forli, ready to advance into Lombardy. The base of this force was established at Rimini, a well fortified town on the coast, and thither the bulk of its supplies were brought by sea from the Neapolitan ports on the Adriatic. As the army moved to the northward supplies could be brought to the mouth of the Po and carried up the river. Thus, although both Bourbon armies were operating in a theatre remote from their own countries, their line of communications would have been a comparatively short and secure one, if they had continental adversaries only to contend with.

The forces opposing the advance into Lombardy were, in the early months of 1742, an Austrian army of about 11,000 men under General Count Traun in the Milanese, and a Piedmontese army of observation of about 11,000 under Charles Emanuel, King of Sardinia. For a long time the attitude of Sardinia had been doubtful—we have seen how it was regarded in relation to Haddock's failure to stop the Cadiz squadron. Even now there was some mistrust as to the sincerity of the King's intentions. He was, indeed, in a very difficult situation and found it hard to decide as to whither expediency pointed his steps. As a descendant of a granddaughter of Philip II he had claimed the Milanese, but this relationship was only a pretext. His real reason for the claim was his fear as to what would happen to his kingdom in the alternative events of a Bourbon or Hapsburg victory. The crushing of Maria Theresa would leave the Bourbons supreme in Italy. Then, with France pressing him on one side, with another branch of the French ruling family in Lombardy, while yet a third held Naples, the prospects that Sardinia would remain an independent kingdom were slight. Although a Bourbon victory was thus opposed to his interests, he could hardly hope to prevent it as the forces arrayed against the Queen were so formidable. An eventual partition of the Imperial dominions seemed inevitable and by being on the winning side he might secure a share. He had lent therefore a favourable ear to a proposal, made in May 1741, that Prussia should maintain her conquests in Silesia, Glatz and Niesse; Upper Silesia should fall to the King of Poland; Bohemia, the Tyrol and Austria proper to the Elector of Bavaria; and Northern Italy should be divided between the House of Bourbon and himself. There was everything in favour of his joining the Bourbon coalition except the one factor—that he had no guarantee that he would be able to keep his spoil. Paper treaties, as Prince Eugene had truly warned Charles VI and as Europe at that moment was experiencing, were of little avail unsupported by armed force. Sardinia, weak and powerless in comparison with her greedy neighbours, would be a tempting object to them.

The great and unexpected patriotic rising in the Queen of Hungary's own dominions in the latter part of 1741, and the immediate successes which followed, assisted the King to make up his mind. England at the same time was evincing a strong sympathy with the Queen and appeared likely to give active support to her cause. Charles Emanuel decided therefore, temporarily and tentatively, to throw in his lot with Austria. In February 1742 an agreement was entered into between the two countries that they should unite in a defensive alliance to prevent the invasion of Milan, Parma and Placentia by the Spanish and Neapolitan armies that were advancing against those territories.

In pursuance of this convention a Piedmontese army of twenty-two battalions and eighteen squadrons, under the personal command of King Charles Emanuel moved into the Duchy of Parma in March and joined the Austrian forces under Marshal Traun. No movements of importance took place until the beginning of May; but while reinforcements were joining both the Piedmontese and Austrians, none were reaching the Spaniards. Both Hapsburgs and Bourbons tried to induce Venice to throw in her lot with their own sides, but the Republic withstood their solicitations and remained neutral.

In May the Bourbon army advanced towards Bologna, the Sardinians at the same time moving on Modena which they straitly invested; and a further series of bold movements on the part of King Charles Emanuel paralysed the Spanish Commander.

The importance to the Spanish army of their sea-communications with Rimini had not escaped the notice of the King of Sardinia, who requested that a naval force might be sent to act against them. Mathews received this request in the first days of June. On the very next day he detached three ships under Captain Lee of the 'Pembroke' with instructions to intercept any vessels carrying stores or provisions to the Spanish or Neapolitan armies. An immediate success followed. The whole of the Spanish heavy artillery which was about to sail for Rimini from Brindisi was unable to move, and its services were lost to the enemy.

The same fear of compromising Tuscany which had induced the Grand Duke to permit the Spanish troops to march through his Duchy, was also the cause of hampering in some measure, though but a small one, the movements of Lee's squadron. Having no charts of the Adriatic, Lee had opened negociations with the Tuscan Minister for the hire of some pilots from the Duke's galleys. The loan was most definitely refused by the Minister. Such a step, he said, would be most improper; the Spaniards might put a hostile interpretation on the Grand Duke's action and Tuscany would then be exposed to Spain's resentment. When those in whose interests our squadron was operating behaved in such a manner, the difficulty of the British commanders may well be imagined. We can understand the feelings of Lee when he wrote to the Admiral, with reference to this refusal: "I leave to your prudence to consider whether these people are as hearty in our service as we seem to be in theirs."

Lee's stay in the Adriatic was short. He reached Rimini on July 22nd, made some useful captures of Neapolitan vessels with stores, and remained off that part of the coast until August 12th; the Spaniards and their allies then being in full retreat there was no further need for his services, and he rejoined the main squadron at Hyères.

While his sea-communications were thus being threatened by the British navy the Spanish General found his army being far more seriously endangered on land. The reinforcements which had reached the allies enabled the King of Sardinia to detach a considerable body to the southward of the Spanish army, with the result that in July Montémar found himself in danger of being surrounded in the district of Ferrara. Hopes ran high in Turin that this would be brought about. A hurried retreat, however, saved the Spaniards, and they and their Neapolitan allies retired first to Rimini and thence to the borders of the Kingdom of Naples, where they arrived in August[1].

While the Spanish invasion was meeting with this severe and unexpected check in Italy, due in a great measure to British action at sea, strenuous efforts were being made in Spain to reinforce the army or to restore the balance by providing a diversion elsewhere. It had originally been intended that a third army should, like the others, be sent by sea, and shortly after the departure of the second convoy in January this force, consisting of twenty battalions and twenty-eight squadrons of horse was assembled at Barcelona ready for embarkation. But the allied Franco-Spanish fleet, damaged by the bad weather it had experienced in the Gulf of Genoa, had put into Toulon instead of returning to Barcelona. Passage by sea unescorted was impossible, delay was undesirable. It was therefore decided not to wait but to send the army by land to Antibes, where it should be embarked and thence escorted by the fleet to Spezia. Permission to pass through France was requested and obtained, and on March 4th the army set out on its journey. It reached the neighbourhood of Antibes in the middle of May. Here the transports were assembled to carry it to Spezia; but here also was the British Mediterranean squadron, reinforced since Don Navarro and de Court had defied it in December. Still, the allied fleet was superior in numbers; and unless the ships of which it was composed were in no condition to put to sea again it is hard to understand why an endeavour was not made to clear the way and repeat the previous coup. Possibly the ships were not yet refitted after the bad weather they had experienced in February; possibly France did not wish to risk an indecisive engagement with forces so nearly balanced. Whatever the reason, however, it was accepted that the passage by sea was closed.

The alternative of marching into Lombardy from Lower Provence was equally barred. Twelve battalions of Piedmontese troops held the line from Nice to Coni and had it in their power effectually to block the Col di Tenda. Genoa was neutral, and it was not possible to march through the territory of the Republic; though even if such a route could be taken, it would be open to attack from the sea at all

[1] His route was: Rimini, August 9th; la Cattolica, 10th; Fano, 11th; Sinigaglia thence across the Apennines and 18th, Foligno.

parts. Direct aid to Montémar being thus impossible, it was decided to attack and occupy the Duchy of Savoy, the absence of whose King with a large body of troops on the other side of Italy left it exposed.

Such then was the situation with which Mathews had to deal when he assumed command. The Spanish troops had just arrived in Provence and the transports were at Antibes. This he knew; but he did not know by what measures the Spaniards intended to assist Montémar, and not without good reason he expected that they would try to pass the troops by sea. Naturally his first concern on his arrival on the coast was to ascertain how things stood at Toulon, and he had proceeded direct from Minorca for that port. He found however that he could gather but little intelligence, for the enemy's ships were all in the inner harbour and their state of readiness could not be seen from the offing. He therefore passed on to join Lestock at Villefranche where he arrived on May 26th.

It is said that at this first meeting Mathews treated Lestock with great discourtesy, reproving him publicly, in the presence of Sardinian officers, for not communicating with him at Gibraltar by means of a frigate when he arrived on the station[1]. If he did so it was a bad beginning to their service. The Admiral was certainly dissatisfied to find the whole fleet at Villefranche instead of being spread along the coast; not one single ship was cruising—so he reported to the Duke of Newcastle—between Barcelona and Cape Garoupe, and in consequence the Spaniards had been able to land more troops and all their artillery at Marseilles[2]. To remedy this Lestock was directed to return to cruise off Toulon, and he sailed thither with nine ships[3] on June 2nd. Mathews remained at Villefranche[4] in order to get into communication with the Sardinian authorities and inform himself as fully as possible as to the situation.

Ignorant of the decision already made by the Court of Spain to march through Savoy, the Sardinians were convinced the Spaniards intended to make their advance through Genoa, beginning with an attack on Villefranche. They also drew Mathews's attention to the fact that the French garrison of Monaco was being strongly reinforced by troops who were passing by sea from Antibes. Now a strong French garrison at Monaco, of greater force than was necessary for the actual

[1] Beatson, *Naval and Military Memoirs*, vol. I. p. 153.

[2] Mathews to Duke of Newcastle, June 6th, 1742, S.P. Dom. Naval.

[3] 'Neptune,' 'Marlborough,' 'Elizabeth,' 'Russell,' 'Ipswich,' 'Somerset,' 'Lancaster,' 'Bedford' and 'Nassau.'

[4] Villefranche, or Villa franca as it then was called, was at that time a possession of the King of Sardinia.

defence of the place, could only be regarded as a serious threat to Villefranche. If the Spaniards made their direct advance through Nice, these French troops might co-operate with them and attack the defences from the other direction. To prevent such assistance from being given to the enemy was within Mathews's instructions, and accordingly, to stop any further reinforcement, he issued orders to all his cruising vessels to arrest any French vessels carrying troops from Antibes to Monaco. The boats of the fleet, manned and armed, patrolled the coast. On the first day they were out—June 3rd—three polaccas with French soldiers on board were taken and brought into Villefranche harbour. French tartans, laden with timber and plank for Toulon which might be intended for the use of the Spanish squadron, were also taken prize—a somewhat high-handed proceeding as these cargoes were not contraband, being free goods under the treaty with France, nor was there any evidence to shew that their final destination was on board the Spanish ships. These actions drew a strong protest from the Governor of Antibes. Mathews in reply bluntly pointed out that the French were obviously intending to assist the Spaniards by moving troops to Monaco; and though he subsequently agreed to release the soldiers he had taken, he insisted on their return to Antibes, and intimated his fixed intention to allow no more to pass. The possession of Villefranche was of too vital an importance to both the British and their Sardinian allies to permit an unfriendly neutral to establish himself in force in a position which rendered its tenure uncertain.

The importance of Villefranche was two-fold. On land it was the principal barrier to an eastward advance of the Spanish army; at sea it was the base of the fleet, the only place where ships could lie in security and where water and provisions could be obtained.

As early as the 6th of June, less than a fortnight after his arrival, Mathews was urging the Sardinian authorities to strengthen the defences. He himself landed twelve swivel guns from the fleet and a good supply of ammunition, and offered also to land heavy guns and to put 200 marines and 400 soldiers ashore to assist in the defence. But the dilatory methods of his allies made him fear that an attack would be pushed through before the defences were completed, and he therefore held himself in readiness to sail as soon as he should hear the Spanish advance had begun from Antibes, as he could not run the risk of being caught in the harbour of Villefranche where, if bad weather should prevent their sailing at short notice, his ships could be destroyed by land batteries on the surrounding heights.

On June 16th a small but useful service was rendered by one of the squadrons off Cape Garoupe. This squadron[1], under Captain Richard Norris, sighted some Spanish galleys with guns and military stores for the army in Italy leaving the anchorage at St Marguerites. Norris at once chased, and the galleys fled into San Tropez and took refuge under the mole. Norris brought to off the port and sent a message in to the Governor requesting that the enemy's galleys might be denied shelter and sent to sea, a request which was refused. At six in the evening, therefore, Norris prepared to attack them. The 'Kingston' and 'Oxford' sailed up to the mole and anchored close to it, and at 1 A.M. the fireship was sent in with all the boats of the squadron to burn the galleys, covered by the guns of the ships. The action is thus described in the log of the 'Spence':

"At 5 P.M. anchored before San Tropez in 9 fathoms: found riding here H.M. ships 'Kingston,' 'Oxford' and 'Duke,' fireship, and found in the Mould of San Tropez five Spanish galleys which Captain Norris demanded of the Governor. Made a clear sloop and brought a spring on my cable. The Commodore finding me too much exposed to the enemy ordered me to weigh and anchor further out. Weighed and anchored against Mould head in 10 fathoms water. The Commodore and 'Oxford' warp[ed] nearer in and brought springs on their cables. At 2 A.M. the galleys not coming out the 'Duke' fireship was sent in to burn them which was done accordingly by being all burnt without any damage to the French. My Lieutenant was ordered [with] the boats attending the fireship in order to bring off the officers and men belonging to her. Just as the fireship entered the Mould the galleys began to fire as did the Commodore and the rest of the ships and then left off. At 3 my boats returned with two of my men shot in her: at the same time my yawl was shot from the stern and lost with the oars and furniture in her. At 4 A.M. weighed and came to sail...."

A protest was of course lodged by the French for this breach of neutrality, for such it unquestionably was. Norris's action has been severely criticised by modern writers, but it may well be borne in mind that international law was still in a very fluid state, and moreover that the French were deliberately assisting our enemies and giving them the use and shelter of their ports. The main Spanish squadron was lying in safety behind the boom and the fortifications of Toulon; and to criticize Norris's conduct by the light of modern views of neutrality would be wholly wrong. We must consider what the doctrine was at that time, and judge by that; and that it was not looked upon as greatly exceeding the rights of nations at war is shewn by the fact that beyond the local protest made by the Governor of San Tropez nothing further was said about it. Modern fulminations describing it as an unheard of outrage are quite out of keeping with the event. Contemporary opinion judged it differently; Captain Callis of the 'Duke' was given a gold medal by the King.

A few days after this, on June 18th, Mathews held a conference at Villefranche with Villettes, our representative at Turin (who had

[1] 'Kingston,' 50; 'Oxford,' 50; 'Spence,' sloop; 'Duke,' fireship.

arrived the day before in the 'Feversham' from Genoa), de Corbeau, the Sardinian Commandant at Nice, and de Vettes, the Commandant at Villefranche. In discussing the situation Mathews repeated his representations to the Sardinians to take immediate steps to defend Villefranche as it was absolutely necessary, in the interest of the common cause, that the fleet should have a safe anchorage. It was decided in consequence to raise four new batteries, the squadron was to aid in the defences to the approaches to Villefranche by watching the mouth of the River Var, the Piedmontese troops were to line the course of the river, and six hundred troops which were offered by Mathews were to be landed at La Turbie directly the enemy's advance should be reported. At the same time, as Mathews learned there was a great quantity of spars and naval stores in Villefranche which were to have been brought by the French for their squadron at Toulon, he purchased them all himself for the service of the British fleet and embarked them, thus making it impossible for the enemy to use them for the purpose of building a bridge across the Var. Finally, as he learned that the Genoese were preparing magazines of stores and provisions in their territory for the use of the Spaniards, Mathews agreed that he would burn any stores falling into his hands which might be destined to the service of the enemy.

Having made these arrangements with his military colleagues, the Admiral left Villefranche on the 29th of June to examine Toulon, leaving a force of four detachments of soldiers and a number of gunners from the fleet to man the eighteen guns which he had put ashore in the batteries round Montalban. After looking into the Var on his way, he joined Lestock at Hyères on July 2nd, and reconnoitred Toulon. New batteries had everywhere been erected and a boom was across the mouth of the harbour. In his letter to the Duke of Newcastle of July 25th he expressed regret that he had not been sent out earlier to take command—a regret tinged with criticism of what he considered Lestock's inaction. "Had it been my good fortune to have been sent out in time to have taken the command upon me before Rear-Admiral Lestock had appeared off of Toulon, it's my opinion good service might have been done; but from the hour Mr Lestock appeared to this day they have been hard at work in raising batteries and mounting guns...." His verbal instructions, as we have seen, had been to attack the French and Spanish ships in Toulon if he found he could do so effectually, and it may be that such an attack would have been possible. But such a criticism on Lestock as is imputed in his letter has a spice at least of unfairness, for the Rear-Admiral had no such instructions. It was only through Mathews having personally asked the Duke what he was to do if he should find that the enemy lay exposed to attack, that he received these instructions himself.

His conference at Villefranche and his reconnaisance of Toulon had now put the Admiral in a situation to form a judgment of the services that would be demanded of the Mediterranean squadron. His view was that a considerable increase would be required to carry out those services effectually. The first necessity was the constant maintenance of a sufficient force off Antibes to be able at all times to deal with the transports and ships that might come out from that port and from Toulon. His own words best place us in possession of his ideas at this time. After saying that he could not keep the sea summer and winter with all his ships, he pointed out how dangerous it would be to reduce the force off Antibes: "It will be making the Spaniards a voluntary present of so many ships," he says, "and without any probability of preventing it. Toulon is but a day's journey from Antibes, often but twelve hours by sea. They can in that time know the exact strength of the ships I leave on this station, viz. between Cape Rous and Cape Delle Mele; they have 17 sail there, many of them already cleaned, the rest careening, without mentioning the French. My ships all foul. They can double-man as many as will be sufficient to destroy those I leave, and return again into Port before I can possibly have any intelligence of their being at sea; whereas had I been supplied with a few more ships I could have kept some constantly a-refitting and cleaning, by the doing of which I should have had a squadron in good order to have kept the sea in the winter of sufficient strength for the Spaniards, whereas as the case stands I have not dared to part with but one ship at a time[1]." This was not Mathews' first reference to the need of clean ships. On June 6th he had written asking that eight ships, all completely fitted for a winter cruise, should be sent out in September, in order that he would have them available for the winter service, sending home the eight ships most in need of repair. "Such a rotation, spring and fall," he had then written, "will greatly contribute in every respect to his Majesty's service." He had also asked for more sloops. "It is next to an impossibility to intercept any of their small vessels and feluccas who pass from Antibes to Genoa and back again every week, though our boats are out constantly all night, which is a very great fatigue to those ships that have the stations from Cape Rous to Cape Delle Mele[2]." In reply to these applications, which the Duke of Newcastle transmitted to the Admiralty, Mathews was informed that the state of the ships at home would not

[1] Mathews to the Duke of Newcastle, July 25th, 1742, S.P. Dom. Naval.

[2] Letter of June 24th.

permit the request regarding the eight ships to be complied with, but that two ships would be sent. As to the small vessels, said the Duke, they were no less distressed at home for want of them, "though new ships are continually building and though they purchase all the Spanish privateers taken by our cruisers which are fit for his Majesty's service, there being so many stations which require such vessels to curb the insolence of the small privateers and row-boats of the enemy which at this time infest all parts of our Channel[1]."

In reply to this Mathews pointed out that his principal objects were, by his instructions, to destroy the Spanish and French fleets, to prevent the Spanish army under Don Philip from getting into Italy, and to protect and defend the Italian territories of the King of Sardinia and the Queen of Hungary and those of the Grand Duke of Tuscany, besides carrying out any enterprises agreed upon for the common cause. With the force he had he considered it impossible to prevent the Spanish army from passing if it should really desire to do so, since he could not keep all his ships cruising, and no less than all would suffice. He therefore intended to gather his main strength at Hyères, with two or three cruisers out off Toulon to watch the Spanish squadron so that it should not put to sea without his hearing of it. This plan he considered a bad one—a "desperate expedient" he called it—but the best that could be arranged with the forces he had. Hyères therefore was to be his base, and from thence he hoped to be able to control the sea-communications along the coast.

The narrative has been interrupted in order to make Mathews's view of the position clear. We see him entering upon an extensive blockade with the conviction that his forces are inadequate to maintain it effectually; indeed, if the Spaniards had acted with any decision or energy, he would have found it impossible. Much less could he have carried out his instructions if the French had continued to work in the spirit of benevolent neutrality which had enabled the second embarkation of troops to pass into Italy in defiance of Haddock's squadron.

Although his interpretation of the intentions of the enemy was wrong, Mathews cannot be blamed for anticipating that the Allies would act as they had acted before, and make use of the great naval strength that lay in Toulon harbour to further their ends. In requesting that he might be furnished with a squadron of ships of the line sufficient to deal with the main squadron of the Spaniards, and of a sufficiency of frigates to deal with the lesser vessels of all kinds which were assisting

[1] Duke of Newcastle to Mathews, July 29th, 1742.

the army in Italy he was doing no more than common prudence dictated.

Mathews had other preoccupations besides the blockade of the Riviera. His instructions authorised him to take action against Naples whose King had furnished troops to assist the Spaniards[1]. On July 18th the first two[2] of the bomb-vessels promised to him arrived, and a third—the 'Salamander'—on the 22nd. Mathews, on the arrival of the first, at once prepared an expedition to assist the Austrians in North Italy. He ordered Captain William Martin to go to Naples with a squadron[3] of frigates and small vessels, with directions that he was "to bring the King of the two Sicilies to a just sense of his errors in having attacked in conjunction with the Spaniards the Queen of Hungary's territories in Italy." Martin's instructions were to take, sink and burn all vessels belonging to the Two Sicilies laden with any kind of provisions, ammunition or warlike stores, and "to use his utmost to lay the said city in ashes, unless the King of the two Sicilies shall agree forthwith not only to withdraw his troops now acting in conjunction with those of the King of Spain in Italy, but to forbear from giving in future any assistance of what kind soever." He was to send an officer ashore for a "categorical answer," and to direct the said officer to insist that it be made in half an hour. If the King should refuse to comply he was to put his orders in execution at the expiry of that time; after which he was to cruise along the coast destroying all vessels belonging to the King of the Two Sicilies. These orders Mathews first sent to the King of Sardinia and Marshal Traun for their concurrence, in case they should consider them too severe. They agreed to them[4].

Captain William Martin was an officer about 46 years old. He had served in the Mediterranean squadron since it came out under Haddock in 1738, but had not so far had any particular opportunity of distinguishing himself. The abruptness of his proceedings off Naples and

[1] See *ante* p. 198.

[2] 'Terrible' and 'Firedrake.'

[3] 'Ipswich,' 70; 'Panther,' 50; 'Oxford,' 50; 'Feversham,' 40; 'Dursley' galley, 20; 'Guarland's' prize (zebeck); 'Terrible,' 'Firedrake,' 'Salamander' and 'Carcass,' bombs. Martin's instructions were dated July 22nd, 1742.

[4] Writing to Horace Walpole on August 18th Mann says: "Admiral Mathews rides triumphant before Toulon and prevents all stirring.... The Lord of the Mediterranean has sent a considerable detachment to Naples under the command of Captain Martin with a compliment to King Charles as how he wishes his Majesty would withdraw his troops from Lombardy—or else. I really don't know what else, but they say the four bomb vessels that make part of the seventeen have about 6000 shells on board." Mann expected that the operation would force Montémar as well as the Neapolitans to return to Naples. *Dr Doran's "Mann and Manners at the Court of Turin."*

the lack of any nicety of diplomatic manners might lead to the belief that he was a rough Tarpaulin of the Benbow school; but it would appear on the contrary that he was a most polished and finished gentleman. Charnock says of him: "He not only possessed a very considerable degree of classical learning, but spoke the French, Spanish, Italian and German languages with the greatest ease and fluency. In his person he was remarkably handsome, and particularly attentive to his dress, manners and deportment.... When in command he always lived in the greatest splendour, maintaining his rank in the highest style; so that, viewing him in every point, we scarcely know which most to admire, the finished gentleman, the elegant scholar, or the brave Commander." It is well to guard against the impression which might be gathered from Smollett's and Horace Mann's descriptions of the sea-officers whom they met, that all the naval officers of the time

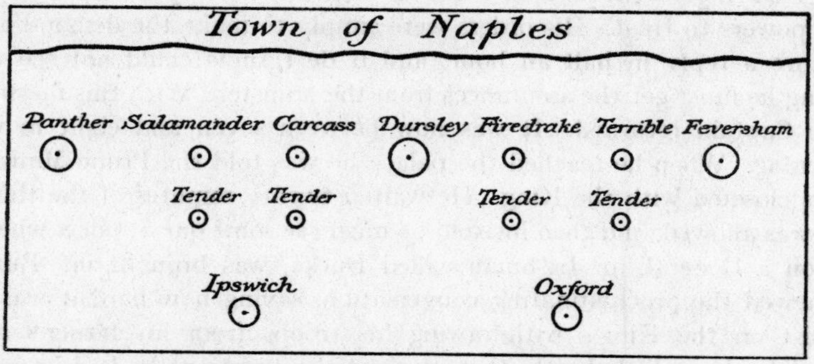

Town of Naples

Panther Salamander Carcass Dursley Firedrake Terrible Feversham

Tender Tender Tender Tender

Ipswich Oxford

Anchorage of Martin's squadron off Naples.

were mere blustering Commodore Trunnions, or of the types described by the "Author of the London-Spy" with much forcible language and breadth of illustration[1].

Martin had only arrived from a cruise on the forenoon of the 22nd. His ship was watered with all imaginable despatch[2] by the 'Bedford' and 'Essex,' and the squadron sailed at 4 P.M. on July 24th. By August 8th he was off Naples where he at once began disposing the bomb-vessels in a line about a cable apart off the town, with the 'Panther,' 'Feversham' and 'Dursley' covering them. The 'Ipswich' and 'Oxford' came to outside, and the bomb-tenders got into position soon after dark. The British Consul, Mr Allen, came on board soon after the squadron anchored, with a message asking whether Martin

[1] *The Wooden World dissected in the Character of a Ship of War: as also the Characters of all the Officers from the Captain to the Common Sailor*, 1706.

[2] *Journal of Captain Martin*, July 22nd, 1742.

came in a friendly manner or not, but as the bombs were not yet in correct position, Martin detained him on board until everything was ready, and then sent him ashore again with Captain Merrick de l'Angle[1] to carry Mathews's message to the King. De l'Angle went to the Palace and there saw the Duke of Montallegra and gave him the message exactly in the terms of Martin's instructions, including the demand for a categorical answer in half an hour. The Duke replied that the King was at Church and would not be back within that time, and protested mightily that he was not to be threatened into compliance with anything that was unreasonable. He spoke about the indignity that was being offered to the King's honour, asked what guarantee he would receive that Naples would not be molested, and finally requested the Captain to go back and represent this to Martin, promising him his answer when he should return.

De l'Angle went on board and saw Martin, who replied that he had no powers to treat. His orders were simply to make the demand and secure a reply in half an hour, and if de l'Angle could not see the King he must get the assurances from the Minister. With this message the Captain returned. It was now between seven and eight in the evening. When he reached the palace he was told the Prime Minister was closeted with the King. He waited twenty minutes of the thirty he was allowed, and then insisted he must see some one at once, whereupon a General, an Irishman called Burke, was brought in. Burke renewed the procrastinating conversation, saying how hard it was to insist on the King's withdrawing his troops from his father's aid. De l'Angle replied shortly that was not the question; he had brought a plain message and wanted a plain answer, and there were only five minutes left in which to give it. The General, replying quaintly: "Yes, the message is plain enough," went off and brought back the Secretary of State at once, who assured de l'Angle that the King agreed to all that was demanded of him. This verbal message was obviously not sufficiently satisfactory and de l'Angle desired it might be put in writing. The Duke demurred to signing anything, and requested him to accept his assurance and carry it to Martin, taking Burke with him. When they arrived on board, Burke again attempted to gain time, asking for guarantees, whereupon Martin told him shortly that he was sent as an Officer to act and not as a Minister to treat. He could give no guarantees, but required his answer. Turning to de l'Angle he said: "Sir, you will go on shore and insist on an answer being given to your message, yes or no, in half an hour, or return without one,

[1] De l'Angle had been detached to Leghorn on the way to get the latest news of Montémar's army. He heard it was then at Rimini.

which I shall look on as a refusal of compliance and put my orders in execution; do you understand me, Sir?" No doubt could now remain in Burke's mind as to what would happen if Martin did not get his answer, and when de l'Angle returned to the palace he received his reply in writing, and took it on board with him. The letter did not wholly satisfy de l'Angle, but as he was promised that he should receive one on the following morning, embracing the points to which he took exception, he accepted it. The letter duly reached Martin next day. It ran thus:

Au Palais. 20 Août 1742.

Monsieur,

Le Roy avait déjà résolu et ordonné que ses troupes qui sont unies à celles d'Espagne, se retirassent pour veiller à la sureté de ses états, et sa Majesté m'ordonne de vous promettre en son Nom, qu'elle va réitérer ses ordres pour que ses troupes rentrent incessamment dans ce Royaume en se retirant de la Romagne, où elles se trouvent à présent, et qu'elle n'aidera ni assistera plus celles d'Espagne en aucune manière dans la présente guerre en Italie.

LE MARQUIS DE SALES[1].

The effect of Mathews's action, so adequately carried out by Martin, was definitely to detach the Neapolitans from their allies and leave Montémar alone with his Spanish army in the Romagna. This depletion of force came at a most opportune moment, for at that very time the Sardinians had been obliged to withdraw a large portion of their own army from their Austrian allies, Don Philip's advance into Savoy[2] constituting so serious a threat to the Duchy that the King of Sardinia, so soon as he heard of it, carried his own troops back to his western frontier; a withdrawal that would have left Traun very inferior to Montémar but for the valuable diversion effected by the British Admiral.

The movement through Savoy relieved the situation on the Riviera; there was now no longer any fear of an advance on Villefranche. Mathews therefore re-embarked his soldiers and sailed for Toulon on the 5th of September to cruise with a strong force off that port, but he left the cannon he had landed at Villefranche, that the defences should still be complete if the Spaniards should alter their minds and return to Antibes. Even if they should do so Mathews was not anxious, for he would be able to have news of their return before they could reach Antibes, and he could send 1000 men from the squadron off Toulon more quickly than the Spanish army could reach Antibes. He considered that in consequence of the impossibility of trusting France

[1] Narrative of Captain de l'Angle, Stowe MS. 256; Martin's letter enclosed in Mathews's of August 16th, 1742, S.P. Dom. Naval; *Log* of 'Ipswich'; Mathews's orders to Martin, July 22nd, S.P. Dom. Naval.

[2] See *ante* p. 206.

no less than twenty sail of the line would be necessary off Toulon; otherwise twelve would have been enough[1]. His intention therefore was to keep this number constantly in a state of readiness at Hyères to deal with the French and Spanish squadrons, which were reported to be ready for sea at 48 hours' notice. He hoped to be able to maintain this force throughout the winter by keeping up a succession of reliefs from the remaining ships of the line. His cruising services would thereby be greatly crippled, but this he could not help.

Besides France, Mathews had Genoa to reckon with. Notwithstanding his notification to her in June, she was again reported to be making magazines, or permitting them to be made in her territories, which would serve a Spanish army. He therefore sent a strong representation to the Government of the Republic on August 29th, through Mr Birtles, our Consul at Genoa, pointing out that their conduct in this matter, and also in endeavouring to seduce the troops of Sardinia and Austria to desert, was such that unless it ceased, it would be necessary for him to "make them still more sensible of their errors." Commodore Martin was ordered to Genoa with instructions to send an officer on shore to "demand of the magistrates to be taken to the magazines and to desire them at once to be burnt"; failing compliance in half an hour, Martin was to "lay their town in ashes," and to complete the business by landing all his men to destroy the magazines, and if opposed, "to repel force by force, and beat the town about their ears" in such way as he considered desirable. This action produced the desired assurance from Genoa that her assistance should cease to be given. All of these measures received the full approbation of the Home Government.

In the meantime Mathews had been made a Plenipotentiary, in accordance with his own request[2]. This appointment has been characterised as a mistake. There were however very good reasons for giving the Commander-in-Chief these extended powers. As the representative of Great Britain's forces in the Italian war it was of great advantage that he should have authority to partake in all the discussions that took place on the plans of campaign. As a seaman his opinion on the possibilities of such functions as were ascribed to the fleet was necessary. A Plenipotentiary unacquainted with the sea, the requirements of the squadron, the demands of its services in many directions, and the questions connected with its administration which affected the number of ships at any moment available for service—such a Plenipotentiary would be less able to express an opinion as to whether the squadron

[1] Mathews to Duke of Newcastle, August 30th, 1742.
[2] Duke of Newcastle to Mathews, July 29th, 1742.

could take part in any particular operation. The similar appointment of Sir George Byng in 1719 had been attended with the happiest results. The successful issue to which the Mediterranean campaign was brought on that occasion was due very largely to the powers extended to the Admiral, which allowed him to interview other Ministers, to persuade them to undertake concerted measures and to act in co-operation with each other. It has been objected that Mathews' duties as Plenipotentiary took him away from the fleet and obliged him to spend his time at Turin. This is not correct. For one thing the number of days he was at Turin might be counted on the fingers of the two hands. For another, as Commander-in-Chief of the fleet his duties extended from Gibraltar to the Adriatic. He needed constantly to be in touch with his military colleagues; and there was no particular reason why he should confine his attentions to Toulon at all times. The squadrons in that harbour were not always ready for sea. When he heard of their readiness he could move thither: but until then he had ample duties to employ him in regulating the operations of the remainder of his ships, which in point of numbers made up over two-thirds of his command. He was however at Hyères with the fleet without intermission for nearly ten months—from September 13th, 1742, to June 26th, 1743.

We have seen that Mathews joined the squadron at Hyères in September in consequence of two causes—the altered line of advance of the Spaniards and the preparations of the allied squadron in Toulon. The withdrawal of his ships and his 600 soldiers from Villefranche drew a letter "full of fright and fears"—in Mathews's words—from Arthur Villettes. The Minister feared that Mathews's absence would be taken advantage of by Don Philip to return to Antibes at once and so push by sea into Italy. Mathews was able to reassure him that from his position at Hyères he could deal with any force coming down to Antibes to embark. The anchorage was not a good one and if it were not for the French, he said, he could have kept half his squadron in a far better bay within sight of Antibes; but circumstances being as they were he must make the best of his position at Hyères.

During September a new element appeared. It was reported that a squadron was fitting out at Brest which was not improbably destined for the Mediterranean. On the last day of the month the Duke of Newcastle warned Mathews that this force was preparing, and gave him additional instructions to meet the situation that might arise in consequence. Beginning by repeating that the Admiral was to keep a sufficient force on the look out for the French and Spanish squadrons in Toulon the Duke continued: "But if the French and Spanish squadrons, or either of them should escape you and get through the Straits, and if you get news that after the French squadron was passed the Straits it is intended to proceed to Brest to join the squadron there, you are to send home as many ships as you can spare, keeping with you in all events a force superior to what France and Spain can bring against you."

This news that he might find the Brest squadron on his back caused a further demand on Mathews' frigate force. He detached the 'Romney,' 50, and two bomb-vessels to act as cruisers in the Straits of Gibraltar and give him timely warning of the enemy's approach, "so as the better to enable me to prevent the conjunction of the two squadrons which if not prevented may prove fatal to the nation." Action by France might undoubtedly be expected at any time, for the main British squadron had now established itself definitely at Hyères Bay, and from that anchorage controlled the movements of all ships going in and out of Marseilles and Toulon. Mathews at this time gave orders to Martin, who was in command of seven ships cruising off Toulon, and Barnett who had another squadron of three off Barcelona, to intercept all stores and provisions going from Spain into any French ports. This gave rise to protests from the Governor of Toulon, who said that if Mathews continued to forbid the entry of provisions to Toulon, he would be constrained to refuse him the conveniences of the harbour of Hyères. Mathews allowed this threat to trouble him not at all. He informed the Duke of Newcastle that he intended to continue to prevent the entry of provisions to Toulon and Marseilles, and that if wood and water were refused him at Hyères, he would reply that he should regard such refusal as a declaration of war and act accordingly. To be driven from Hyères would have made the operations of the British squadron more difficult. A conjunction of the ships from Brest and Toulon could only be prevented, and the defence of Italy secured, by his maintaining this station. The situation was unquestionably galling in the extreme for France, but the attitude she adopted in sheltering the Spanish squadron made it inevitable that consequences inconvenient to her should follow.

The bad weather which came on towards the end of October made Mathews's position precarious. Heavy gales from the north-west and north-north-west rendered it very difficult for Martin to keep his squadron at sea. Losses of spars and sails were continually occurring, and the lack of stores made their replacement a serious question. "Scarce a day," he wrote on October 26th, "but some or other of the squadron come in crippled." Mathews husbanded the ships as much as possible, relieving them continually from the main body at Hyères;

but the service was very trying, and was accentuated by the lack of small ships to keep close watch on the harbour of Toulon. If the Spaniards should abandon their endeavour to pass into Piedmont and return to Antibes Mathews foresaw that his position, without an adequate number of small craft, would be nearly impossible.

The Spanish advance on Piedmont produced the satisfactory result of banishing the last scruples of the King of Sardinia in regard to how he should act, and to a small extent served to ameliorate the position of the squadron in the matter of small craft. The King now became a declared enemy to Spain. He abandoned his purely defensive attitude and moved to attack the Spanish army that was advancing towards Piedmont. At the same time he placed his Sardinian galleys at the disposal of the British Admiral. These craft, though they worked poorly in bad weather, were nevertheless useful, for in calms and light weather, when the small vessels of the enemy crept along in shore and were out of reach of the larger ships of the British fleet, the Sardinian galleys could intercept them.

As the year drew to its close the military campaign became more intense, and the efforts of the Spaniards to effect the junction of their armies in the east and in the west were increased. In the Alps a series of operations left the Spaniards in possession of the whole of Savoy. In the east, where General de Gages had replaced Montémar, the Spanish army, though reinforced by some Neapolitan troops in spite of the King's assurance to Martin, retired northward to Bologna, and the Austrians under Traun fell back to the Panaro. It was now fully anticipated that the next move of de Gages would be on Tuscany. An intercepted letter from Paris, communicated by Horace Mann to Mathews on November 6th, stated that the intentions of the enemy were to wait till the season should oblige the British squadron to leave the coast, when the troops from the west would be embarked on board the combined Toulon and Brest fleets and carried to Spezia. The army under de Gages would at the same time advance, probably to Leghorn; and the desired junction would thus be effected. Magazines were in formation in Tuscany; Neapolitan troops were daily joining the Spaniards.

To deal with this situation Mathews gave orders to capture and burn all Neapolitan craft, and sent a small squadron of four ships to reinforce Captain Peter Osborn[1] in the defence of Leghorn, in case Tuscany were invaded. De Gages's advance, however, did not ma-

[1] Captain of the 'Salisbury.' This ship, sometimes with the 'Folkestone,' had been employed at Leghorn since July, protecting British interests and preventing supplies going through Tuscany to de Gages's army.

terialize. He received some reinforcements from Naples[1], but Traun was able to keep his own numbers up to an equality with the help of troops sent him by the King of Sardinia.

The end of the year saw the armies in both theatres of the Italian war facing each other in winter quarters. The Sardinian army was in Piedmont, the army under Don Philip in Savoy; de Gages was at Imola, Traun on the banks of the Panaro. The main body of the British squadron remained at Hyères, cruising squadrons watched Toulon and Barcelona[2], a small squadron lay at Leghorn, another of two ships was in the Adriatic; watch was being kept on the Straits of Gibraltar; separate vessels were cruising on the coast of Naples and the Papal States[3], in the Straits of Bonifaccio, between Sardinia and the squadron at Hyères, and on services of trade protection. The Franco-Spanish squadrons amounting in all to twenty-eight sail of the line were partly ready for sea in Toulon harbour. The Spanish ships were refitted and rigged but had not bent their sails, the French had about six ships cleaned which were as yet unready, but they were keeping a tight hand on their seamen, none of whom were allowed to leave the Port. Although he had no knowledge of the enemy's intention one thing appeared clear to Mathews—that above all he must keep as many as possible of his ships constantly ready in Hyères. "It is lucky, very lucky," he wrote to the Admiralty, "that there is such a place as Hyères Bay, else I should not have been able to have executed any one part of his Majesty's commands, for to keep the sea was wholly impracticable; and had I been obliged to have retreated to Minorca I could never have answered for it as an officer to have put out to sea with such crippled ships in all respects, the consequence of which might have been fatal to Italy." His perseverance had its reward in the Alps. The threatened return of Don Philip to the coast did not take place, and the invasion of Lombardy through Piedmont was stopped for the time by the strong positions held by the King of Sardinia.

[1] The attitude of the Court of Naples in sending troops after the King's engagement to forbear from doing so, is explained by the fact that Neapolitan troops came under two separate headings. About 10,000 were actually Spanish troops, lent to Don Carlos by the King of Spain. The King of Naples himself maintained about 15,000. The troops that were being sent to de Gages were a portion of the Spanish troops which the King of Naples was under an engagement to restore to Spain.

[2] A large body of vessels laden with provisions, powder, ball, grenades, etc., for the army and provisions for the Spanish ships in Toulon lay in Barcelona for months unable to sail. In letters, January 18th, 1743.

[3] Finding that corn was being imported into the Papal States Mathews ordered his cruisers to stop the importation as "the Pope cannot want it for the use of his own subjects, whatever corn is brought into this country by sea must be for the service of the Spaniards." (Mathews to the Duke of Newcastle, December 22nd, 1742.)

CHAPTER XI

THE MEDITERRANEAN COMMAND (CONTINUED)

THE difficulties with which Mathews had to contend were not confined to defeating the enemy or co-ordinating the efforts of his allies. His relations with the Admiralty were not good. Instead of help he received rebuffs; and the strain of an acrimonious correspondence with the Board concerning his needs must have reacted on his health and his powers of conducting the Mediterranean campaign.

The numerous services the fleet was called upon to perform in connection with the military campaigns left the Admiral very few ships to employ on the protection of trade; and trade in consequence suffered. The winter season was too severe for the Sardinian galleys, and such help as they had given earlier in the year now ceased whenever bad weather came on, so that the Admiral could not depend on their services. To his intense dissatisfaction he found it necessary to employ his 60- and 70-gun ships for cruising. "I am at this instant distressed for small ships," he wrote in December, "...I am forced to use the 70 and 60 gun ships upon stations I would not do had I more ships, especially at this critical time." But to all his appeals for more small craft he received one answer only—that there were no small ships to send him. Nevertheless sententious reproofs were sent for permitting the trade to suffer, and he was advised to hire barcolongos and other small craft to cruise in the Gut of Gibraltar for protection against the privateers. But no men were provided to make up crews for such craft, nor did the suggestion get over the difficulty that many more small frigates were needed on the coast of Italy, for which service barcolongos were quite inadequate.

The letters written by Mathews at this time and the replies sent to him are not pleasant reading, but they explain more clearly than anything else the reason why in this war the navy failed to fulfil the expectations of the country.

In February 1743 Mathews wrote as follows to the Duke of Newcastle: "It will not be in my power to hinder the French and Spanish fleet coming out of Toulon except I totally neglect all other services; for to be able to hinder effectually the combined fleet putting to sea, I must keep my whole strength together: if so, I cannot have any ships on the coast of Italy. Should that be the case, I cannot prevent any embarkations taking place; besides which, I must take leave to acquaint your Grace that it is not possible in the nature of things to keep ships perpetually at sea without their being fitted and careened; being when all together but barely a match for the combined fleet will not admit of my parting with any ships of force, and the want of them being refitted, etc. must inevitably prove in the end the ruin and destruction of this squadron: without I have more ships I dare not part with any: it would be good husbandry and greatly for the service if I had constantly with me a sufficient number of ships to keep two or three constantly a-refitting, or that the great ships were relieved every year. I know but one inconvenience attending my proposition, viz.: the fresh ships being generally sickly whereas the other crews are seasoned men, consequently better able to do their duty[1]." On the day of writing this letter, the disposition of the squadron was as follows:

In Hyères Road	Sixteen of the line, one 50 and two fireships
On Catalonian coast	Three 60's, one 50, one 40
At Minorca refitting	Three of the line, one 50, one 20
On the coast of Italy	Two 50's, one 40, one 20, one galley, one sloop
At Genoa for supplies	One 50, one 20
Between Gibraltar and Malaga	One 50
Off Cape St Vincent[2]	One 50
Off Marseilles	One 70
Between Gibraltar and C. Spartel	Four bomb-vessels (as cruising ships)
Off Majorca	One zebeck

The correspondence on this subject, which continued for some months, places in a clear light the difficulties under which Mathews laboured and the attitude of the Administration towards those difficulties. In March he again wrote twice asking for an increase in his force as the French and Spaniards had now thirty-two sail of the line in Toulon, of which nineteen were ready. He received no reply. In May he wrote asking that some 50-, two 40- and two 20-gun ships might be sent out, as he was being obliged to use 60- and 70-gun ships on services proper for frigates. In answer to this the Admiralty in

[1] Mathews to Duke of Newcastle, February 24th, 1743.

[2] The station out to St Vincent came within the Mediterranean command. Mathews was also responsible for the protection of the trade in the Gut of Gibraltar. "Their Lordships having received strong complaints of the many prizes taken in the Gut by the enemy's small privateers, and charging the captains of his Majesty's frigates and sloops stationed there with great remissness in the performance of their duty...will certainly dismiss them upon the next complaint." Secretary of the Admiralty to Mathews, August 1st, 1743.

June sent one 40, two 20's and two sloops, and proposed to send two 50's in lieu of two 50's which Mathews would be told to send home. On June 4th Mathews again called attention to his want of small ships: "most of the few I have are old and whenever they are sent in to be careened and fitted they are kept so long in port that the service suffers, not having others to send on their stations. On June 13th he wrote once more in the same sense: "Such has been my unhappy condition that I have not been enabled to clean the small ships in eleven months, though they ought never to exceed ten weeks, occasioned for want of ships to relieve them[1]. I am at this instant obliged to employ 70-gun ships where small ships are wanting, and the fire ship, and a bomb vessel with her mortar in, to cruise with them. It is what I cannot in strictness justify. But absolute necessity must be my justification should any unforeseen accident happen to them." Again on June 30th he repeated his statement of his need of more ships of 50 guns and downwards. "Ten sail," he said, "is barely sufficient for the coast of Italy, besides two or three for the Adriatic, two perhaps for the Archipelago, besides all the coast of Catalonia and Provence." All these requests were passed on by the Duke of Newcastle to the Admiralty, who informed the Duke in reply that Mathews had been reinforced with a 40-gun ship and two 20-gun frigates. This reply shewed the economy of truth employed by their Lordships, for the forty had not sailed until June and could not arrive for an indeterminate time; the two small frigates were not a reinforcement but were in replacement of two that had been lost no less than a year before. Mathews, when he received a copy of this letter, was not slow to point out the manner in which the Admiralty evaded the real facts. Writing on July 19th he shewed how untrue the reply was, and strongly represented once more his want of ships. At length, in August, a typical answer was drawn from the Admiralty, who said that Mathews's letters consisted of a "disagreeable repetition of complaints." "If you compare the squadron you had then [*i.e.* when he left England] with that which is now under your command you will find the former inferior both in force and number, tho' the Spanish squadron is fewer and in general in worse condition than at that time both in respect to men, stores and provisions. So that they cannot see any foundation for the constant complaints you have made on that head when it appears that notwithstanding the many other services which call for his Majesty's ships they have not only supported the same strength

[1] It will be recollected (*vide* p. 188 *ante*) that in the proposed Bill for the protection of trade in 1742 it was laid down that the ships should be cleaned *every four months without fail.*

you set out with, but have rather increased it." To the Lords Justices the Admiralty wrote: "Your Excellencies will please to judge by these lists[1] whether the Admiral is not superior in ships of the line of battle to all his Majesty's enemies in those parts, and whether he has not a sufficient number of frigates and small ships to protect the trade and perform other contingent services."

Thus the Admiralty brushed all Mathews's complaints on one side. Because his force was slightly stronger than it had been when he sailed from home eighteen months ago it was big enough. No notice of the entirely changed situation is taken, nor of the fact that before Mathews left he had expressed the opinion that the force was not strong enough effectually to perform the services. His arguments as to the necessity of careening and refitting his ships are ignored; his requests for more small ships, and the need for these above all to be kept cleaned, are not even referred to. There is no doubt that Mathews's complaints were disagreeable; but it is also clear that great difficulty was experienced in supplying him with more ships, large or small, in consequence of the state into which the navy had been allowed to fall and the lack of men. To say that they could not increase his force might have been a correct, though a regrettable, reply. But to say that he had enough ships without taking the pains to examine his complaints in detail was a different matter and less easy to justify. If the Board had consisted of persons whose opinions were entitled to respect from the fact that they were acknowledged authorities on war and on seamanship, it would still have been desirable to support the authority of their names with argument. But they were not. The signatories of the letter were Lord Winchilsea, a politician jobbed into the office of First Commissioner; Lord Baltimore, a man who took some interest in sea-affairs but whose knowledge of the technical requirements affecting the maintenance of ships could only be that of an amateur; John Cokburne, a man who had been a Commissioner for trade in 1716 and a Commissioner of the Admiralty in 1717, but who had no special attainments or experience which entitled him to put aside the Admiral's reasons without discussing them; and Sir George Lee, a lawyer and politician, recently appointed to the Admiralty through the influence of Lord Carteret. These gentlemen failed to appreciate the fact that a ship to be efficient required frequent cleaning, and that while she was on the careen or under refit she was not ready for employment against the enemy; and also that in the services upon which the Mediterranean fleet was employed, a mere counting of the numbers

[1] These were comparative lists of ships of the squadron when Mathews sailed in April 1742 with the squadron he had in August 1743.

of ships of the line was no solution of the strategical situation[1]. Because Mathews had a slight superiority in that class of ship it by no means followed that he had a force suitable for the services of an extensive and continuous blockade.

Besides the Commissioners who thus traversed Mathews's opinions there were also seamen on the Board. But no seaman's name is appended to the letter referred to, nor to many others of the same and later times. The reason for this was the First Commissioner's habitual disregard of the advice of sea-officers. Admiral Cavendish, one of the Commissioners, told Vernon that Lord Winchilsea paid no regard to his advice, or the opinion of those who knew anything of sea affairs, and "that the only method left him of shewing his dislike to the absurd and ridiculous orders which were issued from that Board was to refuse signing them[2]." Mathews, indignant at the Board's reply, went so far as to draw the Duke of Newcastle's attention to the lack of qualifications of his critics at the Admiralty. He quoted how, in July of the preceding year he had been ordered to send home eight ships, but that he had then pointed out how impossible it was to reduce the squadron by so considerable a detachment. "My answer," he said, "gave great offence: yet had I complied with it I should have justly incurred his Majesty's displeasure and convinced the world of my being ignorant of my duty and unworthy of the trust his Majesty has honoured me with. Had some of their Lordships been bred to the sea they would have been better acquainted with discipline and consequently would not have sent an order they would have known not to have been within my power to have complied with, but as is before excepted." The most influential of their Lordships had however not been "bred to the sea," and this, combined with their being kept in ignorance of the instructions under which the Commander-

[1] Mathews's fleet on April 1st, 1743, was as follows, including 4 ships of the line which had not yet reached him:

2nd rates (90-gun ships)	4	5th rates (44-gun ships)	2
3rd rates (80- and 70-gun ships)	18	6th rates (24- and 20-gun ships)	6
4th rates (60- and 50-gun ships)	14	Sloops	3
	—	Zebeck	1
Total ships of the line	36	Bomb-vessels	4
Of which were 50-gun ships	8	Fireships	2
	—		—
Ships of the line proper	28		18
		50-gun ships	8
			—
		Cruising vessels	26

Also a store-ship, a hospital ship and a lighter.

[2] Vernon in the Debate on appointing a Committee of Enquiry into the conduct of the Fleet, April 16th, 1744. *Parliamentary History*, vol. XIII.

in-Chief in the Mediterranean was acting, served to make the conduct of the operations very much of a game of cross purposes.

Notwithstanding the attitude of the Board towards the Admiral, the Mediterranean campaign had been far from unsuccessful. The enemy had made no use of their great fleet locked up in Toulon, no progress had been made by the allied armies, and the conquest of Lombardy was as far off in the end of 1742 as it had been a year before. A great army was wasting its strength in Provence, another was dwindling perceptibly for want of reinforcements in the region of the Panaro. The twin barriers of the Alps and the sea kept these two forces separated, and the Austrian army in Lombardy was still undefeated.

The new campaign opened early in 1743. The Queen of Spain, anxious to bring about a decision without further delay, sent categorical orders to de Gages, who was then in the neighbourhood of Bologna, to attack the Austrian army at once, beginning his advance within three days of receiving the order[1]. Much against his own judgment, based upon his knowledge of the poor condition of his army, de Gages obeyed the orders. He met the Austrians at Campo Santo on Jan. 28—Feb. 8 and fought a bloody but indecisive action. The Austrians held their ground, the Spaniards retired, first to Bologna and later in Neapolitan territory. Thus the first attempt to break through in this theatre was a complete failure.

The news of the battle reached Mathews on the 12th of February at Hyères, where he was lying with seventeen ships. This sudden opening of the campaign on shore was accompanied by reports of considerable preparations at Toulon, where ships were being hastened into readiness, troops were being assembled, defences were being thrown up, and a very high tone was being taken by the local authorities who were boasting that they were soon going to drive the British into the sea. It seemed probable that a move of the combined fleet would shortly follow. Mathews therefore recalled his outlying 50's from Spezia and Leghorn and sent orders to Mahon for all ships refitting to be completed with the utmost despatch and to join him.

Some vessels however he could not recall. He had heavy ships off Gibraltar and Barcelona the former of which were preventing some 3000 seamen from coming from Cadiz to reinforce Don Navarro's crews, while the latter were holding a considerable body of troops at Barcelona. By retaining these minor blockades Mathews was forcing the enemy to march their men by land—a lengthy process in the course of which a large number deserted.

[1] Pajol, *Les Guerres sous Louis XV*, vol. III. p. 23.

There was no radical change in Mathews's instructions. He was given a free hand to take a part in any operations against Naples that might be decided upon by the King of Sardinia and the Austrian General[1], but he found it extremely difficult to persuade his allies to come to a common understanding and to agree to concerted action on a definite plan. Suspicion between the Sardinians and Austrians was rife. Each looked upon any proposal of the other as directed by motives of self interest, and Mathews's position was singularly like that of Sir George Byng in 1719, whose principal labour had been to arrive at a settlement between the representatives of the same two Powers.

Numerous reports had been received in the latter end of 1742 indicating that Don Carlos of Naples was sending troops to help the Spaniards, and the Admiral had communicated with our Consul, Mr Allen, on the subject. Allen reported that the rumours were untrue, but as the Consuls of the other Powers continued to repeat them, and as considerable strengthening of the fortifications of Naples was in progress, Mathews was inclined to believe them. The Neapolitan assistance was of great importance and must be stopped, and an expedition to Naples, which Mathews had discretionary powers to undertake, appeared to him the only means of checking this dangerous movement. He therefore made ready a squadron of six ships and some bomb-vessels which he placed under the orders of Martin, to pay the city a second visit. At the same time he wrote to Villettes and requested him to arrange a meeting with the Sardinian and Hungarian Ministers to discuss the question of combined action against Naples.

Villettes saw M. d'Ormea, the Sardinian Minister, and urged the desirability of striking a blow to prevent Naples from assisting Spain. D'Ormea was averse from taking action. He explained that the Sardinian alliance with the Court of Vienna was only "provisional and defensive," and would not extend to offensive operations, as the King of Sardinia did not wish to involve himself too deeply, or raise up new enemies against himself. "As any attempt you can make on Naples," wrote Villettes after this interview, "must turn to the advantage of the Queen of Hungary, we cannot be too cautious in giving credit to intelligence that comes through the hands of the Generals and Ministers of the Court of Vienna[2]." D'Ormea fully appreciated the value of such a stroke, but he was for temporising and doing nothing until the Neapolitan troops were known to be in

[1] Duke of Newcastle to Mathews, January 18th, 1743.
[2] Villettes to Mathews. Enclosed in Mathews's to the Duke of Newcastle, March 4th, 1743, S.P. Dom. Naval.

motion. Yet it was already quite clear from witnesses uninfluenced by Hungary's interests that the Neapolitans had begun to move and were joining de Gages in the northern parts of the kingdom. Mathews therefore wrote back to Villettes intensely regretting that the Sardinians would not agree to his proposal, and pointing out how necessary it was to have a settled plan of action before a campaign began[1], and how these dilatory methods would spell eventual ruin. Mutual suspicion was at the bottom of this hesitancy; an ineffectual campaign was the result.

A small British military force would on this occasion have been invaluable to bring Naples to a better frame of mind. Mathews had suggested earlier in the year that he should be supplied with a few thousand troops with which to produce a diversion in Spain. He had asked for three or four thousand soldiers, with which, he said, "I could demolish very easily the works before Gibraltar, destroy Malaga and many other places along the coast which perhaps might oblige the King of Spain to recall part of his troops: if my intelligence is true, Cadiz is by no means in a condition to make any great defence." It is interesting to speculate what effect an army of such a size under an able general, or a larger force of eight or ten thousand men as suggested by the Duke of Argyll, acting in conjunction with the fleet, might have produced on the operations in Italy during this war. Such a force might have carried out those expeditions on which Sardinia hesitated to embark from jealousy of Austria; but more important than that, it would have served as a guarantee to Sardinia and would have gone far towards consolidating the alliance, which was still by no means secure, between that kingdom and Austria. Both Spain and France had made overtures to Charles Emanuel during the winter, offering him the possession of the Milanese as the price of his friendship; and Carteret's efforts had been directed towards bringing the Courts of Vienna and Turin[2] to a closer alliance.

The attitude of Genoa was less equivocal. Her inclinations were plainly in favour of Spain and she had already permitted magazines of provisions to be prepared in her territory for the use of the Spanish army. These, as we have seen, Mathews had destroyed. In February it was reported to the Admiral that Genoese seamen were being recruited

[1] Napoleon's saying that "Rien ne réussit à la guerre qu'en conséquence d'un plan bien combiné" is well exemplified in this campaign. (*Quatrième Bulletin*, November 15th, 1808.)

[2] "The King is using his endeavours to bring the Courts of Vienna and Turin to a perfect unison: at least he is in hopes that he will be able to prevent the King of Sardinia from taking part with the enemy." Duke of Newcastle to Mathews, April 26th, 1743.

for the Spanish squadron, and that a Spanish ship of the line had embarked men in the Genoese island of Corsica and carried levies into Italy. In consequence of this Mathews sent Martin in the 'Ipswich,' with the 'Revenge' and 'Ann' galley, to destroy the ship, though she lay under the guns of the Corsican batteries in the neutral harbour of Ajaccio.

Martin sailed from Hyères on the 13th of February and anchored off Ajaccio on the afternoon of the 18th. The ship, the 'San Isidro,' was at anchor in the harbour. Her Captain, a French officer named de Lage, prepared to resist and hauled himself close in to the batteries. Martin weighed at 4 A.M. next day, warped in to her and anchored with a spring on his cable to bring his broadside to bear; the 'Revenge' did the same, about 300 yards from the Spaniard. De Lage boldly opened fire, the British vessels returned it, and in a very short time the 'San Isidro' was in flames. At noon she blew up, and Martin returned to Hyères[1]. The Corsicans, very impatient of Genoese misrule, made no protest. Corsica was, in fact, rather an encumbrance than an advantage to Genoa, and it was reported that the Genoese proposed to sell the island to France or Spain; a rumour which reached Mathews and caused him to write to the Genoese Senate to inform them that in the present state of affairs this sale could not be countenanced by Great Britain.

France, who had now definitely decided to take an active part in assisting Spain to gain her ends in Italy, was occupying herself busily during all these early months of the year in securing her coasts and the port of Toulon from attack by sea. Work on the ships was also proceeding diligently, and a squadron was expected to be shortly fit for service. The French officers were also being actively drilled in tactical exercises. "They have rigged 20 odd long boats," wrote Mathews, "which they propose to send out to teach their young officers how to work a ship and to form a line of battle," and it appeared as though they were at last going to be of some positive assistance to their Spanish friends. The months however went by without their completing their work, but the expectation that they soon would be ready, and the imperfect intelligence that Mathews received as to their exact state, made it impossible for him to relax his vigilance or weaken his force at Hyères. Hence he was unable to carry out those repairs and refits which were so greatly needed in order to keep his squadron fit for the sea.

No movements of any importance, either of fleet or army, took

[1] *Log* of 'Ipswich'; Mathews to the Duke of Newcastle, February 24th, 1743. De Lage was subsequently Chief of Staff to Admiral Navarro.

place during the months preceding June, but the strain on the Admiral was incessant, and in May he was constrained by ill-health to write home asking to be relieved in his command, as he had been indisposed since October, and the long confinement on board ship had told seriously upon his health[1]. The Government were anxious he should not give up the command at this juncture; the Duke of Newcastle however gave him permission to go ashore for his health if it should still be necessary, but desired that he would continue to carry out the duties of the chief command from Villefranche, where he could land and get both exercise and medical treatment. The preliminaries of the Treaty of Worms, which pledged the King of Sardinia to assist in driving the Spaniards out of Italy, were at that moment under discussion, and Mathews was informed that the difficulties attending combined operations would soon be removed; a plan of campaign embracing the armies of Sardinia and Austria and the fleet of England could then be formulated. An attack on Naples would probably be included, but however this might be, that part of the plan relating to the sea would be left, he was told, entirely in his hands, "since your knowledge of the present situation of affairs in the Mediterranean and the constant attention you have shewn to his Majesty's service must have enabled you in the best and most effectual manner to answer his Majesty's expectations upon any great occasion that may arise[2]."

In spite of the permission to go ashore Mathews felt he could not give up his duties while such matters were in the balance; and moreover at this moment trouble with Genoa had again become acute. A quantity of arms and ammunition had been run into the harbour of Genoa in a flotilla of fourteen zebecks which had evaded both the blockading vessels off Barcelona and the frigate 'Kennington' which was watching Genoa. A cautionary letter, implying that this should not have occurred, was written by the Admiral to the captain of the 'Kennington'; the Government of the Republic was also informed that it was not to permit any supplies to pass out of its territory to the Spanish army. The British Consul, Birtles, conveyed this message to the Senate, but as he was unable to obtain from them any assurance that the powder would not be forwarded to its proposed destination, Mathews, leaving Lestock with a strong squadron at Hyères, proceeded himself to Genoa with six ships of the line and three bomb-vessels to enforce his demands. Deputies came on board to see him directly he arrived. They explained how helpless they were in the matter, and how completely they were under the thumb of Spain, but "I cut

[1] Mathews to the Duke of Newcastle, May 22nd, 1743.
[2] Duke of Newcastle to Mathews, June 17th, 1743.

the matter short," said Mathews, "by telling them I had no time to spare and that I was determined the Spaniards should not have the use of the cannon, powder, etc., during the present war in Italy." He gave them thirty hours in which to make up their minds, and while they were doing so he moored his ships and bomb-vessels to cover the town. The Deputies first proposed that the zebecks should be allowed to return to Spain, but to this Mathews would by no means agree. He had one demand and one only to make, namely, that the guns, stores and ammunition should be lodged in the Castle of Bonifaccio in Corsica, there to remain until the end of the war. As the Deputies demurred to this, he said he should take the Spanish vessels out from the Mole and destroy them. In the face of the Admiral's determination, and the force with which his proposals were backed, the Deputies consented. His point being thus fully gained Mathews left two ships to see the transportation and deposit of the stores properly carried out, and returned himself to Hyères.

It was now the end of June. The situation was increasing in seriousness each day, as it became more certain that France was about to join Spain and to declare war with England, for the battle of Dettingen, fought on June 27th, was bound to increase French animosity, while the continued presence and arbitrary acts of the British Mediterranean squadron could not fail to be exasperating to France. Although the Treaty of Worms was approaching completion, Sardinia and Austria were far from being yet in agreement, and indeed so hostile to each other did they appear to Mathews that on the 6th of July he wrote asking for instructions as to how he should act if the King of Sardinia should join the Spaniards. Finally, the one great advocate of peace was dead, and a man of different sentiments held the reins of power in France. When Cardinal Fleury died in January 1743 his place had been taken by Cardinal Tencin, an ecclesiastic known to be devoted to the Stuart cause, and believed to be in active communication with the Pretender and to have promised him assistance.

With such great events impending as must follow the declaration of war by France Mathews naturally was disinclined to abandon his post. Greatly, however, as he wished to remain with the fleet, his health made it impossible for him to do so. For thirty-eight weeks he had not been out of his ship, and he now found it absolutely necessary to remain at Villefranche and endeavour to recover his health. He therefore went ashore, but not to rest. Once more he tried to obtain a conference of the Allied Powers, but until he could be sure of Sardinia's agreement to the proposed terms of the Treaty of Worms, he could make no arrangements. The difficulty of the position may be easily imagined. His instructions were to protect the dominions of Sardinia, Tuscany and Hungary against the Spaniards, and, if the French joined, against them also. While the French shewed every sign of preparing to take part by land and sea, it seemed possible that Sardinia would desert the cause of the Allies and also join the Spaniards. If a blow were successfully struck by the French army on the Rhine it appeared certain that their forces in Dauphiné would be able to join the Spaniards and push into Italy. Placed as they were they might move up to Savoy or down to Nice, and as it was impossible to predict their line of advance, or to tell whether Sardinia would be fighting for or against them, Mathews could not make any plans for the employment of the fleet. One thing seemed certain: he must keep all his large ships as much concentrated as the various services would admit, and as many small ships as possible constantly ready to work along the coast of Provence and Genoa in case of a military advance in that part. To effect this concentration he was obliged to withdraw ships from other services; one of the immediate effects was that trade suffered considerable losses, losses which drew remonstrances from the Admiralty and further recommendations to protect commerce more effectively.

The disposition of the squadron in September was as follows:

At Hyères	18 ships of the line: of these 8 were acting as cruisers between Marseilles, Porquerolles, Levant Island and Cape Roux
At Villefranche	4 of the line with Mathews, assisting in the preparation of the defence of Villefranche
Off the mouth of the Var	1 50-gun ship
About Elba and Civita Vecchia	1 50, 1 40, 1 20 and 2 bombs, cruising to prevent supplies going to the Spanish army through the Papal States and Naples
Cleaning at Minorca	4 of the line and 1 50
Off St Vincent	1 50
Off Gibraltar	1 50
Off Cape de Gat	1 50
In the Straits' mouth	5 small vessels
Between Toulon and Ventimiglia	4 small vessels
In the Archipelago	1 small frigate
Convoying stores from Genoa	1 small frigate
On special cruising service	2 50's

In the beginning of September Sardinia's attitude was at length defined by the Treaty of Worms, to which, after long negociation and with great distaste, the Queen of Hungary agreed. By this treaty Charles Emanuel recognised the Pragmatic Sanction, ceded all his rights in the Milanese to Maria Theresa, and bound himself to defend Lombardy with 40,000 foot and 5000 cavalry. In return for this the Queen agreed to assist the defence of Lombardy with 30,000 men, and to cede the Upper Novarese, Piacenza and some territory on the left bank of the Nura to the King; she abandoned all her claims to Finale, in taking possession of which the Sardinians were to have the assistance of the British squadron. The supreme command of the allied army was placed in the hands of the King of Sardinia, who was to regulate all military operations in concert with the Queen of Hungary. The clauses of the Treaty which referred to Great Britain's obligations committed her to pay a yearly subsidy of £200,000 and to maintain a fleet in the Mediterranean. The clause relating to the fleet and the orders it would receive ran as follows:

"*Article VII*. Aussi longtemps qu'il sera nécessaire de favoriser et de seconder les opérations et aussi longtemps que le danger des alliés de l'Italie le demandera, Sa Majesté le Roi de la Grande Bretagne s'engage de tenir dans la Mediterranée une forte Escadre de ses vaisseaux de guerre, des galiotes à bombes et des brulots, dont les Amiraux et les officers commandants auront ordre de concerter constamment et régulièrement avec Sa Majesté le Roi de Sardaigne ou avec ses Généraux, ou avec ceux de la Reine de Hongrie qui seront les plus à portée, pour les mesures les plus convenables pour le service de la Cause Commune."

While this treaty brought Sardinia into line and facilitated joint action on the part of the Allies, it had an opposite effect on Genoa, who saw her own possessions in Finale being transferred to Sardinia without consultation or compensation. Her relations with Spain, which had hitherto been merely benevolent, now became more actively friendly; and she prepared to dispute the possession of Finale with an army of 10,000 men. France and Spain at the same time concluded a counter-treaty at Fontainebleau by the terms of which France agreed to declare war upon Sardinia, to assist Spain to recover Minorca and Gibraltar, to recognise Don Philip's claim to the Milanese, Parma and Placentia, and to declare war upon Austria and England[1]. On the signing of this treaty a contingent of eleven French regiments which had already been assembled in Dauphiné under M. de Marcieu proceeded to Briançon to join the Spanish general, the Marquis de la Mina.

The relations with Sardinia being now satisfactorily established, every effort was made to strengthen the defences of Villefranche in case the Franco-Spanish armies should advance in that direction. The King of Sardinia arranged to hurry reinforcements to that part in such a case, and Mathews, besides lending 54 guns from his squadron

[1] October 14th, 1743. The clauses relating to declaring war on Austria and England were of a later date.

to strengthen the batteries, kept a landing party of 800 soldiers ready to put ashore at the shortest notice. He also furnished transports and made all preparations for a retirement of the garrison to Vado Bay in the case of the capture of Villefranche by the enemy.

The enemy's advance was however made through the Alps, positive orders having been sent from the Spanish Court to march by the route of Monte Viso. The movement began on September 13th, and a week later the enemy was on Piedmontese soil. But the positions held by the Sardinian army were so strong and so well defended that the enemy were unable to pierce them, and, after a ten days' campaign in which the Franco-Spanish army lost over 8000 men, many guns and much moral, they retired into Savoy and Dauphiné. The first round had been fought and had resulted in the discomfiture of the enemy. Lombardy was now safe for the winter, provided the British squadron could continue to hold the route of the sea.

On the other side of Italy things had been quiet from the time of the battle of Campo Santo until September. The enemy had retired to Bologna unmolested; for this Marshal Traun was censured and superseded in his command by Prince Lobkowitz. The new Austrian Commander arrived at Carpi on September 5th with a reinforcement of nine battalions, and proceeded immediately to infuse a more energetic spirit into the campaign. Advancing rapidly against de Gages he drove him from Bologna to Fano. Once more the campaign was upon the Adriatic littoral. The need for using the sea was felt immediately and Lobkowitz therefore wrote to Mathews asking that the frigates which had been in the Adriatic, but had been withdrawn, might be replaced as soon as possible. The 'Seaford' and 'Dartmouth' were at once sent; their removal from the other services was an appreciable drain, and Mathews, writing on October 30th, again took the opportunity of pointing out his need of more vessels of the frigate class. "There must be ships," he wrote, "constantly in the Adriatic and cruising from Cape del Colonne and Otranto while the two armies in Italy continue in their present motions and situation, not only to prevent the enemy's receiving any succours or provisions by sea, but also Prince Lobkowitz being distressed for want of his provisions and thereby losing the fruit of his glorious labours and endeavours to destroy M. de Gages' army, or drive them to the necessity of taking shelter in the Kingdom of Naples which the Marquis d'Ormea writ me the 6th November N.S. is generally thought they will do. In that case many more proper ships will be absolutely necessary. Sixty or seventy gun ships are by no means proper for these coasts at this season of the year, as I full well know by experience."

There were indeed many services calling for the ships of the navy. At this very moment the Pope was permitting cannon and stores for the use of the Spaniards to be landed at Civita Vecchia, an unneutral action with which Mathews was not slow to deal. He sent Captain Powlett with the 'Oxford' and 'Kennington' to cruise in the neighbourhood of Orbitello with instructions to destroy all the galleys in the harbour. It had first been his intention to bombard Civita Vecchia itself, but in deference to the request of the King of Sardinia for a less severe punishment he contented himself with this stroke.

The signing of the Treaty of Fontainebleau was still unknown in England, but every day was bringing about a greater tension with France. The British cruisers were making prizes of all vessels, French or Spanish, intercepted carrying military stores into Antibes. M. Mirepoix protested against this treatment of a neutral power, but Mathews, in reply to the French Minister's objection, pointed out with some pertinence that in acting as he did he was only performing the duties of an auxiliary to the King of Sardinia whose dominions he was assisting to protect, in the same manner as the French themselves were acting as auxiliaries to the King of Spain whose forces were attacking the Sardinian Kingdom.

Notwithstanding his requests for more vessels for cruising, no reinforcements were sent to him. There are indications that a wretched jealousy may have been a factor in the friction between himself and the Admiralty. The military direction of the Mediterranean fleet came immediately under the Secretary of State, who, as a clerk of the King, transmitted his Majesty's orders. Thus on all questions concerning the operations of the war, the Admiral communicated direct with the Duke of Newcastle; and he was led to believe that the Admiralty took no notice of his complaints owing to his not being under their Lordships' immediate command in regard to his military operations[1]. In the end of the year the Admiralty wrote in the following terms: "Though their Lordships think it incumbent on them to keep up the strength of Mr Mathews' squadron by supplies of fresh ships in the room of those disabled, they cannot take upon them to send out an additional force of ships to him without express direction, as they are not informed of the reasons or necessity for it[2]." There lies the whole petty quarrel. The Admiralty declined to give the Commander-in-Chief the ships he so greatly needed for the services he had to carry out, because they had not been consulted as to the military requirements. The excuse

[1] Mathews to Duke of Newcastle, June 13th, 1743; September 21st, 1743.

[2] Secretary of the Admiralty to Mathews, October 26th, 1743. Yet Mathews had written *seventeen letters* giving reasons.

was also made that Mathews had not informed the Admiralty as to the strength and fitness of the French and Spanish squadrons in Toulon[1]. This, however, was an incorrect statement, for Mathews had kept them informed in nearly every despatch of the disposition of his ships and the requirements of the situation. In addition, all those parts of Mathews's letters to the Duke of Newcastle relating to his needs were transmitted by the Secretary of State to the Board. The plea that the Admiralty were not acquainted with his requirements is wholly insufficient to justify their failure to meet his wants; some other motive was at work.

In the end of November the Admiral received information that the French authorities in Toulon had orders to fit out all the ships in port, numbering twenty-one vessels. The Spaniards had at the same time eighteen ships, so that the situation was now one in which it was necessary for the British ships to be kept together to meet any move which might be made by the combined fleet[2]. Just before receiving this letter the Duke had written another set of instructions, outlining the conduct Mathews was to follow, but remarkable for nothing except its reiteration of earlier orders. Mathews was again told to concert with the Powers appointed in what manner the fleet should be employed for the execution of the Treaty of Worms. He was to keep himself informed as to how soon the ships at Toulon would be ready, and ascertain what they were expected to do: whether in particular, any attempt on Mahon or Gibraltar were likely, in which case he was to take steps for the securing of those places. "The war," wrote the Duke, "in all probability will now be carried on with great vigour in Italy; and as his Majesty's fleet must have a material share in it, it will require great conduct and attention how that may be most usefully employed." Letters from Paris of November 12–23 confirmed the reports "that all the men of war in French ports are to get ready for sea by a date in January: it is not doubted that this is done at the instigation of the Court of Spain to oblige Mr Mathews to retire from the coast of France in hopes to carry and convoy troops to Italy[3]"; about which the Duke remarked: "His Majesty doubts not you will be able to disappoint their designs." The Duke this time backed up his instructions with some practical help and gave orders for a reinforcement of three ships[4] to sail with the first fair wind, and

[1] Out letters. December 9th, 1743.

[2] An extract from this letter is given *post* p. 238. The letter reached the Duke on December 14th.

[3] Extract of a letter from Paris enclosed in Duke of Newcastle's letter of December 13th, 1743.

[4] 'Burford,' 70; 'Boyne,' 80, and 'Chichester,' 80.

another, consisting of two large ships and a frigate, as soon as they could be ready. Some steps to give Mathews the help he needed were thus at last taken, but considering how long reinforcements had been in reaching Haddock, there was no small danger of these not arriving until after the crisis was over.

This despatch had not been received at the end of November when the Admiral, ill in health and weary of the way in which his proposals had been received[1] again asked leave to come home. The mere statements of his wants appeared, he said, to be regarded as a crime. Permission was given; but the Duke hoped he would not leave unless his health absolutely demanded it[2]. Everything pointed to renewed attempts on the part of Spain to force her army into Italy, and to the probability of France taking an active part in the war with her Atlantic squadrons. On the first of these points the Duke was under no misapprehension as to what the Mediterranean fleet should do. "You know," he said, "how necessary it is in all events to prevent the Spaniards from pouring more troops into Italy: and nothing could so effectually tend to the disappointing of the views of his Majesty's enemies in Italy as the destruction of the combined fleet at Toulon." He then added such information as he had as to the second point. The Brest and Rochefort squadrons were preparing for sea and it was reported that seven ships from Brest and five from Rochefort were about to sail, or might even already have done so. "It has been conjectured," said the Duke, "that the real destination of the ships that are to be sent from Brest is to place themselves in the Straits of Gibraltar in order to prevent any reinforcement of ships, or any supplies of provisions, etc., from being sent from hence.... I am also authorised by my Lord Winchilsea to assure you that you shall have further reinforcements according to the advices he shall have of the number of ships that sail from Brest and Rochefort, and such as shall be sufficient to oppose any force they shall meet with in their passage to you, and as may enable you to resist the combined fleets of France and Spain now at Toulon, even tho' they should be joined by any ships from Brest." And he concluded by observing that it was "very material that any such junction should be prevented." He reiterated the instructions given to Haddock on November 11th, 1741, to intercept any French men-of-war coming from any of the Western ports and going to Toulon.

[1] "I am sorry to see the pains their Lordships have taken to throw dirt so thick at me, but I have the pleasure of knowing where it must of necessity stick at last." Mathews to Secretary of Admiralty, November 25th, 1743.

[2] Duke of Newcastle to Mathews, December 23rd, 1743.

Thus every element in the situation indicated the importance of the Mediterranean command at this moment, and it is obvious that no one who felt himself capable of carrying out the duties, could relinquish it at such a critical time. Mathews's position must have been doubly difficult, inasmuch as the man on whom the command would devolve was one whom he considered unfit for the responsibility. Not improbably his personal feelings towards Lestock went some way towards influencing Mathews, but this can be surmise only. At all events he decided to retain the command, and prepared to take the first opportunity of going to Turin to meet Villettes and the representatives of the allied Powers in conference; Villettes had begged him to do this in an express letter of November 26th.

On December 8th therefore Mathews landed at Villefranche on his way to Turin. He left Lestock at Hyères with a force of as many ships as he had been able to muster[1]; but the fleet was still greatly scattered. The following list shews how the outlying ships were employed on December 19th, the remainder of the fleet being either with Lestock or at Villefranche:

At Minorca refitting and cleaning	'Marlborough,' 90; 'Princessa,' 80; 'Elizabeth,' 70; 'Kingston,' 50; 'Norwich,' 50; 'Winchelsea,' 20; 'Folkestone,' 40 (unserviceable); 'Berwick,' 60 (with 200 men sick)
Cruising off Malaga, Cape St Vincent and Lisbon	'Dragon,' 60; 'Newcastle,' 50; 'Guernsey,' 50
In the Adriatic	'Dartmouth,' 50; 'Seaford,' 20
On the coast of Calabria	'Feversham,' 40
On the coast of Romagna	'Oxford[2],' 50; 'Kennington,' 20
At Genoa	'Salisbury[2],' 50

The situation at the end of the year as it appeared to Mathews cannot be better shewn than by an extract from a letter written a fortnight before he went to Turin. The Admiral's views not only of the position in the Mediterranean but also of the way in which he was being treated by the Admiralty are therein set out most clearly:

"My last letter to your Grace was dated the 13th instant. I only hinted at some particular things which I judged absolutely necessary to be for his Majesty's service, but as I send this to your Grace through Germany I shall speak plainly.

I have received certain intelligence that orders are come to Toulon to fit out with the utmost expedition all the ships great and small in that port; their number is twenty-one. One of the persons I have had for a considerable time in pay was about ten days since seized and carried to prison, but after searching his person and house and not finding one scrip of paper by which he might be discovered he was after twenty four hours confinement released, but I have reason to believe is narrowly watched in regard he has quitted the Spanish service in which he was a master of one of their ships, on purpose to serve me.

[1] See Mathews's letter to Duke of Newcastle, November 23rd, 1743.

[2] These ships were being called in by express letter.

...Mr Villettes writes me that he believes a meeting[1] will be agreed to soon. I shall therefore continue here[2] some few days longer, but I shall send away tomorrow morning all the great ships to prevent Mr Lestock's being surprised. When they join him he will have the ships in the enclosed list which I am of opinion are sufficient at present for any number the French can put to sea in three weeks. I daily expect ships from Minorca but I am apprehensive that it will not be prudent to send any more ships there to refit, etc. I shall govern myself in that agreeable to such intelligence as I shall be able to get, having sent another person for fear the former should be refused admission or should be detained. They talk confidently that they are to be joined by twelve sail from Brest. My man writ me that he had read a letter from Brest to one of the Master-Builders at Toulon giving him an account that two were actually sailed.

I must now take leave to state facts, at least those I judge must be such in a little time. The French will have twenty-one sail at Toulon only. The Spaniards have eighteen great and small and I take it for granted that the scheme I formerly mentioned to your Grace was talked of at Toulon will now take place, viz.: the French to take some of the Spanish ships and to man them, without which, it is my opinion, that all the Spanish ships cannot possibly get manned. And the strength that I can depend upon having with me against January is twenty-eight, fifty gun ships included, and they all to be in a condition to keep the sea; and then all other parts of his Majesty's commands must be totally neglected, by the Spaniards and French having the whole coast of Italy open to them to carry by small embarkations recruits into Italy. That is not all, for when the conjunct fleet is kept ready for the sea, how shall I, or the person his Majesty shall judge proper to relieve me, be able to assist at the reduction of the Kingdom of Naples? To divide the fleet will be imprudent and he would justly deserve to be censured as no officer that should do so. Therefore one of these two things must inevitably happen, viz., either the conquest of Naples must be postponed if the assistance of the fleet should be absolutely necessary (as it is generally thought to be); or the conjunct fleet must be left at liberty to go and do what they please. In the latter case they may transport what troops they please to Port Especia [Spezzia] and thereby endanger the liberty of Italy, and after all if joined by any number of ships from Brest, may come and make me (or as I have said before, whoever may be appointed to command) a visit, the consequence of which is submitted to your Grace.

I flatter myself that I have fairly and honourably stated the facts in regard to the present situation of affairs without magnifying the strength of the conjunct fleet. The French ships will be in good order and well manned. The Spanish ships are generally speaking in bad order and ill-manned, and except they should be greatly assisted by France (as I have said before) they will be incapable of putting to sea. They have eight sail in sufficient order and these they can man to put to sea for a short expedition. That number is full sufficient to prevent his Majesty's commanding officer to divide his present strength, and I think it my indispensable duty to acquaint his Majesty in order to undertake the attacking Naples by sea in regard they have put it in the best posture of defence it possibly can be; having been at work in raising batteries all along the coast, and fortifying the Mole heads ever since Captain Martin was there, it will require at least fourteen sail of capital ships besides frigates to protect the bombs. With a less number, according to the account given me of the additional works made, I should be unwilling to undertake the expedition, because I judge that with a less force I should not have any probability of success. I send this by express messenger and must entreat your Grace to lay what I have now the honour of writing before his Majesty for his consideration and farther instructions before the expedition takes place.

As to his Majesty's commands in regard to Finale, I flatter myself that a few of the small ships will be sufficient for that service, though Consul Birtles acquaints

[1] *I.e.* a meeting with the allied commanders, to discuss a plan of campaign.
[2] Villefranche.

me in his letter of the 30th inst. N.S. that the Republic[1] has got and is getting together 10,000 men and that they are determined to dispute it with the Savoyards, inch by inch; these are his words. Should that be the case I am of opinion that my going with the bombs to Genoa will be the surest method for saving the King of Sardinia's troops, and the most expeditious way of reducing that Republic to reason. I shall therefore propose it to his Sardinian Majesty when his Majesty's commands are to be put into execution.

I sincerely wish the severe reflections the Lords of the Admiralty were pleased to make in their letter of the 1st of August may not soon be retorted upon them, by their being convinced that what I have all along complained of, viz. want of ships to enable me to execute his Majesty's commands, was not without just grounds: which in my humble opinion they cannot justify but by confessing they are unacquainted with the different services to be performed by virtue of his Majesty's commands. And I must take leave to add, that severe manner of writing is grounded upon notorious mistaken facts as will plainly appear to any sea-officer in the list of ships I sent your Grace with my letter of the 30th ultimo, wherein are the dates when ships were detached from me, and when those sent out joined me. By their Lordships' manner of representing things one would imagine that the ships ordered out to me were to join me the very day they received their sailing orders, when God knows I never saw any of them until ten weeks or three months after, and then they were so sickly, and some disabled in their passage out, that they have been useless for a considerable time after, particularly the 'Cambridge,' 'Stirling Castle, 'Newcastle' and 'Nonsuch.' I am not afraid to declare that the discouragement and severe treatment I have constantly met with from their Lordships, not to mention the difficulties I have laboured under, greatly to the prejudice of the service, has not assisted to the bettering of my constitution."

Such was the situation and such the state of mind of the Admiral on the eve of the important events which were about to take place; but before following further the course of the war in the Mediterranean we must return to the West Indies, where the nature of the operations was modified by the development of affairs in Europe.

[1] *I.e.* of Genoa. Finale was to fall to Sardinia, by the Treaty of Worms.

CHAPTER XII

THE WEST INDIES. END OF COLONIAL OFFENSIVE. OCTOBER 1742 TO FEBRUARY 1744

UNDER the British system of colonial defence the naval forces in West Indian and North American waters were practically divided into two categories, the active squadron and the stationed ships. As we have already seen, the latter comprised a number of small craft allocated definitely to the local protection of certain colonies and their trade. They were under the Commander-in-Chief of the Jamaica squadron, but at the same time he never interfered with them nor called them away from the waters in which their particular duties lay, except upon pressing occasions. The main force of the squadron was at Jamaica, since Port Royal was the harbour most suitable as a base of operations against Spain, and from that centre the Commander-in-Chief directed the operations of the ships in all parts of the West Indies. But as the conditions of war changed, and the probabilities of French interference increased, the Leeward Islands which were contiguous to important French possessions received more attention. When the French attitude became more actively hostile a small increase in the number of ships in the Leeward Islands was made, and when in October 1743 it became practically certain that France was about to join Spain, there was a further increase, and the Leeward Islands became a separate station under its own Commander-in-Chief. Thenceforward increments were made to cope with the more powerful squadrons that France was maintaining in those waters.

Sir Chaloner Ogle received his instructions to relieve Admiral Vernon on September 23rd, 1742, and the command was definitely transferred to him on October 19th when Vernon sailed for England. The force to be left on the Jamaica station was laid down in a letter from the Duke of Newcastle dated August 5th, 1742, part of which ran as follows: "Mr Vernon is directed, in determining the number of ships to be left with you, to consider the strength that de Torres has with him at the Havana, if he is still there; and in all events to take care that the force he shall leave with you may be superior to any strength that the Spaniards can bring together against you in those parts, and though this may not be to be done without leaving some ships in the West Indies which may not be in so good a condition as were to be wished, yet, in these circumstances, they must remain till others can be sent from home to relieve them." The information[1] Vernon had as to the Spanish squadron was that it consisted of twelve ships, and that only half were ready for service, while the whole squadron was very short of men from death and desertion; the squadron he left with Ogle presumably represents his views as to the fighting value of the ships at Havana.

The naval forces in the three areas of these "Plantations" stations when Ogle took over the command are shewn upon the opposite page. The disposition of the ships of the Jamaica squadron made by him for the protection of trade and other services was as follows:

	Ships of larger classes	Smaller vessels
Off Cartagena: to attack trade to Porto Bello	1	
Off Cape del Vele cruising up to Rio de la Hacha	1	
In Windward Passage to protect trade and attack privateers	1	
Off the South Keys ("where three galley privateers are reported")	1	
Convoying 500 troops sent for relief of Georgia and South Carolina	—	2
Going to Ruatan Island for its protection and to cruise	—	2

The remainder of the squadron were at Port Royal or in American waters, mostly refitting, but a few ready for sea.

A report was current that those ships of de Torres's which were ready were shortly to sail for Europe with the trade. Judging by the use the Spaniards had hitherto made of their squadron it appeared unlikely that they would now use it offensively, but would more probably continue to devote it to the protective duties of convoy. Ogle could therefore afford to send out his ships of the line to cruise independently, relieving them from time to time by those ships which were refitting at Jamaica. But although the English squadron was in a better condition than the Spanish, Ogle found the greatest difficulty in keeping even a proportion of his ships at sea. Ships would be tediously refitted from the store-houses at Port Royal, proceed to the Caraccas coast, and in the strong winds which prevail in those parts, the repairs that had taken months to make might be rendered useless in a week. Not only were the rope and the canvas at Port Royal rotten and insufficient, but it was no uncommon thing for ships to be laid up for months owing to the want of stores to supply them.

[1] Report of Captain Brodrick, of Shoreham dated 8th of July. The ships he reported at Havana were the 'Reyna,' 80; 'Principe,' 74; 'Leon,' 70; 'San Ysidro,' 64; 'Africa,' 64; 'Andalusia,' 64; 'Hercules,' 64; 'Fuerte,' 64; 'Glorioso,' 64; 'Vittoria,' 54; 'Nueva España,' 54, and 'Real Familia' cruising between Cape Antonio and Cape Corrientes. Some of these names would appear to be wrong—*e.g.* 'Africa' and 'Hercules'; a ship of the former name having been destroyed the year before at Cartagena, and a ship of the latter name being at this time blockaded in Toulon by Mathews.

Squadrons in North America and the West Indies, October 1742.

A. *The Jamaica squadron*

	50 guns and above	40	Smaller vessels
'Cumberland,' 80; 'Kent,' 70; 'Grafton,' 70; 'Lyon,' 60; 'Mountagu,' 60; 'Rippon,' 60; 'York,' 60	7		
'Assistance,' 50; 'St Albans,' 50; 'Litchfield,' 50	3		
'Eltham,' 40; 'Fowey,' 40; 'Ludlow Castle,' 40; 'Adventure,' 40	—	4	
'Shoreham,' 20; 'Experiment,' 20; 'Seahorse,' 20; 'Astraea,' 20; 'Bonetta,' 4; 'Spry,' 6; 'Strombolo,' 'Vulcan,' fireships; 'Thunder,' 'Basilisk' and 'Blast,' bomb-vessels	—	—	11
	10	4	11

B. *The Leeward Island and Barbados stationed ships*

	50 guns and above	40	Smaller vessels
At Barbados: 'Norwich,' 50; 'Advice,' 50; 'Scarborough,' 20	2	—	1
In Leeward Islands[1]*:* 'Launceston,' 40; 'Gosport,' 40; 'Eltham,' 40; 'Lively,' 20; 'Pembroke's' prize	—	3	2
	2	3	3

C. *The North America stationed ships*

	50 guns and above	40	Smaller vessels
Newfoundland: 'Sutherland,' 50	1		
North Carolina: 'Swift,' sloop 8.12	—	—	1
South Carolina: 'Rye,' 20; 'Flamborough,' 20; 'Hawk,' sloop, 8.12	—	—	3
Virginia: 'South Sea Castle,' 44; 'Hound,' sloop, 8.12; 'Cruiser,' sloop, 8.12	—	1	2
New York: 'Launceston,' 44	—	1	
New England: 'Gosport,' 44	—	1	
	1	3	6

[1] The 'Otter' joined the Leeward Island command in October.

Empty store-houses played their part in the strategy of this war, both in the West Indies and the Mediterranean.

In November Ogle received sufficiently full information of the situation in the Mediterranean to form a picture of what was passing there and an anticipation of the consequences. The squadron under Mathews was then definitely established off Toulon and along the coast of Provence and the Riviera. French ships were being arrested for carrying troops, French interests were being flouted and a practical blockade of the principal French naval port was in progress. To Ogle it appeared that the hands of France would soon be forced; and her open espousal of the cause of Spain against Austria gave colour to this belief. It was therefore necessary to be ready for eventualities in the West Indies. There were no French men-of-war in those waters, but as the first intimation of war might be the arrival of a French squadron from Europe it was undesirable to have his ships scattered. Concentration was also to be aimed at for offensive reasons, in order that any attack upon French possessions might be put in hand immediately hostilities were declared. Ogle therefore recalled all his cruising ships, and made preparations, in consultation with Governor Trelawny, to attack the French settlements at Petit Guave and Léogane, destroy their fortifications and naval facilities, and so begin the war by clearing the board of these two naval bases. Trelawny arranged to embark 400 troops from the Jamaica garrison to serve as a land force in those operations; but month after month went by and still advices shewed that France did not intend to be goaded, at least for the present, into any overt act. In the spring therefore Ogle again sent out his ships cruising against Spanish trade.

In the meantime the Admiralty had decided to prosecute the war against the Spanish settlements, though on a different scale from that of the great expeditions of 1741 and 1742. The harbours of Puerto Cabello and La Guayra on the coast of Caraccas which were selected for attack were both important trading settlements of the second order. Puerto Cabello was the careening port of the Caraccas Company, whose ships had rendered great assistance to the Spanish navy during the war in carrying troops, arms, stores and ammunition from Spain to her colonies, and its destruction would be a severe blow both to the Company and the Government[1]. La Guayra was—as it still is—the port of Caraccas and an important shipping centre. It was believed by the Admiralty to be very weakly defended, an opinion possibly based on the report of the ships which attacked it in 1739[2].

[1] Duro, *Armada Española*.
[2] See vol. I. p. 43.

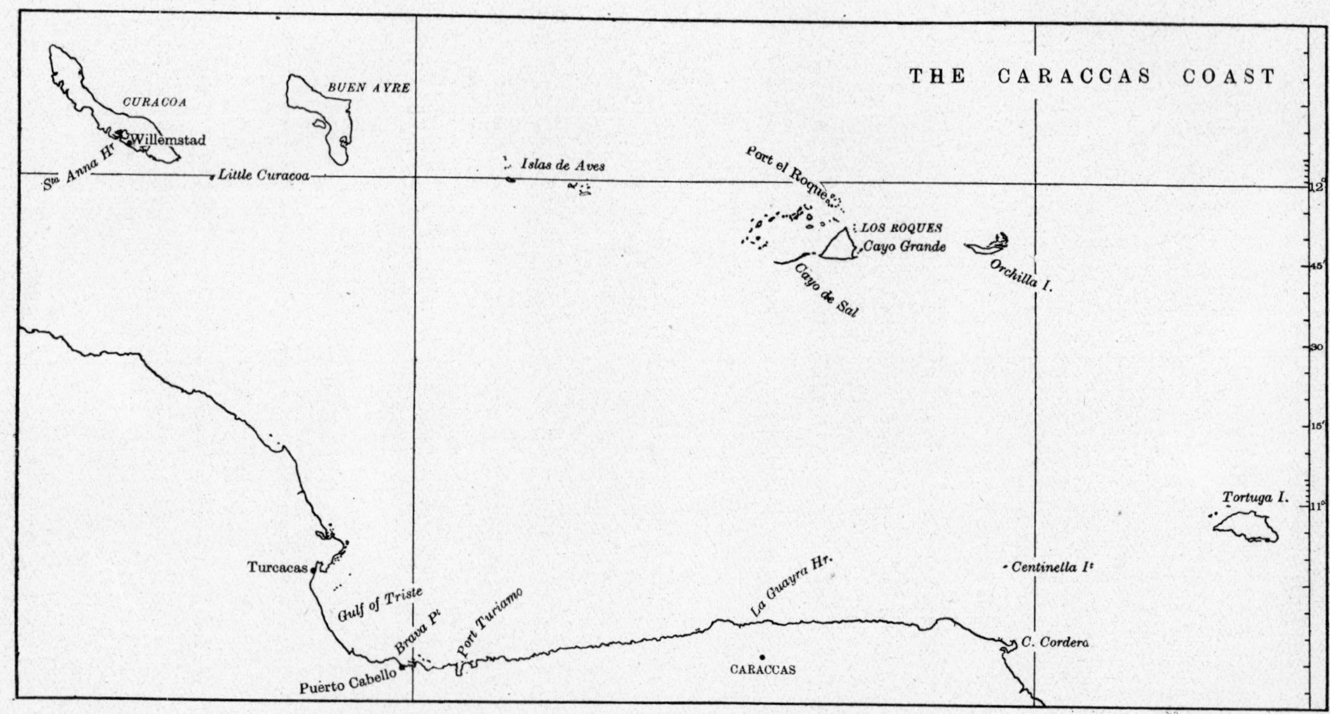
THE CARACCAS COAST
CURACOA
Willemstad
Sta Anna Hr
Little Curacoa
BUEN AYRE
Islas de Aves
Port el Roque
LOS ROQUES
Cayo Grande
Cayo de Sal
Orchilla I.
Tortuga I.
Centinella It
C. Cordera
CARACCAS
La Guayra Hr.
Port Turiamo
Brava Pt
Puerto Cabello
Gulf of Triste
Turcacas
12°
45
30
15'
11°

Against these two ports the Admiralty decided to send an expedition, the scope and intentions of which were set out in the instructions to the officer selected to command—Captain Charles Knowles. Knowles had returned to England in the 'Weymouth' which he paid off on 24th of March 1742. He held strong views as to the best manner in which to prosecute the war, and it is possible that the suggestion to attack these ports emanated from him, and that he was in consequence entrusted with the command[1]. He rightly looked upon the destruction of the enemy's bases as one of the most important measures in attacking and defending trade, and was strongly averse from confining operations merely to cruising and convoy.

Knowles's instructions, dated October 14th, 1742, ran as follows:

Instructions to Captain Charles Knowles, Captain of his Majesty's ship the 'Suffolk,' and Commander-in-Chief of his Majesty's ships and vessels designed on a particular service.

1. Whereas we have thought fit to entrust you with the command of a squadron of his Majesty's ships to be employed on a particular service, you are hereby required and directed carefully to observe the following Instructions.

2. You are to take his Majesty's ship the 'Burford' under your command, whose captain is directed to follow your orders, and as soon as the said ship and the 'Suffolk' are supplied with all the provisions and naval and ordnance stores ordered for them, and are ready in all other respects for the sea, and the wages and advance money due to their companies paid at the Nore, you are to proceed with the said ships to Barbadoes, and if you meet with any of his Majesty's ships named in the margin[2], either at that island or anywhere else, you are to deliver the inclosed pacquets to their commanders, and to take them under your command, and without making any unnecessary stay at Barbadoes, to proceed on without loss of time to Antegoa; but if you meet with none of the said ships in your way thither, you are to leave such orders for their commanders to follow you, as you shall judge proper.

3. When you arrive at Antegoa you are to cause the pacquets directed to the Governor of the Leeward Islands, and to the officer commanding in chief Lieut[t] General Dalzell's regiment of Foot to be delivered to them, the same containing his Majesty's orders, that four hundred men of the said regiment with a proper number of officers shall embark on board the ships under your command to serve in the intended expedition; and you are accordingly to make a proper distribution of the said officers and soldiers on board the ships with you, and to see that their embarcation be made with all possible despatch.

4. And whereas we have ordered the Captain of his Majesty's ship the 'Falmouth,' which ship and the 'Assistance' are going out with a convoy of victualling ships to Jamaica, to proceed himself no farther than Antegoa, and keeping with him such one of the victualling ships as he thinks fit, and also the 'Comet' bomb vessel and her tender, to send the 'Assistance' on with the rest of the victuallers and trade to Jamaica, you are to take the said ship 'Falmouth,' and 'Comet' bomb vessel with her tender, under your command, and to retain the said victualling ship with you, she being laden with dry provisions, and to supply the wants of your ships from her; and if you apprehend that you shall want flesh provisions or any other species of provisions, when you return from

[1] Beatson wrongly attributes the origin of this expedition to Ogle.

[2] 'Scarborough,' 'Advice,' 'Norwich,' 'Eltham,' 'Lively,' 'Pembroke,' prize, 'Otter,' sloop.

the expedition you are going upon, you are to give the contractor at the Leeward Islands timely orders for providing the same.

5. And whereas you carry out an eight inch mortar for his Majesty's ship the 'Scarborough,' you are to order the same to be fixed in her, and to supply her with shells and other necessaries, and proper persons for the service of the mortar.

6. And whereas we are informed there is an eight inch Howitz on board his Majesty's ship the 'Pearl,' you are, if you meet with her, to take the same Howitz from her, together with the officers, and shells and other materials thereto belonging, which her captain is hereby directed to deliver to your orders, and you are to cause the same to be put on board such ship of your squadron, as you think fit.

7. You are at liberty to communicate these our Instructions to Mr Mathews, Governor of the Leeward Islands, and you are to consult and advise with him about the best methods to be taken for performing the intended service; and also to get privately what intelligence you can of the state and condition of the enemy, where you are going.

8. Having got all things in a readiness to go upon service, you are to put to sea with the squadron and forces aforesaid and proceed over to the coast of Caracca where the Guipuscoa Company have established settlements for their trade, at the towns of La Guira and Puerto Cabello, the taking of which places, or any others upon the Main, together with the merchandise and treasure that shall be found there, as also such ships as you shall meet with, and their ladings, are the services that you are sent upon and which you are to endeavour to perform and execute with your whole force and power.

9. But whereas many designs have miscarried by not making an immediate attack upon the enemy after arrival, but wasting the time in deliberation, whereby, their first fears being over they have time given to strengthen themselves and prepare for their defence; you are, before you arrive in sight of the coast to call a consultation of the captains of the ships under your command at which the officer commanding in chief the land forces is to have a vote and the second place in rank, and to lay these our instructions before them, as also such intelligence as may have been received concerning the state and condition of the enemy, and there to settle fully the whole plan of operation against the enemy so that nothing may remain to be done after your arrival but to go immediately upon the attack and perform the whole service, according as shall have been agreed upon at a general consultation.

10. And for the better distinction of command and dignity of the expedition we do empower and direct you to wear a broad pendant while you are in sight of the Spanish continent aforesaid.

11. In case it shall be thought proper to send any soldiers or marines on service ashore, they are to be under the command of the officer who commands in chief the detachment of soldiers sent from the Leeward Islands; but both the landing and re-imbarking the troops, as also all other operations whatsoever in this expedition, either by land or sea are to be performed according as shall be agreed on at a general consultation as above mentioned.

12. In case you shall succeed to take La Guira, Puerto Cabello or any other place on the Main, you are to refer it to a general consultation whether it may be advisable to keep or abandon the same; and in case of keeping any places, you are to appoint the 'Falmouth' and a small frigate or sloop to attend on the same, for the protection and service thereof, and of the forces that shall be left there: and you are likewise to apply to the Governors of Barbados and of the Leeward Islands, for a supply of negroes to assist in fortifying the said places and for such other succour as shall enable the commanding officer to maintain and secure the same, as it is a settlement that may very much redound to the security and advantage of the trade of those islands; and you are to apply the cannon and other warlike stores taken on shore, towards fortifying the said places.

13. You are likewise at liberty to draw from his Majesty's ships under your command such cannon and other warlike stores as shall be judged necessary, at

a general consultation, to be landed and left there for the better security of the settlements.

14. You are to inform yourself of the disposition of the native Spaniards established in the Province of Venezuela before the settlement of the Guipuscoa Company, and if you find encouragement, you are to publish and disperse among them declarations, setting forth that it is not the design of the English nation to make a conquest of their country or to meddle with their property religion and liberty, but only to free them from the tyranny and oppression of the Guipuscoa Company and to open a free and equal trade with them of their mutual commodities, without any exorbitant duties, charge or imposition whatever: and you are to make such provisional agreement with these people, if you find them disposed to it, as shall be thought proper at a general consultation, subject to his Majesty's pleasure and determination.

15. If you keep possession of any place you are to settle the form of Government there 'til his Majesty's pleasure shall be known, and in order thereto you are to give such instructions to the senior captain of his Majesty's ships that you shall leave there as you think proper for the protection of the place by sea, and to the officer commanding the garrison in whatever relates to the defence thereof by land. And whereas Captain Thomas Somers, who is well acquainted with the coast of Caraccas, has voluntarily offered his services to go upon this expedition, and whose advice and assistance will be very necessary towards facilitating the success of the undertaking, we do therefore hereby direct and order that he shall be called to, and have a vote at, all general consultations: and you are to appoint the said captain to take charge of all the stores and provisions on shore as also of the collection and receipt of the Duties or Revenue that shall be settled there, and likewise of the repair of the Garrison, and all other contingent expenses, as also of providing hospitals for the seamen and soldiers, and other necessaries; and you are to direct the said three officers to advise and consult together in all matters relating to the settlement of the colony and of the duties to be established, and to forward as well everything relating to the general service, as the respective services with which they are entrusted in particular, and to continue acting in their employments until his Majesty's pleasure shall be known, recommending it to them above all things to cultivate and maintain a fair correspondence with the natives, and to comport themselves so towards them as may dispose and incline them to have a good opinion of the English nation, and to be assured of a free and peaceable commerce with us, without any fears or apprehension of danger.

16. In case you do not succeed in your attempts upon the coast of Caracca you are to call a general consultation to consider whether any attempt may be made upon the island of Porto Rico, or on any other place, and to proceed according as shall be agreed on, at the general consultation.

17. But if, when you return from the coast of Caracca to the Leeward Islands, you shall have certain information from Governor Mathews that there is a rupture with France, you are to consult with the said Governor how to annoy any of the neighbouring French settlements, and to proceed therein as shall be approved and agreed on at a general consultation as before mentioned.

18. You are to send us early and particular accounts of your proceedings and success on the coast of Caracca by a small sloop or frigate, as you are likewise to do of any other services you may afterwards go upon, with the opinion taken at a General Consultation of what may be necessary to be done here for the furtherance of the service you are employed on.

19. When the service of the expedition is at an end, and it shall not be thought advisable to attempt any further enterprise upon the enemy by land, you are to order the captains of the ships stationed at Barbados and the Leeward Islands to repair to their respective stations and pursue their former instructions, and to come home yourself to England with the two 70-gun ships and the 'Norwich.' And if you have made no settlement for the 'Falmouth' to attend on you are to send her to Jamaica, directing the captain to put himself under the command of the Admiral or Commander-in-chief at that place.

20. In case of your inability by sickness or otherwise you are to leave these our instructions with the next commanding officer who is hereby directed to put them in execution.

Given, etc., the 14th of October, 1742,

WINCHELSEA, J. COKBURNE, PHILIP CAVENDISH, GEO. LEE.

An additional and more specific order of the same date followed:

Whereas the taking the town of Puerto Cavallo, with the forts in and about the same, and keeping possession thereof, is the first and principal object that you are to have in your view, in the expedition you are going upon; you are hereby directed, in addition to our instructions to you of this date, not to make any attempt with the land forces on any other place until you have first tried what can be done at Puerto Cavallo. But you are at liberty, in your way to that place, if it shall be thought proper at a general consultation, to range along the coast of La Guira, and seize on any ships that you may find there, or elsewhere along the coast, and also to insult the said town from the sea, taking care not to waste so much time there as may alarm the people at Puerto Cavallo, and enable them to put themselves into a posture of defence. For which, etc.,

Given, etc., the 14th of October, 1742.

W., J. C., P. C., G. L.

These instructions present several interesting features. While going into a good many details they allow a considerable latitude in execution to the commanders. They provide for what is to be done if it be decided to retain any places in the event of capture. They emphasize the importance of surprise and rapidity of execution and the need of complete preparation, so that the attacks by land and sea can be set in motion immediately on arrival, in full co-ordination with each other. The command was a joint one, according to our usual custom; Knowles was in command of the squadron only (paragraph 1), and any soldiers or marines serving on shore are placed under the command of the military officer (paragraph 10); and all operations connected with landing or on land are ordered to be agreed upon in a joint consultation at which the military officer is to have the second place. But whether, in preparing the plans for the specific conduct of affairs on shore, the judgment of the military officer could be overridden by that of the naval officers who would be in a majority of the council ordered in the same paragraph, appears to be left in some slight doubt.

While the aim of the operations was fairly outlined, a clearer distinction might have been drawn between merely annoying the enemy and developing a strategical situation which would be of permanent injury to him. The attack on Puerto Cabello was of the latter nature, that on La Guayra of the former. The latitude accorded to Knowles to perform the minor operation of destroying shipping at La Guayra was a weak point without a distinct provision that it was in no way to prejudice the success of the major operation. Concentration upon the achievement of the principal object is a fundamental principle which cannot lightly be disregarded; and while every latitude in execution must be extended to a commander, no loophole should be left which can hinder the successful attainment of that object.

Besides issuing these instructions the Admiralty took steps about a fortnight earlier to assemble the Leeward Islands stationed ships in readiness for the expedition[1]. The sloop 'Otter' was sent out to Barbados and Antigua with despatches ordering all the ships on those stations to assemble at Antigua and there complete with provisions and water, and hold themselves "in a constant readiness to proceed on service according to such orders as shall be sent to you. But if you hear of any enemy's ships cruising in the neighbourhood of that island you are at liberty to go in quest of them, taking care to return to Antigua when the service is performed or that there shall be no longer hopes of meeting with the enemy's ships according to the intelligence you had received." This last part of the instructions is to be noted. It constantly recurs in all instructions to ships sent on particular service. Thus a squadron cruising in the Channel, to which certain limits are assigned, is invariably given the same permission to extend its cruising ground beyond those limits if it shall receive information of enemy's ships in a part outside its patrol; and the same sentence about returning to its station when there is no longer hope of meeting the enemy is also a constant formula[2].

The senior officer in the Leeward Islands was Captain Peter Warren of the 'Launceston.' He had been appointed to her on the 18th of January 1742 for Channel service. On the 31st of March he was ordered to fit for New York and after a cruise on the French coast after privateers, sailed for that station on August 23rd, 1742. His instructions were to fall down to the Leeward Islands in the winter when the weather was unseasonable on the American coast, returning to his station in the spring. He was senior to Knowles, and a letter of the same date—October 14th—was sent to him, informing him that Knowles was appointed Commander-in-Chief of a squadron going on a particular service, and directing Warren not to give him any orders "that may anyways interrupt or delay the service he is going upon, nor to take any of the ships or vessels from him that are appointed to his command." And further, to avoid the chance of friction which the situation might produce, Warren was ordered to take the 'Launceston' and 'Gosport' cruising "on such stations either separately

[1] Out letters. September 27th, 1742.

[2] Similar instructions were given to the Admiral commanding the Western squadron who was permitted to chase an enemy squadron so long as there was any reasonable expectation of overhauling it.

or together as may best protect the aforesaid islands and the trade going to or coming from thence from the ships of the enemy until the season will admit of your returning back to your proper stations at New York and New England."

Knowles sailed from Spithead with the 'Suffolk,' 'Burford' and 'Comet.' He picked up his squadron at Antigua, embarked a detachment of Colonel Dalzell's regiment, and sailed from St Kitt's on February 11th and anchored off the Tortugas on the 16th. There he called a council of war of the captains of the ships, the Commander of the land forces and Captain Somers, to communicate to them his sealed instructions.

It is said[1] that the Spaniards had two months' warning of the attack; whether this be true or not cannot definitely be stated. Duro makes no mention of any such information having been received; and that precautions for secrecy had been taken is shewn by a letter of September 1742, written by Lord Winchilsea to the Director General of Ordnance, the Duke of Montagu, in which he *very privately* informed the Duke that two ships were being fitted out for a public service which would require some special stores from the Ordnance Board. "As all designs for the public service," wrote Winchilsea, "are generally defeated by being known long before our ships sail, and by the manner of fitting out our ships.... I must beg to know from your Grace who it is at your Board to whom you would direct me to apply that these things might be provided privately[2]." Besides this, Knowles's orders were sealed and not opened till he reached Tortugas. If therefore the Spaniards had the information, it could only have been from some person in close touch with the Admiralty who had seen the instructions. Rumour of such leakage is common and frequently untrustworthy; but its possibility was suspected by Anson after he had been at the Admiralty for nearly two years, and had learnt something about the ways of the place; in August 1746, when sending some information to the Secretary this well-balanced officer concluded: "When you have communicated this letter to their Lordships I desire you will keep it in your possession and not let it go into the office, that the clerks may not see it."

The instructions were opened by Knowles in the presence of the officers forming the council of war. The capture of Puerto Cabello was clearly the principal object; but it was observed that "we were left at liberty to take what vessels we might see in La Guayra Road and insult the fortifications as we passed." The instructions contemplated

[1] Beatson, vol. I. p. 164.
[2] Montagu Papers, *Hist. Man. Comm. Report.*

the squadron going to windward, passing La Guayra and taking any shipping that was exposed, and passing rapidly to leeward to Puerto Cabello without any delay. But the council reasoned thus: if any ships were seen at La Guayra, the Spaniards, on sighting the squadron, would haul them in under protection of the fortifications. Therefore, before the vessels could be taken the defences must be destroyed, "which, by the intelligence laid before us, would not be difficult." Also, if Puerto Cabello were first attacked, and the squadron damaged aloft, it would take a long time to beat up to La Guayra against the strong winds and currents on that coast. The garrison would in that interval get news of the presence of the squadron and be better prepared than if the attack were made by surprise "which we had great reason to believe would be the case, from the secrecy of our expedition." On the other hand, even if damaged aloft at La Guayra, the squadron would be able to drop down to Puerto Cabello in less than 24 hours, a shorter time than a courier would take by land. Provided, therefore, the spars were not too crazy to stand enough sail to carry the ships past the forts, success would depend more upon anchors and cables than masts and rigging[1].

Upon these arguments the council decided to avail themselves of the latitude in their instructions, and to attempt first to destroy such shipping as might be at La Guayra, and then drop rapidly to leeward on Puerto Cabello and attack and capture the town. The arguments are interesting; they have all the appearance of being dictated by good sense and seamanship. The decision was nevertheless an unfortunate one.

Arrangements for the attack on the defences of La Guayra were made. In a well locked up line of battle the squadron was to sail in and anchor, each ship as close to her next ahead as possible, abreast the forts in the following order: 'Burford,' 'Eltham,' 'Norwich,' 'Suffolk' (flag), 'Advice,' 'Assistance,' 'Lively.' The 'Scarborough' and a bomb-ketch, from a position on the off side of the squadron, would join in the bombardment, the 'Scarborough' having, as the instructions had laid down, an eight-inch mortar specially fitted into her—an innovation, it would appear, introduced by Knowles, who had also mounted mortars on the poop of his flagship.

The discussions and preparations for the attack lasted two days. On the evening of February 18th the 'Otter' was detached to reconnoitre and report what ships were in the port. Reconnaissance is of high importance in many of the operations of war; but when surprise

[1] Account of the La Guayra Expedition described in a letter from Captain Watkins of H.M.S. 'Lively' to Sir John Norris. *Naval Chronicle*, vol. I. pp. 204, 314.

is aimed at, a reconnaissance which, unlike the work of scouts on shore, cannot be concealed from the enemy, furnishes him with a warning and puts him on his guard. So it was in this case. The Spaniards sighted the 'Otter' and instantly took alarm. Seven or eight vessels hastily got under sail and hurried to leeward in the direction of Puerto Cabello, and thus both that port and La Guayra were warned of an impending danger. This was a distinct failure to observe the tenth clause of the instructions in which the importance of secrecy was so insistently enjoined upon the Commander.

At daylight on the 19th of February the squadron stood in in a line of battle as arranged. When within a short distance of the town sail was shortened to fore and aft sail only, in order that there should be as little canvas as possible to handle while anchoring, and to ensure bringing the ships in good order into a close range of the forts. As the squadron approached, the batteries opened a heavy fire to which the ships replied. There was little wind and the smoke of the squadron hung so heavy that vision was obscured[1]. Instead therefore of anchoring as Knowles intended within pistol shot of the walls, they found themselves much farther off, and indeed too far to use their small arms which in such an attack were invaluable. The top riflemen in such a case, firing into the open batteries from their high situation aloft, were of great importance, as the attack at Porto Bello had shewn.

It took about an hour to get the whole squadron anchored. The forenoon had gone by, and it was now near 1 P.M. For over two hours a tremendous fire was maintained by both ships and batteries in which the former, in spite of the drawback of the long range and the swell, were getting the upper hand and driving the gunners from their forts, when came a mishap. A lucky shot cut the cable of the 'Burford,' and about the same time the 'Eltham' also parted her cable. The two ships dropped foul of the 'Norwich'; all three ships then drifted out of action, and although the remainder of the squadron maintained their place, the garrison was encouraged, returned to its guns and reopened fire, while at the same time the bombardment of the ships began to slacken owing to the necessity for refilling cartridges. A magazine in the fort was however blown up, and fighting only ceased at 8 P.M.

Knowles now prepared to send in his boats to attack the enemy's shipping under cover of darkness, but his men were so worn out with

[1] Vernon's orders of March 21st for the attack upon Fort St Louis had anticipated this difficulty. It will be recollected that he forbade the men being placed at the guns until the ships were in position. See p. 115.

the long day's fighting, and so many of his boats were shot through, that he was unable to carry out his intention.

The next day was spent in repairing damages, bombarding the west end of the town and the shipping with the bomb-ketch, and making preparations for a night attack on the shipping. At 3 A.M. the launches were sent in, with strict orders to burn all the ships and not to attempt to bring any of them out. No opposition was encountered in entering the harbour and the first ship was boarded without the smallest difficulty. Then the whole enterprise was spoiled. Notwithstanding Knowles's strict orders, a lieutenant of the 'Suffolk,' tempted by the possession of a fine new ship, partly laden, cut her cable and began to tow her to sea, while others of the men went plundering. An alarm was raised; the forts sprang into life and opened fire and all the boats except one immediately retired,—a retreat which Knowles characterised as "scandalous." He ordered a court martial upon the lieutenant who had so flagrantly disobeyed his orders, but before it could be held the officer was killed in the attack at Puerto Cabello.

The attack thus became a complete failure. Four hundred men had been killed and wounded[1], among whom was the captain of the 'Burford,' and many of the ships were badly damaged aloft. Knowles was therefore unable to proceed to Puerto Cabello until he had refitted. He had appointed a rendezvous at the Keys of Barbaratt, about four miles to the eastward of Puerto Cabello, and thither he sailed next morning, only to find on arrival that the ships damaged in the action—the 'Burford,' 'Norwich,' 'Assistance' and 'Otter'—which should have been there, were missing. These ships were reported to have been sighted to leeward, and Knowles sent a sloop to order them to anchor anywhere on the coast to enable him to join them. The search was

[1] The losses of the squadron in the whole affair at La Guayra were as follows:

	Shot received	Killed	Wounded
'Suffolk'	146	29	80
'Burford'	94	24	50
'Assistance'	54	13	71
'Eltham'	41	14	55
'Norwich'	9	1	11
'Advice'	10	5	15
'Lively'	10	6	24
'Scarborough'	3	0	2
	367	92	308

The enemy are said to have lost about 700. (Charnock, vol. IV. p. 352; Beatson, vol. III. p. 39, gives nearly the same figures.)

fruitless; and, knowing that they were badly damaged, he concluded they must have gone to Curaçoa to refit. Thither therefore he next proceeded, and there found them, and expressed to their captains his severe displeasure at their disregard of his instructions.

Having got his ships together at Curaçoa he proceeded to make as complete a refit as possible, to enable him to carry out his operations against Puerto Cabello. Powder, plank and rope were obtained, but men were lost from sickness and desertion. As good a refit for the immediate purpose could have been made at an anchorage on the coast and less delay incurred. Although surprise was now out of the question, for Curaçoa was in constant correspondence with the Spaniards at Cabello who procured their own supplies from the Dutch island, the delay was a serious matter on account of the extra time given to the enemy to strengthen his defences. The action of his disobedient captains had involved him in this situation and all Knowles could do was to make the best of it. Hastening his repairs to the utmost, as soon as he was able—on March 5th—he sent four of his small ships to prevent further succours from getting in, or any vessels already there from escaping. As his ships were made ready he detached them to Barbaratt to stiffen the blockade.

By March 21st his last ship left Curaçoa. The winds and currents were strong and adverse, and it was not until April 14th that he reached the Keys of Barbaratt, after having been obliged to make a board right over to Hispaniola in order to fetch the place.

The harbour of Puerto Cabello is formed by an isthmus, stretching to the westward from the main land to a cape called Point Brava. On this point a fascine battery of fifteen guns was erected. The neck then turns sharply south and ends in a point on which a castle stood, commanding the entrance to the harbour. Between Point Brava and the castle a second fascine battery of eight guns had been built, designed to rake ships as they made their approach towards the castle and harbour mouth. The entrance is narrow, a bare pistol shot across, and the prevailing wind being easterly it is clear that any attempt to force the entrance by naval action alone was impossible.

After a personal examination made by Knowles from the masthead of the 'Suffolk,' the plan decided upon was to land the seamen and capture the fascine batteries, supporting them with 1100 land troops under Major Lucas. The 'Assistance' was to move close in to that part of the isthmus which runs towards Barbaratt, command it with her guns, and prevent the enemy from reinforcing the crews of the batteries. The landing was to be made in the evening, the actual attack to be made in the dark. Surprise was hoped for; if the two

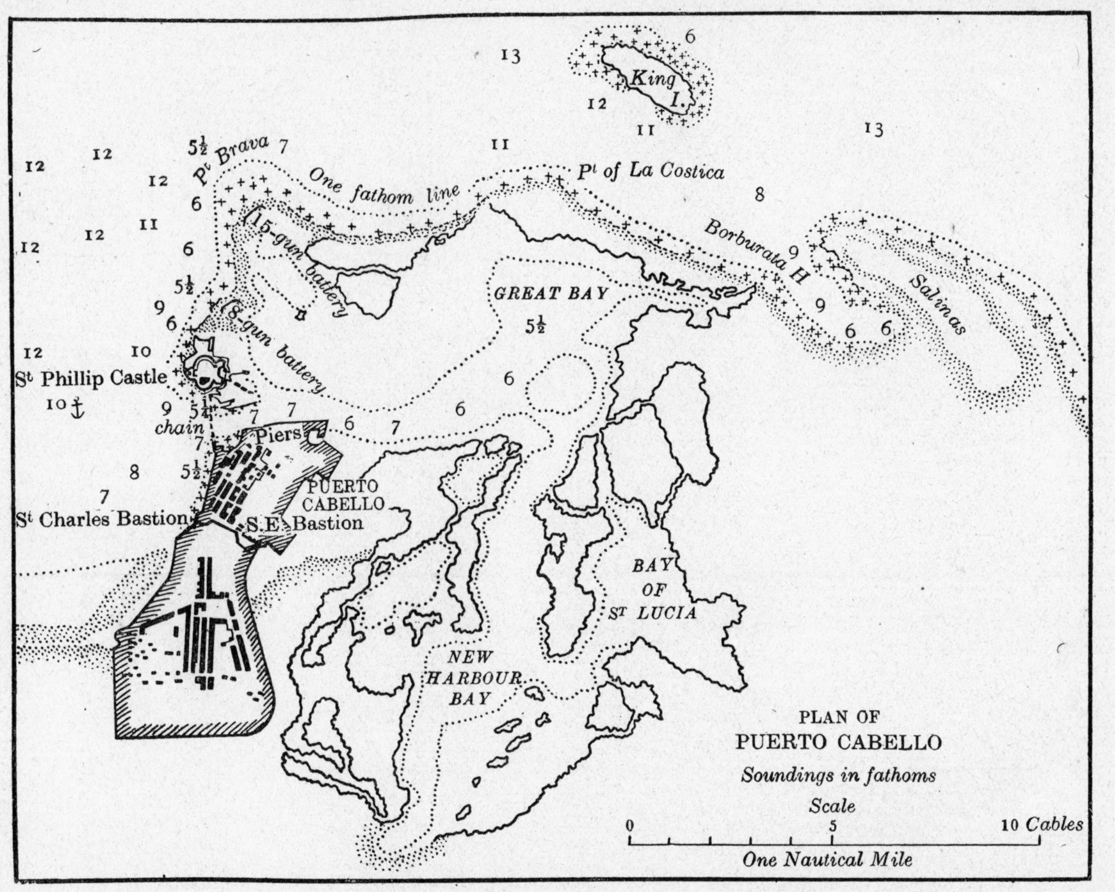
King I.
Pt Brava
One fathom line
Pt of La Costica
Borburata H
Salinas
15-gun battery
8-gun battery
GREAT BAY
St Phillip Castle
chain
Piers
PUERTO CABELLO
St Charles Bastion
S.E. Bastion
NEW HARBOUR BAY
BAY OF ST LUCIA
PLAN OF
PUERTO CABELLO
Soundings in fathoms
Scale
0
5
10 Cables
One Nautical Mile

batteries were taken their guns could be turned on the castle, a breach made, and a general assault by the land troops and squadron would follow.

In order to provide a diversion and weary the enemy, the 'Norwich,' 'Lively' and 'Eltham' were to bombard the fascine batteries all day from the earliest moment. No particular execution was expected from this. It would be enough if the Spaniards was well harassed and tired out, so that when the night attack came a sleepy and fatigued enemy would be either unready, or if ready unfit, to repel the assault. Success was looked upon as certain.

There was some delay in beginning the bombardment, a delay the cause of which gives some insight into the discipline of that time. The captain of the 'Norwich' was dilatory in taking up his position, and when called on by the Commodore to hasten, replied that he would consult with his officers about doing what he had been ordered. Knowles acted promptly. He suspended him and sent another officer to command the ship. The batteries were kept busy all day, and at sunset their crews, jaded and shaken, were in need of repose; the ships were little damaged.

The landing party was put on shore after dark without being seen or opposed, and marched along the isthmus. Fighting began about 11 o'clock. An advanced guard of the enemy had been stumbled upon asleep and might have been taken prisoners quietly, but a naval officer shot one of them. Some of the seamen began firing wildly, volley followed volley, men shot each other, and in the middle of the confusion some guns from a fascine battery, whose garrison was now alert, opened fire. A complete panic seized the whole party, and though Knowles, who in his barge was pulling along in shore abreast the landers, did all he could by hailing to stop the rout, and the officers on shore endeavoured to check the men, the whole party bolted back to their boats without any efforts on the part of the enemy.

A surprise on shore was now as impossible as a surprise attack by sea. Knowles sent in the same three ships next day to renew the bombardment, but no great harm could be done, and the enemy set themselves strenuously to add to their defences. At a council of war held on the 21st, it was decided that the only chance of success lay in a general attack by the squadron. The 'Assistance,' 'Burford,' 'Suffolk' and 'Norwich' were detailed to batter the castle, the 'Scarborough,' 'Lively' and 'Eltham' the fascine batteries. This attack was to be made on the 23rd, but the wind failing it had to be postponed till the 24th. As at La Guayra, difficulty was experienced in getting close to the castle, and though a fierce bombardment was kept up from 2 P.M. till 9, in which the castle was greatly damaged, the range was too great for the ships to have the advantage necessary for success. Finally, when most of their ammunition was exhausted, some 90 to 100 men killed and wounded, and the ships much shattered in both hulls and rigging, Knowles gave up the attempt and signalled the ships to cut or slip and stand to sea.

The squadron then returned to Barbaratt where the council of war came to the conclusion that in view of the shortness of ammunition, and the state to which the ships were now reduced, it would be impossible to execute any further service either here or at Porto Rico; Knowles therefore ordered the ships to disperse and to return to their stations.

The decision to attack La Guayra before proceeding to Puerto Cabello, notwithstanding the apparent soundness of the arguments already given, was assuredly an error. It involved a violation of principle. Puerto Cabello was Knowles's main objective, and to run the risk either of frittering away strength in advance of his attack on that place, or of giving notice of his coming, must be considered a mistake. The law of concentration upon the principal object, to the exclusion of everything else, was not being observed; and though victory may often attend operations conceived upon lines which violate correct doctrine, those who do so not only throw away some of their chances of complete success, but leave more than a loophole for complete failure.

In the actual attack upon La Guayra the ships lost their bearings in the smoke through not withholding their fire, and thereby anchored too far off for a fully effectual bombardment—a mistake Knowles took to heart and provided against in his later attack upon Fort Louis in 1748. In the landing at Puerto Cabello the advance was spoiled by the letting off of a pistol, an occurrence which on more than one occasion has had the same effect. By removing the flints, as Grey did in his successful attacks in the West Indies at a later date, this mischance would have been impossible.

These initial mistakes in the plans, unfortunate and avoidable as they undoubtedly were, might yet have been retrieved if better fortune had attended the squadron. The cutting away of the cables of the ships in the attack upon La Guayra at a moment when victory seemed in their hands, and the immediate loss of the services of three ships, was a stroke rather of ill-luck than anything else. At La Guayra there was no want of gallantry on the part of Knowles or his men, as the heavy losses testify. At Puerto Cabello the attack was well conceived and begun successfully. The panic following the letting off the pistol was one of those incidents which occurs even in the best troops, inexplicable by any form of reasoning. If the attacks on the outlying batteries at Cartagena form any guide, it seems probable that if cold steel had been the order Puerto Cabello would have been taken. It is interesting to note that in spite of the failures of this carefully considered expedition, no enquiry was made into the causes of the miscarriage, nor does it appear to have been anywhere suggested that blame attached to the Commanders.

No operations other than those of trade-attack and protection were carried out during 1743. Ogle remained continually at Port Royal, his cruisers in the various channels used by shipping. But although he sent out all the small craft under his orders they were unable adequately to protect the merchants against the privateers. So great was his need of small ships that in August he took the mortars out of the bomb-vessels and converted them to sloops, but for every small ship he sent to cruise, the Spaniards sent a dozen privateers. The merchants complained both to him and to the home Government of their losses, but he pointed out that he had every ship employed, and remarked, in writing to the Duke of Newcastle on the subject, that it was quite impossible to do more with the force he had, especially as the merchant ships would not help themselves, even well armed ships surrendering without an attempt at defence. In such circumstances a far greater number of small vessels than was at his disposal was needed; but the best answer to the privateer would have been a well armed and well manned merchant service.

Towards the end of the year 1743 the operations were further hampered by a renewal of the French danger. So threatening was the outlook that Ogle was forced to keep his cruising ships in such stations that he could readily assemble them if a rupture took place with France, giving them orders to rejoin him immediately if they should have information that war was declared. The Spanish squadron which appeared to be in a very unsatisfactory condition still remained inactive. Ogle was in no fear of them, for they were reported to be in bad repair and lacking in cordage and stores of all descriptions; these they were trying to buy from the French, who themselves were not well provided, in order to fit the ships for return to Europe. One rumour certainly disturbed him for a moment. In February 1744 Captain Taylor of the 'Fowey' brought in a report that four of the Havana squadron[1] with some thirty small vessels had sailed to retake Ruatan, leaving eight large ships in fair order at Havana. Ogle had at that time a

[1] 'Nueva España,' 'Real Familia,' 'Castilla,' 'Europa.'

squadron of four ships[1] at or about Ruatan, and he left matters to take their course, confident that these four could deal with whatever situation arose; but the affair never came to anything, and no more was heard of the prospective expedition.

It was after this false alarm that the long threatened intervention of France became a reality, and the importance of the Leeward Island theatre developed. Until this time, while Spain had been the only adversary, operations had necessarily centred in the waters round Jamaica, Cuba and the Spanish Main, in which the respective trading interests of England and Spain focussed and clashed. When however it appeared that France was about to join Spain definitely as an ally instead of an auxiliary, the Administration considered it prudent to make a different disposition of the forces for the area of the Lesser Antilles where French and British islands were close to each other. Lying so far to windward of Jamaica they could not be promptly succoured from that station. It therefore became necessary not only to have more ships on the spot but also to constitute them an independent squadron with a separate Commander-in-Chief.

The first officer appointed to the new command was Captain Knowles, with the title of "Commander-in-Chief of his Majesty's vessels at Barbados and the Leeward Islands and the Islands adjacent." It is curious to observe that Captain Warren was given a similar appointment on the same day. The latter was to exercise the command during the winter months when he came down to the West Indies from North America, and Knowles was to resume it again after his departure.

The gist of Knowles's instructions ran in the following sentence: "You are to employ the said ships either separately or together in such manner as you judge best for his Majesty's service, making the security and protection of his Majesty's islands in those seas, and the free navigation of the trade to and from hence, the principal point of your care and attention: and, in the next place, how to annoy the enemy's trade, ships and settlements[2]." He was appointed Captain of the 'Superbe' and ordered to hoist a broad pendant on board her, and to take the 'Biddeford' and 'Comet' bomb under his orders and proceed with them to his station.

Some changes in the ships in the Leeward Islands and Barbados had taken place since the preceding year and reinforcements were also about to be sent. The squadron which Knowles was to command was to be made up as follows:

1 'Mountagu,' 'Greenwich,' 'Adventure,' 'Assistance.'

2 Out letters. October 3rd, 1743.

Over 50 guns	Frigates and Sloops
'Boyne,' 80*	'Lynn,' 40
'Suffolk,' 70*	'Launceston,' 40‡ (Flag of Warren)
'Burford,' 70*	'Hastings,' 40‡
'Superbe,' 60 (Flag)	'Biddeford,' 20§ (to relieve 'Scarborough')
'Severne,' 50	'Deal Castle,' 20
'Argyle,' 50†	'Lyme,' 20
'Woolwich,' 50†	'Otter,' 14
	'Comet,' bomb

* These ships were to have followed in November, but events in Europe made it necessary to keep them at home: they were sent to reinforce Mathews.

† These ships were sent from the West Coast of Africa.

‡ From New York and Virginia: for the winter season only, then to return to their stations.

§ Did not leave England till January 29th, 1744, with a convoy.

From the above it will be seen how large an increase was intended in October 1743 to be sent; a wholly new squadron of considerable strength was to be constituted; but the state of affairs in the Mediterranean and the urgent need for reinforcing Mathews prevented this from being done.

The question of strengthening the Leeward Island squadron at this time opens up one of the fundamental principles of strategy. The reason for doing so was to protect these British possessions against France if she should declare war. France, and France alone, was the danger. But if that Power declared war, where could she strike her most effectual blows? She had three main theatres in which she might employ her sea-forces—the Channel, the Mediterranean and the West Indies. It is true she might make an attack on the last named her opening gambit; but she might equally, or even more probably, attempt to overwhelm our forces in Europe. War was raging on the Continent from the Rhine to Naples; would not France's navy be better employed in co-operating with her land forces either in Italy or elsewhere? The area in which a defeat would most seriously compromise England at this moment was clearly the European theatre of war, and before any British sea forces were detached to outlying parts, superiority in that theatre should be assured. The loss of the West Indian Islands would have been a serious, but not a fatal, blow. The crushing of the Mediterranean fleet, or the invasion of the United Kingdom—and either might follow as the result of the other—would have been an irretrievable disaster. Unless therefore a superiority in European waters were assured it would clearly be a mistake to send ships to distant stations, the protection of which moreover would be better provided for off Ushant and Finisterre. If an adequate watch were maintained whereby early knowledge of the departure and course of any enemy's squadron could be conveyed to the

Admiralty or the Commander of the cruising squadron, a force could be sent in pursuit, which, sailing unhampered by transports, might reasonably be expected to arrive in the threatened area in time to prevent any serious harm from being done. The greater the force in home waters, the less was the danger to the colonies, as cruising squadrons could be more nearly maintained constantly at an adequate strength and the chances of intercepting any expedition at the point of departure would thereby be proportionally increased. It was on this principle that all our subsequent wars were conducted down to 1815: its truth was similarly realized in 1743. As the danger of war with France passed from the region of possibility into that of imminent probability, statesmen began to look round to see whether the force in Europe were adequate. Danger quickens the perceptions; they saw that it was not, and the order to send the ships to the West Indies was rescinded. Strategical dispositions, however, should not depend for their propriety upon the fortuitous stimulus of danger—a stimulus which not infrequently acts in a highly unscientific manner.

In this case however no harm was done. Knowles reached Barbados on December 4th and hoisted his pendant as Commander-in-Chief; Warren arrived on the 22nd from North America and the two Commanders met at Antigua. Here Knowles transferred the command to his superior and went ashore to superintend the defensive works of the island while Warren cruised in the 'Superbe.'

This closed the events of the year 1743; and in the early months of 1744 there is little to record. Very few Spanish and no French ships were in West Indian waters and the part played by the British squadron was governed by the necessity for readiness to meet a French declaration of war which was expected at any moment.

APPENDIX I

A LIST OF SHIPS IN SEA PAY IN SEPTEMBER 1739 WITH THEIR STATIONS[1]

Plantations.

Ship	Guns	Station
'Burford,'	70	At Jamaica under Admiral Vernon
'Hampton Court,'	70	
'Windsor,'	60	
'Strafford,'	60	
'Pr. Louisa,'	60	
'Worcester,'	60	
'Norwich,'	50	
'Falmouth,'	50	
'Diamond,'	40	
'Torrington,'	40	
'Sheerness,'	20	
'Shoreham,'	20	
'Blandford,'	20	
'Drake,' sloop,	4.10	
'Anglesea,'	40	Leeward Islands
'Lowestoft,'	20	
'Saltash,'	8.12	
'Spence,' sloop,	6.10	Bahama
'Roebuck,'	40	Barbados
'Phoenix,'	20	South Carolina
'Tartar,'	20	
'Hector,'	40	Virginia
'Wolf,' sloop,	8.12	
'Flambro,'	20	New York
'Squirrel,'	20	New England
'Deal Castle,'	20	Canso
'Romney,'	50	Newfoundland
'Adventure,'	40	
'Salisbury,'	50	Africa

[1] Papers relating to the Navy, B.M. Add. MS. 19030. The Admiralty Lists of ships give the same information for September 1st.

Mediterranean.

'Somerset,'	80	'Eltham,'	40	
'Lancaster,'	80	'Dursley,' galley,	20	
'Edinburgh,'	70	'Greyhound,'	20	
'Ipswich,'	70	'Dolphin,'	20	
'Berwick,'	70	'Guarland,'	20	
'Augusta,'	60	'Aldborough,'	20	
'Dragon,'	60	'Solebay,'	20	
'Plymouth,'	60	'Kennington,'	20	Under Rear-
'Canterbury,'	60	'Grampus,'	6.10	Admiral Haddock
'Pembroke,'	60	'Ann,' galley,	8.6	
'Jersey,'	60	'Duke,'	8.6	
'Oxford,'	50	'Mercury,'	8.6	
'Gloucester,'	50	'Terrible,' bomb		
'Chester,'	50	'Alderney,' bomb		
'Falkland,'	50	'Salamander,' bomb		
'Tyger,'	50	'Deptford,' lighter		

Coming Home.

'Pearl'	From Lisbon
'Seaford'	From Carolina
'Hawke,' sloop	From Georgia

Ireland.

'Hound,' sloop	8.12	Waterford and Cork
'Dublin,' yacht	6.10	Attends on the Government

At Home.

'Namur,'	90	
'Pr. Caroline,'	80	Spithead
'Russell,'	80	
'Princess Amelia,'	80	Portsmouth
'Boyne,'	80	Deptford
'Cumberland,'	80	Woolwich
'Norfolk,'	80	Plymouth
'Lenox,'	70	
'Kent,'	70	
'Elizabeth,'	70	
'Orford,'	70	Spithead
'Buckingham,'	70	
'Pr. Orange,'	70	
'Grafton,'	70	Portsmouth

Ship	Guns	Station
'Superbe,'	60	Ordered to Spithead
'Lyon,'	60	To Plymouth
'Dunkirk,'	60	Sheerness
'Sunderland,'	60	Portsmouth
'Centurion,'	60	
'Deptford,'	60	Plymouth
'Warwick,'	60	
'York,'	60	
'Rippon,'	60	
'Defiance,'	60	Chatham
'Tilbury,'	60	
'Weymouth,'	60	Ordered on a cruise
'St Albans,'	50	
'Argyle,'	50	Downs
'Newcastle,'	50	Sheerness
'Greenwich,'	50	Ordered to the Downs
'Colchester,'	50	
'Chatham,'	50	Sheerness
'Portland,'	50	Portsmouth
'Bristol,'	50	
'Rochester,'	50	
'Ruby,'	50	
'Panther,'	50	
'Severne,'	50	Plymouth
'Assistance,'	50	Sent to Ireland for men
'Advice,'	50	Plymouth
'Litchfield,'	50	
'Winchester,'	50	
'Ludlow Castle,'	40	Portsmouth
'Trial,' sloops	8.12	Sent to Rotterdam for seamen
'Otter,' sloops	4.4	Attend the Herring Fishery
'Fly,' sloops	8.12	
'Swift,' sloops	4.4	Pressing off the Isle of Wight
'Bonetta,' sloops	8.12	Sent to Vernon with despatches
'Cruiser,' sloops	8.12	Bristol Channel
'Spy,' sloops	8.12	
'Success,'		Portsmouth
'Eleanor,'		Nore
'Cumberland,'		Sheerness
'Deptford,' store ship		Deptford
'Royal Escape,'	4	30 men. N. coast of Scotland surveying
'Royal Carolina,' yachts	10	In the river
'William and Mary,' yachts	8	
'Catharine,' yachts	8	
'Charlotte,' yachts	8	
'Fubbs,' yachts	8	Pressing about the Nore
'Mary,' yachts	8	
'Queenbro,' yachts		Attends Sheerness garrison

ABSTRACT

	Ships and vessels	Men
Plantations	29	6,825
Mediterranean	32	8,122
Coming home	3	440
Ireland	2	120
At home	62	18,762
	128	34,269

A 90-gun ship has 800 men
80 ,, ,, 600 men excluding retinue
70 ,, ,, 480 men
60 ,, ,, 400 ,,
50 ,, ,, 300 ,,
40 ,, ,, 250 ,,

APPENDIX II

CONTEMPORARY CRITICISM (1740) OF THE CONDUCT OF THE WAR

THE following extracts from a contemporary pamphlet entitled "Britain's mistakes in the commencement and conduct of the present war, by a Merchant and Citizen of London," dated 1740, are of interest. After discussing the general conduct of the Administration, the author proceeds as follows:

"However, if our Ministers saw, as I suppose they did, that the spirit of the nation would not allow them to make such compliances as were necessary for satisfying the pride of the Spanish nation, I must from thence conclude that before the end of March, even our Ministers began to look upon a war with Spain as inevitable. What in this case were we to do? It was not, 'tis true, proper for us to issue any letters of Reprisal, or to commence hostilities, till the 24th of May because we could not till then judge certainly of the King of Spain's intentions; and it was prudent in us to wait till the first breach of the Convention, I mean the articles ratified by His Majesty, should be made by the Court of Spain. But surely we ought to have begun that moment to prepare, at least in a private manner, for war; and how were we to prepare?

"Spain, we knew, was a nation that durst not look our squadrons in the face at sea. A squadron of 15 line of battle ships before Cadiz, another of a like number in the West Indies, and a third of the same number upon our own coasts, was, we knew, sufficient to lock up their men-of-war in their ports, and to prevent their attempting to make an invasion upon any part of our Dominions. By having three such squadrons at sea we should have made it impossible for them to do us any injury except by their privateers; and for preventing this a few 4th or 5th rates to serve as convoys to our own ships and to lie in the way for intercepting their ships bound to or from the West Indies; and a great number of 6th rates and armed sloops to cruise upon their coasts in order to intercept their privateers, and to give notice to our merchant ships not to approach the ports or coasts of Spain, would have made it difficult for them to annoy our trade and very dangerous to carry on any trade of their own.

"For this purpose we should, in my humble opinion, have had at least eight 20-gun ships and armed sloops with three or four 4th or 5th rates, stationed in the Mediterranean, and actually upon duty there; together with at least twelve 20-gun ships and armed sloops and six 4th or 5th rates stationed upon the coasts of Portugal and Gallicia and in the Bay of Biscay, and actually upon duty in their several stations before we had published reprisals or committed any act of hostility in Europe. As for the West Indies, we had no occasion to send many 20-gun ships or armed sloops to that part of the world. If we had taken care to have had a squadron of fifteen line of battle ships there, with three or four 20-gun ships besides the guard-ships usual in time of peace, we might have trusted for the rest to our own people in that part of the world for fitting out such a number of privateers as would have been sufficient to protect their own trade, and intercept that of the enemy; especially if we had taken care to give proper encouragement to the armed vessels fitted out by private adventurers to attack those of the enemy. And as for our own coasts, a squadron of fifteen men-of-war with our usual guard-ships and Custom House sloops would have been sufficient to have protected our trade at home and to have secured us against any invasion that could have been made by so impotent an enemy."

The writer then proceeds to argue that instead of publicly issuing orders for reprisal on the 25th of May we should have issued them secretly to the Commodore in the West Indies and avoided giving the alarm; and in European waters to withhold orders for reprisal till July at least, but instruct Haddock privately to seize any *rich* ship he should find sailing to or from the West Indies; one reason for this course being that by issuing orders for reprisal we warned the Spaniards, who therefore kept their large ships in harbour, leaving nothing but the small fry for our squadrons to attack. If by the middle of July no rich capture had been made by Haddock, operations might openly have been begun in Europe, and some additional men-of-war sent off the north capes of Spain to look out for the Azogue ships; having thus got our squadrons in position we could proceed to put other schemes in operation for bringing Spain to a peace. By beginning to increase our land forces in March and raising Marines to man the fleet, we might have had 40,000 or 45,000 regular troops in the country, and of these 14 or 15,000 could have been spared for an attack on Spain by land, preferably in the West Indies. "And," continues the Merchant, "that we might have been ready to set out upon such an expedition as soon as we declared war, we should have begun to contract for Transports, and prepare for victualling them, by the beginning of June, so that they might have been all ready to sail by the end of September at farthest.... My reasons for saying that the month of August or September is the proper season for sending out a fleet and land army to attack the Spaniards in America are these. First, about that time of the year the air is more temperate than it is either in summer or winter; and therefore the soldiers could not suffer so much by being penned up in transports as they would do in the summer or winter months. Secondly, they would probably be landed in some of the Spanish settlements in the West Indies in the month of November or December which is the coldest season of the year in all the Spanish settlements on this side of the continent of America; so that they would probably have done their business before the hot season came on[1], and would by degrees be accustomed to bear the excessive heats of the summer in that part of the world." The writer gives two other reasons, the avoidance of the hurricane season and the possibility of bringing the forces home again before it begins, and then goes on: "Now as we cannot propose to compel the Spaniards to agree to reasonable terms, or to make any conquests upon them that can be of advantage to this nation but by attacking their settlements in America, we should have thought of this, and begun to prepare for it, as soon as we saw that a war would be the necessary consequence of our disputes with them. If we had done this we might have been ready by the end of August to have embarked 12,000 of our best troops, which in my opinion is the smallest number that ought to be sent upon such an expedition, because it would be of the most dangerous consequence to the nation to miscarry in any such expedition...and particularly we ought to have taken care to have the troops we sent thither provided with clothing fit for a march in that hot country: for I must observe that the clothing they have in this country would be very unfit for them in that: which I hope those whose duty it is will take proper care of if we ever do send any troops to that part of the world.

"But in order to have rendered ourselves the more secure of success, and to have saved the public expense as much as possible, we should, the moment we declared war, have published a proclamation promising all the rewards and encouragements we could give to such private adventurers and volunteers as should join in the intended expedition: which we might have done without declaring the place against which it was designed. And at the same time we ought to have sent orders to all our Colonies in America to raise as many men as they could spare and to have them ready to rendezvous at St Christophers or Antigua, some time in the month of November.

"By these means we might have invaded the Spanish settlements in America with an army of at least 20,000 men; and such an army, with the assistance they might and would certainly have received from our seamen, would in all human probability have been sufficient not only

[1] It is to be noted that this was written before the West Indian expedition, which concluded so disastrously.

for taking but holding any of those settlements we might have thought most convenient and advantageous for this nation. Nay, as the Spaniards could no way guard against this danger by sending any relief or assistance from Old Spain, the very apprehension of it might have forced them to give us a sort of Carte Blanche: which would have restored the Honour and Character of this nation at every court in Europe, and would have secured the freedom of our trade and navigation in all parts of the world much better than it is possible for us to do by any treaty we can make."

At the end of his suggestions of this nature the writer observes: "that it has always been reckoned ridiculous in any nation to declare war till they were fully prepared to undertake some important expedition against the enemy; and this method of beginning a war is now become more usual than it was in ancient times. The declaration of war is generally now accompanied by an army, and often first published by an army's entering the territories of an enemy."

APPENDIX III

THE MARINES AND THE MANNING QUESTION

THE difficulties of manning the fleet played so large a part in this war, particularly in its early stages, that a reference to the intentions underlying the formation of the corps of Marines is necessary to their proper appreciation. The principal cause which led to the introduction of the corps was the need of rapidly providing men to man the fleet. It had no relation, as is sometimes supposed, to the preservation of discipline, to the provision of soldiers for landing work, or to an assumed necessity for having two different types of fighting men on board a man-of-war.

During the wars of the seventeenth and eighteenth centuries the bulk of the fleet was laid up in the winter season; the three-deckers, for instance, in King William's time never went to the westward after the 10th of September. In the spring the squadrons required for the ensuing campaign had to be fitted out, and proclamations were then issued offering a bounty, frequently of two months' pay, to all seamen and able-bodied landsmen who came into the service of the King within a certain time. In addition to this voluntary entry, warrants for pressing men were issued to all captains by the Lord High Admiral, and officers were sent from place to place to receive volunteers and to impress those who would not come willingly. Ships fitting out were provided with tenders, specially hired for the purpose, which cruised in likely spots in the Channel to pick up seamen, principally from home-coming merchantmen.

The bounty and the press-gangs provided a proportion of the men required, but were rarely a sufficient source of supply. The merchants who offered higher wages, and the privateers whose service promised more immediate and greater rewards under less irksome conditions of discipline, absorbed a large number of the available seamen. In consequence, when the fleet was fitting out, many of them retreated into the inland counties in order either to avoid service altogether or to postpone joining until the period of the bounty was nearly expired. Besides this a large number of the seafaring population, calculated to amount in 1741 to some 14,800 men, was protected from the press, including men employed in the coasting and fishing trades, colliers, watermen and outward-bound ships' crews.

Under these conditions the manning of the fleet was a constant difficulty, and when it was desired to fit out a squadron for a campaign early in the spring, serious delays which not infrequently compromised the whole of the operations of the year were experienced[1].

It is not therefore matter for surprise that a means should early have been sought to overcome this grave defect, and in 1664 a regiment, called "the Duke of York and Albany's Maritime Regiment of Foot" was raised by Charles II specially for sea service. This regiment was always to be held in readiness for manning the fleet. In 1669 two three-battalion regiments were raised by William III, each battalion consisting of 500 men. The intentions as to their employment are indicated in two paragraphs of the Order in Council of February 22nd, 1693.

"*Para. VI.* That the two regiments be not at any one time kept both on shore together, but during the winter season when the gross of the fleet is laid up, one of them be alternately kept abroad upon the 3rd and 4th rates of the winter squadron; by which means they will in a little time be capable of doing their Majesties the service of Mariners at sea, as well as by what follows render themselves no less useful to them on shore.

"*Para. VII.* That the same regiment during its being quartered on shore be at or in the neighbourhood of their Majesties' yards as following, viz.:

Companies	Yards	Companies	Yards
Four ...	... Portsmouth	Two ...	... Woolwich
One ...	... Sheerness	Two ...	... Deptford
Five ...	... Chatham	One ...	... Plymouth

to be employed from time to time at the call of the Commissioners of Chatham, Portsmouth and Plymouth and at the desire of the Master shipwrights of the other yards (where no Commissioner resides) upon all extraordinary occasions of service, such as, assist in heaving in and out of ballast, manning the cranes, taking up and removing goods and stores, transportation of ships, laying of cables and of various other works; with the encouragement of sixpence a day per man over and above their

[1] This state of things continued into the nineteenth century. See Sir Vesey Hamilton's remarks on the fitting out of the 'Desperate,' which left Sheerness in 1837 after being three months in commission "with only 12 Petty officers and seamen and half our complement of stokers." Byam Martin's *Memoirs*, N. R. Society, vol. I. p. xiii.

military pay to be allowed them for every day they shall be so extraordinarily employed.

"*Para. X.* That the captains of each ship on board of which the soldiers shall serve do send yearly to the Lord Admiral a list of the names of such soldiers as shall in any measure be made seamen, and how far each is qualified towards being an able seaman."

This last paragraph was further amplified in an Order in Council of February 17th, 1694, which reads:

"That the captain of each ship on board of which the soldiers shall serve do send once in two months to the Lord High Admiral or Commissioners of the Admiralty a list of the names of such soldiers as shall in any measure be made seamen, and how far each of them are qualified towards being made an able seaman; and that upon a certificate signed by the commander, master and boatswain of any of his Majesty's ships on board of which the said soldiers serve that they are so qualified, they shall be discharged and the captain of the Marines to be allowed recruit money to raise others in their stead."

One hundred and fifty able seamen could be raised yearly out of the corps: "it being one of the chief uses of the establishment that those regiments may prove nurseries whence the severe necessities of their Majesties' service may be abundantly supplied." So much indeed was the Marine a seaman in the early years of the establishment, that when a captain of a man-of-war impressed seamen from home-coming merchantmen in the Channel it was the practice to put on board those ships a number of Marines in lieu of the impressed men to carry her up Channel with a sufficiency of hands, the Marines on landing returning to their depôts.

Out of the fifteen companies, eight were commanded by land officers and seven by naval officers. "In the attack upon St Christophers," says Burchett, "we had killed or wounded upwards of 150 men, and Captain Keigwin, a sea commander who was appointed Colonel of the Marine Regiment which consisted of about 230 seamen, was shot through the thigh."

At the Peace of Ryswick in 1697 the army was reduced and the Marines were disbanded. But in 1702 when the difficulty of getting the fleet manned and to sea was again experienced, the Marines were revived. Burchett, then Secretary to the Admiralty, wrote: "The French had a great advantage in manning their fleet, their sea trade being very little compared with ours and their seamen not therefore drawn away into the merchant service[1].... We had indeed some part of the last war several Marine regiments designed as a nursery for seamen, but for want of being put at first on a good footing, they did by degrees dwindle away and were at length laid aside, a fate I hope will not attend those six regiments now allowed for sea service." The advantages which would accrue to the public

[1] A statement which seems to contradict itself. For where were the seamen to come from except from the merchant service, the source of supply of France as well as of ourselves.

services if the regiments should be kept entire are argued by the Secretary: they would be useful as labourers and riggers, and also for the protection of the ships and magazines.

These new regiments of Marines were however on a different footing in one respect from those earlier established. The purpose of making foremast hands of them, which as Burchett tells us was "one of the principal motives for the first raising of such a body of men," was not continued. Their usefulness however as a means of rapidly increasing or completing ships complements remained. "Experience hath shewn," says the same authority, "that these regiments have been very useful, but more especially in fitting out squadrons of ships for any immediate expedition. For as they are constantly quartered when not at sea as near the principal ports as possible, viz., Plymouth, Portsmouth and Chatham, so they were with great facility put on board such ships as had most occasion for them, for they were under the immediate direction of the Admiralty."

The Peace of Utrecht, which brought the war of the Spanish Succession to an end in 1714, also terminated the existence of these Marine regiments, which were disbanded in the following year. Sir George Byng's squadron, which was sent up the Mediterranean in 1718 to deal with the Spanish invasion of Sicily, carried soldiers. Three regiments were embarked from the Isle of Wight with whom, said Byng, he should "endeavour to complete our complements, and the best of what shall be left I will put on board the fire frigates in the harbour, and discharge the remainder." Writing later on the subject of the pay of these men, Byng urged that they should receive sea-allowances, pointing out that "they actually serve in the fleet and do the duty as Mariners, whether called so or not." The soldiers borne in the squadron during that two years' campaign were throughout the time part complements of the ships and not auxiliaries of the army; they did not serve ashore at any of the operations.

When the war with Spain began in 1739 the manning difficulties at once became acute. As early as September, 1739, Norris was urging that soldiers should be embarked to make up the deficiencies in the ships' complements. At a meeting of the Council on the 25th of that month he said: "If all the foot soldiers that shall be kept up in the country were by detachments to enrol in the naval service it might be of the greatest utility to the public service, and with those detachments of about 100 to a ship of the line, or if they were a fourth part of the ship's complement, there would never need to be above a lieutenant or a captain to be with them; and if this were a method to be observed in all sea service to have such an establishment, and a register for all seamen going upon the water, or such a number upon an annual allowance as once passed in a Register Act, the nation would never want on any sudden occasions to have their ships manned and at sea as any other nation."

Norris's advice was not heeded. Nothing was done, and the ships lay idle for want of men to man them; and when war was declared the unreadiness of the fleet was largely, indeed principally, due to this cause. Norris then returned to the subject, urging that the Marines should be re-established, using nearly the same arguments as Burchett. He suggested "whether it might not be proper from the example of France to establish about a number of 80 or 100 Marine companies, the captains and under-officers being made out of the elderly (i.e. senior) sea-lieutenants commissioned from the Admiralty as all other officers are at sea, and when on shore to be quartered about our docks, and a party of them when on shore to keep a daily guard. And that every ship of the line of battle should have upon fitting out one of these companies to be borne as part of their complements that would be a means always to have in every ship a number of men disciplined (i.e. trained) to the small arms, and is what the French have in every ship, a third part of their complements being marine. And none of them are regimented but always keep in pay for the sea service as they have occasion to arm their ships. And if we should come into this method it would put our ships upon an equal footing with the French...but we have so many proofs of our misfortunes for want of small arms that the necessity of putting ourselves at least upon an equal armament with France cannot be denied by any reasonable person."

In the discussion which followed this proposal, Lord Harrington (another member of the Council) argued that unless Marines were regimented they could not be of proper service on shore. "To which I replied," writes Norris in his ***Diary***, "that it was proper that land troops should be regimented, as was the custom of all nations; and yet the French did not regiment their Marines. And experience has shown from their example: when M. du Guay Trouin took Rio Janeiro he had only Marines with him, commanded by his sea officers: and when he landed them he ordered them into battalions commanded by his captains and himself as commander-in-chief, and as they were all under one naval direction so without any dispute of power he attacked a more numerous regular force in a strong town and succeeded beyond what could have been expected had they been veteran troops[1]."

Vernon, who was on his way to the West Indies at this time, expressed a similar opinion as to the desirability of embarking troops. His views coincided with those of Norris, even to the point of turning foot soldiers into Marines. Writing to the Duke of Newcastle he said: "I could wish we had each of us a company of regular troops on board of us which would have strengthened us in numbers as well as by their expertness in their arms to have excited our seamen to the imitation of them. If we should come to a general war with France as well as Spain, I believe your Grace will have already perceived, from the difficulty of manning those ships, the necessity there may be of converting most of our marching regiments into Marines. And if they become seamen, and were admitted to be discharged as such, that would make a good nursery for breeding them at a time we might probably find such a necessity for them."

It was at length decided to raise troops who were to be called Marines; but they were to be in regiments and were not to form part of the comple-

[1] *Diary of Sir John Norris*, Add. MS. 28132.

ments of the ships fitting out for the Cartagena expedition. As soon as Norris heard of this, he pointed out to Sir Robert Walpole—who appears to have been responsible for the decision—that those regiments of so-called Marines would be of no help whatever so far as the manning of the fleet was concerned, and in fact would not be what was generally understood in the country by the term "Marines." "It would," he said, "disappoint the trade of our country, as they believed the regiments to be raised as Marines were to serve as part of the complements of the fleet whereby an equal number of seamen might be spared out of the fleet for the merchant service." In similar terms Lord Polwarth criticised the proposal in Parliament. "The Marines," he said, "as they are proposed to be raised at this juncture are very different from the Marines that were raised at the beginning of the last war and are indeed no other than an additional number of standing troops."

When it was necessary to denude merchant ships of their seamen in order to man the fleet, suffering was imposed upon trade. Parliament, while averse from voting soldiers, were ready to vote men for the sea service, who in manning the fleet not only served actively to protect trade but also prevented the ships which carried that trade from being laid up for want of hands. Walpole's proposal would have turned the Marines into an expeditionary army, and all the difficulties of manning the fleet would still have remained to be solved. On Norris's representations the proposal was reconsidered, and the decision made that some of the Marines should be allocated to the fleet—a bad solution as all compromises must be which vitiate a correct principle.

A debate of very considerable length took place in November of this year—1739—when the manner in which the Marines should be recruited was discussed by Parliament. It hinged largely on whether they should be regimented or raised and kept in companies, and whether the men should be newly recruited or transferred from the regular regiments. The cheapest way, in Walpole's views, would be to take newly raised men, and this would he said be the quickest as well: "for a great many fellows that called themselves seamen have been rejected or turned out of our men-of-war because they were found not to be expert seamen, nor any way fit for their business. These men will immediately list as Marines, and will make good Marines, though they could not be accepted of as good seamen." Sir William Yonge, the Secretary at War, was of the same opinion as to the method of recruiting Marines. "Newly raised troops are as good on board a man-of-war as disciplined soldiers," he said. "In fighting a ship there are no marches or counter-marches, there is no part of the land discipline required but that of loading and firing the musket, and a country fellow from the plough may in three days be taught to do this as adroitly as the most expert soldier in the army[1]." Lord Pulteney expressed what were clearly the contemporary views as to the functions

[1] The same view as to the limitations of field training necessary for Marines will be found at later periods, in *A Discipline of the Marine Force*, 1763: and in the description of the battle of Alexandria by the contemporary historian of the corps.

of Marines. "I shall most readily join in opinion," he said, "that a body of Marines ought to be formed, and that it ought to be such a one as may on occasion be fit for the land as well as the sea service. But gentlemen seem to mistake the principal design of having a body of Marines. They ought to be principally designed to come in aid of our national stock of seamen, and that we may not be obliged to draw away from our trade too many of that necessary body of men. If this be, as it ought to be, the chief design, there is no occasion for forming them into regiments or for putting ourselves to the expense of having any Generals or field-officers of Marines.... I know that Marines ought to be men bred to land as well as sea discipline, and for this reason: men who have already learned the land discipline are more fit for Marines, especially as we have immediate use for them, than new or fresh men that know nothing of the land or sea discipline. But gentlemen I find mistake the land service which Marines ought to be designed for. If Marines were to serve a whole campaign at land, and to be made a regular part of a land army, I shall grant that they ought to be formed into regiments and be officered in the same manner as the other land forces are. But this is a service that Marines ought never to be employed in. When such an army is to be formed, a sufficient number of land forces ought to be sent out for the purpose. The only land service that Marines ought to be designed for, or employed in, is to support our seamen in storming a town or castle after a squadron of men-of-war has so battered and bombarded it as to make an assault practicable; or to make an incursion upon some open country where there are no regular troops as can be called an army to oppose them. And for both these services a body of Marines formed as independent companies are as good as if they were formed into regular regiments." Full and lucid as was the debate the matter went no further. The men were not raised and the fleet continued to go short of crews for all sagacious men could urge.

The Admiralty in the meantime was trying to find out some method of raising more seamen, and a Committee was appointed on January 13th, 1740, under the presidency of Sir John Norris "to consider of such means and methods as may be taken for the speedy and effectual a-manning of our fleet[1]." Their task was confined to the question of seamen and did not touch the Marine problem. Their recommendations were:

(1) Payment of same bounty as in preceding year.

(2) Pay to men entering to date from day of being entered and men to join in fourteen days from then.

(3) Commanders of frigates on the coast to press and receive seamen. Lieutenants employed on pressing to know that their diligence will be noted and contribute towards their advancement.

(4) Justices of the Peace and Magistrates of inland towns to be charged to seize all straggling seamen, watermen and others.

(5) Masters of fishing-vessels not exceeding 15 tons to be liable to

[1] Admirals Cavendish, Stewart and the Earl of Granard, Captains Stewart, Vanbrugh, Hardy and Gregory, all senior officers, were the members of this Committee.

impressment. Protections to men employed on the rivers or coast only to extend six months, and to be renewed personally and not generally.

(6) Protections to be allowed to Master, Mate and Carpenter, and one seaman per 100 tons; to servants under 18 and to old people unfit for service belonging to colliers or coasters.

(7) An embargo to be laid on all merchant ships and vessels outward bound: this to be continued until the fleet was manned, and a severe press to be begun at the same time[1].

These recommendations formed the basis of a Bill, introduced by Wager. It was violently resisted in Parliament and did not pass, but some of the recommendations were adopted. The means in any case could not have been effective, since none of them struck at the root of the matter, the grievances which prevented men from joining the navy. The unpopularity of the service at sea in men-of-war—it was popular enough in privateers—was due to these grievances, and to redress them should have been the endeavour of the Government. How averse the seaman of the day was from the service was well understood, and his reasons appreciated, by Vernon. In a lengthy speech in 1749 the kindly Admiral appealed for justice and better treatment of the seaman, and gave an impressive picture of the hardships under which they suffered. "Our fleets," he said, "which are defrauded by injustice, are first manned by violence and maintained by cruelty. When our ships are to be fitted an impress is sent into the streets to bring those who shall fall in the way by force into the vessels From that time they are in effect condemned to death, since they are never allowed to set foot again on shore, but turned over from ship to ship; and when they have finished one expedition, hurried into another without any regard for the hardships they have undergone or the length of the voyage." Vernon foretold that unless better treatment, more regular pay, and a fairer distribution of prize money were given, a mutiny might break out at a time when the security of the Kingdom was in danger—a forecast of what actually occurred forty-five years later. Others saw the root of the problem not less clearly. "Since my leaving Plymouth," wrote the captain of a sloop, "I have pressed in all forty-five men, four of whom notwithstanding a strict watch kept, swam away from the ship in the night when it blowed so hard that a boat could not row ahead, two of which in the attempt were drowned some time before on an attempt of a like nature. This I mention to show their Lordships the aversion they have to the service and the reason why I have raised no more volunteers. I have raised only eight volunteers since my being out[2]."

Thus, as no improvement was made in the inducements to seamen to serve, and as compulsion provided an insufficient quantity besides hampering the trade of the country, the wants of the navy had to be met by the embarkation of soldiers or Marines. In May, 1740, in spite of the embargo which had been imposed, the fleet was still unready at the time when what appeared to be an invasionary force was assembling

[1] The embargo was laid later. The press was not ordered until June 2nd, 1741.

[2] Captain James Douglas, H.M.S. 'Ferret,' December 26th, 1743. Captain's letters.

at Ferrol, and France was adopting a contumacious attitude. To meet the difficulty two marching regiments and 1000 so-called Marines were put on board the ships of the Home Guard which was sent in July off Ferrol under Sir John Norris. In September of the same year when the French squadrons sailed for the West Indies and the intervention of France seemed certain, a proposal was made to increase all our regiments by one battalion and thus furnish another 6000 or 7000 men to man the fleet; but it was not put into execution. Throughout the war the Commander-in-Chief of the Mediterranean fleet had power vested in him to call on the Governor of Minorca to complete his complements from the garrison of Mahon.

The original reason for raising Marines, as expressed by Burchett, was not entirely lost sight of, although it had disappeared in fact. The Marines were still to be afforded opportunity of becoming seamen. In 1746, Brigadier Jeffreys having written to the Admiralty that he might be informed what was expected of Marines on board concerning their going aloft and handling the sails, the Board replied that "though their Lordships would not have Marines beat or punished who do not show an inclination to go aloft to handle the sails, provided they do their duty on deck and assist there in working the ship in the same manner as the rest of the ship's company do, yet their Lordships are very far from giving a liberty to the officer of Marines to discourage their men from going aloft who shall show an inclination to learn seamanship; but on the contrary, do expect they shall endeavour to qualify themselves as seamen: and if their Lordships shall be informed that any officers of Marines shall act otherwise, they shall resent it in a proper manner." The spirit of this letter is again to be found in Lord Howe's standing orders of 1776[1], which say: "the Marines are not to be forced to go aloft, nor on the other hand are to be restrained from rendering themselves expert in a seaman's duty, at proper opportunities agreeable to the standing instructions."

The principal sources of the difficulties of getting the fleet ready for service—difficulties which had so great an effect particularly upon the campaigns in the beginning of the war—are to be traced to the omission to raise Marines for the sea service and the failure to treat the seamen with a proper regard. The second of these could not be remedied at a moment's notice: it would involve inducing confidence into a number of men, and confidence in Parliamentary promises was not a plant of rapid growth. But the former might have been done, and it was not for want of advice either from sea officers or members of Parliament that it was left undone. No change was made in this war or later, and throughout the long struggle in which the British Empire was built up the Navy was manned under the old system; the introduction of the continuous service seaman, of whom the Marine was the first representative, did not take place until the middle of the nineteenth century.

[1] *Signals and Instructions*, p. 89, Navy Record Society.

APPENDIX IV

CONSIDERATIONS ON WAR WITH FRANCE AND SPAIN

A sidelight upon contemporary thought is thrown by a paper[1], written in 1738, in which the existing political situation, and the measures required to meet it, are discussed. The writer does not appear to be a naval officer, though he clearly appreciates the covering functions of the fleet in home waters: "Our men of war being thus at leisure to watch the motions of the French and Spaniards at home, our people in America can meet with little or no opposition, since it will be difficult for the enemy to find means to send succour to their friends in the West Indies when our fleets are masters of the seas at home." He belongs to that school of thought then represented in Parliament by Heathcote and others, and at sea, to a great extent, by Vernon; and later by Pitt and Hardwicke. He desires to concentrate upon offensive war which he argues can only be conducted at sea and in the colonies; he is utterly opposed to continental alliances; he believes in the policy of expanding British trade by destroying that of her competitors; and he attaches high importance to the influence of finance as an element in national strategy.

War, he argues, has now become inevitable. Neither England nor Spain can afford to let matters continue in their existing condition in relation to West Indian trade. He allows full weight to, and recognises the fairness of, the Spanish point of view. "The Spaniards very justly observe," he says, "that if they were to let all English ships pass on pretence of coming to Jamaica, they would lose half their annual Treasure that comes from New Spain; which every reasonable man must certainly admit to be true." The treasure which would otherwise go to Old Spain would be drawn away into the local trade by the contraband traffic and so lost to the home Government. But Britain's point of view is not less important and deserves equal weight. Unless the British colonies could trade with the Spanish settlements they could not continue to exist, since all their ready money came from those parts: "they have no other way of getting one shilling of ready money for their commodities...not having one penny of gold or silver but Spanish money in the country." Hence, the writer argues, "the affair is brought to this dilemma; that Spain must either be content to give up half of their yearly treasure from the West Indies at once, or that the English must give up their Plantations and entirely lose their whole West Indian Trade. Therefore it is clear that this dispute can never be determined but by war."

[1] P.R.O. State Paper Miscellaneous 200. Endorsed "*State of the land forces of France* 1738."

Starting from this basis of political economy—the natural outcome of the mercantilist theories of the period—the writer proceeds to shew that the opportunity is a favourable one; that it is advantageous to Britain to capture Spanish trade; that the effect of French intervention is not to be feared, for Britain could fight the combined French and Spaniards, and, if France should not intervene, each power could be dealt with separately; also that, while so long as the quarrel is maritime and colonial, France has no cause to attack Austria and so weaken our position in the Netherlands, Great Britain can exercise her full strength with greater effect if she is not hampered by continental alliances. Thus, first having reasoned that war is inevitable, the writer proceeds to shew why it should be brought about at once. The headings of his arguments for war on these lines run as follows in his text:—

"I. Because England is at present in a much better condition than at the beginning of 1702, and France in a much worse than they were at that time.

II. Because our Plantations are both able and willing to fit out 50 large ships of force[1] and to raise land forces sufficient to take Cuba, Hispaniola and Porto Rico.

III. Twenty galleys with 500 men to each, added to the guard ships upon our coast, would effectually secure England against French invasions.

IV. Because the success is more certain, and the expense much less to England, of a war carried on against France and Spain without the alliances of the princes of the continent.

V. Because in this present case France and Spain have no pretence to attack the Emperor or the Dutch if they take no part with us in this war.

VI. Because our Trade will not suffer in this war.

VII. Because of the great strength which our colonies in America have acquired since the last war, and the facilities of taking Cuba, Hispaniola and Porto Rico[2].

VIII. Because the war cannot be of any long duration, and the annual expense thereof cannot amount to one half of what we expended the last war.

IX. Because in so just a war there will be no difficulty at home of raising the necessary yearly supplies."

The writer discusses in detail and at some length the military, naval and financial powers of France and Spain. Great stress is laid on the last of these. The emphasis with which he urges the inability of the prospective enemy powers to sustain a long war when their oversea trade is cut off affords a measure of our reasons for attacking French and Spanish oversea commerce. Far from being mere piratical warfare, or predatory operations maintained, as some writers argue, at the instance of fortune-hunting naval commanders, trade attack held, as it had for over a hundred years,

[1] The "ships of force" subsequently described are "galleys of 500 men each, built in the nature of the French and Spanish galleys," and not what seamen understood by the term, viz. ships of the line and heavy frigates.

[2] An extension of II above, dealing more with the supply of troops from the various colonies.

a clearly understood and logical place in our national strategy. As Blake's destruction of the Spanish Treasure fleet at Santa Cruz in 1657 had been a determining factor in the campaigns in Portugal and Flanders, so in 1738 it was proposed to cripple France and Spain by cutting off their principal sources of revenue—the West Indian trade and treasure—without which they could neither pay their armies nor build, fit out and maintain their fleets. The survey of the problem made by the writer shews no sign of that narrowness which regards war merely as a matter of conflicts between armies and fleets, nor of a watertight subdivision into "naval" and "military" operations. It exhibits it on the contrary, as a struggle between two antagonists, each with a definite object in view and making use of all the available resources at its disposal to attain its end; and it does not leave out of account, among the elements that go towards national strength, the willingness of the whole people.

END OF VOLUME ONE

INDEX

Acapulco, 16; proposal to intercept Acapulco ship, 32, 98, 99
Admiralty, First Commissioner, 23, 23 *n.*; Lord Winchelsea as, 180; Norris's claim to, 180–1, 181 *n.*; trade protection, 182–192; manning of fleet, 82; differences with Mathews, 221–6, 235, 236, 240
Adriatic Sea, squadron in, 204, 234
Africa, west coast of, squadron in (1738), 5, 6
Alexieff, Admiral, 107 *n.*
Anson, Captain G., xi, xii, 32, 90 *n.*, 91; his expedition, 97–100
Antibes, Port of departure of Spanish troops, 152, 176–9, 205–7, 210
Antin, Admiral, Marquis d', 57, 81, 109, 110 *n.*, 111
Argyll, Duke of, on coastal attacks, 228
Army, strength of, British, 14; Spanish, 14; French, 15 and *n.*

Balchen, Admiral Sir J., off Ferrol (April 1740), 78–83; commands Cathcart's escort, 90–2
Baltimore, Lord, 224
Baradera battery, 114–117
Barbados, 5, 243
Barbaratt, keys of, 253–5
Barcelona, defences put in order, 9; projected British attack on, 29; Spanish plan to assemble army at, 30; military preparations reported at (1740), 62; influence of threat, 63–7; success of plan, 70; preparations at (1741), 154–5, 159, 160, 163–4; first expedition sails from (Oct. 1741), 165–6; second expedition sails from (Jan. 1742), 171; Newcastle and the blame, 172–8; observation of (June 1742), 201; (Dec. 1742), 220; (Feb. 1743), 222, 226
Barlovento, squadron, 14
Barnard, Sir J., M.P., 182
Barnett, Captain Curtis, xi, xii, 155; skirmish with de Caylus, 160–3, 170–1
Bene, Admiral, de la, 28, 152, 164
Bermuda, 18
Bilboa, 17
Bladen, Colonel, 30, 31
Bland, Colonel, Acts under Norris on Spanish coast, 91
Boscawen, Captain E., 49, 93
Brest squadron, threat of (1740), 79, 81, 82, 87–91; squadron sails (Aug. 1740), 92–4; effect of arrival in W. Indies, 105–111, 114, 135; influence of in European campaign (1741), 148–9, 195–6, 237
Brown, Commodore C., his instructions (1738), 5; duties, 10–11; further instructions, 24; executes reprisals, 39, 43; at Porto Bello, 46–8
Buenos Ayres, ships, 14, 16, 17, 26
Burrard, Colonel, 121 *n.*
Byng, Captain John, his command off Cadiz (Oct. 1740), 71, 151, 154

Cadiz, watched by Haddock (1738), 9, 10; squadron at (June 1739), 14, 17, 24, 25; Ogle sent off, 26–30; shipping entering (1737), 38 *n.*, 53; Haddock off (Oct. 1739—Feb. 1740), 59–63, 73, 74; movements of first concentration (Mar., April 1740), 62–70, 78–82; Byng sent off (Oct. 1740), 71, 151; reinforced, 152, 153; considerations of attacks upon, 74, 84, 86, 228; movements of second concentration (May—June 1741), 144–150, 154–9; neutrals entering, 163; campaign off (Sept.—Dec. 1741), 163–176; Mathews's instructions as to, 198, 264
Campo Santo, battle of, 234
Carolinas, squadrons at, 5, 7, 243
Cartagena (America), place in Spain, trading system, 16–18; discussion as to attacking, 32–5; Vernon reconnoitres (1740), 51; cruises off, 55; de Torres reinforces, 57; expedition to, 101–123, 134–137; report of capture, 144–5; failure, 146
Carteret, Lord, 12; asks for Haddock's instructions, 71, 181
Carthagena (Spain), 14; squadron at (Aug. 1739), 28; detachment off (Jan. 1740), 61; threat from, 62–64, 66, 67, 74, 81, 82; situation at (Jan. 1741), 152, 157
Cathcart, Lord, selected to command expedition to W. Indies, 35; delays in arrival, 56–8; in sailing, 73–94; departure, 102; death of, 103
Cayley, Consul at Faro, 158
Caylus, Chevalier de, skirmish with Martin, 153–4; with Barnett, 160–3

Chagres, 16, 17, 31; capture of, 52–54
Charles Emmanuel, King of Sardinia, 202–3, 227, 233
Chile, expedition to, planned, 31, 32
Clinton, Captain, 8
Cokburne, John, 224
Colonial system, 1, 2
Concentration before war. Haddock to prevent cruising of Cadiz and Ferrol squadrons, 28; Norris to prevent Brest squadron entering Ferrol, 89; Vernon's measures to prevent cruising of French and Spaniards, 107; Mathews to prevent Brest squadron entering Toulon, 199, 237; Nelson in 1803, 199*n.*
Convoy system, 183–6, 188
Cornewall, Captain, 32, 150, 163, 165, 167
Coruña, 17
Council, Committee of, constitution, 23, 24–28; discusses plans for war, 30–37, 50*n.*, 61, 62; Spanish escape from Cadiz (April 1740), 67–9; direction of war (Jan.—April 1740), 73–9; sends Balchen off Ferrol, 78; concentration at Ferrol, 79–89; attitude towards France (Sept. 1740), 94–5; on annexing Cartagena, 124, 141*n.*, 144, 150, 152, 166, 181, 196
Court, Admiral de, instructions to, when escorting Spanish army, 172
Criticism, Parliamentary, 71–2, 72–5; of defence of trade, 182–190

Dandridge, Captain, his reconnaissance of Port Louis, 106–9, 106*n.*
Darien, proposed attack upon, 30, 31, 32
Diversions, divided idea in Spanish war plan, 30; divided effect of expedition to Naples (1742), 215; Mathews's proposals for attacks on Spanish coast, 228

Elibank, Lord, opinions on ships *v.* forts, 115, 117*n.*, 120*n.*, 122*n.*; on holding Boca Chica, 125

Fanshaw, Captain, 7
Ferrol, 14, 19; squadron at (July 1739), 29, 30, 34, 51; movements for first concentration at (Mar., April 1740), 53, 68, 69, 78–82; offensive sally from, 83; proposal to attack with fleet, 84–5; Norris ordered to watch, 86–9; sailing of Ferrol squadron (July 1740), 91–3, 102; arrival of Ferrol squadron in W. Indies (Oct. 1740), 57, 103; second concentration at Ferrol (May 1741), 144–7, 157–9
First Commissionership, 23, and *n.*; Lord Winchelsea as, 180; Norris's claim to, 180–1, 181*n.*
Fleury, Cardinal, 22, 23, 118, 135, 140*n.*; death of, 231
Flota, 17, 24, 25, 28–9, 60, 61, 74
Forts *v.* ships, Waterhouse at La Guayra, 43; Vernon at Porto Bello, 46–50; at Chagres, 52; Norris's views on, 84; Vernon at Port Louis, 107; at Cartagena, 111–113; attempt on the Castles at Cartagena, 114, 115; the 'Gallicia' used as bombarding ship, 123; Rentone at Santiago, 125–6; Mathews off Toulon, 209; Martin at Naples, 213–5; Knowles at La Guayra, 251–3; at Puerto Cabello, 254–6
François, Cape, 18

Galleons, 16, 25, 74
Gascoigne, Captain, 89, 90, 91, 102
Georgia, defence of, 6, 7; Spanish expedition against, 10
Guantanamos Bay, 56, 127, 130
Guayra, La, attacked by Waterhouse, 43; by Knowles, 245, 254, 256

Haddock, Admiral Nicholas, his instructions (May 1738), 8, 9, 11–13, 25, 26; begins reprisals, 28–9; begins war, 59; his instructions (Feb. 4, 1740), 61; operations (Oct. 1740), 62–5; Cadiz squadron escapes home, 66–8; second escape of Cadiz squadron, 155–160; difficulties with neutrals, 163; Haddock and Toulon squadron, 165; and Barcelona expedition, 165–7; and second Cadiz squadron, 167–171; blamed for miscarriage, 173–5; illness and retirement, 176–7
Harrington, Lord, 25*n.*, 61*n.*, 77 and *n.*, 141*n.*
Hardwicke, Lord, modifies instructions to Ogle and Haddock, 26, 61*n.*, 73, 86*n.*, 89, 95*n.*, 141*n.*
Hardy, Admiral, 273*n.*
Havana, 10; its place in Spanish trade system, 16–18; question of attack upon, 32–5; Brown cruises off, 39, 43, 45; Vernon's objections to attempting, 55; potential fleet at, 126, 129; squadron at (Oct. 1742), 242; sally against Ruatan, 257
Hervey, Captain, 64
Hervey, John Lord, 69

Illicit trade, 2–4, 11
Instructions, Vernon's additional, 41, 42, 47

Jacobite, restoration feared, 20, 75, 135
Jalapa, 17
Jamaica, squadron at (1738), 5, 6, 43, 50; Vernon ordered to protect, 53–4; want of stores at, 55; Ogle ordered

to reinforce Vernon at, 68–9; expedition to assemble at, 101; Vernon expects French attack on, 105; Kennington goes to, 155; separation of Jamaica and Leeward Island stations, 241; squadron at (Oct. 1742), 243
Jenkins, Captain R., 3*n.*, 4, 5

Keene, Mr, Ambassador at Madrid, 3, 13
Kempenfelt, xi, 175 and *n.*
Knowles, Captain Charles, 7; on course of Spanish trade, 18; at Porto Bello, 49; engagement with d'Épinay, 103; at Port Louis, 107; at Cartagena, 117–9; at Puerto Cabello and La Guayra, 245–260

Lage, Captain de, 229
Laton, Captain, 195
Lee, Captain, his initiative, 155; in Adriatic, 204
Lee, Sir G., 224, 248
Leeward Islands, squadron at (1738), 5; reinforced, 6; separated from Jamaica station, 241
Leogane, 109, 244
Lestock, Captain Richard, 106, 112, 115; leaves W. Indies, 126; in Mediterranean; temporary command, 175–8; Mathews's opinion of, 197, 206, 209, 238
Lingen, Captain, 168–9
Lisbon, ships stationed off (1739), 25; convoy puts into, 157

Manila, 31, 32
Marines, 35, 36, 83, 142, 265, 267–275
Marlborough, her voyage to Mediterranean, 167–9
Martin, Captain William, 152–7; character of, 212; his diversion at Naples (1742), 212–5; at Genoa, 216, 218; destroys San Isidro, 229, 239
Martinique, French arrive at (1740), 57, 58, 97
Mathews, Admiral Thomas, early career, 197; his instructions, 198; his views (June 1742), 199–201; arrives Villefranche, 206–210; orders action against Naples, 212; against Genoa, 216; made Plenipotentiary, 216–7; operations Sept.—Dec. 1742, 218–220; differences with Admiralty, 221–225; campaign of 1743, 226–234; further differences, 235–8; views on situation Dec. 1743, 238–40
Mattagorda, Fort, Rooke's failure to take, 84
Maurepas, de (Minister of Marine), 88, 107, 162
Mayne, Captain Covill, 78
Mediterranean squadron, strength before war, 4, 5; reinforced (1738), 8; recalled, 12, 28; remains out, 13, 28; disposition (Oct. 1739), 59; reinforced (Jan. 1740), 60; weakness of (April 1740), 67; Norris urges strengthening, 74; Cornewall's reinforcement (1741), 150, 163, 166–9, 174; Lestock's reinforcement ordered, 165; arrives, 175; strength (June 1742), 199–202; Mathews on weakness of (1742), 210; (1743), 221–6; military direction of, 235; general situation (Dec. 1743), 239
Medley, Captain H., 148

Naples, Neapolitan galleys assist Don Philip, 176; Mathews's instructions as to (1742), 198, 199, 200; Neapolitan help to Spain, 202, 204; Mathews sends Martin to, 212–215, 219, 210, 220*n.*; renewed Naples help, 227–8, 234, 239
Newcastle, Duke of, 12, 25, 35; correspondence with Vernon, 44, 45, 53–58; attitude towards French intervention (1740), 77; reasons for not sending veteran troops to Cartagena, 135; correspondence with Norris (1741), 147–150; blames Haddock for Spanish evasion (Dec. 1741), 173–4; correspondence with Mathews (1742) 199, 201, 209–211, 216, (1743) 221, 227, 235–240
Newfoundland, Defence of, 5, 243
Norris, Admiral, Sir John, 23; early career, 24; appointed to command fleet in home waters, 25; discusses war plans, 31–37; proposals for Mediterranean (Jan. 1740), 61; on Spanish escape from Cadiz, 67; plans for 1740, 73–5, 80–83; views on attack upon forts by ships, 84–5; his instructions (June 20, 1740), 86; takes command, 88; attitude towards French, 89; windbound, 90–1; final operations of 1740, 91–7; on Anson's instructions, 98; on holding Cartagena, 124; on manning, 142, 270–4; his instructions (June 18, 1741), 145–6; Biscay cruise, 147–150; relinquishes his command and position in cabinet, 181; consulted on state of fleet, 195

Ogle, Admiral Sir Chaloner, misses Azogue ships, 26–7; opens Cadiz (1740), 62–8, 70, 78–9, 81, 82; brought home, 83, 89, 93; appointed to command escort to Cathcart, 94; sails for W. Indies, 96, 102–106, 111; Vernon's instructions to, 112, 113, 115, 119; leaves Cartagena, 125,

127, 132; assumes command at Jamaica, 241, 242–5, 257
Oglethorpe, Colonel, 31
Ostend, Company, 20, 21
Owlers, 3

Pacte de Famille, 21
Paita, taken by Anson, 99
Panama, 16, 31; Anson and, 97
Pearce, Captain Vincent, failure at San Augustin, 50, 51
Peru, trade of, 17
Peyton, Captain Sir Yelverton, 7
Pintado, de, Admiral, 53
Pizarro, de, Admiral, 27; in command against Anson, 98, 99
Plantations, squadrons at (1738), 5; (1739), 261, 264; (1742), 241–3
Port Louis, 55, 104
Porto Bello, 16, 17, 33; capture of, 45–50, 54; Anson and, 97, 133
Porto Rico, 7, 17; proposed attack upon (1742), 247
Pretender, the young, 75
'Princesa,' capture of, 78
Puerto Cabello, 43; attack upon, 245–8, 253–7

Reggio, Admiral, 53
Register ships, 17
Rentone, Captain, 108*n.*, 126
Rochalart, Admiral, 58, 84, 93, 95, 110*n.*
Roquefeuil, de, Admiral, 110, 111
Ruatan, 133, 257, 258

Steuart, Admiral Charles, 3
Strangford, Mr, Consul at Alicante, 9
Strategy, opposing views on, xiv–xix

Tencin, Cardinal, 231
Tinker, Mr, his plan to attack Darien, 30, 31
Torres, Admiral de, appointed to command Ferrol squadron, 83; his sailing reported (Aug. 1742), 92; effect of French squadron on de Torres's movements, 109, 110; his instructions, 111, 129, 144; Norris ordered to intercept, 145–7, 149; Windham to intercept, 193
Trelawny, Governor of Jamaica, 45; at councils of war, 106, 125, 130, 244
Tyrawley, Lord, prompt action of, 158

Vera Cruz, 45
Vernon, Admiral Edward, xii, 26, 27; early life and character, 39, 40; his instructions (July 1739), 40, 41; additional instructions initiated by, 41, 42; views on territorial attacks, 43–5, 55–6; takes Porto Bello, 45–50; off Cartagena and Chagres, 51–2; movements to Dec. 1740, 53–8, 68, 73–4, 79; views on French intentions, 105–7; at Cartagena, 106 *et seq.*; instructions to fleet, 112–3; operations, 114–124; Santiago, 125–30; Panama, 130–2; recalled, 133; blame for failure, 134–7, 225
Villefranche, British naval base, 178, 206–9, 232, 238
Virginia, naval defence of, 5, 7, 243

Wager, Sir Charles, First Commissioner, 23; discusses plans, 31–4, 83–4, 87, 142; resigns, 180
Waldegrave, Lord, 36, 65, 77, 81
Walpole, H., 22
Walpole, Sir R., 19, 21, 33, 36, 81, 89, 94, 180
Warren, Captain Peter, at San Augustin, 51, 109; Commodore in West Indies and North America, 258, 260
Waterhouse, Captain, 43
Watson, Captain T., 114; captures Baradera battery, 115, 117, 122
Wentworth, General, 103, 106; at Cartagena, 113–124; Santiago, 125-130; Panama, 131, 132; recalled, 133; blame for failure, 136, 137
Winchelsea, Lord, First Commissioner, 180; opposes Bill of 1742, 189; 196, 197, 224, 225, 237, 248, 250
Worms, Treaty of, 230–2

24/115

CAMBRIDGE: PRINTED BY J. B. PEACE, M.A., AT THE UNIVERSITY PRESS.